The Tragedy of a Generation

The Tragedy of a Generation

THE RISE AND FALL OF
JEWISH NATIONALISM
IN EASTERN EUROPE

JOSHUA M. KARLIP

HARVARD UNIVERSITY PRESS
Cambridge, Massachusetts, and London, England   2013

Library of Congress Cataloging-in-Publication Data

Karlip, Joshua M., 1971–
  The tragedy of a generation: the rise and fall of Jewish nationalism in Eastern Europe /
Joshua M. Karlip.
    p. cm.
  Includes bibliographical references and index.
  ISBN 978-0-674-07285-5 (alk. paper)
  1. Jews—Russia—History—20th century.   2. Jewish nationalism—Russia—History—
20th century.   3. Yiddishists—Russia—History—20th century.   4. Jews—Russia—
Politics and government—20th century.   5. Jews—Russia—Intellectual life—
20th century.   6. Jewish socialists—Russia—History—20th century.   7. Labor Zionism—
Russia—History—20th century.   8. Jews—Russia—Identity—History—20th century.
9. Russia—Ethnic relations—History—20th century.   10. Cherikover, I. M.,
1881–1943.   11. Kalmanovitch, Zelig, 1885–1944.   12. Efroikin, Isroel 1884–
I. Title.
  DS134.8.K35 2013
  320.54095694—dc23
  2012050489

To Shoshana

Contents

A Word about Transliteration

THE SUBJECTS OF THIS BOOK were fluent in at least three languages—Yiddish, Hebrew, and Russian—and also knew German and French. Given this reality as well as the multiethnic nature of Eastern Europe in the first half of the twentieth century, the transliteration of names, places, and terms was an issue. As a basis, I relied upon the YIVO system of transliteration for Yiddish and the Library of Congress system for Russian and Hebrew. In keeping with contemporary scholarly usage, however, I eliminated most of the diacritical marks when transliterating Hebrew, only retaining them for the letter ʿayin and for in-between independent vowels and consonants. When transliterating Hebrew, I had to decide between the contemporary Israeli pronunciation and the traditional Ashkenazi one, which all the subjects of this study used. My compromise was that in independent words, terms, and titles I transliterated according to the modern Israeli standard. When, however, I was quoting or referring to a Hebrew word or phrase invoked by the subjects of this study, I transliterated according to the Ashkenazi standard. Even more complicated, when transliterating Hebrew words that have entered mainstream Yiddish vocabulary, I had to choose between the Hebrew and Yiddish systems of transliteration. With words that have been thoroughly assimilated in Yiddish, I translated according to the YIVO system for Yiddish (thus kheyder, not ḥeder). In instances where the Hebrew word has not been as integrated into Yiddish, I transliterated according to the Hebrew standard. In the case of names of people, I have tried to Romanize them as they did themselves even when their usage contradicted rules of transliteration (e.g., Efroikin, not Efroykin). Also, when it came to both first names and well-known words, I transliterated them according to popular usage rather than according to the YIVO or Library of Congress system (Chaim instead of Ḥayim, for instance).

The Tragedy of a Generation

Introduction

ON THE EVE of World War II, the following words appeared in an essay by one of the editors of the Yiddish
journal *Oyfn sheydveg:*

> And who knows, perhaps the Jewries in the Fascist and half-Fascist lands
> would have been devoured internally if not for Jewish historical provi-
> dence, which imparted to the contemporary Hamans the idea to build the
> anti-Semitic movement on principles not of religion but rather of race.
> And from this standpoint, it is perhaps true that "the Holy One Blessed Be
> He made a blessing for Israel" that this illogical theory has rendered apos-
> tasy purposeless. What would become of these Jews, if they would be able
> to save their lives and property through conversion?[1]

The other editor of the journal compared Nazism to a whip, which
God used to chasten his wayward people and bring them back to
their Jewish identity.[2] Still another central contributor to the journal
introduced his essay, titled "Under the Hammer of History," with the
following Talmudic argument: "Rabbi Eliezer says: If Israel repents,
they will be redeemed, and if not, they will not be redeemed. Rabbi
Joshua said to him: If Israel will not repent, it won't be redeemed?
Rather, the Holy One Blessed Be He will cause a king to arise whose
decrees will be as harsh as those of Haman and [thereby] return them
to do good."[3] The Jewish people, argued this writer, had disappeared

through assimilation under the conditions of emancipation. Now, in an era of counter-emancipation, perhaps they could forge themselves once again into a unified whole.[4]

All three writers thus envisioned Nazism as serving as a potential catalyst for the strengthening of Jewish identity, which they argued had disintegrated in modernity. Similarly, all three employed a historiosophy steeped in religious tradition to deal with the ensuing persecutions. The two passages cited above invoked the traditional religious beliefs that the Jews suffered as a result of sin and that their persecutors served as divine agents of this punishment. Given the internally destructive nature of emancipation, these writers hoped that some positive results might come from Nazism's negation of this negative force. Throughout their essays, they voiced a call for political and cultural retreat at the moment of European Jewry's greatest crisis. Each of these men called upon his readers to retreat from European politics in response to the betrayal of both the Fascist and democratic countries. Similarly, they castigated their generation as one beset by a cultural assimilation that robbed it of the power to spiritually weather the Nazi storm. One of the editors of the journal even openly called for political and cultural retreat to the "ghetto."[5]

Who was this "*Oyfn sheydveg* group," which voiced such conservative opinions at the moment of European Jewry's greatest crisis? The passages read like the statements of East European rabbinic leaders who, during the late 1930s, pointed to Nazism as proof of the futility of attempts by Jewish nationalists at normalization. Oftentimes, these same rabbis also viewed Nazism as the divine agent to turn Europeanized Jews back to their religious roots.[6] Yet the editors and contributors to *Oyfn sheydveg* were far from being Orthodox rabbis. Rather, they served as leaders of two of the same secular nationalist movements, Diaspora nationalism and Yiddishism, that these rabbis so vigorously condemned. Elias Tcherikower, the journal's coeditor, was a former Menshevik activist who then embraced Yiddishism and pioneered the discipline of Yiddish historiography. Yisroel Efroikin, the other coeditor, had served as a leader of SERP (Jewish Socialist Workers' Party) during the 1905 Revolution and then of *di yidishe folkspartey* (the people's party) in the aftermath of the February Revolution in 1917. Zelig Hirsh Kalmanovitch, the contributor to

Oyfn sheydveg who had framed his article with the Talmudic quote, functioned as a Yiddishist scholar and activist, occupying a central administrative role in YIVO (Yiddish Scientific Institute).

A reading of their *Oyfn sheydveg* articles in light of their biographies unsettles our assumptions regarding the categories of the secular and the religious, the culturally and politically radical and the conservative. More fundamentally, it questions the long-held assumption of historians that secular Jewish nationalism's break with traditional religious Judaism proved total and irreversible. What does their religious rhetoric of persecution as a catalyst to national preservation say about the relationship between Diaspora nationalism and Yiddishism and the religious tradition that these ideologies had come to replace? To what extent were the opinions expressed in the pages of *Oyfn sheydveg* a rejection of the ideologies that these men formerly had espoused, and to what extent were they an articulation of them in extremis? What does the yearning for a lost premodern golden era of religious faith and solidarity tell us about the nature of East European Jewish nationalism, a movement that defined itself in opposition to religious Orthodoxy? Could it be that Jewish nationalism and Orthodoxy through their shared commitment to the survival of the Jewish people with a unique culture (admittedly humanistic for nationalists and religious for the Orthodox) had more in common with each other than they could have realized? Perhaps the phenomenon of *Oyfn sheydveg* demonstrates the extent to which modern secular nationalism had built itself upon the roots of traditionalist religion. If modern nationalism is a public religion, as some scholars have asserted, then it makes sense that some East European Jewish nationalists attempted to marshal their religious tradition's most unifying values and beliefs when they sensed that their modernist experiment had failed.[7]

All these questions led me to study the ideological journey of Tcherikower, Efroikin, and Kalmanovitch from its beginning around the 1905 Revolution to its end during the Holocaust. The portrait that emerges from this forty-year journey is a story of a Jewish political and cultural revolution and counterrevolution, largely catalyzed by surrounding events and trends but with an internal logic of its own. Historians and theorists of Jewish modernity long have viewed East

European Jewish history from 1881 onward as a period of political and cultural revolution, when many Jews replaced their traditionalist religious identities with secular ones, rooted either in nationalism, socialism, or acculturation. This revolution allowed for the emergence of secular Hebrew and Yiddish cultures, which, in the words of Kenneth Moss, served as two prongs of the same "cultural project." Former Jewish identity, rooted in religious beliefs, practices, and customs, would have to yield to a national identity rooted in language, literature, culture, and activist nationalist politics. This revolution had two endings: one tragic and the other triumphant. The Holocaust, Stalin's purges, and Jewish acculturation in America destroyed the cultural system created by Diaspora nationalists and Yiddishists. However, the State of Israel solidified the achievements of Zionists and Hebraists, allowing for the continuing flourishing of modern Hebrew culture.[8]

Broadly schematic, this conceptualization of a secular Jewish cultural revolution of course obscures the very real fault lines between Zionism and Diaspora nationalism, Hebraism and Yiddishism, aesthetic culture and nationalist ideology, and socialist versus liberal variants of nationalism. Yet, in general, scholars of this cultural and political transformation have studied the relationship of the Jewish religious tradition to these movements as largely unidirectional. Making a complete break with the past, the articulators of a new Jewish identity supposedly never looked back. Fewer studies have addressed the subtler anxiety of influence of the religious tradition on the new humanistic culture. Nor have recent studies generally explored the nexus between the religious notion of transcendence through Torah study and the secular nationalist search for the equivalent in the production of culture and scholarship.[9] My study reveals that Diaspora nationalists and Yiddishists, long before the crisis of Nazism, constantly sought both to rebel against the religious tradition and to draw inspiration from it.

The ways in which these men invoked the religious tradition changed as the prospects for the success of their cultural revolution shifted. If the 1905 Revolution proved a major catalyst for the articulation and implementation of Diaspora nationalism and Yiddishism, then the period 1939–1945 served as their effective end. Between

1905 and 1917, both political opportunities and adversities contributed to the perception of the inevitability of the recognition of the Jews as a national minority in Eastern Europe. A hallmark of this national status was the possession of a national language, Yiddish, that proved capable of producing a modern national culture. Despite narrowing political horizons, the first decade and a half of the interwar period witnessed the full flowering of modern Yiddish culture. However, the rise of Nazi Germany, Stalinist purges in the Soviet Union, and growing anti-Semitism in the successor states of East Central Europe contributed to the decline of Diaspora nationalism and Yiddishism as viable alternatives for East European Jews. Even as official anti-Semitism extruded the Jews from economic and political life, increasing numbers of young Jews continued to abandon Yiddish for the languages of their lands of residence.

The combination of all these factors led many Diaspora nationalists and Yiddishists to forge an ideology for an age of counterrevolution, in which they believed that they were witnessing the failure of their political and cultural dreams. Tcherikower, Efroikin, and Kalmanovitch thus heralded both the Jewish revolution and then its decline. On the eve of World War II and during the Holocaust, they paradoxically sought to salvage their cultural vision by severing it from its base in the Jewish revolution. Whereas proponents of all the trends of the cultural revolution had sought to synthesize Jewish with European cultures, these men struggled to save Diaspora nationalism and Yiddishism by envisioning their return to a state of premodern Jewish political and cultural isolation.[10]

Diaspora Nationalism and Yiddishism

The creation of the State of Israel in 1948 assured the place of Zionism and Hebraism in the story of Jewish nationalism. Yet this historical outcome obscured from both scholarly and popular view the fact that Zionism served as only one in a variety of Jewish nationalist ideologies popular among East European Jews during the first half of the twentieth century. Diaspora nationalism, also referred to as autonomism, served as the political and cultural ideology of those Jewish nationalists who, at the turn of the twentieth century, accepted the

Zionist premise of the national nature of Jewish identity but rejected Zionism's belief that a national renaissance could occur only in Palestine. Diaspora nationalists rather believed that Jews would achieve this national renaissance in their lands of residence in Eastern Europe.

The original theoreticians of Diaspora nationalism, the Jewish historian Simon Dubnov and the socialist Chaim Zhitlovsky, envisioned the Jews attaining national autonomy in a democratically reformed, multiethnic Russian state. Throughout his long life, Dubnov combined the roles of nationalist historian and architect of Diaspora nationalism. Beginning in the late 1880s, he came to believe that Jewish historical consciousness would prove the key to preserving Jewish national identity in the Diaspora in an age when traditional religion was losing its sway. Between 1897 and 1907, Dubnov penned his *Pis'ma o starom i novom evreistve* (Letters on old and new Judaism), in which he argued that Jewish national autonomy in the Diaspora would serve as the Hegelian synthesis between Jewish medieval separatism and modern emancipation. Unlike Dubnov, Zhitlovksy was a committed socialist and prominent member of the Russian Socialist Revolutionary Party who sought to synthesize his Jewish nationalism with socialism. According to Zhitlovsky, in a new socialist order, each national group would receive the right to govern its own cultural, social, economic, and political affairs. To Dubnov, the modernized Jewish community (*kehile* in Yiddish, *obshchina* in Russian) would serve as the building block of Jewish national autonomy. Membership in the *kehile* would prove compulsory for Russian Jews, who would pay an income tax to help fund this local body's cultural and social work. On the national level, Jews would convene a Jewish National Assembly. Zhitlovsky, in contrast, concentrated more exclusively on the cultural aspects of this autonomy: recognition of Yiddish as a Jewish national language, the creation of independent Jewish schools, universities, scholarship, and literature.[11]

Perhaps because so many Jewish intellectuals and politicians adopted Dubnov's, and to a lesser extent Zhitlovsky's, vision in the aftermath of the 1905 Revolution, Diaspora nationalism lacked a single political party to which its adherents rallied. In 1906, Dubnov founded a Jewish Folkspartey, or people's party, which in reality was not a political party at all but rather a small group of intellectuals. Dubnov's Folkspartey envisioned the transformation of the Russian Empire into a liberal, democratic, but not socialist, multiethnic state. Unlike this group of intellectuals, the Jewish Labor Bund of Russia, Poland, and Lithuania emerged as a major political party with mass support. A Social Democratic Party, the Bund saw itself as the independent representative of the Jewish proletariat.[12] Given its adoption of Marxist ideology, the Bund advocated for autonomy in matters of culture alone, refusing to participate in a national autonomy that would recognize the Jews as a unified nation across class divisions.

The smaller Jewish Socialist Workers' Party (SERP) occupied the middle ground between the *klal yisroel* (united Jewish) politics of Dubnov's Folkspartey and the class position of the Bund. In fact, Zhitlovsky was one of SERP's founders. SERP emerged as the heir of a small group of young Russian Jewish intellectuals who sought a synthesis of socialism with full-fledged Jewish nationalism. Labeling their group and their periodical *Vozrozhdenie* (Rebirth), these young intellectuals came from the ranks of mainstream Zionism but rejected it in favor of voluntarist socialism and a commitment to Jewish national renaissance in the Diaspora. The *vozrozhdentsy* (adherents of Vozrozhdenie) and later the members of SERP combined allegiance to the non-Marxist Socialist Revolutionaries with demands for maximal Jewish national autonomy in a future socialist Russian state. Because of their call for the Jews to form a *seym*, or parliament, to serve as a representative body of their national interests, members of SERP referred to themselves as Seymists.[13]

In the immediate aftermath of the February Revolution, SERP merged with another small socialist nationalist Jewish party, the SSRP (Socialist Zionist Labor Party), to form the Fareynikte, or United Jewish Socialist Labor Party. At the conference of Russian Zionists held in Helsingsfor in November 1906, the Russian Zionist Organization incorporated the demand for Jewish national autonomy in Russia into its political platform.[14] The Russian Socialist Zionist Party, ESDRP (Jewish Social Democratic Labor Party)–Poale Zion (Workers of Zion), advocated both for the emergence of a political and cultural center in Palestine and for Jewish national autonomous politics and culture in the Diaspora. For this reason, some Diaspora nationalist activists and thinkers allied themselves with this party.

The relationship of Zionism to Diaspora nationalism has proven far more complicated that once imagined. Scholars of Jewish nationalism recently have begun to argue that it was Zionists who often were the most vocal advocates of Jewish national autonomy in Eastern Europe. Joshua Shanes, in his study of fin de siècle Jewish politics in Galicia, argued that it was Zionist politicians who spearheaded the fight for Jewish national rights in the Habsburg Empire. Simon Rabinovitch, similarly, has demonstrated that Russian Zionists took the lead in the organization of an All-Russian Jewish Congress in the aftermath of the February Revolution. During those heady months, support for Jewish settlement activity in Palestine took a decidedly back seat to autonomist politics among Russian Zionists. In a recent book, Noam Pianko sought to recover the lost voices of three interwar and mid-twentieth-century Zionist thinkers, Simon Rawidowicz, Mordechai Kaplan, and Hans Kohn, whose definitions of Zionism conflicted with the model of the sovereign state. Although each of these thinkers differed in terms of their political visions for the future of Palestine, they all agreed upon the importance of Jewish national autonomy both within and outside Palestine. Like the Diaspora nationalists discussed in this book, Pianko's subjects sought alternatives to the sovereignty model of nationhood. Dimitry Shumsky has taken Pianko's argument still further by stating that throughout the interwar period, the political leaders of the *Yishuv,* no less than leading Zionist intellectuals, championed what he has termed "autonomist Zionism." According to this "autonomist Zionist" vision, the future state in Palestine would function as a nationalities state, in which both Jews and Arabs would enjoy autonomy in all their internal national affairs. Leading Zionists, from Hans Kohn to David Ben-Gurion to Vladimir Jabotinsky, linked their calls for national autonomy for the Arabs to their struggle for Jewish national rights in Eastern Europe.[15]

Limiting the definition of Diaspora nationalists in this book to those outside the Zionist camp makes sense despite the recent scholarship on autonomism within Zionism. Throughout the first half of the twentieth century, Zionists, no matter how involved in the struggle for Jewish national rights in the Diaspora, still envisioned the creation of some form of Jewish national home in Palestine. At least until the 1930s, Tcherikower, Efroikin, and Kalmanovitch all dismissed this goal, even in its most minimalist incarnation, as at best a sideshow and at worst a diversion from the task of creating a modern Jewish nation in Eastern Europe. Consequently, in their battle with the Zionists, they often mischaracterized Zionism as monolithically opposed to both Jewish national autonomy in the Diaspora and to Arab national rights in Palestine. In fact, the similarities between Diaspora nationalism and Zionism only heightened the battle between these two ideologies, as their respective representatives staked their claims as the true champions of Jewish national rights and the architects of national renaissance. Another benefit of studying these two ideologies as distinct from one another is that an understanding of the successes and failures of each can help to illuminate the fate of the other. Thus, in the immediate aftermath of World War I, when Diaspora nationalists were euphoric regarding the possibilities of Jewish national rights in Eastern Europe, Zionists of all stripes turned to autonomism and to alternatives to territorial sovereignty. Similarly, the crisis that led Tcherikower, Efroikin, and Kalmanovitch to despair of Diaspora nationalism in the late 1930s also led Zionist thinkers and activists to a rejection of autonomist models in favor of more exclusively territorial ones.

Also indispensable for this study is the strong link between Yiddishism and Diaspora nationalism. In an era when the religious tradition no longer would determine Jewish belonging, Yiddishists envisioned the Yiddish language and culture as serving as the unifying force binding Jews to their Jewish identity. Proponents of Yiddishism reacted against both the traditional subjugation of Yiddish to Hebrew and the maskilic (Jewish Enlightenment) disparagement of Yiddish as a corrupt jargon. Rejecting both views, they understood Yiddish as a national value that would prove capable not only of mobilizing the masses who claimed it as their mother tongue but also of serving as the medium of a secular modern Jewish national culture. By creating a rarefied culture in the mother tongue, argued Yiddishists, Yiddish would prove capable of bridging the gap between the Jewish masses and the intellectual elite. Such a process also would allow for the Jewish intelligentsia to satisfy its intellectual and cultural needs in Yiddish, without having to turn to high Russian and Polish culture as many had done until that point.[16]

Given Yiddishism's connection to the quest for Jewish national autonomy, it is not surprising that in time it became closely intertwined with Diaspora nationalism. Dubnov, though very sympathetic to modern Yiddish culture, was not a Yiddishist but rather envisioned Russian Jewry as producing national culture in all three of its historical languages: Hebrew, Yiddish, and Russian. Zhitlovsky, in contrast, was a founding architect both of Diaspora nationalism and of Yiddishism. During the inter-revolutionary years, most of Dubnov's disciples abandoned their mentor's linguistic pluralism and embraced the Yiddishist ideology. Yiddishists, despite their not belonging to one political party, almost always embraced the political ideology of Diaspora nationalism. Such a political orientation made sense, given that Yiddishists anticipated their cultural revolution as occurring in the East European Diaspora, where the majority of Jews spoke Yiddish in their daily lives. The organs of national autonomy, these ideologues hoped, would ensure state recognition of Yiddish as the language of Jewish schools and other cultural and social institutions. In 1908, Yiddishists convened a conference for the Yiddish language in Czernowitz, Bukovina, where the participants declared Yiddish a national language of the Jewish people. During the inter-revolutionary years, Yiddishist and Diaspora nationalist intellectuals transformed Yiddish into a language of highbrow political and cultural discussion and made the first steps toward the creation of a Yiddish scholarship.[17]

Ideologies in Action

As second-generation Diaspora nationalists and Yiddishists, Tcherikower, Efroikin, and Kalmanovitch, in varying degrees, were the disciples of Dubnov, Zhitlovsky, and the great Yiddish writer and early Yiddishist, I. L. Peretz. As such, they had to adapt their mentors' ideologies to the dramatic changes that occurred during the forty-year period from 1905 to 1945. This book thus operates as a case study of Diaspora nationalism and Yiddishism in action at several key moments of hope and crisis for East European Jewry. Although the book moves in chronological order, it addresses several tensions that preoccupied these men during almost all the stages of their careers. Those tensions were the following: commitment to Jewish socialism versus *klal yisroel* nationalism; a cultural radicalism that fought the influence of the Jewish religious tradition versus a conservatism that drew from it; competition with Zionism over the nature of Jewish national rights versus mutual influence; the search for state support for Yiddish culture versus antipathy toward the avowedly antinational Yiddish culture in the Soviet Union; the balance between realism and utopianism within these movements. Although the same tensions remained throughout the period, the balance between them shifted according to historical circumstance. For instance, the utopianism engendered by the 1905 Revolution led to partisan ideology and commitment to socialism, only to be followed by a turn to practical, nonpartisan, and non-socialist organic work in the aftermath of this revolution's failure. Similarly, as long as these men understood religious Orthodoxy as the greatest impediment to the implementation of their political and cultural visions, they fought it strenuously. Later, when they recognized linguistic acculturation and anti-Semitism as their greatest enemies, they looked backward to the religious past, and even to the contemporary Orthodox, for nationalist inspiration. In the late 1930s and during the Holocaust, they likewise sought to sever their nationalism from liberal European culture, to which they long had looked for inspiration. This book will evaluate the successes and failures of such attempts to refashion, revise, and sometimes reject these ideologies in the wake of progressive historical upheaval.

The first to chart the ideological trajectory of a cohort of Diaspora nationalists, Yiddishist intellectuals both at the dawn of these ideologies and at the moment of their decline, this *longue durée* study fills a lacuna in the historiography of these movements. Given the importance of Diaspora nationalist thought and modern Yiddish culture to twentieth-century East European Jewish history, it is surprising that, until the past several years, very few historians have researched these movements. Those few who have studied them, moreover, often have concentrated exclusively either on politics or on culture and on the careers of the founding ideologues of these movements. Over the last decade, several scholars, mostly young, have studied the interplay between Jewish political and cultural nationalism in Eastern Europe. However, with rare exception, these fine studies have concentrated on one era in the history of these movements, to the exclusion of others.[18]

Another lacuna that this book fills is the ideological reaction of European Jewish intellectuals to the crisis of Nazism. From 1933 until the eve of World War II, Jewish intellectuals and publicists throughout continental Europe had to react to the Nazi reversal of Jewish emancipation first in Germany and then in Austria and Czechoslovakia. In some ways even more troubling, they confronted a crisis of liberalism and a rise in xenophobic anti-Semitism both in France and in the successor states of East Central Europe. The reaction of Jewish intellectuals to this crisis relates to the larger question of Jewish participation in the crisis of humanism that occurred on the eve of World War II. To what extent did European Jewish intellectuals reevaluate the legacies of the French Revolution and its promise of emancipation in light of these crises? As darkness enveloped the European continent, did Jewish intellectuals seek refuge in the historical memory of emancipation, or did they abandon it as illusory? If they did the latter, then to what other usable past did they turn? Can we speak of a European or even worldwide Jewish intellectual reaction to the crisis of Nazism, or must we only speak of local responses? Guy Miron recently addressed some of these issues through a comparative analysis of French, German, and Hungarian Jewish intellectual and publicistic responses to Nazism and Fascism. He concluded that overwhelmingly these Jewries continued to embrace the historical memory of emancipation and of Jewish integration. Yet, because Miron concentrated on acculturated Jewish communities with officially integrationist ideologies, he only tangentially discussed the very different reaction to the crisis by Yiddish-speaking Jews.[19]

No study has thoroughly analyzed the reaction of Diaspora nationalists to the crisis of the 1930s. Diaspora nationalists in the 1930s had to react to a twofold tragedy. European Jewry, they concluded, had failed to secure even the most basic civil and political rights promised by emancipation, let alone the national rights championed by Diaspora nationalist ideology. Even in the best of times, Diaspora nationalists had reacted to the legacy of emancipation with ambivalence. They envisioned their ideology as the natural antidote to the loss of premodern Jewish corporate identity, the foremost casualty of emancipation, and to the assimilation that accompanied Jewish modernization. In the late 1930s, Diaspora nationalists looked at the collapse of emancipation through the prism of the earlier failure of their own ideological vision. Emancipationist ideology, they concluded, had wrought destruction on Jewish collective identity without delivering its most basic political and social promises. Through this lens of double failure, some former Diaspora nationalists collapsed the 150-year time frame of 1789 to 1939, dismissing it as one of unmitigated failure and national disintegration. Diaspora nationalists thus turned to the premodern past of Jewish corporate identity as a historical model of how to salvage their vision of Jewish national autonomy from the wreckage of liberalism. To those Diaspora nationalists such as Tcherikower who advocated a return to the "ghetto," this term primarily served as a code word for a reconstitution of a Jewish corporate identity in the absence of emancipation. The call of return to the ghetto thus functioned as an attempt to implement the Diaspora nationalist vision in the absence of liberalism.

Similarly, this book evaluates the crisis of Yiddishism as it reacted to the rise and spread of Nazism. Yiddishism had envisioned itself as the synthesis of Jewishness and humanistic European culture. With European culture's increasing embrace of anti-Semitism and exclusive national myths, some Yiddishists sought to sever their ideology from its European context. The greatest symptom of their crisis of humanism was their rhetorical reappropriation of the Jewish religious tradition that they had rejected in their youths and their expressed desire to find refuge from the tragedies of history in sacred text. Yet Tcherikower spoke for nearly all the contributors to *Oyfn sheydveg* when he expressed the tragedy of the "neither nor" proposition that he and his fellow secular nationalist intellectuals faced. In his words:

> The tragedy of our generation does not consist in the amount of afflictions that have befallen our lot, but rather in that the generation has lost the old beliefs and has despaired of the new. Through and through individualistic, skeptical, and rationalistic, our generation is devoured by assimilation—right or left—and has lost its past strength. It stands now empty, expelled, without the innocence of a believer and without the primitive strength of a fighter—without any consolation in its afflictions.[20]

This book will attempt to reconstruct this moment of crisis, bereavement, and soul-searching within the contexts of the careers and lives of Tcherikower, Efroikin, and Kalmanovitch as Diaspora nationalists and Yiddishists.[21]

Even rarer than a discussion of Jewish intellectual reactions to Nazism on the eve of the war is the integration in one book of a discussion of key Jewish political and cultural actors in the late tsarist and interwar eras with a portrayal of these actors' reflections on the destruction of East European Jewry during the Holocaust. As David Engel recently argued, the bifurcation of the discipline of Jewish studies from Holocaust studies has diminished our understanding both of pre-Holocaust European Jewish history and of Jewish agency and reaction during the Holocaust. Many modern Jewish historians have chosen not to discuss the ultimate fate of their subjects in the Holocaust so as to avoid the bias of "backshadowing," through which the prewar lives of European Jews are interpreted through the dark prism of their horrific deaths. This study seeks to redress the imbalance about which Engel spoke by studying the subjects of this book both at the beginning and at the end of their political and cultural careers.[22]

This approach allows for a new perspective of the years 1905–1945 in the modern Jewish experience. Naturally, most historians have concentrated upon the radical discontinuities in this forty-year period: three revolutions (1905, February and October 1917), two world wars, the disintegration of empires, the rise of successor nation states and the Soviet Union, the rise of Nazism, and finally the obliteration of European Jewry. Yet, often forgotten is the fact that the generation that came of age in 1905 reacted to the subsequent cataclysms through the prism of the ideologies that its members first had forged in their youths. Thus, to Tcherikower, Efroikin, and Kalmanovitch, the February Revolution of 1917 appeared as the event that would allow their long-deferred political and cultural dreams born in 1905 to come to fruition. In a very different way, these men looked backward at the end of this era for personal and historical explanation of their plight. Thus, in a transit camp in the South of France in 1940, Tcherikower reacted in his diary to the ideologies that he first had espoused three decades earlier. Incarcerated in the Vilna ghetto in

1942–1943, Kalmanovitch likewise reacted to the unfolding genocide through the prism of the ideologies of which he had first believed and then despaired. Similarly, in exile in Montevideo, Uruguay, Efroikin edited a journal that sought to salvage Yiddish culture by severing it from the European civilization that he believed had betrayed it and by reconnecting it to its roots in the religious tradition.

Mindful of the pitfall of "backshadowing," this book tells a compelling story of ideological belief and despair, ideological tenaciousness and flexibility, utopianism and realism, cultural radicalism and romanticism, struggle against the Jewish religious tradition and longing for it during the first four and a half decades of the twentieth century. It analyzes the ideologies and actions of these three men both within a general historical context and within the context of their own unique personalities, ambitions, hopes, and fears. Despite their different backgrounds and experiences, all three men experienced the trajectory from political and cultural revolution to counterrevolution in a strikingly similar manner. At key moments, moreover, they worked closely together. For this reason, in addition to their collaboration on the 1939 journal, they merit attention as members of the same cultural and political cohort.

The Context of Small-Nations Nationalism

The strong link between Diaspora nationalism and Yiddishism illuminates the long-standing debate over the place of Jewish nationalism within the larger context of Central and East European national movements. Given the multiethnic composition of the Habsburg and tsarist empires, it is not surprising that the "small nations" of Eastern Europe often engaged more in a struggle for national autonomy and legal recognition of their national languages and cultures than in a battle for territorial sovereignty. Most of the co-territorial national groups among whom East European Jews lived were stateless to one degree or another. Although Polish nationalists never ceased to struggle for the reconstitution of the state that they had lost, they turned throughout the nineteenth century to the creation of a national culture in the Polish language as a vehicle through which to preserve their national identity. According to the theorist of nationalism

Miroslav Hroch, Lithuanians, Ukrainians, and Belorussians experienced "the belated type" of nationalism. In all three cases, the economic and cultural elites had assimilated into the dominant national culture, leaving the national language and culture in the hands of the peasantry. Similarly, with the advent of modernization and capitalism, the bourgeoisie in Lithuanian, Belorussian, and Ukrainian territories became the Jews and other urban minority groups, rather than members of the majority nationality. Given this socioeconomic and cultural reality, the architects of national revival in all three cases were urbanized intellectuals, one or more generations removed from the countryside. These intellectuals researched and celebrated the folk language, all the while seeking to transform it into the medium of a high culture.[23]

To some extent, the rise of Jewish nationalism in late tsarist Russia followed Hroch's model, paralleling that of the Jews' Polish, Lithuanian, and Ukrainian neighbors. In all four cases, these national movements developed and thrived despite, and in good measure because of, increasing tsarist oppression. In the western provinces of the Russian Empire, the tsarist government followed an inconsistent nationalities policy whose primary goal was the maintenance of the empire at any cost. Attempts at the Russification of Poles and Jews, for instance, stemmed less from a consistent policy of forced acculturation than it did from a deep fear of the separatism and inherent revolutionary nature of nationalist movements. Following the suppression of the Polish Revolt of 1863, Polish nationalists first embraced Positivism and dreams of a rapprochement with Russia and then, when gradualism seemed to fail, turned to more militant forms of ethnic nationalism and socialism. The Jewish responses to the Great Reforms of the 1860s and the subsequent discrimination of the 1880s somewhat paralleled the Polish example. When Tsar Alexander II ameliorated the legal status of "useful" Jews, *maskilim* (proponents of Haskalah) greeted his reign with euphoria and with calls for Jewish acculturation. In the aftermath of the pogroms of 1881–1882 and the anti-Jewish legislation of Alexander III's government, this same Jewish intelligentsia turned increasingly to Zionism, Diaspora nationalism, and to socialism.[24]

Like their neighbors the Ukrainians, Russian Jews spoke a language long disparaged by both non-Jewish and Jewish elites as a jargon and as a bastardization of a dominant language. Refusing to recognize any real national distinction between the Russian people and the Ukrainians—whom it referred to as "Little Russians"—the tsarist regime actively repressed the Ukrainian language and culture. When Ukrainians insisted upon the independent existence of their language, arguing that it was more than a dialect of Russian, they staked a claim to the status of an independent nation, worthy of autonomy and language rights. Similarly, for the stateless Russian Jews, the development of a modern culture in Yiddish could lead to the recognition of East European Jewry as a national minority deserving of national autonomy.[25]

Yet these similarities should not obscure the very real differences between East European Jewish nationalism and its co-territorial equivalents. In very fundamental ways, the Jewish nationalist movements described in this book deviated from Hroch's model. According to Hroch, small nationalities pass through three stages of growing national awareness. In the first stage, a small cadre of intellectuals cultivates the national language and engages in national scholarship centering on ethnography and national history. During the second stage, ever greater numbers of the cultural elite become involved in the tasks of national renaissance. Only in stage three does the national movement attain a mass quality, spreading among the common folk. As Cecile Kuznitz has observed, the case of Yiddishism occurred in reverse of Hroch's model. In the second half of the nineteenth century, a Yiddish literature, press, and theater developed. The loosening of censorship restrictions during the 1905 Revolution allowed for the Yiddish press to reach a mass audience. However, only on the eve of World War I, and then principally during the interwar era, did Yiddishists turn to scholarship as a tool of nation building. Even more fundamentally, with his focus on either peasant or dominant nationalities, Hroch left no room in his model for the unique circumstances of the Jews, who belonged to neither group. Functioning as the middle class that Poles, Lithuanians, and Ukrainians alike sought to replace, the Jews, unlike the bourgeoisie in Hroch's model, did not come from the ruling class.[26]

The late historian and theoretician of nationalism Ernest Gellner succeeded more than Hroch in fitting East European Jews into his typology of nationalisms, defining Jewish nationalism as diasporist.

According to Gellner, diaspora nations, such as Greeks, Armenians, and Jews, combined the seemingly mutually exclusive features of economic advantage and relative political powerlessness. Somewhat deterministically, Gellner explained that ruling empires often feared to hand the keys to financial capital to members of their own national groups, preferring instead the use of marginal, pariah national or religious minorities that would have no designs on ultimate power. In the transition to capitalism and to modernization, the national majority then turned on this pariah nationality of middlemen, seeking to usurp its economic role. Although this model fails to account for the economic diversification and increasing pauperization of East European Jewry, it explains much better than Hroch's the turn to nationalism by groups such as the Jews that combined certain economic advantages with relative political powerlessness.[27]

This study of Diaspora nationalism and Yiddishism also belies the division, posited by leading theorists of nationalism, between "civic" and "ethnic" nationalisms. Whereas civic nationalism defines national belonging based on citizenship, ethnic nationalism limits membership in a nationality to ties of blood. In the eyes of many scholars of nationalism, civic nationalism proved liberal and therefore "good," whereas ethnic nationalism was chauvinistic and therefore bad.[28] However, as Pianko has demonstrated, both Diaspora nationalists and Zionists alike sought to create a synthesis between civic and ethnic forms of nationalism. To Jewish nationalists of all stripes, both civic nationalism, with its calls for the integration of all ethnic minorities into one overarching civic culture, and ethnic nationalism, with its exclusion of ethnic minorities not from the dominant nation, proved equally problematic. Instead, both architects of Diaspora nationalism and some Zionists sought to correct the abuses of both these models by envisioning the creation of a liberal multinational state that would at once grant civic equality to the Jews and recognize their rights to a national culture. Dubnov and others thus sought to transform the Jews' anomalous situation as a stateless nation into a new norm that would allow for the flourishing of liberal states that would recognize and celebrate national difference. Even as they appropriated the language of immutable national difference from ethnic nationalists, Diaspora nationalists and Yiddishists such as Dubnov, Zhitlovsky, and Peretz turned this rhetoric on its head by identifying the Jewish national essence with such universal values as progress and the primacy of spirit over the physical.[29]

By tracing the lives and thought of three Diaspora nationalist, Yiddishist intellectuals through the first four and a half decades of the twentieth century, this book demonstrates the successes as well as the limits of this attempt to forge a Jewish nationalism at once humanistic and ethnically particular. As the xenophobic nationalisms of the interwar era progressively crushed this synthesis, Diaspora nationalists increasingly turned to both territorial nationalism and to less universal, more particularistic, claims of Jewish national exceptionalism. Yet even when attempting to untangle Diaspora nationalism from liberalism, intellectuals such as Tcherikower, Efroikin, and Kalmanovitch only deepened their belief that ethical refinement rather than brute force distinguished the Jewish national essence from that of other nationalities. Thus, the Jewish ethnic nationalism of Diaspora nationalists and Yiddishists bore only a superficial resemblance to its European equivalent. Although the Nazi era led the three subjects of this book to embrace the "ghetto" and essentialist, even racial, definitions of Jewish identity, they still maintained some hope to implement their humanist vision under extreme conditions.

Another division often drawn by historians of nationalism, between political and cultural nationalism, also proves problematic. Jewish cultural nationalism avowedly emphasized national culture over national politics. It was Aḥad Ha-'Am's emphasis on the creation of a modern Hebrew culture that established him as a cultural nationalist whose particular ideologies were Zionist and Hebraist. Zhitlovsky and Peretz, on the other hand, were cultural nationalists who espoused Diaspora nationalism and Yiddishism. Still, these men linked their visions of national culture to the distinctly political goal of elevating the Jews to the status of a nation deserving of national rights. The distinction between Jewish political and cultural nationalists, just as that between Zionists and Diaspora nationalists, was thus often one of degree rather than kind. Yet cultural nationalists often sought to create an independent modern Jewish culture unfettered to ideological constraints, a goal that often clashed with the goals of the political nationalist movements to which they belonged.[30]

One of the central creative tensions of both modern Hebrew and Yiddish cultures was the tension between the latent religious inspiration that lay behind their redemptive view of culture and the blatant secular nature of their contents. The exploration of this tension rests at the heart of this book. In analyzing this tension, this book makes use of several recent studies that understand the "religious" and the "secular" as not two completely distinct realms but rather as two areas that constantly influence one another.[31] Hebraism and Yiddishism both rebelled against traditional East European Jewish culture and drew upon it both for content and for human recruits. From its beginnings, the creators of modern Yiddish culture recognized their begrudged indebtedness to traditional Jewish culture and society. The combination of the crumbling of this traditional society coupled with other processes such as the increasing linguistic acculturation of modernized Jews contributed to the ideological crisis that the subjects of this study experienced beginning in the late 1930s.

Another tension that operated within Yiddishism was that between populism and elitism. Unlike its Hebraist counterpart, Yiddishism emerged as a populist version of Jewish cultural nationalism. Jewish populism celebrated the Jewish masses for their retention of Jewish identity and their continued use of Yiddish and derided the Jewish intelligentsia and bourgeoisie for their assimilation and abandonment of Yiddish in favor of Russian and Polish. Yiddishists thus at least rhetorically celebrated the masses' popular culture even as the former attempted to refine the latter aesthetically. This tension between populism and elitism, between a desire to serve the folk and to create a rarefied highbrow culture, contributed both to creativity and to conflict among representatives of modern Yiddish culture.[32]

From its beginnings in the first decade of the twentieth century, Yiddishism possessed two competing trends: radical Yiddishism and national-romantic Yiddishism. Radical Yiddishism, championed by Zhitlovsky, attempted to forge a modern Yiddish culture "Jewish by virtue of its language, not by virtue of its particularist content."[33] Radical Yiddishism served as an example of the de-parochialization process that accompanied the modern Jewish cultural revolution. To participants in this revolution, the use of a Jewish language, either Hebrew or Yiddish, would liberate modern Jewish culture from a specific Jewish content and demolish the artificial boundary between the Jewish and the universal.[34] One of the most cogent articulations of this non-essentialist position came from the pen of the Zionist and Hebraist Ḥaim Greenberg, who in 1917 argued that Zionism was "a struggle not for the preservation and fruitless conservation of this or that fixed trait of this individuality, but for the establishment of a free background for its unceasing re-formulation."[35] Zhitlovksy similarly spoke for this trend in Yiddishism, arguing that a culturally open, secular Yiddish culture would replace the old religious Judaism as the basis of modern Jewish national identity.[36]

Yet, at the same time, many Jewish cultural nationalists, both Hebraist and Yiddishist, opposed this trend, arguing instead for the preservation of a Jewish national essence that survived the transformation of the Jews from a religious ethnicity to a modern nation. To Ahad Ha-'Am, this national essence equaled Jewish ethics as reflected in the biblical and rabbinic traditions. Peretz applied this essentialism to modern Yiddish culture. Himself a religious agnostic and proponent of Jewish secularism, Peretz argued that modern Yiddish culture and literature had to appropriate the best values of the old religious heritage and incorporate them into the new humanistic culture. According to Peretz, Yiddish literature and culture served as the latest link in a "golden chain" that extended back to the Bible and therefore had to remain true to the spirit of Jewish national treasures.[37]

In reality, most Yiddishists did not neatly fit into one of these categories, but adopted radical and national-romantic positions at different moments of their careers.[38] In both the Hebraist and Yiddishist camps, a split developed regarding these two competing trends between literati on the one hand and publicists, historians, and folklorists on the other. In general, Yiddish and Hebrew literati tended to champion the de-parochialization of their respective literatures.[39] Historians, folklorists, and many publicists, in contrast, tended to the more essentialist, or neo-romantic, wing of their respective movements, searching for the antecedents of their modern secular culture in the nation's traditionalist past. Both Yiddishism and Hebraism, moreover, possessed unique forces that shaped the balance between radical and national romantic trends. The elevation of Yiddish as a highbrow language itself was a radical, revolutionary act. Yet Yiddishism's populism tempered this radicalism by understanding Yiddish as the repository of the collected wisdom of East European Jewry—a claim that necessarily bound the movement to the Jewish past.

This book attempts to bridge the fields of political and cultural history, seeking to explore the nexuses and tensions between Diaspora nationalist politics and Yiddishist culture. It is my hope, moreover, that this study tells a compelling story because of the backdrop of dramatic historical events against which Tcherikower, Efroikin, and Kalmanovitch acted and thought. Since these three men left behind a prodigious record of their thought and activity over a forty-year period, I have chosen to focus on the major historical moments in which they forged their ideologies, sought to implement them, and then despaired of them. The first three chapters of the book cover the years 1905–1921; the remaining chapters focus on 1939–1945.

The book revolves around key moments in the life (and ultimately the death) of East European Jewry: 1905 and its aftermath, World War I, the Russian Revolution, and the eve of World War II through the Holocaust.[40] Moreover, whereas others have told the story of Diaspora nationalism and Yiddishism during the interwar era, none yet have linked the ideologies born in reaction to the 1905 Revolution to the era of the Holocaust nearly forty years later. For that reason, this book does not attempt a comprehensive biography of Tcherikower, Efroikin, and Kalmanovitch but rather analyzes their political and cultural ideologies at their greatest moments of ideological hope and despair. It will only delve into the nuances of its protagonists' lives to the extent that they impacted upon their ideologies.

This study of the ideological vagaries of a group of intellectuals captures the ambivalent synthesis between traditional Judaism and modern European culture that marked the expression of Jewish secular nationalism in Eastern Europe. It also speaks of the interconnectedness of Zionism and Diaspora nationalism, Yiddishism, and Hebraism in historical perspective.

This interconnectedness of seemingly mutually exclusive movements reveals a historical irony. For much of the period that this book covers, its subjects advocated Diaspora nationalism and Yiddishism and rejected Zionism and Hebraism in the name of realism. Diaspora nationalism and Yiddishism asked of its constituents only to remain in their lands of residence and to continue to speak and to celebrate their native language. The fact that Diaspora nationalism occupied the center position in Jewish politics between Zionism and socialism is evidenced by the fact that all Jewish political parties incorporated its basic tenets into their platforms. And the fact that Yiddishism, too, occupied a centrist position among Jewish cultural movements can be seen from the fact that a majority of East European Jews, though not avowedly Yiddishist, served as consumers of modern Yiddish culture. Yet in the volatile environment of interwar twentieth-century Eastern Europe, the seemingly most realistic movements became the most utopian. During the interwar period, even as most East European Jews consumed Yiddish culture, they decidedly rejected Yiddishist ideology in favor of their co-territorial language or of Hebrew. By the second half of the 1930s, the forces of Diaspora nationalism and Yiddishism lost their attraction in favor of more radical options for Jewish national survival.

These phenomena led the subjects of this book to conclude that the Jewish nation suffered from a pathology that led it to disdain its own language and culture. This dark conclusion led them to question the whole experiment of Jewish normalization and to seek a return to the exceptional conditions of premodernity in order to preserve Jewish identity. In reality, however, Kalmanovitch came much closer to the historical truth in his *Oyfn sheydveg* essay: if his claim that modernity had destroyed the Jewish people proved an exaggeration, he certainly was correct in sensing that the interwar period had destroyed the possibility of creating an independent, self-sustaining national Yiddish culture backed by government support. Both external and internal historical processes militated against this outcome, which just several decades before had appeared so realistic. The political and cultural revolution that Tcherikower, Efroikin, and Kalmanovitch had helped to initiate had been crushed "under the hammer of history."

CHAPTER ONE

Diaspora Nationalism and Yiddishism in Late Imperial Russia

THE REVOLUTION of 1905 catapulted Tcherikower, Efroi-kin, and Kalmanovitch into the arena of Russian Jewish politics and culture. For members of their generational cohort, the revolution served as the catalyst that allowed them to move their ideas regarding a dramatic reordering of the Russian Empire into a social-ist, nationalities state from the world of theory into action. In many ways, the Revolution of 1905 was a revolt of the youth, which carried a unique resonance among young Russian Jews. At once, young Russian Jews were rebelling against the tsarist regime and against the Jewish place within that regime as defined by their parents' genera-tion. A transitional generation, the parents of these revolutionaries lived with one foot steeped in the world of traditional East European Jewish society and one foot standing in the world of the new Jewish politics of auto-emancipation and Zionism. The involvement of Rus-sian Jewish youth in the Revolution of 1905 functioned as much as a rebellion against this compromise as it did against the tsarist regime. For many young Russian Jews, what they perceived as the half mea-sures of Russian Zionism, with its call for bold national renaissance in Palestine coupled with relative political quietism in Russia, no lon-ger would suffice. Instead, they hoped to implement the Jewish na-tional renaissance in the present, by refashioning Russian Jewry into a secular, socialist, and autonomist nation.[1]

Like many other socialist nationalists, Tcherikower, Efroikin, and Kalmanovitch rejected both general Russian Zionism as escapist and as bourgeois and the Bund as insufficiently nationalist. Still, the heroic shadow that the Bund cast in revolutionary Jewish society in the years 1905–1906 led these same intellectuals to adopt an orthodox Marxist approach to class struggle that oftentimes undermined their maximalist nationalist positions.[2]

With the quelling of the revolution in 1907, these socialist nationalist revolutionaries gradually became an autonomist intelligentsia, which sought to implement its transformation of Russian Jewish society and culture incrementally. During the years of reaction between 1907 and 1914, these young intellectuals created a new autonomist public Russian Jewish culture, which secularized and nationalized increasing numbers of Russian Jews.[3] Just as the generation of 1905 saw no half measures when it came to tsarist autocracy or traditional Jewish society, so too did it subsequently not brook any compromise when it came to the language question. The turn from politics to organic work and culture led to the marriage between Diaspora nationalism and Yiddishism, a union that previously had existed only in the minds of lone intellectuals such as Zhitlovsky. Taking up the cause of Yiddish, these young intellectuals refashioned themselves from a Russian-Jewish into a Yiddishist intelligentsia.

In different ways, Tcherikower, Efroikin, and Kalmanovitch all traveled this same trajectory. The relationship of each of these activists to traditional Russian Jewish society and culture differed. To Tcherikower, born into a somewhat Russified, Zionist family, his rebellion was more against the half measures of the Russian Jewish culture born in 1881 than it was against the world of East European Jewish tradition. As a result, Tcherikower's revolutionary activity traversed the borders of Jewish socialist nationalism and Russian Menshevism. Yet it was Tcherikower's deep immersion in Russian revolutionary culture that in part led him to espouse a romantic Jewish cultural nationalism, which glorified martyrdom. Efroikin, both a product of a Lithuanian yeshiva and a maskilic family, rebelled against the unique Lithuanian Jewish compromise between tradition and modernity that had allowed for the synthesis of first Orthodoxy and Haskalah and then Orthodoxy and Zionism.[4] From the beginning, Efroikin felt equally at home in Yiddish culture and in Russian-language Jewish culture.

Kalmanovitch, the only of the three born into abject poverty, seemingly mostly rebelled against the traditional world of the *besmedresh* (study house).[5] At least on an unconscious level, Kalmanovitch's view of Yiddish scholarship as a sacred calling came from his youthful dedication to the study of Torah, seen by traditional Jewry as a transcendent enterprise. Yet it must be remembered that of the three, Kalmanovitch alone was born officially outside the Pale of Settlement, in Courland, where German vied with Yiddish as the spoken language. The tension between Kalmanovitch's traditionalist upbringing versus the marginal status of Yiddish in his hometown goes a long way in explaining his lifelong passion for Yiddish and his zealous need to defend it against its detractors.

Having rebelled against the perceived half measures of their parents, this generation ultimately came to its own compromises between tradition and secularism—compromises that would profoundly shape East European Jewish politics and culture for the next four decades. From a socialist dogmatism that eschewed national unity, each of these three men eventually moved more toward a democratic nationalism, which strove to remake Russian Jewry in a populist vein. Similarly, each of these activists, like so many in their generation, came to espouse the ideology of Yiddishism, which sought to synthesize the authentically Jewish with the European to arrive at a modern Jewish national culture.

The Revolution of 1905

For Jewish youth in the Pale of Settlement, the revolutionary period began not in 1904, as it did for many others in Russia, but rather in April 1903 with the Kishinev pogrom. Much more deadly than the pogroms of the early 1880s, the Kishinev massacre mobilized a generation of Jews in their teens and twenties to seek new radical solutions to the Jewish plight in tsarist Russia. In contrast to the aftermath of the pogroms of 1881–1882, socialism, rather than Zionism, emerged as the most popular ideology among Russian Jewish youth in the aftermath of the Kishinev pogrom. The synthesis of Jewish nationalism and socialism, as represented by the Bund and other parties, contributed to a belief that Jews did not have to compromise their national loyalties to participate in the revolution. In contrast, Zionism seemed out of touch with the life-and-death struggles of the Jews in the Pale of Settlement.[6]

Within this context, it is not surprising that a group of young Russian socialist Zionists distanced themselves from Zionism by creating their own movement that sought to synthesize Jewish nationalism and socialism in a manner that spoke to the immediate needs of Russian Jewry. This group, led by Moyshe Zilberfarb, Ben-Adir (Avrom Rosin), and Mark Ratner, called itself Vozrozhdenie (Rebirth). Holding its first conference in September 1903, Vozrozhdenie began publishing its own journal several months later. Vozrozhdenie at once was more Diaspora-centered than early socialist Zionism and more nationalistic and voluntarist than the Bund. The *vozrozhdentsy* continued to believe in a Jewish territory as an ultimate goal, but believed that in the meantime, Russian Jewry should create organs of Jewish national autonomy in the Diaspora. Unlike the Bund, which limited its conception of autonomy to cultural matters alone, Vozrozhdenie imagined Russian Jewry creating organs of Jewish national autonomy that would undertake such maximalist tasks as regulating social services and emigration. The ultimate political institution of Jewish national autonomy would be a national *seym* or parliament. The *vozrozhdentsy* borrowed this demand from certain members of the Socialist Revolutionary Party, who imagined a socialist Russia as run by a series of national parliaments. Like the Socialist Revolutionaries, the *vozrozhdentsy* approached socialism from a non-Marxist, gradualist, and voluntarist perspective. This voluntarism carried over to their Jewish nationalism as well. Rather than waiting either for mass emigration to Palestine, on the one hand, or for Marxist revolution, on the other, the *vozrozhdentsy* attempted to transform Russian Jewry into a proletarian nation with the trappings of national autonomy in the here and now. By 1905, Tcherikower, Efroikin, and Kalmanovitch all had joined the ranks of the *vozrozhdentsy*.[7]

If the years 1903–1905 brought an increase in revolutionary activity among Russian Jewry, all of Russia followed in this direction in 1905. When in January troops fired into a crowd of peaceful protesters marching to the Winter Palace to submit its demands to the tsar, the residents of St. Petersburg and then other Russian cities erupted in massive protests and strikes. From January through October 1905, the autocracy floundered as Russia slid into disarray. On October 17, 1905, after months of vacillation, Tsar Nicholas II promised his subjects broad, sweeping reform through the creation of an elected parliament, or Duma, with legislative powers, and freedom of the press and of assembly. Although the wording of the October Manifesto was ambiguous, it created the potential for transforming Russia into a constitutional monarchy. With elections held in January 1906, the first Duma convened in April of that year. Unsatisfied with its deputies' demands for more freedoms, the tsar and his minister of the interior, I. L. Goremykin, dissolved the first Duma in July 1906, after it had convened for only seventy-two days. Although elections occurred again in December 1906, the second Duma lasted only several months longer than the first. P. A. Stolypin, the new interior minister, dissolved the second Duma on June 3, 1907, when he grew tired of working with it. Although an election campaign for a third Duma immediately began, it soon became clear that Stolypin had effectuated a coup d'état. Committed to building a constitutional system that would not challenge the autocracy, Stolypin greatly reduced the franchise to the third Duma and limited its powers. Whereas Russian liberal parties such as the Kadets (Russian Constitutional Democratic Party) dominated the first and second Dumas, the Octobrist Party, with its minimalist, conservative interpretation of the October Manifesto, and far-right parties dominated the third and fourth Dumas. Historians categorize the period from June 3, 1907, onward as the end of the revolution and the onset of political reaction.[8]

From the beginning to end of this initial revolution, Russian Jewry participated actively. In the pitched battles between revolutionaries and tsarist troops in the first months of the revolution, Jews joined forces and suffered casualties with the revolutionaries. Mirroring the broader split in the Russian revolutionary camp, Jewish revolutionaries divided themselves between those who advocated for the orderly transition to a constitutional monarchy and those who hoped for the transformation of Russia into a socialist society. Members of the first camp organized themselves into the Union for the Attainment of Full Rights for the Jews of Russia. Within this organization, loosely connected to the Kadets, Jewish integrationists and non-socialist Diaspora nationalists cooperated in uneasy tension. Although integrationists such as Maksim Vinaver and Genrikh Borisovich Sliozberg advocated for full Jewish national rights, their paramount goal remained individual liberties within a democratically reformed Russia. In contrast, for Diaspora nationalists such as Dubnov, the legal recognition of Jewish national autonomy and the creation of organs for its implementation emerged as their chief concern.[9]

In the immediate aftermath of the issuance of the October Manifesto, Russian Jewry's euphoria turned to despair when pogroms erupted in the Ukraine in response to what tsarist loyalists perceived as the tsar's forced capitulation to Jewish revolutionaries. From the months of October through December 1905, pogroms claimed the lives of over one thousand Jews throughout the Pale of Settlement. Jewish nationalists interpreted the meaning of the pogroms within the context of the revolution in varied ways. On the one hand, the pogroms dampened the revolutionary euphoria of many Jewish nationalists of the older generation. Dubnov, for instance, wrote that the widespread participation of the Russian people in the pogroms demonstrated that these attacks were not merely the desperate tool of Russian reaction but demonstrated the durability of Russian anti-Semitism. For many young Jewish socialist revolutionaries, however, the pogroms represented the last throes of the old Russia in the process of disappearance.[10]

Just as they reacted differently to the pogroms, so too did Jewish nationalists and socialist nationalists react differently to the elections to the first Duma. When they realized that the electoral law disqualified the majority of Jewish workers from voting, the Bund and the other Jewish socialist parties boycotted the election. In contrast, the Union for the Attainment of Full Rights led a campaign to organize Jewish voters and supported both Kadets sympathetic to Jewish rights and Jewish nationalist candidates. In the end, Russian Jews succeeded in electing twelve Jewish representatives to the first Duma: nine members of the Kadets and three members of the Trudovik (workers') Party. After the tsarist regime dissolved the first Duma, the Bund and the other Jewish socialist parties learned their lesson from the Union's successful campaign and participated actively in elections to the second Duma.[11]

During the three months of the first Duma's existence, internal conflict eroded the Union for the Attainment of Full Rights. The uneasy alliance of Jewish liberals and nationalists proved capable of surviving an election campaign but not actual parliamentary politics. In response to the nationalists' call for the twelve Jewish Duma representatives to unite into a Jewish faction, the liberals formed their own political party, the Jewish People's Group, or the Folksgrupe, which limited its national demands to communal, but not fully national, Jewish autonomy. The Zionists in the Union, in the meantime, also went their own way. Under the influence of a new young leader, Vladimir Ze'ev Jabotinsky, the Russian Zionist Congress in 1906, held in Helsingsfor, incorporated the call for full-scale Jewish national autonomy in the Diaspora into its political platform. Within this context, Dubnov led those most ideologically committed to autonomism in forming their own political party, known as the Folkspartey. The Union, though still existent on paper, now contained within it representatives of four political parties: the Jewish People's Group, the Russian Zionist party, the Folkspartey, and the Jewish Democratic Group (composed of non-Marxist socialist nationalists).[12]

The splintering of the Union for the Attainment of Full Rights was symptomatic of a larger factionalism among politically active Jews as the revolution progressed. Vozrozhdenie, too, constituted an amalgam of Jewish political activists and thinkers, in this instance dedicated to a reinterpretation of socialist Zionism that would emphasize work in the Diaspora. In the politically fractious environment of 1905–1907, these socialist nationalist circles split into three parties: the Poale Zion; the SSRP and SERP. Poale Zion remained Palestinocentric, seeking to reconcile Marxism with Zionism, while at the same time demanding Jewish national rights in the Diaspora. The SSRP, known by its first initials SS, sought a territorial solution to the Jewish question, believing that only in a Jewish territory could Jewish class struggle and the victory of the proletariat occur. SERP, in contrast, served as the successor party of Vozrozhdenie in its deferral of Jewish territorial concentration to the distant future. In the meantime, SERP elevated the creation of a Jewish *seym*, or parliament, with broad coercive powers of taxation, as its central goal. In this regard, members of SERP, known most often as Seymists, were following not only the path of Vozrozhdenie but also the general trend of all major Jewish political parties both liberal and socialist, which included ever-increasingly broad demands for Jewish national autonomy in their political platforms.

Paradoxically, the Seymists also were following the lead of other Jewish socialist parties in adopting a strident Marxism in their political platform and in their party journals. In contrast to Vozrozhdenie's affinity toward the Socialist Revolutionaries, members of SERP drew close to the Russian Social Democratic Labor Party in their Marxist emphasis on class struggle and near-exclusive focus on the Jewish proletariat. It was the close personal relationship between Zhitlovsky and his fellow co-founder of the Socialist Revolutionaries, Victor Chernov, that led to the ties between SERP and this all-Russian party. Both these contradictory demands of SERP—maximal Jewish national autonomy and proletarian victory—emerged from the revolutionary fervor of the era. They also resulted from the Seymist need to become at once more nationalist and more Marxist than the Bund. At the time, Seymist intellectuals felt compelled to justify their national demands according to their socialist beliefs. As long as Russian Jews remained without national rights, they argued, the class struggle would remain subordinate to the national one. Only the fulfillment of Jewish national autonomy could pave the way for class struggle and for the victory of the Jewish proletariat. In this assertion, the Seymists echoed the arguments of other socialist nationalists throughout the Russian Empire, who justified their nationalism along the same lines.[13]

Simon Rabinovitch has noted that even as the Revolution of 1905 led to increasing political fractiousness among Russian Jews, it also led to an almost universal embrace of demands for some form of Jewish national autonomy. Yet the fault line between socialist class-based parties and nationalist *klal yisroel* parties made for interesting political decisions. When, for instance, Jabotinsky called for the creation of an all-Russian Jewish National Assembly to represent the national interests of Russian Jewry, the Seymists refused to go along. In this instance as in many others, they chose proletarian solidarity over the fulfillment of their political goal of founding a Jewish parliament. Partially as a result of this political fractiousness, Jewish representation in the second Duma decreased from twelve to four. The Jewish representatives came from the Jewish People's Group, the Zionists, and the Social Democrats.[14]

In the end, however, it was the political instability and relative powerlessness of the Dumas themselves, rather than Jewish factionalism, that doomed successive Jewish attempts at passing legislation that could ameliorate Russian Jewry's plight. The two Jewish representatives in the third Duma and the three in the fourth had even less success in this attempt, as the rightist majority had little interest in cooperating with the Jews on this matter. As political reaction set in, even the Kadets distanced themselves from Jewish demands, fearing a loss in popularity because of their support of the Jews. The resurgent tsarist government's refusal to ameliorate the Jews' legal plight meant that, ultimately, engagement in the parliamentary politics of the various Dumas would yield no tangible legal results for those Jews who participated in them.

Although political fractiousness had marked the era of the elections to the second and third Dumas, interparty cooperation increased once reaction set in. Particularly significant was the extent to which socialist nationalists proved willing to collaborate with folkists and liberals to advance autonomist causes. When the Jewish liberal leaders Sliozberg and L. M. Bramson called for a conference to be held in Kovno to discuss the future composition of the *kehile*, or *obshchina*, representatives of the Jewish socialist parties, including the Bund and SERP, accepted the invitation to participate. The immediate catalyst for the calling of the Kovno Conference was the fact that Naftali Fridman and Leopold Nisselovich, the two Jewish representatives in the third Duma, had presented a bill that would legalize the Jewish community. At the Kovno Conference, which met in November 1909, a debate ranged over the nature and jurisdiction of the revitalized *kehile*. Whereas Sliozberg and other liberals argued for a religious definition of the community, Bramson together with the nationalists demanded its secularization and nationalization. In the end, the representatives to the conference reached unanimity in articulating their vision of the reformed, revitalized *kehile*. Any Jew by birth, with the exception of converts to Christianity, could belong to the *kehile*, whose leaders would be elected through a democratic, near universal suffrage. The members of the conference also called for the abolition of the hated *korobka,* or meat tax, which socialists and folkists alike decried as a burden on the poor. Instead, they advocated the imposition of a progressive income tax.[15]

The Kovno Conference thus demonstrated the growing consensus among the Russian Jewish leadership on the issue of Jewish national autonomy. The defeat of Sliozberg's religious definition of Jewish communal identity demonstrated that Russian Jewish liberals increasingly thought and acted in autonomist terms. Equally significantly, Seymists and even Bundists participated for the first time in a discussion about autonomy with bourgeois nationalists and liberals. Unlike the Bund, which qualified its support with continued calls for limiting the authority of the *kehile* to cultural affairs and education alone, the Seymists present could not have helped but rejoice in the maximal definition of communal autonomy that the conference called for. In fact, such veteran Seymists as Zilberfarb recognized the confluence of interests between the Seymist call for the organization of a Jewish national parliament and the incremental steps toward nation building begun in Kovno. In 1913, Zilberfarb joined with Dubnov in forming a journal dedicated to the question of reforming the *kehile.* Although still in Berne at the time of the Kovno Conference, Efroikin later would participate in the debate about the future direction of the *kehile.*[16]

As political reaction intensified in Russia, a common response of both the Russian and the Russian Jewish intelligentsia was to turn from political activity to cultural creativity and organic work. Most characteristic of this trend among Russian intellectuals was the publication in 1909 of *Vekhi* (Signposts), whose articles called for a retreat from politics and a turn inward toward the creation of national culture. The development of the national spirit through culture, argued the journal's editor Mikhael Gershenzon, would lead to national liberation much more quickly than the false route of politics.[17] The Russian Jewish intelligentsia followed a similar path. Stolypin's coup had dramatically curtailed the possibilities for direct political action even as it left intact the basic liberties granted in the October Manifesto, such as freedom of the press and assembly. This contradiction led to many former young Jewish socialist nationalist intellectuals shifting their activity away from politics toward the creation of a modern

Jewish public culture largely centered on Yiddish and the establishment of educational and relief organizations. These cultural endeavors often demonstrated a high degree of nonpartisanship, as former political rivals joined to forge a common secular Jewish national culture.

During these years of reaction, Russian Jewish nationalists also created the institutional trappings of a Jewish public culture, especially through the creation of the Jewish Historical-Ethnographical Society and the Jewish Literary Society. It was during this time that folkists and socialist nationalists joined in creating self-help organizations such as the Jewish cooperative movement to ameliorate such pressing issues as Jewish financial solvency. In addition to creating new public institutions, Jewish autonomists, both socialist and liberal, sought to co-opt existing institutions such as the Jewish Colonization Association (EKA) and ORT (Obshchestvo Remeslennago i Zemledelcheskago Truda Sredi Evreev v Rossii) (the Society for the Promotion of Artisan and Agricultural Labor) and to democratize them. According to Rabinovitch, the creation of these cultural and social organizations created a public Jewish space that implemented autonomism in action.[18]

The process of democratization occurred most noticeably in the OPE (Obshchestva dlia Rasprostraneniia Prosveshcheniia Mezhdu Evreiami v Rossii—Society for the Promotion of Enlightenment among the Jews of Russia), which had long served as a bastion of Russian Jewish integrationism and then liberalism. During the Revolution of 1905, autonomists and Yiddishists used OPE's annual meeting as an arena to demand this institution's democratization and nationalization. This process continued during the years of reaction. Swelled from the ranks of former revolutionaries and political activists, OPE membership greatly increased between 1908 and 1911. Great rancor accompanied local and central meetings as Zionists, Bundists, autonomists, and liberals battled over the question of Jewish educational reform. The main point of contention was the language issue, with Zionists arguing for Hebrew, Bundists and autonomists for Yiddish, and liberals for Russian. The Yiddishists themselves were divided between the Bundists, who advocated the use of Yiddish but rejected overtly nationalist content, and the autonomists, who saw the use of

Yiddish as the agent of a modern national culture. After much wrangling, the central committee reached a compromise in 1911 that supported the creation of secular schools that would teach Yiddish and Hebrew literatures, Bible and Jewish history. Each school would decide for itself regarding religious instruction. Similarly, each school would choose the children's mother tongue as the language of instruction. Given realities in the Pale, this compromise spelled a victory for the Yiddishists.[19]

OPE branches continued to thrive following Stolypin's assassination in 1911, despite increased restrictions on freedom of assembly. Yet Yiddishists, Hebraists, and integrationists battled over the proportion of hours dedicated to the various languages in the schools. Within the Yiddishist camp, Bundists and autonomists fought each other over the question of the desirability of the reformation of the kheyder. Despite these internal squabbles, the OPE achieved its greatest success when the All-Russian Congress for National Education approved the OPE delegation's resolution calling for tuition-free Jewish elementary schools that would teach students both Jewish and general subjects in Yiddish.[20]

The Russian Jewish press also served as a major arena for the creation of a public Russian Jewish national culture. Founded in 1909 by a group of Jewish liberals and autonomists, including Dubnov, the journal *Evreiskii mir* (Jewish world) soon reached beyond its original base to include the articles of general Zionists, Seymists, and even Bundists. In general, however, *Evreiskii mir* represented the growing consensus of Jewish nationalists, both folkist and socialist nationalist, regarding the issue of Jewish national autonomy. According to Rabinovitch, the journal accomplished the twin tasks of keeping the issue of autonomism alive in the minds of the Russian Jewish reading public during the era of reaction and creating a sense of inevitability about the triumph of this political ideology in the near future. In drawing members of SERP and the other socialist nationalist parties into the heart of this discussion, *Evreiskii mir* succeeded where the Union for the Attainment of Full Rights had failed.[21]

This success, however, owed as much to the change in attitude of the socialist nationalists involved as it did to the growing consensus on the issue of autonomy. In the process of seeking a broader appeal for Jewish socialism, socialist nationalist activists and intellectuals decided to participate in such bourgeois institutions as the *kehile* and in such democratic, but not socialist, publications as *Evreiskii mir.* Unwittingly, however, this process ended up co-opting them into the centrist "bourgeois" mainstream that, during the heady days of the revolution, they had so resisted. During an era of paralyzed political activity, the opportunity to preach and to engage in practical work for the incremental realization of Jewish autonomy in Russia proved more alluring than adhering to party doctrines. This shift from revolutionary fervor to incremental organic work served as a major factor in the transformation of Efroikin, Kalmanovitch, and many others from socialist nationalists into folkists during the inter-revolutionary period.[22]

As a Russian-language Jewish nationalist periodical, *Evreiskii mir* was ill-timed, since its creation coincided with the rise of the Yiddishist movement. The Czernowitz Yiddish Language Conference, which convened in late August 1908, served as the most dramatic, though not the most successful, example of the consolidation of the Yiddishist ideology among young Russian Jewish intellectuals in the aftermath of the 1905 Revolution. At the same time, two journals appeared in Vilna, *Di literarishe monatsshriftn* (Literary monthlies) and *Leben un visenshaft* (Life and science), that represented the emerging two poles of highbrow and populist Yiddishism. In their introductory essay to the readers, the editors of *Di literarishe monatsshriftn* (Shmuel Niger, A. Vayter, and Shmarye Gorelik) declared the arrival of a Jewish cultural renaissance and vowed to further its spread in Yiddish. They made it clear, however, that their role in the creation of this cultural renaissance decidedly did not rest with popularization but rather with the creation of Yiddish literature on a high cultural level. As such, their journal, which appeared only four times, carried short stories by leading Yiddish writers, who used the journal to experiment with symbolism, decadence, and other literary forms. In contrast, in his introductory essay to *Leben un visenshaft,* the editor, A. Litvin (pseudonym of Shmuel Hurvits), stated that his goal was "not to discover any Americas" but rather "to transmit scientific information in popularized form." Specifically, the editor stated that he intended this journal for those youth who yearned for scientific knowledge yet never had received a formal education because of poverty. This journal, in sharp contradistinction to *Di literarishe monatsshriftn,* understood its goal as functioning as "a Yiddish carrier of culture, which would work for the people together with the people."[23]

Despite their apparent differences, the introductory essays of *Di literarishe monatsshriftn* and *Leben un visenshaft* in reality shared more central features in common than not. Both editorials began by decrying the divide between the linguistically acculturated intelligentsia and the Yiddish-speaking masses. Significantly, both editorials also understood the low level of Yiddish culture as symptomatic of the lack of integration of European culture with Jewish culture and the Yiddish language. Finally, both editorials also emphasized the importance of nonpartisanship in the pursuit of cultural work.[24] Both these journals reflected the shift from politics toward culture during the period of reaction. The call for nonpartisanship, though still resisted by some on the left, indicated a new willingness to subordinate political orientation to cultural work. Litvin spoke for many former political activists when he declared cultural work as the only surviving "city of refuge" during "the difficult and dark period of political reaction."[25] Both these journals thus sought to provide East European Jewry with a new, secular Yiddish culture that would synthesize the Jewish with the European. In fact, *Leben un visenshaft* thus served as an example of the attempt to win over a broad Yiddish-reading audience to the same high-culture version of Yiddish culture articulated in the pages of *Di literarishe monatsshriftn.*[26]

The creation of this highbrow Yiddishist culture had profound effects on many young Russian Jewish nationalist intellectuals, who subsequently rejected Russian for Yiddish as their language of high culture. Ironically, it was outside of the Pale in St. Petersburg that many of these young intellectuals, such as Nokhem Shtif, discovered the national import of Yiddish. In the pages of *Evreiskii mir,* the use of Russian became associated more and more with the great national sin of assimilation. Even Dubnov, who had resisted this trend by advocating for a trilingual Russian Jewish culture, identified the use of Russian over Yiddish as leading to assimilation (even while expressing this opinion in the pages of *Evreiskii mir* in Russian!). Although

Evreiskii mir closed in 1911 because of financial problems rather than ideological concerns, a Jewish nationalist Russian-language journal dedicated to combating linguistic assimilation ultimately was proving itself unsustainable.[27]

Soon after *Evreiskii mir* ceased publication, a group of intellectuals who had written for it formed a new Yiddish journal as its successor, appropriately named *Di idishe velt* (the Jewish world). The editorship was composed of several young autonomists who had embraced Yiddishism: Efroikin, Aron Perel'man, Niger, and Yisroel Tsinberg. On the editorial board they were joined by two veteran Yiddish literary figures, H. D. Horovits and Sh. An-sky (pseudonym for Shloyme Zaynvl Rapoport). No longer claiming nonpartisanship, the journal envisioned itself as the organ of the newly reconstituted Folkspartey. One year later, when the journal moved from St. Petersburg to Vilna, the Kletskin Press assumed control and dropped the official affiliation with the Folkspartey. Still, *Di idishe velt* continued to embody the growing centrist position in Jewish nationalist politics and culture. Non-Bundist and non-Zionist, the journal represented a non-socialist form of Diaspora nationalism that allied itself with Russian democratic parties rather than with socialist ones. The transformation of *Evreiskii mir* into *Di idishe velt* symbolized the ascendancy of a highbrow Yiddishism that sought to create a rarefied culture that would connect the intellectual elite to the folk through the medium of the mother tongue.[28]

At the same time, this journal's metamorphosis served as the most cogent symbol of the refashioning of the generation of 1905 from Russian Jewish intellectuals to members of the Yiddishist intelligentsia. Efroikin, as a member of this generation, previously had expressed his thoughts on the issues of Jewish nationalism and socialism in either Russian or Yiddish, depending on his audience. Once the language question became inextricably bound to plans for national renaissance, however, he, like so many of his contemporaries, wrote nearly exclusively in Yiddish. This marriage between Diaspora nationalism and Yiddishism separated this younger generation of autonomists from their mentor, Dubnov, who, despite increasingly pro-Yiddish sentiments, continued to write in Russian and to champion a trilingual Russian Jewish culture.[29]

Di idishe velt's opening editorial articulated a combination of Diaspora nationalism, Yiddishism, and commitment to an activist politics. The editors began by stating that they had decided to create their periodical for the new, highbrow Yiddish readers who could not satisfy themselves on the Yiddish dailies. The journal, moreover, sought to encourage the return of the Jewish intelligentsia to the national culture of the masses. Decrying the national alienation of the Russified intelligentsia, the editors portrayed a situation in which the old Jewish traditional life proved intolerably stale while the new had not yet produced anything more than national disintegration. Into this breach, the editors of the journal sought to introduce a program of national regeneration that would possess the following features: a modern Jewish school built upon secular, national foundations whose language of instruction would be Yiddish; the rebuilding of the *kehile* as a building block of national autonomy, also upon secular, national foundations; the regulation of Jewish emigration through a national folk organization that could become a constructive national force; and the productivization of Jewish emigrants through their settlements upon farms.[30] In short, the journal, at least in its first year of publication, adopted the Folkspartey program in its entirety. Finally, the editors ended their opening article on a note of optimism, stating their conviction that the dark forces that currently ruled Russia would not long endure. Moreover, they wrote, "We believe in the deeply buried strengths of our people, which will continue to lead it on its bright path of human and national progress." Because national struggle proved so important, the editors condemned social and political apathy as the greatest danger.[31]

Following this introduction, an inspiring article by Dubnov appeared, titled "After the Thirty Years War." In this article, Dubnov chronicled the difficulties of Russian Jewish life from 1881 through 1911. However, he buttressed his readers by refuting those who claimed that the Jews were demoralized and on the brink of national apostasy. Rather, Dubnov praised Russian Jewry for having created a national consciousness in response to its persecution. He also favorably spoke of the creation of two new important centers, the United States and Palestine. In Russia itself, the intelligentsia had stopped leaving the people and had become more national. The Jewish press had proliferated in three languages. He only exhorted Russian Jewry to fortify itself against internal exhaustion. The task of the periodical, *Di idishe velt,* was to encourage Russian Jews to engage in national work, even under the current conditions of repression.[32]

Each in his own way, Tcherikower, Efroikin, and Kalmanovitch all followed the trajectory of revolutionary activity to organic work and cultural production. It is to Tcherikower's journey that we now turn.

Tcherikower's Russian-Language Period

Unlike the other two, who were born and raised in Jewish Lithuania, Tcherikower spent his formative years in the much more Russified environment of Poltava, Ukraine. Typical for the Poltava region, his parents' home combined the features of mitnagdic traditional Judaism, Haskalah, Ḥibat Zion, and Russification. Having grown up speaking Yiddish and Russian, Tcherikower attended first a Russian gymnasium and then an art school in Odessa. As a young man, Tcherikower went not by his Hebrew/Yiddish name, Eliyohu, but rather by his Russian name and patronymic, Ilya Mikhailovitch. For the rest of his life, his friends referred to him by this Russian name, often personally referring to him by the affectionate diminutive, Ilyushe. From his late teenage years onward, Tcherikower's life partner was his girlfriend and then wife, Riva Teplitsky (known by her Russian name Riva Naumnova). As a young couple, they immersed themselves in the world of Russian art and literature. Both coming from a privileged background, young Ilya and Riva traveled outside of the Pale often. In 1902, for instance, Riva even traveled to Alexandria, Egypt.[33] Although Russian served as their cultural language, Tcherikower and Teplitsky peppered their letters with Yiddish and Hebrew phrases. Both young Ilya and Riva grew up in homes that combined moderate religious observance with a commitment to Zionism. Riva, for instance, actively participated in Zionist activities in Poltava. She reported to Tcherikower about the showdown between young Zionists and the anti-Zionist rabbi, which occurred in a central Poltava synagogue on the Sabbath.

Although having joined Vozrozhdenie in 1903, by the outbreak of the 1905 Revolution, Tcherikower had drifted toward Menshevik circles. He revealed his Marxist perspective in his first article for the

Russian Jewish Zionist journal *Evreiskaia zhizn'* (Jewish life), which he published in 1905. Titled "Mendele Moykher Sforim: An Attempt at a Critical Characteristic," this piece served as Tcherikower's first foray into the world of Yiddish literature. Through a harsh critique of the Yiddish works of Sholem Yaakov Abramovitsh (1836–1917; his Yiddish pseudonym was Mendele Moykher Sforim), known popularly as "the grandfather of Yiddish literature," Tcherikower demonstrated that he valued class struggle far more than the nascent Yiddish literary renaissance. Defining his methodology as social literary criticism, he explained that a literary critic must primarily take into account the unique social circumstances of an author, and view him "as a point to which a whole network of social threads accumulates."[34] Tcherikower analyzed Mendele's primary Yiddish works, *Dos kleyne mentshele* (The little man), *Di takse* (The tax), *Di klyatshe* (The mare), *Der priziv* (Military service), "Fishke der krumer" (Fishke the lame), and "Dos vintshfingerl" (The wishing ring), in order to analyze the author's social perspective.

From this perspective, Tcherikower concluded that Abramovitsh belonged to the petit bourgeois maskilic class, which remained bound to the Jewish street even as it criticized it. Typical of his class, for instance, was Abramovitsh's criticism both of the haute bourgeoisie, which he blamed for exploitation, and of the lower classes, which he viewed as parasitical. According to Tcherikower, this petit bourgeois character permeated all of Abramovitsh's works and lowered their literary worth. For instance, Abramovitsh often simply sought to reflect real life, such as when he included real portraits of corrupt community leaders of Berdichev in his play *Di Takse.*[35] Also contributing to the low artistic level of Abramovitsh's work was its didactic material. Unable to see past his own perspective, Abramovitsh crafted not a seamless plot but rather unending character sketches, all "versions of the same life image."[36] As a member of the petite bourgeoisie, moreover, Abramovitsh employed a Yiddish style that never transcended the parochial confines of the *besmedresh,* despite his pretensions of enlightenment. In Tcherikower's words:

Mendele is a poet, who understands and admires nature, but he never seems to penetrate its shoreless profundity. He understands nature from his point of view—he made nature Jewish, as he did with the "klyatshe" and with whatever came in the sphere of his creative imagination. He uses expressions from *selikhes* and *kines* for his images—which add to the *be-smedresh* stylization of his descriptions. The images of the outside world are strange to him.[37]

Tcherikower, though a Jewish socialist nationalist, displayed indifference toward Abramovitsh's contribution to the development of a Yiddish national culture. Rather than praise the author for forging a Yiddish literature that criticized traditional Jewish society in its own language, Tcherikower dismissed this Jewish content as too parochial. The best praise that Tcherikower could offer was the anemic statement: "His great achievement was that he was the first to write in the crooked Jewish jargon for the grass-roots, that he was a realist, and even a rough realist carried his long-suffering word to the audience . . ." Tcherikower tempered even this praise, however, by adding that now that social conditions had changed, Abramovitsh had lost his audience.[38]

Tcherikower's hostility toward Abramovitsh's works demonstrated the extent to which Tcherikower did not link his socialist nationalism to Yiddish cultural nationalism. With the exception of Chaim Zhitlovsky, few socialist autonomists espoused Yiddish language and literature as a national value until the end of the 1905 Revolution. As a Marxist, Tcherikower believed that Yiddish literature only had value to the extent that it could spread socialist ideas to the masses. During this period, the Bund also demonstrated this utilitarian approach to Yiddish literature, criticizing the national-romantic turn of Peretz and other leading Yiddish writers. Tcherikower hinted at this approach when he criticized Abramovitsh's occasional sentimentalism, stating that this style had set the stage for Peretz.[39] Identifying these trends as petit bourgeois, Tcherikower could dismiss the importance of Abramovitsh's work without further thought. Tcherikower's lack of appreciation of Yiddish makes sense within the context of his journey toward Jewish nationalism and socialism, which had occurred completely in a Russian-speaking context.

During 1905, Tcherikower also wrote articles for the general Russian press on the revolutionary struggle. Interestingly, even during the heady months of the 1905 Revolution and its immediate aftermath,

Tcherikower voiced concern that the present euphoria would cause revolutionaries to forget those who had suffered for the movement. In an article titled "In the 'Past,' " Tcherikower bemoaned the loss of romanticism in the revolutionary movement. Whereas before 1905, revolutionaries had mourned those exiled to Siberia, now, he argued, few paid attention to the great number of those suffering from political repression. Typical of a revolutionary with Menshevik sympathies, Tcherikower also attacked the Kadets for what he deemed the outdated methods with which this party of Russian liberals fought the old regime. Expelled from the nobility, members of the Kadets, argued Tcherikower, cared more about fighting for their titles than for expressing the will of the people.[40]

In early 1906, Tcherikower traveled from Poltava to St. Petersburg, where he entertained himself in the Russian theater, which he appreciated for its realism, symbolism, and music. In need of cash, he supported himself by writing for the Russian and Russian Jewish press. In particular, he contributed to the journal *Nauka i zhizhn'* (Science and life) and also wrote an anonymous piece about Heinrich Heine for *Evreiskaia zhizn'*. However, increasingly, it was political work that occupied his time and interest. During the election campaign to the first Duma, Tcherikower demonstrated an interest in the meetings and activities of the various political parties, both Jewish and Russian. However, his loyalties lay with the Menshevik wing of the Russian Social Democratic Labor Party (RSDLP). Increasingly, he explained to Teplitsky, he belonged to "another world," "the world of the Party." Attending their meetings, he especially enjoyed the speeches of Julius Martov, Vladimir Bazarov, and Vladimir Lenin. Typical of his loyalty to the RSDLP was Tcherikower's disparaging comment about the Bund, as made up of "kings without a people, but [who] imagine that a parade is following them." He noted that his party work, though still small, involved agitation with the Russian, rather than the Jewish, proletariat. It would be a mistake, however, to imagine that Tcherikower had completely exchanged his socialist Zionist sympathies for Menshevik internationalism. Rather, during the 1905 Revolution, even Jews involved in the all-Russian revolutionary movements could espouse Jewish nationalist sympathies in a way that the previous generation of the 1880s could not.[41]

Tcherikower's agitation work on behalf of the Mensheviks, however, did not last long. In early April 1906, the Russian police arrested him for his involvement in the organization of a Menshevik demonstration, charging him under the article of the Criminal Code of 1903 that banned political demonstrations and strikes. Tcherikower experienced incarceration first in St. Petersburg and then in Poltava. He took advantage of the generally lax security conditions in the prisons to write letters to Teplitsky, who smuggled notes to him in foodstuffs such as kielbasa. In the Poltava prison, elected chairman of his cellmates, Tcherikower helped to stage a May Day celebration that involved the hanging of red flags outside their prison windows and singing revolutionary songs. As a punishment for these antics, the prison guards transferred him to yet another prison, where he ended up in solitary confinement. Soon after, however, Tcherikower was transferred back to the Poltava region, where he spent the next two years under a very liberal house arrest. Tcherikower's cat-and-mouse experience and non-harsh sentence proved typical of the experience of Russian Jewish revolutionaries during the era of reaction.[42]

Although hardly harsh, Tcherikower's experience of prison and house arrest did end his career as an active revolutionary and led him to return to his roots as a Jewish socialist nationalist. After his release from prison, Tcherikower continued his life as a peripatetic Russian Jewish intellectual. Although based in St. Petersburg, he traversed the tsarist empire, and in 1910 he and his new bride, Riva, even visited the United States. Like so many other Jewish socialist nationalists during the era of reaction, Tcherikower turned to cultural work. In particular, he sought to eke out a living as a writer for the St. Petersburg–based Russian Jewish press. While awaiting trial, for instance, he completed work on a lengthy article, "Essays on the Jewish Revolutionary and Workers' Movement," which he submitted to *Rassvet*. Between 1909 and 1911, he also contributed regular news briefs to *Evreiskii mir*. He began his career as a Jewish historian and scholar between 1908 and 1913 by contributing entries to the *Evreiskaia entsiklopedii* (Jewish encyclopedia), a project initiated by Dubnov and An-sky. With the ambitious goal of demonstrating the Jewish influence upon world history from antiquity to the present, the encyclopedia project demonstrated cultural Diaspora nationalism in action.[43] In 1913, Tcherikower also found steady employment in the OPE, where he edited its journal, *Vestnik OPRE,* and wrote an official history of the early years of the institution. He thus assumed a leadership role in this institution right after it had completed its transition from integrationism to nationalism.

Tcherikower's book on the OPE served as the official history of this organization upon the occasion of its fiftieth anniversary. The unstated goal behind the work was to justify the OPE's integrationist past in light of its national present. Saul Günzberg, the prominent Zionist who headed the OPE in 1913, wrote an introduction in which he defended the Haskalah and its representatives against contemporary critics, who failed to understand the historical conditions under which the *maskilim* had labored.[44] In his introduction, Tcherikower too wrote that the social conditions of Russian Jewry in the 1860s through 1880s explained the activity and ideology of the OPE in its formative years. What followed throughout the book was a detailed description of the OPE's educational and cultural activity during its classical period. Arguing that mid-nineteenth-century Russian *maskilim* had failed to understand the true missionizing intentions of Nicholas I's government, Tcherikower portrayed them as naïve but wellmeaning. He then chronicled the founding of OPE, the projects that it launched to promote education, its complicated relationship with government-sponsored and private Jewish schools, and the society's internal debates. In speaking of the language debate in the OPE, Tcherikower criticized its former disdain of Yiddish. By 1913, the transition of the Russian Jewish nationalist intelligentsia into a Yiddishist intelligentsia had led Tcherikower to understand Yiddish as an integral part of the Jewish national renaissance. Tcherikower's study, moreover, served as a historiographical justification of Russian Jewry's move from emancipationist to autonomist politics. As the Russian government thwarted the society's goal of integrating the Jews into Russian culture, the OPE had to abandon its broad goals of cultural and civic revival and instead concentrate more narrowly on education. In his conclusion, for instance, Tcherikower ironically quoted an OPE committee correspondent from 1866 stating that the government never would deny the Jews their ultimate rights. By the 1880s, these hopes had proven illusory.[45]

A Populist Critique of Jewish Socialism.

Yisroel Efroikin was born in 1884 to relatively wealthy parents in the small, traditional shtetl of Vekshne, Lithuania. In the 1890s, the family moved to the larger city of Libave in Latvia. The family straddled the worlds of traditional East European Jewish culture and modernization. Efroikin's deeply pious mother came from a long line of distinguished rabbis. In contrast, his businessman father considered himself a *maskil* who nonetheless had a favorable view of Yiddish. Under his mother's influence, the young Yisroel, after completing a traditional kheyder, studied in the famed Telz yeshiva. As with many of his peers, Efroikin left the yeshiva to study in a local Russian gymnasium. In 1904, the twenty-year-old Efroikin followed in the footsteps of many modernizing Russian Jewish youth who attended university abroad by studying philosophy at the University of Bern. When revolution erupted in Russia less than a year later, he returned home to participate in political agitation.[46]

An early member of Vozrozhdenie, Efroikin joined SERP when the party was founded in 1906.[47] During 1906–1907, he engaged in party activity in Vitebsk, where he organized workers, registered voters for Duma elections, and involved himself in communal activities. In the summer of 1907, he reported on these activities in SERP's Yiddish weekly journal, *Di folksshtime* (the people's voice). Appearing from December 1906 through August 1907, *Di folksshtime* reported and commented upon Russian Jewish politics from the time of elections to the second Duma through preparations for the election campaign for the third Duma.

The timing of *Di folksshtime*'s publication thus coincided with the movement from euphoria to despair among all Jewish socialist nationalists. The socialist nationalist intelligentsia experienced a sense of crisis over the fact that Russian Jewry overwhelmingly favored the candidates of the Union for the Attainment of Full Rights' election committees over socialist candidates to the second Duma. These election results belied the Jewish socialist leaders' belief that they had a mass following in the cities and towns of the Pale of Settlement. Once the political campaign ended, moreover, party work stagnated. The crisis only deepened with Stolypin's coup d'état on June 3, 1907.

Although few Jewish socialist leaders had great hopes for representation in the third Duma, they used this election campaign as a means to remobilize their party loyalists and followers. At the same time, they searched for other nonpolitical means of reaching their would-be constituents. They began to view work in the *kehile,* which they previously had spurned as a bourgeois institution, as a way to maintain their respective parties' communal influence. Other means that these parties used to retain their relevance were renewed involvement in trade unions and cultural work. SERP participated in both these fields, especially in its stronghold of Vitebsk, where Efroikin functioned.[48]

Di folksshtime reveals the interesting ways in which revolutionary fervor persisted even as crisis set in. The legacy of the revolution had propelled the Seymists as well as all Jewish socialist nationalists leftward, a direction that did not immediately abate after Stolypin's coup. Thus, the articles in *Di folksshtime* concentrated on the plight of the Jewish proletariat, largely embraced Marxist doctrine, and addressed the question of the reconciliation between class struggle and the struggle for national autonomy. On the other hand, the writers of *Di folksshtime* fully shared in the crisis of Jewish socialism in the aftermath of the coup, actually feeling its first signs before other parties. It was Moyshe Zilberfarb who made the case in the journal's pages for SERP's involvement in the reformation of the *kehile.* Zilberfarb argued that since the tsarist authorities had imposed the current *kehile* on the Jewish community, Seymists did not have to wait for the revolutionary future to attempt its democratization.[49]

In the summer of 1907, Efroikin worked to win support for his party among the Jewish workers of Vitebsk. However, he had to fight an uphill battle because of the low morale caused by political reaction and economic stagnation. In this environment, he complained, Jewish workers had abandoned SERP for "adventurists of all sorts," such as anarchists to the left and Zionists to the right.[50] Like so many of his contemporaries in all the Jewish socialist nationalist parties, Efroikin located the origins of his party's crisis in the party itself, which had emphasized the election campaign to the second Duma over internal party organization. As a result, once the election campaign had ended, the party lost its grassroots support and existed "only on paper."[51]

Efroikin, therefore, had to recruit members anew. When SERP, like its political rivals, passed a party resolution to recruit members from the labor unions, Efroikin helped to organize lectures on such topics as "the crisis of the Jewish working class" in order to win back old members and attract new ones.[52]

Efroikin's decision to influence the decisions of the *kehile* demonstrated his following of his party's lead as well. The first opportunity for such influence occurred when the Vitebsk Synagogue Council, or *v'a'ad*, held a meeting over the issue of sending delegates to the city duma, whom the latter institution had handpicked in advance. At issue was the fact that, according to the law, Jews were barred from sitting on the city dumas, even in places such as Vitebsk where the Jews constituted a majority of the population. Jewish socialist nationalist leaders such as Efroikin used open forums such as this synagogue *v'a'ad* meeting to seek to impose their party ideals on the community. In his report, Efroikin thus concentrated upon the speech of a certain Alexandrov who argued at the meeting for boycotting the city duma. Alexandrov, whose name closely resembled Efroikin's Russian pseudonym "Alexander," articulated SERP's party platform in the resolution that he proposed. The resolution called for the condemnation of the city duma as an undemocratic institution that only interested itself in the needs of the wealthy rather than the masses. The city duma's handpicking of several token Jews to join it served as no more than alms meant to pacify the Jews. As a good socialist autonomist, Alexandrov called for the resolution to end with the demand for the democratization of the city duma and for its handing over the administration of Jewish affairs to an autonomous Jewish representative body best suited to defend the interests of the "wide folk masses." In the pages of *Di folksshtime*, Efroikin similarly argued that the city duma was doubly estranged from the Jewish workers because of its bourgeois, undemocratic nature, its lack of Jewish representatives, and its discrimination against Jewish workers when assigning work relief.[53]

In 1907, the socialist nationalist turn to communal work did not signify a cooling of socialist fervor but rather a desire to refashion the *kehile* in its image. Efroikin thus fulminated against the retrograde, elitist leadership of the Vitebsk *kehile* that he witnessed at the synagogue *v'a'ad* meeting.[54] Although the *v'a'ad* ultimately decided not to send the government's handpicked delegates to the city duma, the head of the *v'a'ad* vetoed Alexandrov's resolution as too provocative. He also bowed to the wishes of the Zionists, who feared making a general statement about the undemocratic nature of the city duma. Decrying what he perceived as the undemocratic, oligarchic nature of the *v'a'ad*, Efroikin commented bitterly:

> That is how public opinion is created amongst our bigwigs [*redelfirer*] and *kahal* people. In general, the meeting made the worst impression. It could appear that before our eyes it was a meeting of an old-fashioned *kahal-shtibl*. . . . In one word, we must put a lot of work into it just to clean off the Jewish *kehile* from its external filth, to give it a bit of a cultural face. Finally, I must add in particular that the comportment of the Zionists, who came out against the resolution very fiercely, is simply beyond comprehension. If the everyday *bale-batim* simply were in fear of the small shopkeeper, not immersing themselves in the essence of the resolution, the Zionists as "politically educated" people should have understood that there was no danger, God forbid, in it. It appears that the Zionists are in the meantime very close friends of the *kahal-shtibl*.[55]

Efroikin's charge that the Zionists pandered to traditional Jewish leadership resonated with the general Jewish socialist critique of Zionism as a force of conservatism that obfuscated class consciousness.

Efroikin's attitude toward the Vitebsk *kehile,* moreover, reveals the extent of the fault line that existed between Seymists and *klal yisroel* autonomists. In fact, he ended his reportage by commenting upon the activity of a democratic group seeking to reorganize and democratize the *kehile*. In his outline of the terms for its success, Efroikin demonstrated the Seymist refusal to abdicate proletarian solidarity in the name of national autonomy:

> And if the democratic group will be truly democratic, if it will completely renounce the utopia of introducing the reforms without any struggle with the old bigwigs and *kahal*-people and will not [seek to] unite fire and water, will not want to live in peace with everybody, it can accomplish a lot. It must once and for all clearly know and understand that only through relying on the masses, emerging from their interests and needs, making a break with the wealthy [*gvirim*] and bigwigs of a well-known type, supporting the working class and the party, which will take a lead in the struggle for its interests in the Jewish *kehile,* will it be able to bring use to the Jewish masses.[56]

Another means that Efroikin used to fight despair was to register Vitebsk Jewish workers for the elections to the third Duma. In the weeks following Stolypin's coup d'état, all the Jewish political parties discussed the question of whether to boycott the elections. Although deeply disillusioned by the political reaction, all the Jewish socialist nationalist parties, with the exception of Poale Zion, decided not to boycott the elections.[57] Siding with the anti-boycott majority of the party, Efroikin participated in party meetings in which he and his fellow activists explained to others that they still could accomplish much through the Duma, even under these conditions. According to Efroikin, these speeches proved enough to banish the "mood of resignation" and "apathy" reigning among the party members and workers.[58] Stolypin's new electoral law, however, posed serious challenges to voter registration. The law divided each city into two curia based upon property ownership. The first curia, comprising the wealthiest members of the community, received more electors than the second, less-affluent curia. The new electoral law also stipulated that non-taxpaying apartment renters had to register themselves for the elections by acquiring certification from the police of their residential status. Through this bureaucratic hurdle, the regime sought to disenfranchise the urban poor. Representatives of the Bund, SS, and SERP all tried to overcome this obstacle to participation in the elections by sending party activists door to door to help apartment renters register their residences. Time was the biggest obstacle that these party activists faced in their voter registration campaign. Only beginning their work at the end of June, they had to submit their petitions to the authorities by the beginning of July.[59]

Efroikin helped to lead this campaign of voter registration in Vitebsk. He took great pride in the fact that the SERP-run Jewish Workers' Voters Committee succeeded in registering six hundred voters, far more than any other Jewish party, liberal or socialist. It is not surprising that Efroikin contrasted the organized voter registration drive of SERP with the disorganized one of the Bund, which only succeeded in registering fifteen voters. In this regard, Vitebsk, a Seymist stronghold, proved an exception to the overall trend of Bundist success in voter registration. Efroikin's victory, however, proved ephemeral. Through various obstacles, including by limiting the time allowed for registration, the city mayor succeeded in invalidating a large number of those registered from voting.[60] Still, through his persistence, Efroikin demonstrated what would become a central feature of his political perspective during the years of reaction: continued hope in the efficacy of the Duma and insistence upon the continued political organization of the Jewish masses.

As early as March 1907, a SERP leader openly called for the organization of nonpartisan workers' committees to organize the older, less politically conscious Jewish workers. The secretive party structure of SERP, this SERP leader argued, had proven too narrow to attract a mass following.[61] Efroikin adopted this strategy in the pages of *Di folksshtime* as a means to maintain Jewish workers' political interest during the era of reaction. In essence, Efroikin and SERP borrowed the idea of nonpartisan workers' committees from the Menshevik Pavel Axelrod, who had proposed this plan at the 1905 Non-Partisan All-Russian Congress of Workers. Efroikin's application of this call for nonpartisanship to the Jewish socialists came within the context of growing cooperation between the various Jewish parties in light of the more difficult circumstances of this election. Even the Bund parted with its previous policies by calling for nonpartisan technical bureaus, in which members of the various oppositional parties would engage in united activity such as voter registration.[62]

Despite its call for nonpartisanship, Efroikin's proposal did not transcend the SERP's vision of the relationship of class struggle to national autonomy. For instance, Efroikin lamented that whereas greater class differentiation within national minorities had occurred during the elections to the second Duma, a parallel process had not taken place among the Russian Jewish proletariat. The fact that most Russian Jewish workers and poor had voted for the bourgeois democratic parties had forced the Jewish socialist parties to realize that they had "little significance not only in Jewish society but also even among the wide working masses."[63] The success of the Jewish bourgeois parties in attracting working-class voters resulted from their Jewish Election Committees, which united Jewish members of the Kadets, Zionists, folkists, and others. Unlike the proletarian parties, the bourgeois parties recognized their lack of appeal among the Jewish masses and therefore banded together in a nonpartisan alliance.

Success would come only to *"mass organizations, built on the foundation of the most necessary, generally recognized needs."*[64] In contrast, the Jewish socialist leaders and organizers had remained out of touch with the masses. Jewish socialism possessed only "distant goals, see[ing] before itself only distant horizons and beautiful heavens, and cannot because of their [*sic*]direct character of struggle give any answers to its [the masses'] daily life questions and needs."[65]

Efroikin, therefore, proposed the creation of a parallel nonpartisan election committee, composed exclusively of the various socialist parties. In making this suggestion, he rejected the two prevalent responses to the success of this unity among the bourgeois parties. On the one hand, he adamantly rejected the calls of the bourgeois parties to the socialists to merge with them. In this regard, Efroikin vehemently rejected a *klal yisroel* politics. In fact, Efroikin had nothing good to say about the *klal yisroel* political parties that had incorporated autonomism into their platforms. He thus dismissed the three new political parties to have emerged during the election campaign to the second Duma, the Folkspartey, the Folksgrupe, and the Democratic Group, as nothing more than "a few lawyers, doctors, and plain 'intellectuals.'" The Russian Zionist Party, moreover, only transcended its roots as a colonization society and developed a program of its own at the Helsingsfor Conference. Although adamantly rejecting *klal yisroel* politics, Efroikin also criticized the leaders of the socialist parties, who declared their class doctrines every day when rising and lying down, yet who had no influence on the masses.[66]

Political fractiousness, believed Efroikin, only served to alienate the Jewish workers, who had grown more independent. The time had passed that the Jewish worker would not answer the question "what time is it" without consulting his central committee, joked Efroikin.[67] In contradistinction to sectarianism, Efroikin thus proposed the following goals for the nonpartisan workers' election committees:

> The general workers' organization must be built upon the ground of such a program minimum, which every Jewish worker must adopt, as long as he does not deny his existence as a Jewish worker. This is, according to my opinion, firstly, the class and secondly, the national principle; that means that the nonpartisan workers' committees should be considered a political organization of a specific class, which is as a foe opposed in political and

social life to all other classes and as a national organization of the Jewish working class, which has its needs, its life-questions and interests, which need an independent formulation and defense. Class struggle and autonomism—these are the only two pillars that must uphold the organization's building of the broad working masses, and I reckon that the two principles are fit to attract to them the largest group of the Jewish workers.[68]

These nonpartisan election committees, argued Efroikin, would serve as the best weapon against apathy in the wake of the growing consolidation of tsarist reaction. Efroikin imagined a permanent role for these committees both as electors for the second curia during elections and as educational networks affiliated with local *kehiles* at other times.[69]

Yet, despite this greater call for nonpartisanship in the wake of political reaction, Efroikin retained a large degree of his party's revolutionary doctrinism and fervor. For instance, he followed his party's lead in both focusing upon class above nation and echoing the Marxist rhetoric of the RSDLP over the more populist, voluntarist ideology of the Socialist Revolutionaries (SRs). This orthodox conception of class struggle emerged in the slogan that Efroikin envisioned for the nonpartisan workers' committee: "Jewish workers, unite yourselves against the unified householders [*balebatim*] and notables!"

Yet his very call for a nonpartisanship committee contradicted the spirit of 1905–1907, when the various Jewish socialist parties had championed greater party differentiation, not unity. Seeking to defend his plan against its inevitable detractors, Efroikin argued that the workers' committee not only would not undermine the political parties but also would stimulate them to further refine their political platforms. Because the workers' committee would elevate the class and national consciousness of the Jewish working masses, it would challenge each of the parties to better articulate its position on the two principles of Jewish workers' solidarity and national autonomy.[70]

As Efroikin predicted, criticism to his plan within the ranks of SERP was not long in arriving. In the next issue of *Di folksshtime*, Y. Solomonov attacked what he labeled as Efroikin's "despairing plan," denouncing it on both ideological and practical grounds. Disagreeing with Efroikin's interpretation of the election results to the second Duma, Solomonov argued that the socialist parties garnered more votes than the percentage of the Jewish working class in Russian Jewish society. Practically, argued Solomonov, Efroikin's plan never would work since the various socialist nationalist parties never would agree on the definitions of class struggle and national autonomy. Ideologically, Solomonov argued that a nonpartisan coalition would impede the Jewish masses' development of a class consciousness during an election campaign, the very moment in which political differentiation naturally occurs.[71]

In addition to his grassroots activity as a party organizer and his planning for the election campaign, Efroikin traveled throughout Russia and even abroad to Germany to represent SERP at various socialist conferences. The central theme of these conferences was most often the relationship between socialism and nationalism. Seymists, as all other Jewish autonomists, looked at the demands for national autonomy of other national groups as both a source of inspiration for their own objectives and as a source of anxiety over the place of the Jews in these various groups' consciousness. For instance, even as Russian Jewish autonomists looked to the Poles as a model, they also increasingly feared that the Polish demand for territorial autonomy left no room for Jews to achieve non-territorial autonomy in Polish lands. Tension between Jewish and Polish socialist nationalists came to a head at the conference of all-Russian socialist nationalist parties, which the Socialist Revolutionary Party convened in June 1907. The uneasy alliance between SERP and the SRs secured the former's invitation to the conference. With the conference largely organized by Zhitlovsky, SERP leaders offered three of the four main speeches. Efroikin participated in the conference as an observer.[72]

The heated debates between Seymists, socialist nationalists of other nationalities, and leading Socialist Revolutionaries demonstrated the difficulties of the Jewish struggle for acceptance of the principles of non-territorial autonomy among socialist circles. Again and again, the leaders of SERP found themselves on the defensive. In particular, a leading Socialist Revolutionary attacked SERP's platform as leading to the weakening of class consciousness in the name of national solidarity. As a defense against this charge, Ratner and Zilberfarb relied on their party's doctrine that the creation of organs of national autonomy would serve as a catalyst to class conflict, not as an obstacle to it. The SERP members, reported Efroikin, also had to defend themselves against the hostility of the representatives of the Polish Socialist Party (PPS), who attacked the concept of extraterritorial Jewish national autonomy as leading to a division between Poles and Jews. In general, SERP received support for its proposals only from small, non-territorial nations such as the Armenians. Nonetheless, Efroikin remained optimistic, reveling in the fact that some of the parties present accepted SERP's resolution calling for the recognition of wide-scale autonomy for the national minorities. Opposition, concluded Efroikin, had come from ignorance rather than from ill will.[73]

Efroikin also traveled abroad on behalf of SERP, serving as one of its representatives to the Second International's annual meeting in Stuttgart, Germany. As other Jewish socialist nationalist parties, SERP had a problematic relationship with the Second International. SERP had permission to participate in the International, not as an independent party but rather as a subdivision of the Socialist Revolutionary Party. Beholden to the Socialist Revolutionaries for his presence at the conference, Efroikin sided with them against their Social Democratic detractors, despite SERP members' growing sympathy for the latter. In one such instance, Efroikin did not even shirk from publicly debating Trotsky. In his reportage of the conference, Efroikin blamed the machinations of the Bund for the lack of SERP and SS representation at the Second International. He particularly expressed anger over the Bundist attempt to block SERP membership in the Second International on grounds that the Seymists instilled despair among their party members and recruited members from the petite bourgeoisie. Between 1907 and 1914, members of SERP and the SS continued to collaborate over the issue of the entrance of their parties into the Second International, without success.[74]

In 1907, the very moment of Efroikin's political activity for SERP, the leading intellectuals of the various Jewish socialist movements emigrated from Russia to the West. By the winter of 1907–1908, the party activists in the field largely had joined them. Both those who emigrated and those who remained in Russia began a slow process of adjustment to nonrevolutionary civilian life. Many used this period of indefinite break in revolutionary activity to receive a university education. Still others sought a livelihood as reporters and commentators in the Russian Jewish and Yiddish press. Still others found employment in Jewish public life or in private industry.[75] During the inter-revolutionary years, Efroikin followed this trend. He first lived as a student in Switzerland, and then returned to Russia, where he earned his living as a writer for the Russian Jewish press and as an inspector for the Jewish Colonization Association.

The anger of those activists Efroikin left behind in Russia when leaving for the safety of Bern led him to defend his decision. The pursuit of an education, he explained in a letter, would allow him to more properly carry on the revolutionary struggle under conditions of tsarist reaction. From 1908 through mid-1910, Efroikin lived in a student colony consisting of young Russian Jewish revolutionaries enrolled in the University of Bern. Despite his concentration on his studies, and his dire economic situation, Efroikin continued to immerse himself in SERP both on a practical and an ideological level. In fact, in the pages of the Jewish socialist press and at various party meetings, he emerged as an internal critic of the party's direction. In his critique of SERP, he sought to establish himself as a close personal and ideological disciple of Zhitlovsky, whom he hailed as his "mentor [rebbe] and friend." Efroikin joined Zhitlovsky in the attempts to create a more authentically Jewish socialism suited to the Jewish masses and to unify the four political parties that had emerged from socialist Zionist circles: Poale Zion, SERP, the SS, and the Jewish Territorialist Association.[76]

Desperate to improve his impoverished existence, Efroikin looked to Zhitlovsky as a potential patron who could help him launch a career as a political commentator in the Yiddish press. In his letters to Zhitlovsky, Efroikin vacillated between ingratiating flattery and increasing annoyance at Zhitlovsky's long silences and tardiness in paying him for his articles. In order to win Zhitlovsky's support, he agreed to organize the dissemination of Zhitlovsky's new Yiddish journal, Dos naye leben (the new life), among his fellow Russian-Jewish students living in Western Europe. Efroikin contributed a series of articles to this journal, expressing the hope that by publishing his work, Zhitlovsky could help him become a true political writer in

Yiddish. Throughout his correspondence, Efroikin praised Zhitlovsky as the leading Jewish socialist thinker of the hour and hailed *Dos naye leben* as the best Yiddish journal to have graced the Jewish street.[77]

Yet it would be wrong to dismiss Efroikin's ideological closeness to Zhitlovsky during these years as resulting from no more than his search for patronage. As a member of Vozrozhdenie and then as a leader of SERP, Efroikin had drawn inspiration from Zhitlovsky's combination of socialism and Diaspora nationalism. It is only natural, then, that he would turn to Zhitlovsky not only for material support but also for answers to the most vexing problem facing Russian Jewish socialist nationalists during the first years of political reaction: how to keep Jewish socialism relevant for the Russian Jewish masses in an era when revolutionary struggle was no longer possible. As the other leaders of SERP, such as Zilberfarb and Shimen Duben, attacked Efroikin's call for ideological revision, he no doubt took solace in Zhitlovsky's encouragement and support.

During the last years of the first decade of the twentieth century, Zhitlovsky applied his romantic socialism, forged in the revolutionary years, to his conception of Yiddish culture and to the nascent ideology of Yiddishism. The influence of such prominent Yiddish writers as Peretz and An-sky led Zhitlovsky to embrace, temporarily at least, a neo-romantic perspective on the place of modern Yiddish culture within Jewish history. In 1908, Zhitlovsky helped to lead the Czernowitz Yiddish Language Conference. In his 1909 essay "The Poetic Rebirth of the Jewish Religion," he adopted the neo-romantic argument that secular national Jews should reappropriate Jewish holidays by emptying them of their supernatural beliefs and concentrating instead upon their deeper national-poetic meaning. In his seminal essay "Yid un mentsh" (Jew and human being) written in 1912, Zhitlovsky invoked the neo-romantic argument that an appreciation of Jewish history and literary heritage should serve as the foundation of a new, secular Jewish national identity. Echoing Peretz and An-sky, Zhitlovsky even spoke of innate Jewish qualities and hinted at Jewish superiority. Zhitlovsky's new journal, *Dos naye leben*, which appeared in New York from 1908 through 1913, embodied in many ways the goals of the Czernowitz Conference by producing highbrow political, publicistic, and literary material that would cater to a Yiddish-reading intelligentsia. *Dos naye leben* also served as Zhitlovsky's latest effort at synthesizing Jewish socialism and nationalism. By providing the intellectual elite with its cultural needs in Yiddish, Zhitlovsky hoped to advance the interests of Jewish socialism by providing the Yiddish-speaking masses with an intelligentsia that could lead them in their own language.[78]

During his two-year sojourn in Bern, Efroikin channeled much of Zhitlovsky's neo-romantic approach to Yiddishism into his own search for a solution to the crisis of Russian Jewish socialism in the era of reaction. During this period, Efroikin grew closer to modern Yiddish culture and to the Yiddishist movement, expressing a desire to attend the Czernowitz Conference as a press correspondent. However, it was the crisis of the Jewish socialist nationalist parties in Russia that attracted most of his energy. Efroikin concluded that the only future for these parties rested in their expansion beyond their narrow working-class base to become national representatives of the Jewish people in Russia. He elaborated on this theme in a series of articles, "Tsayt fragen" (Problems of the era), that he published in *Dos naye leben*. In the first installment, titled "The Jewish Socialist Parties and the Jewish Folk Masses," Efroikin argued that he perceived the signs that Jewish socialism stood at the threshold of a revision of its most firmly held convictions. Since revolution had seemed at hand, the socialists did not attempt to ameliorate the plight of the Jewish working masses in the here and now. Unlike the Russian Social Democrats who had learned the importance of the peasants, the Jewish socialists did not similarly come to appreciate the Jewish petite bourgeoisie, whom the tsarist regime oppressed as much as the workers. Condescension toward the petite bourgeoisie led to a profound alienation of the Jewish socialist activists from poor Jews who were not wage earners. By not connecting Jewish socialism to the Jewish prophetic tradition and by artificially separating the wage earners from the rest of the Jewish poor, Jewish socialist leaders had alienated their own constituency.[79]

It is not difficult to detect the highly populist-nationalist quality of this critique. Political reaction clearly had led Efroikin to abandon the strident Marxist tone and message that had permeated his articles and reportage in *Di folksshtime*. Whereas before he had concentrated on the unity of the Jewish working class, here he stressed more the unity of the Jewish poor. In his populist imagination, the impoverished petit bourgeois Jew emerged as the analogue of the Russian peasant in his natural alliance with the Jewish worker. In fact, Efroikin asserted that every social class of the Jewish people could find a place for itself within Jewish socialism. True, he conceded, the proletariat always would remain the avant-garde, with independent craftsmen and petty merchants playing progressively smaller roles in the movement. If only socialism connected to the lifestyle of the Jewish masses, Efroikin explained, it could become a great unifying ideology for the Jewish people. In his words, *"A Jewish socialism however can only be a people's socialism, or cannot be at all!"*[80]

Efroikin also applied Zhitlovsky's current neo-romantic mood to his vision of the national role of Jewish socialism. The true measure of Jewish socialism's success would not only be the implementation of its platform but also more fundamentally the elevation of the people's consciousness. Romantically, he wrote that socialism transcended the role of a political party and approached that of a "religious sect."[81] In order to root this new "religion" into the soul of the people, socialism had to draw upon the national cultural heritages of each national group to which it preached. Whereas socialists of other nations had learned this truth, argued Efroikin, Jewish socialists had not. Reacting to the Jewish past and its spiritual heritage with apathy, Jewish socialists produced a literature that amounted to nothing more than translations of European socialist tracts. The old world of traditional Judaism and the new world of Jewish socialism never merged to forge a new Jewish identity. He also contended that Yiddish literature had yet to depict a Jewish socialist as a psychological type. Because a conversion to socialism seldom involved a radical break with one's former identity, the Jewish worker easily could abandon his newfound ideology.[82]

Efroikin, then, advocated that Jewish socialist parties adopt a dialectical approach to the Jewish past. On the one hand, in an obvious reference to the Zionists, he derided "conservative nationalism" that venerated the past for its own sake. Moreover, Efroikin understood Jewish socialism as a total experience, which would have to replace traditional Judaism in the hearts and minds of its adherents if it were to succeed. At the same time, however, he was convinced that only by intimately engaging with the Jewish national tradition could Jewish socialists effectuate such a change. In his words:

> What we can and should demand from it [Jewish socialism] is—it should always reckon with the entire historical inheritance of the Jewish people. Fight with the ideas from our past that are hateful to Jewish socialism; adopt and rework those which find themselves in harmony with it. Do not believe, however, that no streams of ideas existed among the Jewish people before we were born into God's world. And it cannot be believed that the two-thousand-year history of a people ... should only consist of "old clothes," should not possess within itself such spiritual treasures, such elements, which can fructify the Jewish freedom idea, Jewish socialism, and be fructified by it. Such did Peretz find in Hasidism an entire source of ideas and feelings, *of life joy and life cheer,* from which we can still draw and draw. Dig deeper and deeper and farther and you will still find new sources and no less life desire and energy for struggle.
>
> Whatever the case may be, one thing is clear: just as Jewish socialism can only be built when it will become an organic part and product of the contemporary Jewish social life..., so too can it only stand when it will become an organic part of our Jewish spirit, when it will create its own, not "translated" ideology, when it will stop to be a strange book and will enter as one page into Jewish history (perhaps the most beautiful page!) and braid itself as one link in our great "golden chain."[83]

This passage reveals the extent to which the national romantic rhetoric of Yiddishists at the time influenced Efroikin's vision of Jewish socialism. From Peretz, he borrowed the term the "golden chain" of Jewish tradition. In his essays from this period, Peretz stressed the need of secular, modern Yiddish culture to serve as the latest link in the chain of Jewish tradition. Because it would serve this role, modern Yiddish culture would have to look to the Jewish past for inspiration for the present and future. Efroikin's challenge to other Jewish socialists sounds very similar to Peretz's exhortation to other Yiddish writers to cease imitating Europe and to produce a modern literature loyal to the entire Jewish cultural and literary legacy.[84] Fundamentally, Efroikin envisioned Jewish socialism in the same manner that national-romantic Yiddishists viewed their new culture: as both the continuity of the Jewish historical tradition and as the substitute for all previous forms of Jewish identity. But whereas national-romantic

Yiddishists understood the creation of a modern Jewish national culture as a goal unto itself, Efroikin sought to invoke Jewish tradition for the more utilitarian purpose of winning over the masses to Jewish socialism. Still, it appears that Efroikin genuinely believed that when Jewish socialists translated socialism into an idiom to which the Jewish masses could relate, it would become the common inheritance of the Jewish people.

According to Efroikin, the Jewish socialists had failed to relate both to the masses' national consciousness and to their most immediate needs. In particular, he criticized the Jewish socialist parties for their failure to formulate a plan to control Jewish mass emigration from the tsarist empire. Commitment to their own political ideologies blinded members of these various parties to the need to address this pressing national need. The only group that had not waited was the Jewish masses themselves, who had emigrated wherever they could. This abdication of leadership led to deplorable results such as profit-making emigration networks in the Pale of Settlement fleecing immigrants and the over-concentration of Jews in certain urban areas and in certain professions, which led to their further economic exploitation. The only organizations to ease these conditions were created by West European bourgeois Jews, who did not have the true interest of the emigrants at heart.[85]

Efroikin therefore called on all socialist and democratic elements to form a central organization to direct emigration that would disseminate information in the Pale about conditions in America, protect the immigrants from the rapaciousness of the large ship companies, and direct the stream of emigration to places with optimal economic and social conditions for the new immigrants. Another major theme to emerge from this series of articles was Efroikin's call on the Jewish socialist parties to engage in organic work. In his criticism of the leaders of the various Jewish socialist nationalist parties for engaging in theoretical hair-splitting rather than ameliorating the most pressing social needs of the Jewish masses, Efroikin echoed the new direction of SERP, which as early as 1907 had called for a shift toward organic work.[86]

Efroikin's series of articles elicited a sharp response from many of his fellow SERP leaders. Zilberfarb, for instance, strongly objected to

Efroikin's claim that Jewish socialism had failed to initiate a profound psychological and spiritual revolution in the hearts and minds of Jewish workers. Despite Efroikin's claim to the contrary, argued Zilberfarb, socialism had not remained a dry theory but rather had initiated a deep internal transformation. Alluding to Vozrozhdenie, Zilberfarb wrote that it took much soul-searching for many of his generation to merge their Zionist commitment to national renaissance with the socialist dedication to general human progress. Particularly for this reason, it bothered Zilberfarb that Efroikin had accused Jewish socialism of not drawing inspiration from Jewish history, a traditional Zionist accusation. Russian Jewish socialists had succeeded in refuting this charge, argued Zilberfarb, by making history rather than simply learning from it. By denying the worth of the Jewish socialist present, concluded Zilberfarb, Efroikin's charges transcended the realm of self-criticism and had entered the dangerous arena of ideological suicide.[87]

Still other leading SERPists attacked Efroikin for his contention that Jewish socialism had to transform itself from a movement of the Jewish proletariat to a movement of the Jewish poor. Kalmanovitch revealed the extent of his socialist commitment by arguing that whereas the Russian peasantry worked by the sweat of its brow, the Jewish petite bourgeoisie survived off exploitation and therefore backed political reaction. Therefore, one could support either Jewish socialism or the petite bourgeoisie, but not both. The SERP leader Shimen Duben carried this critique further by accusing Efroikin of illogically confusing the general questions of the character and composition of Jewish socialism with the unique challenges caused by tsarist reaction. Since the external force of political reaction precipitated the crisis, a revision of the Jewish socialist ideology would not solve the problem but only compound it. Efroikin's call for Jewish socialism to address the needs of the petite bourgeoisie contradicted years of socialist practice and theory.[88]

Even as Efroikin came under attack for his call to revise Jewish socialist ideology, he also became embroiled in a party controversy over the relative wisdom of merging SERP with the other Jewish socialist nationalist parties. On this issue as well, he found himself following Zhitlovsky's lead. In 1909, the leaders of SERP, SS, and Poale

Zion began discussions of merging into one Jewish socialist nationalist party. Within all three parties, some advocated a full-scale merger while others favored continued party independence coupled with heightened cooperation on such pressing immediate national concerns as Jewish emigration. In early April 1909, Zhitlovsky organized a joint conference of the American sections of SERP, the Jewish Territorialist Party, and Poale Zion in the hopes of effectuating a merger. Zhitlovsky persuaded the conference to adopt a platform that called for unification of the parties based on commitment to Jewish national autonomy in the Diaspora, work for Palestine, and work for a Jewish national concentration in Mesopotamia, then the object of diplomatic interest for territorialists.[89] In the pages of *Dos naye leben*, Zhitlovsky argued that each of the socialist nationalist parties wrongly believed that an ideological chasm separated it from its rivals. The reality, however, was quite different: "The program demands of the Jewish-socialist parties are, when they are taken altogether, one single program, which must satisfy *all* the life needs of the Jewish people in the current situation. But every party tore out one life need, one means of rescue, and placed it in the center of its worldview and completely annulled or pushed into a corner all the rest."[90] Zhitlovsky's message was clear: for unification to work, each Jewish socialist nationalist party would have to adopt aspects of the other party programs into its own platform. SERP would have to embrace contemporary territorial work, and Poale Zion would have to turn to Jewish national work in the Diaspora.[91]

Given that SERP included both Diaspora nationalism and territorialism in its political platform, the movement toward unity revolved around it. In particular, Ratner played a leading role in discussing the nature of this unity with the other parties. Efroikin worked toward this goal from Bern. At least at first, he adopted Zhitlovsky's maximalist vision of a full merger of the three into a new party, believing that such a union could help to solve the crisis of the Jewish socialist nationalist parties in Russia. In many ways, this call for unity was the next step from Efroikin's 1907 call for the creation of a nonpartisan workers' election committee. During much of 1909–1910, Efroikin dedicated himself to the goal of organizing a SERP party conference in Bern, which would discuss the possibility of the merger of these parties. Along the way, however, he faced the opposition of many of the other party leaders, including Ratner and Zilberfarb, who envisioned collaboration but not a full-scale merger. They particularly objected to the fact that Zhitlovsky had called for this unification program in the name of SERP at his New York conference. At his conference, Efroikin intended to propose a realistic plan in which members of all three parties would agree to collaborate on practical work such as reform of the *kehile* and organization of emigration, which would pave the way for full unification in the future. Repeatedly, Efroikin implored Zhitlovsky to attend the conference, expressing the hope that only he could convince the skeptical SERP members of the rightness of this plan.[92]

In the process of planning the conference, however, Efroikin came to appreciate his opponents' arguments against complete unification. Particularly vexing to Efroikin was the fact that Poale Zion at the time was a member of the Zionist Organization. Like Zhitlovsky and all other Seymists, Efroikin decried non-socialist Zionism as thoroughly bourgeois. After attending the Zionist Congress in Hamburg, Efroikin dismissed the Russian Zionist Organization for its stale character and lack of vision. "Tiny actions and tiny people [*kleyne mentshelekh*] rule Zionism now, especially in the Russian version, where the '*bal habos*' has spread himself out in length and width."[93] In his lengthy report on the conference in the pages of *Evreiskii mir,* Efroikin decried the calls for retreat among some Russian Zionists from the Helsingsfor platform with its call for *Gegenwartsarbeit.* Another moment of the conference that particularly upset Efroikin was when the audience booed the Polish Zionist leader Yitzhak Gruenbaum when he attempted to give his speech in Yiddish.[94]

A deeper impediment to unity among socialist nationalist parties, Efroikin concluded, was that all four parties viewed Jewish colonization efforts and nation building in the Diaspora as mutually exclusive. With a large degree of exaggeration, Efroikin complained that Poale Zion would prove ready to abandon the entire Jewish people in the Diaspora for the good of one Jewish family in Palestine. This criticism echoed Zhitlovsky's open letter to Poale Zion in which he had accused it of insufficient attention to national needs in the Diaspora.[95] At the same time, Efroikin criticized SERP's exclusive focus on the Diaspora to the exclusion of any possibility for colonization efforts. Efroikin correctly understood SERP's ideology as viewing territorial concentration as the end goal of Jewish national renaissance, not as a means to rescue the Jews from the physical dangers of the Diaspora. Yet Efroikin questioned why Seymists denied the legitimacy of all Zionist and territorialist activity:

> Where is it said that the renaissance-process cannot occur geographically simultaneously in the lands of exile as well as in the future Jewish land? The gathering and growing of national strength in the lands of exile and the growth of the Jewish community in the land of Israel of course do not find themselves in any tension with one another. Yet despite this, it is accepted amongst us in the party that whoever does not believe in this assumption is not a SERPist.[96]

Of course, by writing these lines to Zhitlovsky, Efroikin knew that he was preaching to the choir. As he approached the SERP conference in Bern in March 1910, Efroikin concluded that the best for which he could hope regarding unification was that SERP and the other parties would influence each other to moderate their ideological positions. He hoped that SERP would influence the Poale Zion and SS to look more favorably at work in the Diaspora, whereas these latter parties would convince SERP of the importance of concrete nation building in Palestine or another territory. At the time, Efroikin expressed his resolve to leave SERP if the rest of the party leadership would not incorporate territorialism into its platform.[97]

Yet, in reality, this particular fear proved groundless, since the SERP party leadership was moving in his desired direction. At the SERP Conference in Vienna in June 1910, the party, in an effort to lay the groundwork for collaboration with the SS, changed its party platform to concentrate more on territorial colonization. It now had swung the pendulum from the stance that Efroikin had criticized: whereas during the revolution SERP had pushed off territorial work to the distant future and concentrated exclusively on the achievement of Jewish national autonomy, it now argued the reverse. Its only request from the SS was that it dedicate itself to active work on behalf of Jewish autonomy in the Diaspora even while pursuing its main territorial goal. When in 1909 and 1910 Borochov led Poale Zion out of the Zionist Organization, it seemed that conditions were now ripe for the merger between the three parties that Efroikin so desired. Yet the plan failed after the SS refused to reciprocate SERP's overture by not appreciably changing its stance toward work for Jewish national autonomy in the Diaspora. Although the parties collaborated loosely on broad projects, nothing came of their joint efforts, largely because each had its own specific goals in mind. In the long run, when active political life became possible again in Russia following the February Revolution, SERP and SS finally merged into the Fareynikte.[98]

For Efroikin, the failure of the unity program coincided with his movement away from SERP. Perhaps his marginalization in SERP over both his critique of Jewish socialism and over his vision of unification led to his disillusionment with socialism as a compelling ideology for Jewish national renaissance. In 1911, he acted on this disillusionment by helping to refound Dubnov's autonomist but decidedly non-socialist Folkspartey under the new name "Obedinennaiia natsionalnaiia gruppa"—in Yiddish, Fareynikte natsionale grupe (United National Group). According to Dubnov, Efroikin served as a particularly active member of the committee. Under the influence of Efroikin and several other newcomers, the group adopted into its platform a call for primary education for Jewish children in their native tongue, Yiddish. On the eve of World War I, Efroikin spoke of forming a democratic movement that would wrest political power from the Jewish elites and transfer it to the masses.[99]

Diaspora Nationalism, Yiddishism, and Political Militancy

In the summer of 1910, Efroikin abandoned his studies as well as his political activity in Bern and returned to tsarist Russia. Efroikin's return to Russia coincided with his movement away from SERP and from Zhitlovsky's tutelage toward his embrace of Dubnov's folkist version of autonomism. In what would be his last correspondence with Zhitlovsky for decades, Efroikin curiously struck a distant tone, no longer praising Zhitlovsky or asking him for advice or patronage. Now, Efroikin did not discuss politics but only asked Zhitlovsky to publish in *Dos naye leben* the memoirs of a Jewish merchant, which he had reworked. Whereas only three years before, in *Di folksshtime*, Efroikin had lambasted the bourgeois leadership of Vitebsk's Jewish community, now he waxed poetic over the national authenticity of the Jewish trader's experience. Having initially reached out to the Jewish petite bourgeoisie in hopes of winning them over to Jewish socialism, Efroikin now found himself drawn to them as repositories of the national folk spirit. This embrace of the Jewish petite bourgeoisie proved typical of Jewish socialist nationalists in their turn toward organic work. At its meetings, SERP now addressed the needs of Jewish shopkeepers and engaged in the Jewish cooperative movement. In 1914, Poale Zion founded a journal dedicated entirely to the needs of the Jewish salesperson.[100] Efroikin, however, had gone still farther by arguing for a Jewish socialism that would address the needs of all the Jewish poor, including the petit bourgeois. Ultimately, however, this expansive vision led Efroikin away from socialism altogether.

Efroikin's move toward a *klal yisroel* autonomism suited the environment that he no doubt discovered in St. Petersburg, where he settled in 1910 after his brief sojourn in Vitebsk.[101] Together with his generational cohort, he made the transition from *Evreiskii mir* to *Di idishe velt,* for which he served as a coeditor during its first year of publication. In his debut article for the journal, he applied the journal's emphasis on the democratization of Jewish life to the debate over the revitalization of the *kehile.* Reacting to a report that nothing had come from the Kovno Conference's resolutions, Efroikin took the opportunity to decry the estrangement of the Jewish intelligentsia from the masses. Perhaps not realizing that Zilberfarb and socialist autonomists had attended the conference, Efroikin described the conference as a gathering of plutocrats. Only common suffering bound this intelligentsia to the Jewish masses, he argued. If anyone could revive the *kehile,* argued Efroikin, it would be the folk masses, which had preserved it and democratized it through the means of popular protest. Efroikin ended his article with a call for the emergence of a true Jewish intelligentsia that, faithful to its predecessors throughout history, would stand not above the people but rather with them. These intellectuals adhered to the principles of "purity and honesty, both to God and to the people, loyalty to the Jewish flag and steadfastness in the faith (the content of the faith can change)." If the return of the intelligentsia to the people were to continue, he concluded, "we may still merit seeing with our eyes a unified people, strong in its unity, steadfast in its old-new culture."[102]

In January 1914, Efroikin used the OPE's recent participation in the All-Russian Congress for National Education to once again bemoan the divide between the Russian Jewish intelligentsia and the folk masses. From Efroikin's depiction of the OPE, the reader never would realize that it had won a major victory at this congress. Rather, Efroikin criticized the OPE leadership for not going far enough in implementing its officially pro-Yiddish program adopted in 1911. Unlike members of the Jewish intelligentsia who thought in Russian and therefore still advocated for this language, the representatives of other national minorities at the conference were true *"folksmentshn,"* who presented a strong case for the "mother tongue" as the language of instruction. Efroikin's populist Yiddishist ideology blinded him both to his own level of Russification and to the fact that the OPE had become much more nationalist than it was in the past.[103]

Despite Efroikin's growing interest in Yiddish culture and organic work, he strongly resisted his contemporaries' abandonment of politics. In Efroikin's view, a Jewish national renaissance could not occur in the realms of culture and economics, divorced from political activity. In his words:

> A tenseness grows in the Jewish community—insecurity. And the more the psychological repression grows, the more our creative spirit in the field of our spiritual culture must be weakened, and our initiative must become increasingly smaller, the productiveness of our work in the sphere of material culture. If there are among us pure "culturalists" and "economists" who disparage "politics," let them think about it, perhaps they will then see that we stand before a deep abyss of spiritual and material destruction; if the atmosphere of dread will long endure . . . in such an atmosphere the most elementary conditions for the nation's creativity are lacking.[104]

Seen from a historical distance, Russian Jewish involvement in cultural production and organic work, by creating a Jewish public space, advanced the vision of Jewish national autonomy. Yet, at the time, Efroikin feared that this exclusive concentration on the internal over involvement in general Russian Jewish politics proved a great danger to the future of autonomism. For the Jews to achieve national autonomy, implied Efroikin again and again, they had to feel at home in Russia. Yet Jewish estrangement from all-Russian and Russian Jewish politics in reaction to growing anti-Semitism in effect meant that Russian Jewry had internalized its enemies' charge of Jewish foreignness. As a metaphor to describe the political dormancy prevalent among Russian Jews, Efroikin compared it to the smell of a corpse. In this era of reaction, Russian Jews had returned to "the ghetto philosophy, the old *mah-yofis* Torah."[105] Efroikin's perception was correct in that in the era of reaction, all remaining Jewish political parties, including the Bund, blunted their revolutionary rhetoric, calling on the government only to ameliorate the worst anti-Jewish abuses and to abolish the Pale of Settlement. In an era of proliferating anti-Jewish governmental decrees and the government sponsorship of the blood libel in the Mendel Beilis trial, Russian Jewish leaders engaged in a politics of defensive antidefamation rather than offensive agitation for change.[106]

Efroikin, no doubt also angry over the continued dominance of wealthy Jewish liberals in Russian Jewish politics, labeled this policy of self-defense *"shtadlones." Shtadlones* (*shtadlanut* in modern Hebrew) was the term for Jewish intercession with premodern governments, often conducted by wealthy Jews, to better the plight of the Jewish population living in that government's domain. Axiomatic to the "new Jewish politics" was the conviction that the integration of the Jews in the body politic would render such intercession obsolete. In the Middle Ages, argued Efroikin, when the Jews had placed their faith solely in the hands of God and had considered themselves as strangers in their lands of residence, the submissive tactics of the *shtadlonim* (intercessors) could not lower the Jewish spirit. Among the secularized Russian Jewish leaders who saw themselves as an integral part of Russian and European societies, however, such a "ghetto" response emerged as "either the most serious form of hypocrisy or the basest cynicism."[107]

The process of secularization, implied Efroikin, demanded a more genuine response to anti-Semitism. Whereas the premodern Jew had understood non-Jewish power as no more than a force of nature and "a whip in God's hand, to punish His people Israel when they sin," the contemporary Russian Jew who felt the sting of Russian anti-Semitism needed to combat it through an activist politics.[108] To

Efroikin, politics, in contradistinction to *shtadlones,* meant participation in the life of the state as full members of civil society. Rather than rely on the Kadets for salvation, argued Efroikin, Russian Jewry should develop its own political strategy to best struggle for its civil and national rights. He therefore called upon those still involved in activist politics to persevere, knowing that their efforts eventually would bear fruit. Even in invoking the revolutionary tradition, Efroikin demonstrated the extent to which the cooling of his own revolutionary fervor had allowed him to move into the Diaspora nationalist center. He urged his readers to do something profoundly non-revolutionary: instead of encouraging them to seek to overthrow the government, he wanted them to participate in politics in the present. Realizing the limits of Jewish politics in the era of reaction, Efroikin called upon his readers to "sow the seeds" of national liberation in the present so that they might "reap the harvest" in the future.[109]

Efroikin's role as a political commentator for *Di idishe velt* corresponded with the elections to the fourth Duma. Elections to this Duma followed on the heels of the 1911 assassination of Stolypin, who ultimately had failed in his experiment of controlled constitutionalism. Because of governmental limits imposed on Jewish participation in the elections, a vibrant Jewish election campaign took place only in several central cities, such as St. Petersburg, Odessa, Vilna, and Warsaw. In the end, three Jewish representatives were elected to the Duma, all affiliated with the Kadets. Just as in the third Duma, the right-wing and Russian nationalist parties commanded a solid majority over the opposition, which was composed of the Kadets and Social Democrats. Given this reality, Russian Jewish leaders and intellectuals hoped only that the Jewish Duma representatives would use their position to defend Russian Jewry from further attack.

The three Jewish Duma deputies, in the end, spent most of their time battling anti-Jewish accusations from right-wing members of the Duma, as well as launching inquiries into anti-Jewish bias. Still, when the Kadets adopted the Jewish cause as an integral component of their attack on the reactionary regime, Russian-Jewish political analysts became more hopeful of the possibility of meaningful change. At the very least, they convinced themselves that Russian public opinion opposed the tsarist regime's Jewish policies. This optimism ironically reached a peak during the Beilis trial, in which the Kiev Jew Mendel Beilis was accused of ritually murdering a Ukrainian youth, Andrei Yushchinsky. The drama of the Beilis trial occurred not just in a Kiev courtroom but also in the fourth Duma. The case, prosecuted by the government ministers Nikolai Maklakov and V. G. Shcheglovitov, met with the determined opposition of the Kadets. Historians have argued that tsarist loyalists and the tsar himself used the blood libel as a means to consolidate support. When a Kiev jury found Beilis not guilty, many Russian Jewish intellectuals interpreted the verdict as a tangible symbol of the ultimate victory of the liberal opposition to the regime. This optimism, however, proved itself unwarranted. Tsarist opposition parties rallied around the issue of the Beilis trial not because of their inherent interest in the Jews but rather because of their struggle against tsarist reaction. With the outbreak of World War I, the Kadets patriotically supported the regime, turning a blind eye to the government's still greater abuse of its Jewish population.[110]

Regarding Jewish participation in the fourth Duma, Efroikin persisted in his call for an activist nationalist politics. As such, he decried the Jewish Duma representatives' defensive posture as *shtadlones*. Both the Jewish bourgeois Duma representatives and their radical critics, argued Efroikin, cared about Duma politics only to the extent that they could yield the immediate result of Jewish emancipation. Instead, Efroikin voiced his desire that the Jewish Duma deputies use the fourth Duma as a "free tribunal" to affect change on a slow pace. Instead of endless speeches listing Jewish grievances and apologetically defending the Jews, Efroikin urged action. This nearly universal censure of the Jewish representatives contrasted with his more balanced assessment of the activities of non-Jewish Duma representatives. Harshly condemning the Octobrists as hostile and the Progressives as apathetic to the Jewish question, he consistently praised the Kadets as defenders of Jewish national rights. In his attempt to convince his readers that the Jewish Duma representatives could join with progressive forces to effectuate change, Efroikin naïvely overestimated the Duma's power during the years of reaction.[111]

Nowhere did Efroikin demonstrate more optimism regarding Russian society than in his reaction to Beilis's acquittal in the fall of 1913. Like many other Russian Jewish publicists, Efroikin believed that the

public reaction to the trial demonstrated that the progressive elements of Russian society stood with them.[112] Only in response to the
Beilis trial did the progressive forces in Russia respond forcefully to
anti-Semitism, creating what Efroikin referred to as a mass movement. In dramatic fashion, Efroikin portrayed the trial as a symbol of
the present and future of Russian Jewish relations. The jurors, he argued, had to answer the question, "What is exactly the soul of the
simple Russian people?" Jews awaited the outcome of the trial with
bated breath because it would answer the question, "Among whom
do we live?"[113] Efroikin attributed great significance to the identity of
the jurors as displaced peasants living in Kiev, who were susceptible
to anti-Semitic agitation. Despite all the anti-Semitic incitement of the
prosecution, "the human emerged victorious" and the peasants saw
Beilis as a human being rather than as a *"zhid."*[114] The onus, he argued,
now fell upon the Jews themselves to engage in an activist politics that
would maintain the momentum begun by the trial. In his words:

> The feeling of loneliness, the feeling of the "sheep among the wolves" that
> the Assembly of Israel brought with it from the ghetto, was forced to disap-
> pear. And here in the nation's consciousness was prepared the ground for a
> Jewish politics in the country, which desires to build the fortunes and the
> future of the Jewish people together with others, for ourselves and for the
> entire country. To clean this ground, to carry the light and clearness into the
> minds—this is the task of those, who have not yet despaired of their own
> people, who believe in the fruitfulness of the struggle, of their own work.
> We must expel the dark ghetto-shadows from their last hiding places,
> banishing the pessimism, wherever they raise their head.[115]

Efroikin wrote here in an almost euphoric tone, optimistic that
Russian Jewish relations had changed for the better. Committed to a
national future for the Jews in Russia, Efroikin could not admit to
himself the deep roots and widespread popularity of anti-Semitism
among the Russian people. If only the Jews and the Russian opposition could join forces, they could fight the tsarist regime's use of anti-
Semitism as a political weapon. In so doing, they could allow the
true desires of the Russian people to emerge. In this assessment, as
we have seen, Efroikin was not alone. The impact of World War I on
Russian Jewry would demonstrate, however, the wrongfulness of this
assumption.

Efroikin on Polish-Jewish Relations

Efroikin's misinterpretation of Russian popular opinion toward the Jews stemmed at least in part from autonomism's paradoxical attitude regarding the relationship between Jews and members of the national majority among whom they lived. As a synthesis of liberalism and Jewish nationalism, Dubnov's version of Diaspora nationalism incorporated some of the core assumptions of Jewish integrationism even while rejecting and transforming others. Unlike nineteenth-century Russian Jewish integrationists, autonomists, both liberal and socialist, embraced "auto-emancipation," the foundational premise of the "new Jewish politics." Russian Jewry, autonomists argued, should reject the accommodationist, self-abnegating politics of assimilation and instead demand national rights. Yet autonomists, both socialist and liberals, predicated the implementation of their national aspirations at least in part on the goodwill of their non-Jewish neighbors. It would be the public opinion of the all-Russian people that would serve as the agent of the transformation of tsarist Russia into a state with autonomous rights for its nationalities.[116]

Autonomists, therefore, were often at a loss to explain evidence that pointed to the opposite—namely that Russian public opinion, and even the public opinion of many of the empire's national minorities, gravitated against the granting of autonomous rights to the Jews. In order to rescue their political vision, autonomists, both socialist and folkist, often attributed the growth of Russian anti-Semitism during this era to the desperate bid of the tsarist regime and its supporters to maintain power. This explanation, as we have seen, led Efroikin and other autonomists to exaggerate public sympathies for the Jews. The issue became even more complex when it came to the public opinion of other nationalities, such as the Poles, among whom the Jews lived, who also demanded national rights from the Russian government.

In demanding national rights, Polish Jews had to contend with the results of a profound transformation in Polish nationalism that had occurred during the last third of the nineteenth century. Until that point, Polish nationalists had offered an expansive definition of Polish identity that left room for the incorporation of non-ethnic Poles in the resurrected nation. Although most nineteenth-century Polish nationalists advocated Jewish assimilation, some, during the 1863 uprising, even allowed for the possibility of Jews retaining cultural distinctiveness within their Polish national identity. These intellectuals, as well as the Polish progressives who emerged in the wake of the crushing of this revolt, believed in the march of history, which would right Poland's grievances. In the last two decades of the nineteenth century, a new generation of Polish nationalist intellectuals, despairing of history as a progressive force, argued that Polish nationalists would have to impose order and national discipline on the often recalcitrant Polish masses. Roman Dmowski, the founder of the Polish National Democratic Movement (Endecja), combined this new ideological perspective with xenophobic anti-Semitism. Viewing the Jews as a foreign, parasitical element within Polish society, Dmowski preached not only the futility but also the undesirability of Jewish assimilation into the Polish nation, which he defined in essentialist, integral terms. He and the National Democrats also argued for the extrusion of the Jews from their traditional commercial role. In his zero-sum conception of national struggle, Dmowski believed that only through the extrusion of the Jews could the Poles develop their own middle class. Though opposed by the nationalist, moderately socialist PPS, the National Democratic view of the Jew as Poland's enemy gained increasing popularity in an age of mass national politics.[117]

The revolution of 1905, with its mass politicization of both Poles and Jews and its securing of greater freedom of the press and assembly, led to the ascendancy of this anti-Jewish view. As an ever-increasing percentage of Polish Jews embraced Jewish nationalism, even Polish liberals came to view the Jews as an internal enemy. It soon became evident that the Polish Club, or Kola, in the various Dumas consistently sought to block Jewish nationalist aspirations. When the tsarist authorities promised municipal self-government to the cities of Congress Poland, the Kola joined forces with the tsarist regime in seeking to restrict Jewish representation in cities where Jews constituted a majority. Tension reached fever pitch when Poles and Jews fought over whom to send to the fourth Duma as a representative from Warsaw. Because Stolypin's limited franchise favored property owners, the majority of Warsaw voters for the fourth Duma were Jewish. The Jews feared the anti-Semitic backlash that would result from their election of a Jewish representative to the Duma from Poland's historical capital. Yet Warsaw Jewry could not support the candidate of the National Concentration, the National Democrats' moderate competition, after he backed legal restrictions on Jewish commerce. In the end, the Jewish members of the electoral college cast their vote for a Polish socialist candidate, Eugeniusz Jagiello, who assumed the Duma seat. In retaliation, the Endecja launched a boycott against Jewish businesses that resonated positively with Polish public opinion. Even many Polish progressives voiced their support of the boycott, which they saw as a tool both to strengthen the indigenous Polish middle class and to promote Polish national unity.[118]

The growing Polish public hostility to the Jews proved one of the greatest challenges to the autonomist vision. Complicating matters further was the fact that Diaspora nationalists, as opponents of territorial nationalism, envisioned the future of Poland as part of a reformed Russian state, not as an independent country of its own. This issue deeply divided Jewish socialist and liberal nationalists from their Polish counterparts. Increasingly, Polish nationalists viewed the realization of Jewish national autonomy in its political, economic, and cultural forms as inimical to their national interests. Autonomists such as Efroikin had to somehow salvage their vision of the national future of the Jews in a multiethnic Eastern Europe from what he termed "the Jewish-Polish chaos."

As in the case of Russian public opinion, Efroikin chose to salvage his vision by minimizing the deleterious effects of the boycott. Having ruined only a small number of Jewish businesses in the Christian section of Warsaw, argued Efroikin, the boycott left Jewish businesses in Lodz and in the small towns of the provinces intact. The boycott, by subsidizing the founding of Polish businesses that later fell into Jewish hands, ended up strengthening the Jewish economy. Moreover, he separated the boycott movement, which was anti-Semitic in its origin, from the Polish cooperative movement, which had emerged from the healthy desire of the Polish people to develop their own businesses. Soon, he argued, proponents of the Polish cooperative movement would realize that the boycott's elimination of free competition only hurt their cause. Efroikin's involvement in the Jewish cooperative movement thus led him to express sympathy with its Polish counterpart. At the same time, he saw Jewish cooperatives, rather than counter-boycott, as the appropriate Jewish response to the Polish boycott.[119]

Rather than imitate the Endecja's xenophobic nationalism by patronizing only Jewish-owned stores and products, Efroikin suggested that Polish Jews learn instead from the Poles' creation of institutions of self-help. Underlying this call for Jewish restraint was not accommodation but rather Efroikin's recognition that the future of Jewish national autonomy depended on an improvement in Polish-Jewish relations. His embrace of the cooperative movement and concern with the fate of Jewish merchants, moreover, demonstrate the extent to which Efroikin had shifted away from a class toward a *klal yisroel* version of Diaspora nationalism. Yet, Efroikin's ironic disdain for counter-boycott as "the holy mission of supporting private enterprise in the name of the national interests" reveals traces of his former socialism.[120]

Efroikin also reacted to the renewed attempt of the Endecja to limit Jewish representation in local Polish assemblies. Like all Diaspora nationalists, Efroikin envisioned a future for Poland not as an independent state but rather as an autonomous unit within Russia in which Poles, Jews, Lithuanians, and Ukrainians all would enjoy national rights. When the Kadets attempted to block the limitation of Jewish representation in Polish local assemblies in 1913, as they had done previously in 1906, he praised their efforts. When, a year later, they retreated from this position, he criticized them. However, once again, he placed most of the blame on the Jewish Duma representatives for not having adequately voiced their protest for this impending restriction of Jewish rights.[121]

Zelig Kalmanovitch as Champion of Socialist Autonomism

Kalmanovitch was born in Goldingen, Courland, on October 30, 1885. Although he spent his childhood in conditions of abject poverty, he nonetheless enjoyed the benefits of a traditional Jewish education first in kheyder and then in the Libave *besmedresh*. As a teenager, Kalmanovitch became exposed to Haskalah literature and enrolled in gymnasium. First at the University of Berlin and then at the University of Königsberg, Kalmanovitch studied Semitic philology, psychology, political economy, and ancient history, eventually earning a doctorate. In his memoirs, Joseph Kruk, a Polish Jewish socialist nationalist, recalled that Kalmanovitch organized the smuggling of revolutionary propaganda from Berlin to tsarist Russia. Kalmanovitch's average looks and phlegmatic, scholarly disposition made him the perfect candidate for this revolutionary role.[122]

It was in Berlin that Kalmanovitch also became active in Naḥman Syrkin's socialist Zionist group, Ḥerut (Freedom). In later joining Vozrozhdenie, Kalmanovitch persisted in Syrkin's spirit of revolutionary and national voluntarism, even as he embraced a more positive outlook toward the Diaspora than Syrkin. Like Efroikin, Kalmanovitch returned to Russia from his studies abroad to involve himself in SERP party work, though not as a party organizer but rather as a reporter, translator, and propagandist for *Di folksshtime*. In the course of his revolutionary activity, he even briefly was arrested. At this early stage in his career, Kalmanovitch voiced opinions wholly in keeping with SERP's party line: a militant expression of the primacy of class struggle and the need for Jewish national autonomy.[123]

Kalmanovitch combined these two ideologies in his coverage of the 1907 elections to the Austrian Reichsrat. Seymists, like other Russian Jewish autonomists, looked to Austro-Hungarian Jewry as an example of Jewish political mobilization for national rights in the Diaspora. The 1907 election carried particular importance because it was the first in which Austro-Hungarian subjects participated on the basis of near universal male suffrage. In the elections, the Jews of Galicia elected three Zionist representatives to the Reichsrat. Clearly with Russian Jewry in mind, Kalmanovitch argued that the political organization of Galician Jewry demonstrated that when presented with a concrete political opportunity, Jews could engage in united action. At the same time, Kalmanovitch hailed in equally glowing terms the great victory of the Austrian Social Democratic Party in the elections. He only expressed regret that Austro-Hungarian Jewry did not yet have a socialist nationalist party to best represent its demands for national autonomy in the Reichsrat. Although he admitted that the Austrian Zionists had accomplished much in politically mobilizing the Jewish masses, Kalmanovitch dismissed them as more "clerical-democratic" than purely democratic, often bowing to the demands of the Orthodox. Later, when reporting on the setbacks faced by the Social Democratic Party in the Reichsrat, Kalmanovitch softened his stance toward the Zionists, whom he credited with democratic behavior. Kalmanovitch's commitment to socialism persisted even after his work for SERP and its journal had ended. In 1909, for instance, he published two non-scholarly articles in *Leben un visenshaft* dealing with the history of socialism in Austria and Germany.[124]

During this period, Kalmanovitch synthesized his socialism with his newfound Yiddishism by arguing that modern Yiddish culture owed its creation and continued existence to the Jewish working masses. In a 1913 review essay on Zhitlovsky's works, Kalmanovitch emphasized that Yiddish literature, both belletristic and scientific, unlike other European literatures, originated from the working class and its struggle for "human culture and national determination." Similarly, he asserted that the Jewish bourgeois disdain for Yiddish literature stemmed from its hatred for the Jewish working class.[125]

Between Scholarship and Popularization

In 1908, Kalmanovitch made the transition of so many other members of his generation from political activity to cultural work. Earlier than Efroikin and Tcherikower, Kalmanovitch became a passionate participant in the young Yiddishist movement. He served this movement by engaging in his own original scholarship, in the production of major Yiddish periodicals of both general and scholarly interest, and in the translations of works of Jewish and general scholarship into Yiddish. He engaged in all of this work through his role of administrator and coeditor of the Kletskin Press, dedicated since its founding in 1910 to the publication of quality Yiddish literature and scholarship. It is significant that Kalmanovitch contributed both to *Di literarishe monatsshriftn* and to *Leben un visenshaft*, since his work during these years bridged the gamut between highbrow scholarship and popularization. In his 1913 review of Zhitlovsky's essays, Kalmanovitch praised his mentor for the synthesis of highbrow culture and popularization that he sought to emulate in his own work.[126]

On the one pole, Kalmanovitch tended toward scholarship. Trained in philology as a university student in Germany, he sought to turn this discipline into a tool for asserting the national distinctiveness of Yiddish. He made his debut in this field in the pages of *Di literarishe monatsshriftn,* where he attempted to prove that Yiddish was indeed a language independent of German, formed historically from the Jews' independent cultural and linguistic milieu. Several months later at the Czernowitz Conference, Peretz would differentiate between the historical national language, Hebrew, which had been born with the Jewish people and would travel with it throughout its history, and the folk language, Yiddish, which served an important section of the nation in a particular period of its history.[127]

Kalmanovitch advanced the same argument by distinguishing between Hebrew, the "old national language," which followed the Jews in all their wanderings, and German, which served as just one in a series of "lodging languages." Through a historical trick, German had become a building block of the *folkssphrakh,* Yiddish. The history of the Yiddish language, then, was the story of how the Jews appropriated German and completely rebuilt it, reformulating it in the national spirit. Other Yiddishists, Zhitlovsky most prominent among them, already had advanced this argument about the Jewish creation of a new language from borrowed roots.[128] Similarly, like them, Kalmanovitch took aim at those Jews who rejected Yiddish as a corrupt jargon, and those German philologists who stressed the German origins of Yiddish in order to see this language as an emissary of German culture. In contrast to this view, Kalmanovitch asserted: "The Yiddish language has its own rules of development, its own language structure and style, which emerge from a pure Jewish source, which were tightly tied to the life and thought of the Jewish people."[129]

In attempting to prove the Jewish authenticity of Yiddish, Kalmanovitch articulated a novel thesis that departed from that of previous Yiddishists. When Zhitlovsky argued that the Jews had appropriated a Germanic language and made it their own, he did so in order to reject Hebrew as the national language.[130] However, Kalmanovitch emphasized that it was Hebrew, with its own rules of grammar and syntax, that transformed Yiddish from a dialect of medieval German into an independent language. For instance, he argued that it was the influence of Hebrew that moved the predicate in the Yiddish sentence from last place, as in German, to immediately following the subject. Similarly, the binding word "vos" came from the Hebrew word "asher." Kalmanovitch also attributed to Hebrew influence the fact that in Yiddish an apposition follows the noun (*Moyshe der kremer,* Moses the storekeeper) and that the possessive pronoun often follows the subject.

The influence of Hebrew, Kalmanovitch argued, made itself felt slowly, until it transformed the language. As evidence, he brought quotes from old Yiddish literature, showing that the Hebrew influence on word usage and grammar increased with time. Through quotations from biblical translations, versions of the *Tsene-rene,* and community records, Kalmanovitch sought to document the gradual emancipation of Yiddish from German. Interestingly, Kalmanovitch asserted that the moment of full linguistic independence came as late as the eighteenth century, through Hasidic literature. Only in the mid-nineteenth century did a "pure, classical Yiddish" emerge in the writings of Mendele Moykher Sforim. Kalmanovitch's emphasis on the determinative role of Hebrew in the formation of Yiddish placed him in the paradoxical situation of being a Yiddishist who honored Hebrew as the source of the national authenticity of Yiddish. In the dichotomy between the national and folk languages, this view made the latter derivative of the former. To a large extent, this paradox accompanied Kalmanovitch for the rest of his career.[131]

During the inter-revolutionary period, Yiddish philology remained a marginal enterprise in modern Yiddish culture, eclipsed by the importance of aesthetic literature. Still, Barry Trachtenberg has argued persuasively that Yiddishist philology and literary criticism had their origins in this period. In particular, Trachtenberg concentrated upon the more well-known pioneering Yiddish philological study of Borochov in his and Niger's 1913 *Der pinkes.* In his "Oyfgaben fun der yidisher filologiye" (Tasks of Yiddish philology), Borochov sought to harness Yiddish philology to the task of Jewish nation building. In particular, he presented a plan in which Yiddish philology would become the instrument of standardizing Yiddish orthography, purifying the language from foreign elements, and humanizing and nationalizing it. By the latter, Borochov meant the elevation of Yiddish to the level of a cultural language that could express at once all human sentiments and thoughts and Jewish national culture. Borochov's other major contribution to the field of Yiddish philology was his review of four hundred years of Yiddish philological works. Writing from an unabashedly Yiddishist perspective, Borochov sought to differentiate his nationalist scholarship from previous works that denied Yiddish the status of an independent language.[132] In this review, Borochov listed Kalmanovitch's pioneering study as one of the first examples of Yiddish philology in the "wide national-cultural meaning of the word."[133] Nonetheless, Borochov rejected Kalmanovitch's principal argument that the uniqueness of Yiddish owed itself to the Hebrew component of the language. Was not Kalmanovitch aware, asked Borochov, of similar unique syntactical constructions in various German dialects as well as in Slavic languages?[134]

Regardless of the weaknesses of Kalmanovitch's arguments, the readers of Di literarishe monatsshriftn were no doubt impressed by his attempt to establish Yiddish as a national language independent of German. He continued this task in a harsh review of Zalman Rejzen's Yudishe gramatik: Folshtendige yudishe gramatik; etimilogye un sintaksis (Yiddish grammar: A complete Yiddish grammar; etymology and syntax). Kalmanovitch pointed out five major flaws in the book, nearly all of which had to do with what he perceived as Rejzen's overreliance on German grammatical rules, word usage, and orthography.[135] Kalmanovitch thus emerged as an early opponent of daytshmerish, or the over-influence of modern German in modern Yiddish. Kalmanovitch's scholarly and ideological preoccupation with daytshmerish would persist throughout his career.

Although his philological work remained peripheral to Yiddishism in the inter-revolutionary period, Kalmanovitch's role as the daily administrator and coeditor of the Kletskin Press brought him into the center of the movement's cultural activities. With Boris Kletskin, the press's founder and owner, often traveling on business, Kalmanovitch assumed the daily management of the press. By determining the content of the books and journals published through the press, Kalmanovitch wielded great behind-the-scenes influence regarding the direction of modern Yiddish culture. From the beginning, he articulated an expansive view of modern Yiddish culture, which he believed had to reflect every aspect of the particularly Jewish and the generally human. Yet, because of its nature as fluid and secular, modern Yiddish culture could not espouse any dogmas that tied it to the Jewish religious past. In the spirit of *Di literarishe monatsshriftn,* Kalmanovitch also would not let the press's works become fettered to partisan creed.[136] The freedom that Kalmanovitch demanded for Yiddish culture stemmed in large part from the prophetically redemptive, even religious, role that he assigned to it. Superseding the stifling constraints of rabbinic Judaism, modern Yiddish culture, through its fusion of Jewish tradition with European humanism, would lead the Jewish nation to a moral regeneration. As part of this redemptive vision, Kalmanovitch envisioned the mission of the Yiddishist intelligentsia as elevating the Jewish masses to share in these cultural goals.

A major venue through which Kalmanovitch expressed his Yiddishist vision was his translation of works of Jewish history from Russian, German, and ancient Greek into Yiddish to be published by the Kletskin Press. The study of history featured predominately among Diaspora nationalists and Yiddishists, who hoped to reclaim East European Jewish historiography from the non-sympathetic, and often hostile, hands of German Jewish *Wissenschaft des Judentums* (science of Judaism) scholars. In his introduction to the Yiddish version of his one-volume popular Jewish history, translated by Kalmanovitch, Dubnov transmuted a religious conception into a nationalist one by stating that this translation fulfilled the mitzvah of *hashovas avedoh,* or returning lost property. This translation, he hoped, signaled the beginning of the process of returning Jewish history to both the Hebrew and Yiddish languages.[137] Introducing his historical approach to his Yiddish readers, Dubnov criticized German Jewish *Wissenschaft des Judentums* scholarship for its concentration on literary and religious themes to the exclusion of social, institutional, and cultural history. Beyond the bounds of religion, argued Dubnov, the Jewish people conducted an independent life, "not only in the *besmedresh* but also in the street, the home, in communal matters."[138] Dubnov's goal was to study this secular history from a sociological perspective.

The translation of Jewish scholarship into Yiddish, he argued polemically, belied the Hebraist claim that Yiddish lacked a future in the Diaspora.[139]

As the father of Diaspora nationalism, Dubnov articulated a secular nationalist vision of Jewish history that Kalmanovitch and his contemporaries espoused. Several years later, Kalmanovitch echoed Dubnov's perspective regarding the importance of a secular nationalist history in a review of a new collective volume that told the history of the Jews, which appeared in Russian under the title *Istoriia evreev v Rossii* (History of the Jews in Russia). Like Dubnov before him, Kalmanovitch began this review by emphasizing the shortcomings of the historical scholarship of German *Wissenschaft des Judentums* for its concentration on religious over social and communal history. Kalmanovitch even stated that East European Jewish historians would have to look to national historians of other nationalities, rather than to the great *Wissenschaft* scholar Heinrich Graetz, for inspiration.[140] A secularizing East European Jewry, argued Kalmanovitch, needed a social history to create a usable past: "The East European community—and its offshoot—the North American—demonstrate more and more tendencies to divest from themselves the religious synagogue garment and to take on more and more the form of a modern, secular-cultural nation—that strengthens the desire to find the traces of secularism in its past, as well as in the past of all other Jewish communities."[141]

Kalmanovitch's unique contribution to Yiddishist scholarship was his translations of works relating to ancient Jewish history. In 1914, the Kletskin Press published his Yiddish translation of Josephus's *Jewish Wars*.[142] In his introduction to Josephus's work, Kalmanovitch combined genuine erudition with his socialist nationalist, Yiddishist ideology. As Roman political and economic oppression increased, he explained, the common people of Judaea and especially the peasants joined the zealots. In contrast, the middle class and wealthy proprietors *(balebatim)* of Jerusalem, together with some of the religious element, feared the popular rebellion and therefore sought peace with the Roman oppressor. Only after the zealots had won over the majority of the nation to their side did the elite reluctantly join them, assuming a leadership position. Between the nationally loyal *folksmasn* and the traitorous *balebatim,* Josephus belonged squarely to the latter. For this reason, he failed to unite the Jewish peasants behind his command, instead concentrating on the establishment of a Jewish government in the Galilee. Rather than focusing on the bravery and dedication of the Jewish rebels, Josephus instead exaggerated their depredations. Josephus's antinational stance owed itself not just to his class origin but also to the language in which he wrote his history. Writing in Greek for a Roman audience, Josephus ingratiated himself to it by belittling the Jewish rebels.[143] The best praise that Kalmanovitch had for this national traitor was the following anemic words: "And if in life Josephus was far from a great man, through his literary work he certainly earned an eternal name in Jewish history."[144] In Josephus, Kalmanovitch found a perfect representation of the bourgeois, Russified Jewish intelligentsia, which Yiddishists accused of having abandoned its people. This Yiddishist portrayal of the Great Revolt and Josephus's role in it had a great impact among the young Yiddishist intelligentsia.[145]

Kalmanovitch continued to use ancient Jewish history as an analogue for his Yiddishism and autonomism in an even more original manner in his 1914 translation of Emil Schürer's *History of the Jewish People in the Time of Jesus Christ.* In this work, Kalmanovitch reached his greatest synthesis as translator, popularizer, and scholar. As he himself stated in his introduction, his translation skipped over all the learned investigations, "since the translation is designed for the widest circles of readers."[146] Kalmanovitch's translation, then, served as an exercise in popularization. In a sense, though, Kalmanovitch left his imprint as an author, no less than as a translator, on this Yiddish version of Schürer's history. For instance, he readily admitted that he took the license of changing some of the content of the history, especially when it came to Schürer's biased presentation of the Talmudists. Indeed, Kalmanovitch even changed the title of the work to *Geshikhte fun yudishn folk in der tsayt fun bayis sheyni* (A history of the Jewish people in the time of the Second Temple). Clearly, the goal of this translation was to provide Yiddish readers with a comprehensive history of the Jews in antiquity that would prove both appropriate to their level of intellectual sophistication and to their national consciousness.[147]

In Kalmanovitch's introductory essay, he provided his vision of how the modern, secular Diaspora nationalist could look to ancient Jewish history as a usable past. The three-hundred-year period in Jewish history described in this book, stated Kalmanovitch, had crucial significance for all of world history.[148] Dispensing with the political history of the Jews in Palestine in a few paragraphs, Kalmanovitch clearly understood the greatest contributions of this period as occurring in the Diaspora. Kalmanovitch could have been speaking about his own dream of national autonomy in the contemporary Diaspora when he wrote, "Sharply and clearly these dispersed Jewish communities differentiated themselves from their surroundings through their autonomous, internal organization, through their unique life and customs."[149] Moreover, Kalmanovitch asserted that it was in the Diaspora, rather than in Palestine, that the greatest cultural development of the period occurred: the synthesis between Judaism and Hellenism. This process was not one of assimilation but rather of mutual cultural fructification, in which the Jews combined the best of general and Jewish sources to create "new cultural values" that contributed to the evolution of Judaism.[150] Similarly, in a letter to Niger, Kalmanovitch derided the accusation of a Zionist historian that the Septuagint had led to the bastardization of Palestinian Judaism as "a profanation of the holy, of one of the greatest events in human cultural history." The synthesis of Judaism and Hellenism, Kalmanovitch insisted, derived from "the eternal wisdom" of "He, Who leads history." This divine force "brought together two, in truth different, forms of the same eternal human striving for honesty and truth and justice."[151] It is not difficult to read into this glowing appraisal of Jewish Hellenism the Yiddishist call for a synthesis of the European with the authentically Jewish to create a new, secular Jewish culture in Yiddish.

Whereas Kalmanovitch expressed unrestrained enthusiasm regarding Hellenism in the Diaspora, he articulated a much more ambivalent attitude toward rabbinic Judaism and halakhah, Jewish law, the products of the land of Israel. Although the Pharisees recognized that the prophets' Torah did not depend on ceremonies, he wrote, they surrounded the Jews with rituals in order to strengthen national cohesion. This insistence on ritual proved prescient, since after the destruction of the Temple, the Pharasaic Torah proved "the only real foundation of . . . national existence."[152] Here, Kalmanovitch echoed Aḥad Ha-'Am, Dubnov, and other formulators of a secular national Jewish identity who argued that religion served as a means, not an end, to Jewish existence. Because the Jews constituted a nation, rather than a religious group, Jewish religious laws served as a means to sustain their national existence during a particular period of their history. Although these rituals stifled both the spirit of Judaism and the individual quest for religious edification, they allowed the Jews to transmit their central belief in the unity of the Creator to future generations.[153]

Kalmanovitch sounded most ideologically programmatic when he addressed the contemporary relevance of this history, which, tellingly, announced the impending collapse of rabbinic Judaism:

> Connected with the hope for a bright national future, it [rabbinic Judaism] gave and will still give the Jewish nation strength to endure its bitter destiny, until the time when it will create for itself other, more appropriate means to preserve its existence and, liberated from all established, binding ceremonies and accepted, limiting beliefs, will once again be able to weave the holy thread of its religious thought, which was so suddenly interrupted.
>
> In our time, when the Jewish people has begun slowly to shed itself of the iron fence of the statutes and beliefs, when from various sides voices make themselves heard regarding "expansion of the boundaries," it is perhaps worthwhile to look back at the past, to the roots from which these borders grew, and to become more well-acquainted with them. Also, now the time has come already to take into the circle of Jewish consciousness those thinkers and doers from the Hellenistic period with their work, who until now hardly existed for the broader Jewish world. The Jewish creative men of spirit, to whom belongs the first voice in the renaissance, will certainly find enough points of connection in the evolving cultural life of that period.[154]

In this ideological pronouncement, Kalmanovitch gave voice to a kind of secular messianism that in some ways paralleled Christian messianism in its evaluation of the role of Jewish law. Kalmanovitch shared his evaluation of rabbinic law as having stifled the true spirit of Judaism with Christian theologians, no doubt including Schürer. However, whereas Christians would argue that Jesus's advent liberated the Jews from enslavement to the law, Kalmanovitch implied that the arrival of Jewish secular nationalism served this function. And whereas Christian theologians viewed the synthesis of Judaism and Hellenism as having prepared the way for the advent of Christianity, Kalmanovitch understood it as a model for the creation of a dynamic, redemptive humanistic Yiddish culture.

Implicit in Kalmanovitch's secular messianism was its latent and blatant religious inspiration. Ironically, it was precisely because he invested modern Yiddish culture with messianic, religious significance that Kalmanovitch believed that the persistence of rabbinic rituals could prove so nationally harmful. In a letter to Niger, Kalmanovitch commented on the debate among the Russian Jewish intelligentsia over the national worth of the traditional kheyder. Even as Russian Jewish intellectuals of all stripes derided the kheyder as a retrograde, unsanitary institution, many also came to express a sense of loss over its inevitable disappearance. The same generation of Russian Jewish intellectuals that feared use of the Russian language as a symptom of assimilation also reappropriated the kheyder as a repository of Jewish national wisdom and strength. Nationalist activists thus sought to incorporate the reform of the kheyder along nationalist lines into the purview of the OPE. Other intellectuals, however, understood the kheyder as an exclusively religious institution, over which the OPE had no jurisdiction.[155]

As the acting editor of *Di yudishe velt,* Kalmanovitch ran into opposition from his colleagues in St. Petersburg over the issue of how much space to allot the debate over the kheyder. Soliciting an article on the kheyder from Niger, Kalmanovitch mused to him over the meaning of the debate. Among Yiddishists, argued Kalmanovitch, "the kheyderists" were those who wanted the Yiddish school to narrowly deal only with the "spirit of Jewishness." The anti-kheyderists, in contrast, desired the modern Yiddish school to expand the boundaries beyond Jewishness to reflect the broadened character of Jewish life. Even the anti-kheyderists, argued Kalmanovitch, were not cultural radicals for whom Yiddish meant only the Yiddish language and history.[156]

To Kalmanovitch, the kheyder debate symbolized the larger question of the relationship of traditional Judaism to modern Yiddish culture. He pointed to Vayter's article in *Di literarishe monatsshriftn* on the Yiddish theater, in which the Bundist revolutionary-turned-literary-critic lamented the spiritual emptiness of the Russian Jewish middle class, for whom the national roots of the Yiddish theater had lost all meaning.[157] Kalmanovitch explained that Jewish nationalists found themselves in a unique predicament in regard to Jewish folk culture. Since all other European nations possessed folk customs that predated their Christian religious heritage, their nationalist intellectuals could discard their respective religious traditions without in any way weakening the national worth of their folk cultures. Jewish nationalists, however, did not have this luxury, since nearly all Jewish customs drew their authority from the religious tradition. Kalmanovitch argued that Yiddishists could not hypocritically rely on a religious tradition in which they no longer believed when building their own transcendent humanistic culture:

> And if amongst us, both the young and the old, these customs already have lost, some more and some less, their religious holiness, if we are in the process of building a pure, prophetic religion, and we cannot take the ceremonies with us specifically *because* we are religiously oriented, because we do not want religion to be *socially* determined ... [then the] problem stands before us in its full frightful breadth, of the bourgeois, secular national life forms. And this, essentially, as I see it, is *the* question, the only cultural question, which within it are included all the other partial questions of our life.[158]

In other words, Kalmanovitch fought the influence of the Jewish religious tradition specifically in the name of creating a modern Yiddish culture that would serve as that tradition's "pure, prophetic" substitute. Just as Christianity superseded Judaism, so too would modern Yiddish culture supersede the Jewish religious tradition by distancing itself from its customs. Once these customs lost their original religious meaning, Jewish nationalists safely could incorporate them into the new culture. It was the future Yiddish national school, concluded Kalmanovitch, that could implement this cultural goal.[159] What remained invisible to Kalmanovitch was the irony that this redemptive, messianic role he envisioned for Yiddish culture largely derived from the Jewish religious tradition itself, with its emphasis on the messianic potential of Torah study and the performance of *mitzvot*. In fact, Kalmanovitch brought the religious fervor of his *besme-*

dresh past to his role as administrator of the Kletskin Press. A workaholic, he complained that his responsibilities for the press consumed him from the moment that he rose until he went to bed. Attributing his occasionally perceived lack of productivity to laziness, Kalmanovitch unselfconsciously railed against his *yester hor'o* (evil inclination) and the *sitra aḥra* (a kabbalistic term, meaning literally "the other side" or the demonic forces) that prevented him from working.[160]

On a more conscious level, he applied his redemptive, expansive vision of modern Yiddish culture to his role as one of the press's chief editors. At the beginning of 1913, Kalmanovitch received the opportunity to shape this culture when the Kletskin Press assumed responsibility for *Di yudishe velt*. Kletskin had concluded a deal with the St. Petersburg editors in which he would print the journal but they would continue to have responsibility for its publicistic section. Unsatisfied with this arrangement, Kalmanovitch fought a six-month-long battle against what he termed "the spirit of St. Petersburg," which he deemed as not sufficiently nationalistic. For instance, the St. Petersburg group sought to limit the publication of too much material in favor of rehabilitating the kheyder. In order to rid himself of this interference, Kalmanovitch invited Niger, then a student in Bern, to assume editorship of the journal. Once Niger arrived in Vilna, Kalmanovitch predicted, the St. Petersburg group would abdicate the publicistic section to Vilna. When Niger equivocated in his response to the offer, Kalmanovitch temporarily assumed editorship of the belletristic section of the journal together with Kletskin and the young Yiddish writer, Dovid Bergelson. In reality, Kalmanovitch operated as the de facto editor of the entire journal, micromanaging its contents long after Niger officially assumed the role of editor.[161]

From the beginning, Kalmanovitch reacted to his new responsibilities to the journal as if the entire future of modern Yiddish culture depended on it. Dramatically, he wrote Niger that it tore his heart apart to cut sections of articles by Niger and Dovid Einhorn. More substantively, he hoped that *Di yudishe velt* would reflect his expansive vision for modern Yiddish culture. Consequently, Kalmanovitch envisioned an expanded publicistic section of the journal, in which leading Jewish intellectuals would express their opinions on the pressing Jewish and general issues of the day. Regarding matters of contemporary Jewish religious philosophy, Kalmanovitch hoped to recruit Shim'on Bernfeld. He similarly hoped to attract the Polish Jewish historian Ignacy (Yitskhok) Schiper to contribute articles about Polish Jewish history and economics. Kalmanovitch hoped to encourage these scholars to publish their books on these topics in serialized form in *Di yudishe velt*. As acting editor of belletristics, Kalmanovitch made every effort to secure the publication of the memoirs of Sholem Aleichem and short stories by Peretz. He similarly agreed with Kletskin's proposal to serialize a modernist Yiddish novel, which would take place in Germany and deal with German-Jewish relations.[162] In the journal, Kalmanovitch pursued nothing less than Jewish national comprehensiveness: "because in our journal we cannot miss even a single question, or point," he declared.[163] In contradistinction to "an orthodox Marxist" journal, *Di yudishe velt* would remain nonpartisan and thereby express a multiplicity of views.[164]

Yet, not surprisingly, Kalmanovitch's nationalist pluralism reached its limits when it came to religious Orthodoxy. On the one hand, he hoped that *Di yudishe velt* would have room to express the opinions of those Yiddishist intellectuals who believed in the continued relevance of the Jewish religious tradition. For that reason, he opposed the proposal that Ben Adir serve as editor of the publicistic section. Ben Adir, with his rationalist bent, might not look favorably at the "internal spiritual revolution" that had begun during the years of reaction. *Di yudishe velt*, Kalmanovitch argued, had to be broad enough to include the opinions of Hillel Tsaytlin, who wrote about Jewish chosenness and the value of traditional Judaism.[165] Kalmanovitch's openness to Tsaytlin's opinions did not stem from his agreement with them. Rather, he believed that the journal must accurately reflect the "internal evolution among Jews."[166] This tolerance of religious sentiment, however, reached its limits when it came to actual calls to abandon the nationalist experiment in favor of religious observance. When Nathan Birnbaum, the Yiddishist-turned-religious-penitent, contributed an article to *Di yudishe velt*, Niger asked Kalmanovitch if he deemed it necessary to print an editorial statement distancing the journal from the author's views. Kalmanovitch answered that as long as Birnbaum limited his religious reflections to the realm of the theoretical, such a statement would not be necessary. If, however, Birnbaum openly called on the readers to believe in the divinity of the Torah or wear such ritual objects as phylacteries, Kalmanovitch would refuse to print the article. In the end, Kalmanovitch did print such an editorial statement, expressing disagreement with some of Birnbaum's positions.[167]

Conclusion

Between the years 1903–1914, Tcherikower, Efroikin, and Kalmanovitch followed a trajectory that proved typical for those young Russian Jews who fashioned themselves into a socialist nationalist, autonomist Yiddishist elite. The similarity of their paths appears all the more remarkable when we consider the differing cultural and social milieus in which they grew up. All rebelled against what they perceived as the half measures of their parents' generation to solve the anomaly of Jewish life in Russia, whether those measures included traditional rabbinic learning, Haskalah, Russification, Zionism, or a combination of all four. All three men joined the first socialist Zionist cells that formed in the first years of the century and soon followed these cells into Vozrozhdenie. Their membership in Vozrozhdenie indicated the synthesis of socialism with maximal Jewish nationalism that these three men, together with so many in their generational cohort, believed would lead to Jewish national renaissance in Russia.

During the years 1905–1907, Tcherikower, Efroikin, and Kalmanovitch experienced the opportunity to translate this radical program of national rebirth into action. Typical of their generation, their revolutionary fervor propelled them both leftward in their socialism and rightward in their embrace of an undiluted Jewish nationalism. In the case of Tcherikower, his movement leftward led to his involvement in the general Russian revolutionary political activity of the Mensheviks, even as his Jewish nationalism led him to muse about the fate of Russian Jewry in the pages of the Russian Jewish press. Efroikin and Kalmanovitch joined SERP, which combined dedication to revolutionary socialism with demands for maximal Jewish national autonomy in the Diaspora. In the pages of SERP's Yiddish organ, *Di folksshtime*, they sought an ideological basis for the synthesis of Jewish socialism and nationalism.

It was the prolonged crisis of Jewish socialism in the aftermath of Stolypin's coup d'état that moved all three men into the coalescing autonomist mainstream. When revolutionary activity no longer proved possible, these three men, like most members of their generational cohort, transferred their dream of transforming Russian Jewry from the realm of politics to that of culture and incremental organic work. They therefore found a legal place for themselves within the emerging Russian Jewish public culture. All three, in various degrees, joined in the new marriage between Diaspora nationalism and Yiddishism. Through this process, they persisted in their quasi-messianic dream of preparing Russian Jewry for a secular, Diaspora nationalist rebirth. To Efroikin, this rebirth meant a last attempt to transform Jewish socialism from a movement of the Jewish proletariat to that of the Russian Jewish masses. Subsequently, this vision led him to an embrace of a populist folkism that attempted to forge a Jewish nationally autonomous space by creating an independent Jewish economics and politics. To Efroikin, the task of creating a new Jewish culture could not be separated from that of improving the Jews' economic situation and their political consciousness. Kalmanovitch, in contradistinction, focused more exclusively on the cultural realm, seeking to provide East European Jewry with a Yiddish culture at once secularly nationalist and religiously redemptive. Although not officially switching his cultural language to Yiddish, Tcherikower also turned to cultural nationalism, writing a nationalist history of the OPE that championed the causes of autonomism and modern Yiddish culture.

Between 1908 and 1914, Tcherikower, Efroikin, and Kalmanovitch considered their attempts at Jewish national regeneration as severely hampered by tsarist political reaction. Certainly, these men no doubt were justified in negatively comparing the incremental progress of these years with the revolutionary fervor of 1905–1907. Yet, in historical perspective, these three men, along with their entire generation, achieved a level of stability during the years of reaction that would elude them during the coming apocalypse of world war. World

War I would interrupt and ultimately transform their attempts at Diaspora nation building in ways that they never could have imagined at the onset of the conflict. Ironically, the war also served as a catalyst for the rapid implementation of their autonomist and Yiddishist vision.

CHAPTER TWO

Catastrophe and Renaissance during World War I

BY THE SUMMER of 1914, Tcherikower, Efroikin, and Kalmanovitch all had settled into the routines they had carved for themselves in political, economic, or cultural organic work that sought to incrementally improve the plight of Russian Jewry and to prepare it for its eventual national liberation. The outbreak of war disrupted this work in some ways yet accelerated it in others. To all three, the war with its unprecedented destruction created the potential for the implementation of their Yiddishist autonomist vision. Each in his own way understood his task during the war as preparing Russian Jewry for the political and cultural renaissance that the war's end would inaugurate.

World War I brought unprecedented upheaval and destruction to Russian Jewry. In the immediate aftermath of the outbreak of war, Russian Jewish leaders expressed their patriotism and their desire to sacrifice for their homeland. At least initially, these leaders hoped that Russia's alliance with England and France would influence the tsarist regime to alleviate Jewish legal disabilities. Even Diaspora nationalists supported the Russian war effort, hoping that a Russian victory over Austria-Hungary could unite the Jews of Galicia with those living under Russian rule in the Pale and in Poland.[1] Yet, as the war continued, such fervent patriotism became impossible to maintain.

Because much of the Pale functioned as the war front, its Jews suffered from the normal civilian casualties of war. In addition, however, they fell victim to pogroms, initiated by the army and joined in by locals. Popular anti-Semitism combined with a perception of Jewish grievances against the regime to lead to charges of Jewish disloyalty. In particular, the army and the Russian press accused the Jews, with their usage of a Germanic language, Yiddish, and their close ties to Galician Jewry, of espionage for the Germans and Austrians.

From the outbreak of the war, the Russian government placed most provinces of the Pale under military occupation and empowered the Stavka (the Supreme Military Headquarters) with the ability to determine policies for the populations under its control. The Stavka used its power to expel Jews en masse from the front. This policy of expulsion reached its heights in the spring and summer of 1915, when nearly two hundred thousand Jews were expelled from the Courland, Kovno, and Grodno provinces. Suddenly, hundreds of thousands of Russian Jews found themselves homeless and without means of sustenance and financial support. During the first months of the crisis, these refugees crowded into nearby cities such as Vilna and Minsk, and in the eastern provinces of Poltava and Chernigov. In order to alleviate the overcrowding in these provinces and to curry favor with Jewish capital abroad, the Russian government in August 1915 allowed the Jewish refugees to settle in all towns and cities, but not the countryside, of the Russian interior. This policy led to the de facto, if not de jure, abolition of the Pale of Settlement. In his reflections on his fact-finding mission in Russian-occupied Galicia, An-sky detailed the deep psychological effects of the destruction on the Jewish population. In particular, he and other writers concentrated on the demoralization that led many formerly respectable Jews to smuggling and even to prostitution. The breaking of prewar taboos in the face of catastrophe and dislocation led, in David Roskies's words, to the loss of "that final claim to Jewish sanctity, intimacy, and security." The shtetl as *kehilah kedoshah*, as a sacred community, no longer existed.[2]

Yet, less well known was the attempt by young Jewish relief workers to use the devastation of war as an opportunity to rebuild Jewish communities upon a democratic, nationalist basis. The massive dislocation caused by the war empowered autonomists to translate the theories of Jewish self-government that they had developed for nearly a decade into action. In the immediate aftermath of the outbreak of war, Russian Jewish leaders organized the Central Committee to Aid Victims of War (Evreiskii komitet pomoshchi zhertvam voiny—EKOPO). Initially established to aid the families of fallen Russian Jewish soldiers, EKOPO soon turned its attention to relief activity for the hundreds of thousands expelled form their homes. The leadership of EKOPO consisted of the leading Russian Jewish oligarchs such as Baron Alexander Ginzburg and his family, the banker M. A. Varshavsky, banker B. A. Kamenka, and David Feinberg. To this group were added more recent Russian Jewish leaders, who had emerged on the scene since 1905, such as Maxim Vinaver and Meir Kreinin. At least initially undemocratic, the small organizational committee determined the composition of the Petrograd Committee. Even after EKOPO established branches throughout Russia, the Petrograd Committee continued to wield most of the power.[3]

The predominant role of integrationist oligarchs and liberals and EKOPO's nondemocratic nature initially led young socialist and liberal autonomists to dismiss the work of EKOPO as old-fashioned philanthropy. What the Jewish refugees really needed, they argued, was training in self-help. Yet EKOPO's ability to raise massive sums of money from Russian Jewry, American Jewry, and the Russian government, and its ability to direct the distribution of those funds, made it impossible for these autonomists not to work with it. In fact, as the war continued, EKOPO co-opted all other preexistent Jewish relief societies, such as EKA, OPE, and OZE (Obschestvo zdravookhraneniia evreev—Society for the Protection of the Health of the Jewish Population), which became divisions of the umbrella relief organization. EKOPO thus assumed responsibility for the material, educational, and occupational needs of hundreds of thousands of Jews.[4]

Manning this massive relief effort were thousands of employees of the formerly independent social and cultural organizations such as ORT, OPE, and EKA. The fact that these relief workers largely came from these ranks had a democratizing effect on EKOPO. Steven Zipperstein has emphasized the importance of this so-called "third element," professionally trained young people who belonged neither to the ruling or the working classes, in democratizing EKOPO and its relief efforts. In particular, he emphasized how the thousands of Jewish relief workers from this background influenced Jewish refugees and their communities with their democratic, autonomist principles. These principles of democratization and secularization fell on fertile ground, largely because of the war's destruction of the traditional communal framework. In the absence of traditional leadership, these young relief workers often assumed a leadership role in both devastated Jewish communities in the Pale and emerging ones in the Russian interior.[5]

In practice, EKOPO functioned as an all-Russian form of Jewish self-government. With a centralized leadership in Petrograd, it coordinated Jewish relief work on a national scale. It also implemented the autonomist plan of Jewish self-taxation, demanding of its members that they donate 5 percent of their income to the relief effort. This flowering of Jewish self-government owed itself largely to the tacit encouragement of the Russian government, which directed Jewish refugees and war victims to EKOPO for aid. The government's empowerment of Jewish civil society had its analogue in general Russian society, in which the Union of Zemstvos and Union of Towns assumed responsibility for war relief. This process of democratization led to angst among the Russian Jewish oligarchy. In May 1916, for instance, Alexander Ginzburg complained to Felix Warburg, a leader of the Joint Distribution Committee, that the relief organizations under EKOPO's domain had fallen into the hands of Zionists and subversive Yiddishists. No doubt worried about the loss of control for the elite, Ginzburg and his cohort worried most about the politicization of relief work that democratization implied. Whereas Ginzburg and the other leaders of EKOPO understood their task as providing philanthropic relief for Jewish individuals, younger relief workers insisted on the communal, national nature of their work. Relief work, they argued, did not constitute charity but rather national self-help. In time, the oligarchic leadership of EKOPO bowed somewhat to the demands of the democratizers by including places on its central committee to representatives from OPE, ORT, OZE, EKA, and the refugees. Clearly, this arrangement still could not satisfy the democratic elements, given that power remained consolidated in the hands of the Petrograd leadership.[6]

Another major factor that contributed to the growth of Diaspora nationalism was the attitude of Russian liberalism toward the Jews during the war. With the outbreak of war, the Kadets' sympathy for the Jews as victims of the regime vanished as their patriotism led them to turn a blind eye to the army's abuse of the Jews. Moreover, the fact that during the war the Kadets joined in the Progressive Bloc that welcomed openly anti-Semitic deputies into its midst further diminished the chances of their voicing support for Jewish rights. Increasingly, Kadet leaders feared that outspoken sympathy for the Jews would cost them their popularity and, in some instances, even joined in the charge of Jewish disloyalty and espionage. Although the Progressive Bloc included a vaguely worded statement about the amelioration of Jewish disabilities in its platform, its members in practice did nothing to implement this policy into action. The nadir of the relations between Russian Jewry and the Kadet party occurred in 1916 with the "circulars affair." When two government circulars accused the Jews of hoarding, contributing to the food shortage, and fomenting revolution, the two Jewish Duma deputies (both Kadets) demanded an interpellation calling on the government to inform the Duma whether or not it determined its policies based upon these reports. However, despite the fact that the circulars had led to the arrest of hundreds of Jews, the Kadets pressured these deputies to withdraw their demand, further eroding the image of Jewish liberalism in Russian Jewish society.[7]

In a seminal essay, Jonathan Frankel argued that what he termed "the paradoxical politics of marginality" led East European Jewry, in the midst of its suffering, to believe that the end of the war could bring resolution to its deepest national problems. In his words:

> Never before in modern history . . . had the inherent vulnerability and weakness of the Jews as a scattered minority been exposed with such insistent brutality and impunity. Yet at the very same time, many Jews— movements, groups, individuals—came to the conclusion that the moment of emancipation or autoemancipation (national liberation, however variously defined) had arrived. The Jewish people had it within their grasp at last to solve the Jewish question.[8]

These "paradoxical politics of marginality," in which a myth of Jewish power led both to intense anti-Jewish persecution and to limited concessions, had a direct effect on the growth of Jewish Diaspora nationalism during the war years. The Russian government's abandonment of the Jewish refugees to their own devices ironically led to the consolidation of Jewish self-government through EKOPO and its constituent relief organizations. Abandoned by Russian liberalism, Russian Jews increasingly turned to an autonomist definition of their place within the empire. In grandly paradoxical fashion, the disillusion of Russian Jewry as a compact geographical and cultural unit empowered autonomists to act and speak on behalf of a Russian Jewish nation. It is no wonder then that the subjects of our study sought to build the foundations of a Jewish national renaissance on the ruins wrought by World War I.

A Fighter for Jewish Rights

When World War I erupted in late July 1914, Elias and Riva Tcherikower were abroad, visiting Palestine. Writing to their family and friends from Jaffa, they expressed concern for the situation in Russia, and hoped that soon they would prove able to travel home. Fearful of the Ottoman policy of expulsion of Russian Jews from Palestine, the Tcherikowers then settled briefly in Cairo, Egypt, where they lived among Jewish refugees from Palestine. Still fearful of the political situation in Ottoman Egypt and with Tcherikower desiring to return to his communal and scholarly work, the couple traveled to the United States six months later.[9] The national romantic manner in which Tcherikower described their journey to America became typical of Tcherikower's writing during World War I:

> Together with a small group of unhappy Jews who had been driven out of Jerusalem, Jaffa, etc. consisting of old folks, women, and children, and another small group consisting of young people, we went through the whole emigrational gamut, which took a month. "In one's community [surrounded by one's people], even death is beautiful . . ." is not just a wise saying, but a real and important affirmation of our psyche. It was all quite different when we stepped onto American soil, landing in famous New York. We had not experienced such a sweet, affectionate reception in a long time. We landed in the Jerusalem of America in a city that includes one to one and a quarter million Jews, where Jewish life flourishes on a large scale. Right after our arrival, we happened to meet B. Borochov, who has lived here (with Liuda and their little girl) for seven or eight months.[10]

Years later, Tcherikower recollected that it was precisely this child-hood friend, Borochov, who influenced him to write in Yiddish while in the United States. If Borochov could have mastered a Yiddish literary style despite his having grown up in a Russian-speaking home, then Tcherikower, a native Yiddish speaker, certainly could do so.[11] Even without Borochov's influence, Tcherikower probably would have turned to Yiddish in New York for practical reasons. With no Russian Jewish press in New York, Tcherikower had to look to the active American Yiddish press for livelihood.

Perhaps through Borochov's initiation, Tcherikower immediately became active in the Jewish socialist nationalist circle then active in New York. Starting in 1915, he wrote for *Der idisher kongres* (The Jewish congress), *Der idisher kempfer* (The Jewish fighter), and *Der tog* (The day). In Tcherikower's articles for these journals and newspaper, the issue of Jewish national rights occupied a preeminent position. Again and again, he argued his position that the Jews of Russia needed full civil and national rights. Seeking to educate his American audience about this necessity, Tcherikower often offered them basic lessons in the history of the struggle for Jewish political and national rights, both in Western Europe and in Russia. Immediately upon settling in America, Tcherikower thus joined forces with the nationalist wing of the American Jewish socialists, who demanded nonpartisan struggle on behalf of their fellow Jews in Eastern Europe.[12]

Tcherikower's embrace of an activist nationalist politics led to his close collaboration with Borochov, Syrkin, David Ben-Gurion, and other leaders of Poale Zion living in New York during World War I. Whereas Syrkin and Ben-Gurion represented the Hebraist, Palestine-centered wing of the party, Borochov represented its Yiddishist wing. In America, membership in Poale Zion made sense for socialist autonomists, given that it functioned as the only American Jewish socialist party to endorse a plan for autonomy in the Diaspora. During World War I, Tcherikower collaborated with both the Hebraist and Yiddishist representatives of this party in the publication of a one-hundred-page pamphlet, *In kampf far idishe rekht* (In struggle for Jewish rights). This pamphlet, edited and largely written by Borochov, sought to educate American Jews in the Jewish struggle for civil and national rights so that they effectively could lobby the world powers at the war's end. Although Borochov claimed nonpartisanship, the contributors, Borochov, Ben-Gurion, and Tcherikower, all were adherents of Jewish socialist nationalism. Not surprisingly, the Jewish National Workers' Alliance commissioned this project. The authors of the brochure understood the story of the Jewish struggle for rights as both the most important narrative of modern Jewish history and the most pressing goal for the immediate postwar period. Also significant is the fact that the brochure conceived of the struggles for the political emancipation of the Jewish individual and for the attainment of autonomy for the Jewish nation as two parts of the same political process. Borochov, for instance, argued that three levels of rights existed: human and personal rights, citizenship rights, and finally national rights. Whereas citizenship rights protected the basic human rights of the individual, national rights protected the citizenship rights of members of national minorities against the encroachments of the dominant nationalities.[13]

Dubnov himself invoked this schema in his own attempt to bring the plight of Russian Jewry to the American Jewish reading public through his three-volume *History of the Jews of Russia and Poland*. With the outbreak of World War I, the project, commissioned and translated by the New York Russian Jewish professor Israel Friedlaender, assumed the purpose of bringing the political plight of Russian Jewry to the attention of American Jewry. Dubnov wrote the manuscript for this work during 1915–1916, against the backdrop of the mass expulsion, the refugee crisis, pogroms, and the splintering of Russian Jewry due to the German occupation. What emerged was what historian Salo Baron referred to as "the lachrymose conception of Jewish history," the tendency to paint the Jewish past in black terms.[14] Despite his protestations to the contrary, Dubnov had adopted this historiographical model from his *Wissenschaft des Judentums* predecessors. Dubnov emphasized Jewish suffering at the hands of the Romanovs in order to convince his American readers of the need for Jewish personal and national emancipation at the war's end.

Transforming the meaning of a familiar *Wissenschaft des Judentums* trope, Dubnov implied that *leiden* (suffering) had begotten *lernen* (study), which he understood not as religious study but rather as cultural production. The Jewish national culture forged in the crucible of tsarist oppression would pave the way for a national emancipation that would include the attainment of political autonomy. Belying his secularism in his invoking of the theme of Jewish martyrdom, Dubnov wrote the Russian-Jewish experience into the liturgical pantheon of age-old Jewish suffering.[15] Elsewhere, he sought to further weave the current catastrophe into Jewish liturgical collective memory by seeing in the war the fulfillment of the words of the Book of Lamentations, "from outside the sword bereaves and inside there is dread." In his words: "A new Jeremiah needs to write a new Book of Lamentations in which he will have to add many terrible things to the last chapter ... but the refrain should remain the same: 'Remember, O Lord, what happened to us, behold and see our disgrace.'"[16]

In his emphases both on the continuities between civic and national emancipation and on tsarist oppression as leading to Jewish national renaissance, Tcherikower followed Dubnov's lead. In his chapter for *In kampf far idishe rekht* dealing with Jewish emancipation in Western Europe, Tcherikower criticized the assimilatory excesses of West European Jewish proponents of emancipation, who sought to attain their rights through the loss of Jewish "*national individuality,* with erasing the spiritual physiognomy of the oldest historical people."[17] Yet he decidedly stopped short of declaring these champions of emancipation Jewish national traitors, arguing that emancipation had proven the most pressing political need of nineteenth-century European Jewry.[18] In fact, Tcherikower argued, the national conscience of West European Jewry had revealed itself in the help that it offered its non-emancipated brethren in Eastern Europe. This aid in turn stimulated Russian Jewry to independently battle for its political and, ultimately, national rights. Tcherikower then declared: "So stretches the line of the Jewish battle until our time. From Paris to St. Petersburg to Vilna and from Berlin and Vienna to the United States, this thread of historical struggle for Jewish rights stretches. As much as the means, the place, the intensiveness of the program vary, it is however at heart the exact same process—the struggle of a people for its human and national life."[19] In this conception of Jewish national autonomy as the truest embodiment of Jewish emancipation, Tcherikower echoed Dubnov, who had argued that if the Jewish separatism of premodernity had operated as the historical thesis, and emancipation as the antithesis, then national autonomy served as the new synthesis.[20]

Tcherikower's emphasis on the struggle for emancipation reached its climax in his lachrymose depiction of the conditions of Jewish life in tsarist Russia. The lack of Russian Jewry's political rights despite its demographic importance in Russia's western provinces carried great significance for world Jewry. He asked his readers to imagine that half the population of the cities of the Pale

> are bound, simply bound hand and foot, confused by thousands of chains that do not allow him even the slightest free movement. And imagine further, that nearby, not far, people stand with glazed eyes and hold high, beautiful and echoing sermons about the greatness of modern culture and individual freedom, about the progress of ideas, about order and lawfulness—what a shameful, unnatural picture it would be, how devilish would this game sound? And this painted picture is, without any exaggeration, the daily life of six million Jews in Russia.[21]

In this lachrymose depiction, Tcherikower contrasted the freedom and progress of free Russian citizens with the virtual slavery of Russian Jews. From this emotional outburst, the reader would be unable to realize that no individuals, Jewish or non-Jewish, living under tsarist rule enjoyed citizenship rights in the West European and American sense of the term. Following Dubnov's lead, Tcherikower emphasized Jewish exceptionalism under the tsarist legal system. Successive tsarist regimes, he insisted, had passed more laws regarding the Jews than regarding any other matter. Indeed, he portrayed the history of Russian Jewry since the nineteenth century in the bleakest terms. This history consisted of the military service of the Cantonists, the expulsion of thousands living outside the Pale, and the eruption of bloody pogroms. The latter had caused "the sharpened knife of bloody persecutions, together with the most grotesque tortures, with the rape of Jewish women, barbaric murder of infants" to "hang over the neck of six million Jews."[22] Not Jewish national separateness but rather the tsarist regime's quest for a scapegoat served as the primary cause of this persecution. Only the regime's desire to maintain this scapegoat would prevent it from completely eradicating the Jews. In the meantime, the tsarist refusal to integrate the Jews allowed the Jews to cultivate Yiddish culture even as the regime's desire to integrate the

Ukrainians, Lithuanians, and Poles had led to the suppression of their national cultures.[23]

Behind this observation rested the same anxiety that plagued many Russian Jewish nationalists during World War I, namely that emancipation would lead to assimilation. Rather than hailing the de facto abolition of the Pale as a first step toward Jewish emancipation, Tcherikower thus feared that it would "crumble the Jewish collective, which is so internally national and heartily Jewish, so internally strong as long as it is melded together in one compact mass."[24] In the absence of Jewish civil and national rights, geographic dispersion would lead only to social and cultural degeneration. He therefore decried the plans of Russian Jewish leaders to take advantage of the expulsion of Jews to the interior to establish Jewish communities in Siberia. Such decentralization would culturally lead to a sense of exile and yearning for a spiritual center and economically contribute to the reproduction of the current Jewish economic order in the Pale, thus breeding anti-Semitism. Instead, Tcherikower called for the creation of Jewish agricultural colonies in Siberia, where Jews could maintain their own culture.[25] It must be remembered that from 1905 through 1914, Tcherikower had attempted successfully to transcend the Pale both culturally and geographically. That he of all people would wax nostalgic for the Pale's national role in Russian Jewish life speaks to the extent of the anxieties of emancipation among the autonomist intelligentsia.

As an antidote to this fear of assimilation, Tcherikower, like Dubnov, emphasized Jewish cultural renaissance as emerging from the midst of the current persecution. The cataclysmic suffering of the Jews during World War I led Tcherikower to a romantic appreciation of the durability of the Jewish national culture produced in its wake.[26] In 1916, Tcherikower described in a martyrological tone the Galician refugee crisis and the forced evacuation of thousands of Russian Jews from the front:

> The scenes of the expulsion, the terrible details, the dirty freight cars filled with Jewish souls, with the mentally ill and sick . . . the ninety-year-old rabbi, who lay in the freight car with the cry to heaven—"Because of our sins we were exiled from our land"—these are already moments that have entered the classic Jewish martyr-history of generations, just like Hannah

and her seven sons, the ten martyrs of the Roman government, the stories of the destruction of Jerusalem and the sacking of Betar, about the martyrs of Torquemada, of the decrees of *Taḥ ve-tat* (1648), of the slaughter in Uman and in Kishinev. To recount them is superfluous.[27]

In this passage, Tcherikower compared the current suffering to the classic examples of *Kiddush Hashem* (dying for the sanctification of God's name) in Jewish liturgy. In this national-romantic vision of martyrdom, all boundaries dissolved between the liturgical, the historical, the religious, and the national. Similarly, Jewish history emerged as a seamless chain of suffering. In this enshrinement of the events of World War I into the pantheon of Jewish suffering, Tcherikower followed Dubnov's lead. As early as 1903, Dubnov had compared the Kishinev pogrom to the Haidamak massacre in Uman in 1768. At least since 1912, moreover, he had compared the pogroms of 1881–1882 to such apocalyptic years in Jewish history as 1096, 1492, and 1648.[28]

Tcherikower turned to the study of Jewish martyrology to impart the terrible current events with transcendent meaning.[29] In commemorating the tenth anniversary of the pogroms of October 1905, he turned to martyrology to impart meaning to what he would otherwise dismiss as meaningless suffering. In his words:

Jewish history does not want to change its silent tragic path. We are powerless to understand, to grasp its thread—to where it leads us. The dark despair, the deep, horrifying meaninglessness of our martyrs' history can drive into the coldest skeptic, even the most sober atheist, a restless religious tendency, a mystical mood, to rescue his passionate soul, our thought from the surrounding chaos, from the dark eternity.

On the black anniversary of our murdered brothers and sisters, it remains for us only to repeat after our pious and believing elder brothers the frightful prayer: God full of compassion.[30]

Although Tcherikower, "the sober atheist," repeatedly described the current carnage as meaningless, it seemed that he desperately sought to redeem contemporary Jewish suffering by linking it to the historical martyrdom of the Jewish people. In the spring of 1916, for instance, he wrote a series of articles that described the devastation of the Chmielnicki and Haidamak pogroms of the seventeenth and eighteenth centuries.[31] Tcherikower clearly conceptualized the history of

Jewish martyrology as cyclical, commenting that the forms of torture and martyrdom had remained the same across more than three centuries, from the time of Chmielnicki to that of the current world war. Even the perpetrators of the current pogroms were members of the same historical peoples responsible for past catastrophes. To some extent, Tcherikower's focus on Jewish suffering was practical and political. In September 1915, for instance, he echoed the call of Peretz, Yankev Dinezon, An-sky, and other leading East European Jewish cultural figures to collect documentation of the pogroms. By sending emissaries to the war-torn countries on a fact-finding mission, American Jewry could help in this process of creating documentation for the international Jewish community to present to the victors at the war's end.[32]

On a deeper level, however, Tcherikower invoked Jewish martyrology as part of the schema of national persecution leading to cultural renaissance. For instance, he described the cultural renaissance as "a miracle" that emerged "from the ruins of the pogroms."[33] Indeed, Tcherikower invoked religious terminology to describe this cultural renaissance, applying to it the kabbalistic term *tikun neshomoh* (a repair for the soul). He stated that such spiritual creation often followed on the heels of catastrophe. Echoing Dubnov's historiographical position, Tcherikower explained that Hasidism had emerged in the wake of the Chmielnicki and Haidamak massacres. Dramatically, he applied the verse from Ezekiel recited at a traditional circumcision ceremony, "In your blood shall you live," to describe the meaning of the current cultural productivity of the Jews of Russia. Elsewhere, Tcherikower invoked a well-known midrashic story of how a *Tanna* (Mishnaic sage) attempted to ward off the Angel of Death by studying Torah continuously as a metaphor to Russian Jewry's cultural renaissance in the midst of war.[34] Romantically, he wrote: "Under the most desolate persecutions, surrounded by angry winds, pursued by Satan, which lurks for the Jewish people, the Remnant of Israel does not want to take a break from its spiritual work even for one minute, and as long as it occupies itself with spirituality, the Angel of Death will not have dominion over it."[35]

Committed to secularism, Tcherikower nonetheless turned to the traditional Jewish belief that the Jews as a people remain alive in the merit of their Torah study. Similarly, he attributed the willingness of Russian Jewry to fund new OPE schools for Jewish refugee children to the traditional Jewish preference for *talmud Torah* (Torah study) over *leḥem evyonim* (bread for the poor). The reliance of this cultural nationalist vision on the Jewish religious tradition, however, remained largely unconscious.[36] In fact, Tcherikower argued that the current secular cultural renaissance had absolutely nothing to do with the despair, messianism, and mysticism of Hasidism, a product of oppression, but rather consisted of "a healthy, normal striving toward cultural creation, which carries a pronounced *social* character."[37] As part of this cultural renaissance, Tcherikower praised the self-help initiatives of the OZE, the "Hilf durkh arbet" (help through work) movement, and the schools created for refugee children in the Russian interior by the OPE. Himself a graduate of art school, he also praised the endeavors of the Society for the Development of Jewish Art in Moscow. Turning to Jewish scholarship, he also praised *Istoriia evreev v Rossii* (History of the Jews in Russia), written by various scholars, and Israel Tsinberg's *Istoriia evreiskoi pechati v Rossii v sviazi s obshchestvennymi techeniiami* (History of the Jewish press in Russia). Yet because the cultural renaissance occurred in Moscow and Petrograd rather than in the large Jewish population centers, the cultural movement served the people but was not of the people. Still, the cultural renaissance had demonstrated the falseness of the Zionist charge that Jews could not create national culture in the Diaspora.

As the language war escalated among Russian Jewry, Tcherikower sided with the Yiddishists. For instance, when the OPE created new Yiddish schools for refugee children, he argued that the victory of Yiddish in the schools strengthened its position as a cultural language.[38] Tcherikower manifested his position on the language war in two columns for *Der tog,* in which he responded to an attack on Yiddish by Syrkin. Syrkin stated that now that Germany had occupied vast tracts of Russia and Poland, the language war had become a very practical matter.[39] Yiddishism, Syrkin argued, ignored the Jewish past and future for the narrow East European present. Without the pedigree of a holy tongue, Yiddish could never develop into a cultural language. Nor could it develop a grammar without merging either with German or with Hebrew. As a result, Yiddish served only as "an unfortunate episode in the history of the Jewish exile, just as the many other Jewish jargons." Syrkin ended his polemic by invoking the well-known Hebraist imagery of Hebrew as the mistress that had to assert its rights against Yiddish, the uppity maidservant. In the end, Syrkin argued, Poale Zion, OPE, and the entire Jewish people would have to decide between "great nationalism and small nationalism," between "Mistress nationalism" and "maidservant nationalism."[40]

Syrkin's disdain for Yiddish, responded Tcherikower, emerged as a product of the Zionist belief in *shelilat hagolah,* or negation of the exile. This ideology, which dismissed Jewish cultural production in the Diaspora as a misfortune, had blinded Syrkin to the truth that the best products of Jewish history, from parts of the Bible through the Babylonian Talmud, had emerged in the Diaspora. Tcherikower referred to a "golden chain" that flowed "from Maimonides to the Baal Shem Tov and the Vilna Gaon, from Philo of Alexandria, Egypt to Spinoza and Mendelssohn."[41] Recognition of this truth would lead to respect for Yiddish, the language through which the Jews had experienced the joys of Hasidism, Haskalah, national awakening, and revolutionary struggle. Although firmly Yiddishist, Tcherikower affirmed different roles for each language in the national renaissance. Hebrew conjured the image of his pious, scholarly father, whereas Yiddish evoked the image of his loving, nurturing mother. Hebrew thus served as the language of the "historical past" and Yiddish that of "the harried and busy masses in the gray present." In Tcherikower's words:

> Now, when I have roamed to far-off lands, when the broken soul is injured in the bitter life struggle, only the mother's loving image warms my soul. Can I forget it—the plain, intimate, Jewish image of my mother? . . . We are caught in a tragic division between two worlds, between holiness and worldliness, between the language of tradition and the language of bitter reality. Can we without an operation, without excising a piece of our living soul, choose specifically one of these two languages?[42]

Although an impassioned defense of Yiddish, this statement was a far cry from the highbrow Yiddishism to which Kalmanovitch subscribed during these same years. Rather, here Tcherikower invoked the argument of populist Yiddishists, who venerated Yiddish as the language of the masses.

Tcherikower went still farther in using this Yiddishist argument to criticize Zionism. Such contemporary Zionist thinkers as Aḥad Ha-'Am, Yosef Klausner, and Menaḥem Ussishkin had inherited their combined disdain for Yiddish and enamorment with Russian from the Haskalah. Pointing to the alleged similarity between Syrkin's attack on Yiddish and a recent speech in which Jacob Schiff had disparaged Yiddish, Tcherikower commented, "Compare it, and it will become clear to you that one feeling of disdain and struggle against Yiddish unites the bourgeois assimilationists and the extreme Hebraist Zionists."[43] This labeling of Hebraist Zionists as bourgeois was nothing new to those who combined support for Yiddish culture with a politics of socialist Diaspora nationalism. Still, in Tcherikower's case, this accusation proved a sensitive issue, given his close connections to Poale Zion, a socialist Zionist party that embraced both Hebrew and Yiddish. In fact, Tcherikower called on the party to distance itself from Syrkin's views, which contradicted the party's platform. Had Syrkin expressed similarly hostile views regarding Hebrew or the settlement of Palestine, contended Tcherikower, the party already would have distanced itself from him. Despite his populist defense of Yiddishism, Tcherikower came to appreciate Yiddish culture on its own artistic merits, writing Yiddish theater reviews in which he inveighed against "stupid melodrama and cheap humor" and praised instead high art.[44]

Just as Kalmanovitch and Efroikin did, Tcherikower mused about the relationship of the secular nationalist Jew to the Jewish religious tradition. Following the High Holidays in 1916, Tcherikower confessed that the holiday season had evoked in him feelings of nostalgia for the lost religious faith of his youth. More than a natural yearning for lost childhood, this nostalgia emerged from the secular Jew's yearning for an "inner harmony" that only religion seemingly could provide. Like Kalmanovitch, he believed that the absence of religious ritual had brought desolation into the lives of secular Jews:

And perhaps stronger than everything is the inner demand and yearning for a *yontev,* to whichever holiday mood. The eternal gray commonplace dulls the soul, castrates the spirit. Radicalism destroyed the tradition of the religious holidays and did not give us any new ones, and the protest of our spirit against the eternal commonplace, against the permanent weekday clothing, becomes stronger with the years.

This all leads to the fact that when Passover comes, we search with longing for a traditional seder with the beautiful, childish stories about the exodus from Egypt, with the celebratory holiday mood. When it comes to Rosh Hashana and Yom Kippur, we search for the old *selikhes* mood, the onetime *"U'nesaneh tokef"* and *"Kol Nidre,"* the mood of *"ne'iloh"* and the mystic melancholy of the Remembrance of Souls—and we come to the door of the synagogue. However, we remain "at the threshold of the Study House" [in Hebrew], at the threshold. We have so thoroughly severed ourselves that inside there in no place for us. And when we come to the *besmedresh*, we see that it was a "blue bird" about which we were dreaming, for which we searched for years, but we can never find it. And as we arrive estranged, so too do we leave estranged.[45]

In this piece, Tcherikower invoked Bialik's poem "'Al saf bet ha-midrash" (At the threshold of the study house), in which the poet imagined himself standing "on the threshold" of the ruins of the study house, which he compared to the ruins of the Temple. Returning from the outside world that had rejected him, the poet mourns both the loss of the former spiritual glory of the *besmedresh* and his own spiritual devastation. The poem ends with the hope that both the poet, who symbolizes the Jewish people, and the study house, which symbolizes its spirit, will be rebuilt. Written on Tisha B'av, the day that commemorates the destruction of the Temple, the poem modeled itself on Yehuda Ha-Levi's odes to Zion, which first depicted the ruins of the land of Israel and then imagined the land's rebuilding. In this poem, Bialik gave voice to a major theme in both modern Hebrew and Yiddish literature, which Roskies referred to as *ḥurban bet ha-midrash*, the destruction of the study house.[46]

Whereas Bialik ended his poem on a triumphal note, confident that the study house could symbolically be rebuilt, Tcherikower invoked the poem's beginning to indicate that the modern secular Jew never could re-cross the threshold of this institution that represented the old faith. In both America and in Eastern Europe, he argued, the synagogue and its ceremonies had become devoid of the internal spark of holiness that once had animated them. Given that traditional Judaism was dying on the Jewish street, the search for lost faith proved illusory. Still, Tcherikower, like Kalmanovitch, noted that it was religion that had served as the cement for Jewish national existence. As a result, the Jewish radical intelligentsia, in contradistinction to its non-Jewish counterparts, demonstrated its lack of faith through such dramatic exhibitions as smoking on Yom Kippur and the Sabbath and attending Yom Kippur balls. Having vainly attempted to liberate themselves from the religious tradition, these freethinkers in reality remained "the same religious fanatics, only with their *arbekanfes* [ritual garment] inside out . . . prisoners of the Master of the Universe."[47] Tcherikower's romanticization of the *besmedresh* reveals the extent to which he had changed in the decade since the publication of his article on Mendele Moykher Sforim, in which he had criticized that author's use of *besmedresh* imagery as a sign of provincialism.

Tcherikower as Socialist and Jewish Nationalist

At the time of Tcherikower's arrival in New York, American Jewish socialists found themselves divided over the issue of the establishment of an American Jewish Congress. The fissure in the American Jewish socialist movement over this issue lasted until 1917. The debate pitted the more internationalist representatives of American Jewish labor such as the Jewish Socialist Federation, the Arbeter Ring (Workmen's Circle), and the *Forverts* Association against the socialist nationalist parties such as Poale Zion, the Jewish National Workers' Alliance, and the Jewish Socialist Territorialist Labor Party of America. At question was the desirability of a democratically elected American Jewish Congress to fight for the civil and national rights of East European Jewry during and following the war. Poale Zion and the other socialist nationalist parties desired to work with Louis Brandeis and the other bourgeois leaders of the American Jewish Congress movement in an effort to ameliorate the plight of their Russian Jewish brethren caught in the war zone. In contrast, the other Jewish socialist organizations opposed the congress movement both for its transcendence of class lines and for its Zionist nature. In order to limit the influence of Poale Zion within the future congress, their opponents coalesced into the National Workmen's Committee (NWC).

Between 1915 and 1917, the NWC sought to limit both the role of the socialist nationalists in the congress movement and the role of the future congress itself. The socialist nationalists, in the meantime, continued to demand full civil and national rights for the Jews in the Diaspora as well as the creation of a politically independent Jewish homeland in Palestine. After two years of struggle, the various parties reached a compromise that allowed for elections to be held for an American Jewish Congress. However, America's entry into the war postponed the meeting of the congress until 1918.[48]

It is not surprising that in America, Tcherikower found himself on the side of Zhitlovsky and his followers as opposed to Abraham Cahan, the editor of the *Jewish Daily Forward* with his international socialist contingent. Still, Tcherikower had to justify the breach of socialist doctrine that collaboration with Jewish bourgeois leaders in the formation of an American Jewish Congress entailed. In this search for justification, he was not alone. In the lead editorial of its very first issue, the editors of *Der idisher kongres* explained their willingness to participate in national work with non-proletarians: "Just as the obligation of the proletariat is to divide the Jewish people and to transform it through class struggle, so too is its responsibility to unite the nation, when the foundation of its existence is shaken."[49] In the same issue, Syrkin wrote apocalyptically that in the crucible of World War I, the Jews were experiencing a resurrection to new life as a unified nation. Syrkin then distinguished between two forms of national unity: the false kind that emerges from the exploitation of one class by another, and the true kind that occurs when the nation merges its hopes and interests with that of the working class. For the first time, he argued, the working masses had risen to awaken the Jewish people from its slumber. Zhitlovsky likewise argued that in peacetime, it would not make sense for workers to collaborate with the bourgeoisie on behalf of the nation. However, at a time when the very existence of the nation was at stake, it was the duty of the proletarian parties to work with the bourgeoisie in order to ensure that the latter did not emerge as the sole representative of the nation's interests. Because the bourgeois parties would act only in their economic self-interest, the socialist parties had to join in national decisions. Still, he insisted that the working class enter the congress under its own flag.[50]

Several months later, Tcherikower added his voice to this issue. Whereas Syrkin and Zhitlovsky justified proletarian participation in national work on grounds that the working class would assume leadership of the struggle, Tcherikower argued for the complete separation of the socialist and national spheres. Titling his article "The Boundaries of Our *'sholem bayes'* [domestic tranquillity]," Tcherikower placed the debate against the backdrop of the crisis of the socialist parties during World War I. Although he vehemently opposed the German Social Democrats' decision to halt socialist agitation in the name of *Burgfrieden* ("castle peace" or "party truce"), he rejected any comparison of this phenomenon with the congress movement. Until recently, Tcherikower conceded, the suspicion of *kol yisroel politik* (politics of the entire Jewish people) could invalidate the credentials of a "kosher socialist." Ten years of anti-Jewish persecutions in Russia, however, had forced Jewish socialist nationalists to reevaluate that position. In his words:

> The Jewish persecutions are so below class, or more precisely, above class and nonpartisan, like a plague, a pestilence, an elemental misfortune. It is simply a matter of murder, of a thief with a knife over the throat. Exerting all energies to throw off the knife—does this rest in class interest? Does this have to do with "class ideology"?
>
> It is a simple life necessity, such as freeing oneself from a plague, saving oneself from a fire. We need elementary rights as people, as citizens; and as Jews, just as elementary is the need for a free national atmosphere. These are the boundaries of our *"sholem bayes."*[51]

Tcherikower called upon Jewish socialists to continue in their economic agitation against Jewish capitalists even as he argued for unity in the national struggle. The fact that the Jews were in an anomalous position among national groups explains this seeming contradiction. Possessing no national framework of existence, the Jews had to give priority to their national needs over their internal social divisions. Like socialist nationalists during the 1905 Revolution, Tcherikower assumed that only after the Jews achieved a normalized national status would the internal class struggle occur. As a Jewish nationalist, he understood it as his task to prepare the way for a postwar settlement in which East European Jewry would receive its national rights:

> Our work is a real one: to help our brethren in Eastern Europe to create concrete national positions in their public life—national institutions, folk schools, a wide folk movement, on the cultural and economic plains, so that they can display their national inheritance to the international political world. And secondly—to organize here all our strength, to unify all streams in order to create a national representative, the Jewish Congress, with a steadfast will and clear demands to the general peace conference.[52]

Also following the lead of the American Poale Zion, Tcherikower combined his support of the congress movement with opposition to the European socialists' participation in the war.[53] Possessing the foundations of national life, the various European socialist movements never should have allowed their patriotism to trump their proletarian solidarity. Such a move had exposed European socialist ideology to the charges of falsehood and hypocrisy. Once war erupted, the socialists, enjoying unprecedented power in European parliaments, should have used the moment to foment revolution. Instead, by supporting the war, they had eroded the International, which only could be rebuilt if it were to *become an instrument not only in time of peace, but principally against war. Whether that will truly be—therein lies the main question.*[54] Elsewhere, he decried the split in the Second International that occurred in Zimmerwald, Switzerland, between those who called for continued internationalist socialist solidarity and those who supported their respective countries' forms of patriotic socialism.[55] Despite his pacificism, he opposed the most extreme members of the Zimmerwald Conference, such as Lenin, probably because of this figure's hostile attitude toward Jewish nationalism. Tcherikower also expressed his socialist ideology in his condemnation of President Woodrow Wilson's call for peace even in the absence of a clear winner. The American president had also argued for the rights of small nationalities and for the creation of an international body to enforce peace. Representing the "basic traditions of capitalist domination," Wilson proved unable to "break the holy power of the contemporary social order." War, moreover, would endure as long as the capitalist system continued to predominate. In the absence of social revolution, Wilson's proposed "Peace League" would only succeed in suppressing social revolution, rather than achieve true peace.[56]

In the fall of 1916, watching the war rage in Europe from the safety of America, Tcherikower wrote that the irony of contemporary Jewish life was that the Jewish love affair with world culture was a one-sided phenomenon. Offering the Jews assimilation, even friends could not understand Jewish culture with its "national pathos of our Bialik, the irony of Mendele Moykher Sforim and the hasidic *dveykes* [cleaving to God] in Peretz as we understand their poets and writers." This unrequited love, confessed Tcherikower, led him sometimes to despair:

> Whether they do not want to know us or if they cannot do it, if Christian ignorance or Jewish distinctiveness is guilty—I do not know. I only know that in such an atmosphere where you understand everyone and no one understands you—it is difficult to live.
> We are a people that lives alone—"*'om le-vodod yishkon,*" even though we are spread among everyone and nestle behind every wall. And this tragic aloneness is, especially at certain moments, intolerable and stifling.[57]

This statement encapsulates Tcherikower's complicated relationship both with the outside world of Russian culture and socialist politics and with the internal world of Jewish national politics and culture. From art school in Odessa to Menshevik agitation in St. Petersburg, Tcherikower had transcended the Pale both geographically and culturally. During the inter-revolutionary years, he had expressed his Jewish nationalism from the Russified environment of St. Petersburg. His separation from Russian Jewry during the moment of its great catastrophe, however, heightened his nationalism and his yearning for national cohesion. Adopting Yiddish as his literary language, Tcherikower came to genuinely champion both the populism and the highbrow cultural aspirations of the Yiddishist movement. "The sober atheist" who ten years before had dismissed the grandfather of modern Yiddish literature as too parochial, now elevated Jewish cultural creativity to religious heights. His growing obsession with martyrology fueled his belief in the potential for Jewish national renaissance to emerge from the crucible of apocalypse and war.

Yet Tcherikower persisted in his outer-directed ideologies. For instance, he still believed that the Jews could join forces with other national minorities to secure their rights. Not abandoning his interest in European culture, Tcherikower increasingly believed that it inexorably drove its Jewish participants back to their Jewish roots. Thus, in the Middle Eastern landscapes of the Russian Jewish painter Leon Bakst, he discovered the artist's hidden Jewish spirit. The fact that the Russian police had expelled the returning Bakst from his native St. Petersburg proved the inescapability of Jewish identity and destiny.[58] Despite the vast differences between the two personalities, Tcherikower clearly understood Bakst as a projection of himself, the artist with the cosmopolitan spirit drawn back to his own people. The separation of his socialism from his Jewish nationalism served as the most dramatic example of the bifurcation of Tcherikower's outer- and inner-directed selves. During the period of World War I, these contradictions of ideology and personality—the universal and the particular, the rational and the mystical, the socialist and the national—lived together in an uneasy tension.

Kalmanovitch during World War I

In Kalmanovitch's reaction to the first news of the war, he demonstrated a combination of religious-style resignation and steely resolve, which would accompany him throughout all other major tragedies in his life. In his words to Niger:

> But during the current times, when everyone is so differently depressed, we must accept the blows with love. Now, we must hold on to the old Talmudic principle: "Every wave that passes over you, bend your head to it. . . ." I live with the belief that we will come out of this current difficult test although badly beaten, nonetheless whole, and maybe our brothers in Galicia will even be joined with us. I am certain that "German militarism" is playing its last role . . . the curse of generations will rest upon it. We, however, must begin to build again. . . . I am now completely peaceful. I am filled with hope that the war will not touch Vilna directly.[59]

In this last prediction, Kalmanovitch, of course, could not have proven more wrong. However, in this passage we see an articulation of Kalmanovitch's belief, shared by so many of his contemporaries, that East European Jewry in the end would emerge from the crucible of war strengthened. Despite tsarist persecution and his own socialist leanings, he, like most other Diaspora nationalists, sided with Russia against "German militarism." He even expressed hope that a Russian victory would lead to the unification of Russian and Galician Jewry under one political rule. In both this deep-seated faith and in the religious resignation with which he accepted news of the war, Kalmanovitch demonstrated the influence of the Jewish religious tradition upon his cultural nationalism.

As the war began to affect Vilna Jewry during the first six months of 1915, Kalmanovitch helped to spearhead the Yiddishist autonomist initiative of publishing a weekly journal, *Di vokh* (The Week). *Di vokh* sought to educate its readers about the events of the war from a Diaspora nationalist perspective. Although officially published by Boris Kletskin, the journal functioned as the private initiative of Kalmanovitch, Niger, and Shtif. Given his crucial behind-the-scenes role, the journal listed Kalmanovitch as its editor and publisher. In this journal, Kalmanovitch sought to gather the talents of all the leading Yiddishist intelligentsia, many of whom also had contributed to *Di yudishe velt:* Bazin (Zilberfarb), Wolf Latski-Bertoldi, Baal Makhshoves, Bergelson, Daniel Tsharni, Jakob Lestchinsky, Efroikin, Y. Sosis, and many more. In short, most of the leading young Yiddish writers of the day collaborated in this journal, which dedicated space to both publicistic and Yiddish literary matters. When Peretz suddenly died on Passover, 1915, *Di vokh* dedicated an entire issue to his memory.[60]

Not surprisingly, the journal represented an autonomist political and social perspective. Many articles by Efroikin, Shtif, and others dealt with Jewish self-help, which these writers saw as a national enterprise. As the refugee crisis worsened, the journal reported on the efforts of such relief organizations as "Hilf durkh arbet" and the cooperative movement to alleviate the crisis. Throughout the issues of the journal, the contributors emphasized the need for these self-help organizations to reflect democratic, populist values and practices. Given the tight censorship to which the journal was subjected, it is not surprising that it espoused Russian patriotism. In a series of articles titled "The War and We Jews," Niger argued that a Russian victory would concentrate the combined cultural and economic strength of the Jews of Lithuania, Poland, and Galicia in one political center. Given that reality, Russian Jews should unite with all-Russian progressive forces in helping the war effort.[61] Although perhaps exaggerated, this patriotism did accurately reflect the deep connection of Diaspora nationalism to the Russian Empire as a geographical unit. Although Niger, Efroikin, and others no doubt hoped for the transformation of Russia from an autocracy into a democratic, progressive regime, they also could not have envisioned a future for Jewish national autonomy outside of the empire's current borders.

Just as with *Di yudishe velt,* Kalmanovitch no doubt expended most of his energy as an editor behind the scenes, eliciting articles from leading Yiddishist writers and arranging them for print. However, he also contributed a series of articles that sought to expose his readers to the latest news about the war. In all instances, Kalmanovitch espoused a Russian patriotic stance. For instance, he wrote patriotically about the need of all Russian businesses and industries to support the war effort and organize appropriately for victory. Kalmanovitch also hailed the entrance of Italy into the war on the side of the Allies as the final foreclosure of any chance of a German and Austro-Hungarian victory. Russia now had an opening to the Adriatic Sea in its quest to conquer Constantinople. In a similar spirit, Kalmanovitch hailed the fact that American public opinion had turned away from the Germans and toward the British toward the second half of 1915. The thriving of the British economy despite the war had led that country to resolve to fight the war to the bitter end. It was German militarism and its imperialist ambitions, Kalmanovitch contended, that had led to the poisoning of the relationships between the various nationalities of the Balkans.[62]

It was the sudden death of Peretz in early spring 1915 that lent a sense of urgency and mission to Kalmanovitch's work. Kalmanovitch's role as administrator of the Kletskin Press had led to his personal acquaintance with Peretz.[63] More deeply, however, it was his perception of himself as Peretz's disciple that led Kalmanovitch to mourn deeply. In the immediate aftermath of receiving the news, Kalmanovitch wrote the following words to Dinezon, Peretz's personal secretary and confidant, which captured Kalmanovitch's sense of loss and his mission of commemoration:

> My hand shakes writing this letter. Should I search for words of consolation, which my mood does not want to attempt at all? The words from Asch's telegram constantly ring in my ears: "Be strong in silent mourn-

ing." . . . This mourning will remain for every one of us who had the fortune to benefit even a little from his great light, remain forever in the soul as long as it is destined to carry the burden of life—it must remain depressed internally—but we must, with embittered teeth, carry on the work. We are the heirs—perhaps not worthy to be that. Yet, I must strengthen myself so that *his* life, *his* work, should continue, *his* light should continue to glow, *his* voice should continue to call and awaken. The first task in our edition is that his portrait, his image, should become closer to the audience.[64]

For that purpose, Kalmanovitch dedicated the next issue of *Di vokh* to Peretz's memory and planned a special issue of *Di yudishe velt* for that purpose. This special issue of *Di vokh* contained articles by Kalmanovitch, Niger, Y. Dobrushin, Lipman Levin, and others that spoke about Peretz as a national writer. Niger spoke for all of them when he wrote that Peretz transcended the role of a writer by becoming nothing short of a life force. "Somewhere, we have people. However, there was only one *spectacular* person in our society. And he is no longer here."[65] Similarly, this issue of the journal included reportage of Peretz's funeral as well as letters from readers and organizations expressing their grief. In the coming issues, the journal continued to publish news of Peretz commemorations in various communities throughout Russia.[66]

Kalmanovitch wrote *Di vokh*'s obituary for Peretz. For a description of Peretz's early years, he turned to the writer's memoirs, which recently had appeared in the pages of *Di yudishe velt*. Interestingly, Kalmanovitch, who took these literary memoirs as fact, dwelt on a passage in which Peretz described how his mother's tears had prevented him from leaving home at the age of twenty. Although attempting objectivity, Kalmanovitch commented on Peretz's special relationship to the Kletskin Press, which recently had purchased the rights to publish his collected works. At the time of Peretz's death, the writer was helping the press expand the scope of its publications. Kalmanovitch also emphasized the special mentorship of Peretz toward the next generation of Yiddish writers. Kalmanovitch also disagreed with those literary critics who viewed Peretz's fin de siècle turn to neoromanticism as a new literary phase in his life. Rather, throughout his career, Peretz had emphasized the same perspective *(velt onshoyung)* in various forms.[67]

Another revealing feature of Kalmanovitch's obituary was its stance toward Peretz as a bilingual Hebrew-Yiddish writer. Peretz, argued Kalmanovitch, had made his main literary contribution as a Yiddish writer. Kalmanovitch's Yiddishist ideology led him to mischaracterize Peretz's position on the language question at the Czernowitz Conference. Peretz in reality had fought the proposal of the Bundist Esther Frumkin to declare Yiddish "the national language of the Jewish people." Until all the classics of Jewish literature appeared in Yiddish translation, Yiddish would remain the folk language and Hebrew the national language. The conference's final formulation adopting Yiddish as "a national language" represented Peretz's compromise. Kalmanovitch, however, erroneously reported that Peretz had declared Yiddish "the language of the Jewish people."[68] Given Kalmanovitch's enraptured interest with everything pertaining to modern Yiddish culture, it is doubtful that he did not know Peretz's true stance on the matter. Rather, by misrepresenting Peretz's view, he sought to claim Peretz fully for the Yiddishist cause. Despite his sympathies toward Hebrew, Kalmanovitch thus betrayed the monolingual cultural nationalist vision that Peretz's disciples nearly all had embraced.

When the Germans invaded Vilna in the fall of 1915, Kalmanovitch fled eastward to Petrograd. There, he lived in the same apartment building with Efroikin, Shtif, and other Yiddishist autonomists. With Kletskin having transferred his press to Petrograd, Kalmanovitch continued his administrative and editorial work there. *Di yudishe velt* suffered the same fate as did nearly all other Yiddish and Hebrew periodicals, which the Russian government closed in the summer of 1915. However, it managed to exist under different names into early 1916. In a January 1916 article, Kalmanovitch discussed the state of the relief efforts. True, he conceded, the political backwardness of many of the organizers hampered the relief work. "Yet," he concluded, "overall it must be said that since the national tragedy revealed itself in its full magnitude, the relief organizations, particularly the central one, are attempting, if not always in theory then at least in practice, to lead the relief work as a great, important, national task." Although Jewish attempts at self-help remained in their infancy, Kalmanovitch praised the cooperative movement and its savings and loan societies as the first positive step toward the creation of the refugees' economic self-sufficiency.[69]

Efroikin during World War I

During the years of reaction, Efroikin channeled his desire to incrementally improve Russian Jewish society into his work for the Jewish cooperative movement. This movement sought to create self-sufficient small-time Jewish merchants and artisans by providing them with easy credit and other professional help. Efroikin's leadership of the cooperative movement on the eve of and during World War I reveals the distance that he had traveled from socialism to democratic autonomism. Like many other Diaspora nationalists at the time, he celebrated the Jewish petty merchant as a source of East European Jewish authenticity. The most representative economic class of Russian Jewry, small-time Jewish merchants were threatened by the economic transformation of the Russian Empire at the fin de siècle. Consequently, the rehabilitation of this class assumed national importance. On the eve of World War I, Efroikin implemented these ideals by helping to found a journal, *Di yudishe kooperatsiye* (The Jewish cooperative), which would instruct Jewish merchants and artisans in the principles of the cooperative movement. The Jewish cooperative movement was the creation of the EKA (Jewish Colonization Association), which established savings and loan banks, known as *kassas*, throughout the Pale of Settlement. These *kassas* lent money to Jewish merchants and artisans at low interest rates. After the onset of Russian reaction, socialist and democratic Diaspora nationalists became active in the cooperative movement. In the final years before the outbreak of war, these savings and loan cooperatives both achieved independence from the EKA and dramatically increased in number. For democratic, non-Marxist autonomists, the creation of a self-sufficient Jewish economy served as an important step toward Jewish national renaissance.[70]

The editorial board of the journal *Di yudishe kooperatsiye*, which besides Efroikin included Y. Blum, Kh. D. Hurvits, and L. Zak, understood the Jewish cooperative as a national institution and movement meant to ensure Jewish economic self-sufficiency. The purpose of the journal was to help unite the members of the various savings and loan *kassas* into one cooperative society. Members of these societies, argued the editors, had to understand that the savings and loan societies operated as a middle ground between philanthropy and a banking system. Not wanting to create dependency, the cooperative *kassas* would not function as a traditional communal charity that did not expect return payments. Nor, however, did its leaders want the cooperative movement to treat its savings and loan *kassas* as nothing more than a banking business. Rather, they had to provide credit to those who otherwise could not afford it.[71] The goal of the journal and the movement was nothing less than "*to implant the idea of the Jewish cooperative more widely and deeply in the broad layers of the folk,* to influence their social feelings and to awaken in them a greater interest in practical cooperative work, to strengthen the belief in their own strengths, to encourage their will to struggle for a better future."[72]

The outbreak of war created both new challenges and new opportunities for the cooperative movement. A crisis ensued at the beginning of the war when frightened investors withdrew their money from the *kassas*. This, combined with the fact that some borrowers defaulted on their loans, led to a shortage of available funds in the treasuries. With the onset of mass expulsions in 1915, however, the cooperative movement received a much larger and more urgent mandate: it had to supply credit to thousands of Jewish refugees who had lost their businesses and needed to begin anew. The leaders of the cooperative movement saw this challenge as an opportunity to expand the national role of their movement.[73]

The crisis of the onset of war, wrote Efroikin, brought with it an important lesson about the kinds of loans that the *kassas* should offer. Those treasuries that had specialized in offering short-term small loans, in contrast to those that offered long-term large loans, had remained solvent. Cooperative activists, cautioned Efroikin, needed to learn their lesson by only offering short-term loans. Even in the absence of war, such short-term loans proved preferable both for the borrowers and for the treasuries. The average recipient of the loans, explained Efroikin, was the petty merchant who earned a slow but steady income. Therefore, his needs were best suited by a small loan that he could pay back quickly. Those merchants, on the other hand, who insisted on borrowing large sums for a year's time often had trouble managing the funds in such a way that they could pay the loan back. The savings and loan treasuries then suffered as did the borrower. The whole goal of the cooperative movement, argued Efroikin, was to teach Jewish small businessmen how to manage their money effectively. Lending them large sums for long periods therefore defeated the movement's goals.[74]

As the war continued, Efroikin increasingly came to see the Jewish cooperative movement as playing a vital role in the Jewish national project of economic reconstruction. At the end of January 1915, he reported triumphantly that the *kassas* had weathered the first months of the war better than the Russian banking system. Help from private and state banks together with the hard work of cooperative workers ended the crisis that ensued when investors withdrew their money from the treasuries at the onset of war. Once people realized the stability of the *kassas,* they began to invest in and borrow from them again. With the money of over two million Russian Jews invested in these treasuries, the success of the cooperative banks proved not only an economic but also a great social-national achievement. Both hardened businessmen and Jewish intellectuals, estranged from the masses, now would learn the power of *"the idea of organized and united self-action."*[75]

As more Russian Jews became refugees, they increasingly turned to the cooperative movement for help. Efroikin understood the cooperative movement's task as maintaining its role as a third way between philanthropy and banking. Even under wartime conditions, Efroikin warned, the cooperative *kassas* could not become free-loan societies. Despite popular opinion to the contrary, the cooperative movement based itself not on the principle of *tsdoke* (charity), but rather self-help. If the savings and loan treasuries began to use their funds for job creation for nonmembers, eventually this effort would weaken the economic foundations of the movement. Only members who shared in the "all for one and one for all" mentality of the cooperatives could benefit from its funds.[76]

On the other hand, Efroikin criticized those cooperative leaders who went to the other extreme by lending funds only to those with the best credit risks. Because the refugee problem was a national rather than a private matter, the cooperative leaders had to ensure that those who had no other source of credit could receive it from the savings and loan treasuries. Both the cooperative movement and the refugees, he argued, would have to demonstrate ingenuity in solving this problem. He proposed that refugees organize themselves into *landsmanshaftn* in their new cities of residence, so that fellow towns-people could attest to the reliability of potential borrowers. By the summer of 1915, the refugee crisis led Efroikin to a much less rosy assessment of the *kassas* than he had offered six months before. The failure of these treasuries to recover from the initial panic of the onset of war, he confessed, proved a major problem for the cooperative movement. Why had the savings and loan treasuries in the interior provinces of the Pale, where economic conditions were stable, refused to accept new members, to extend large-size loans and decent credit? These policies hurt precisely those who needed credit the most. Rather than making any blanket rules, the leaders of the treasuries needed to evaluate each potential borrower on an individual basis.[77]

Besides for the cooperative movement, Efroikin had very little good to say about Jewish relief organizations. Early in the war, he criticized the various relief organizations for not encouraging Russian Jews to register the sum of their lost property with the government. Although the Russian government now allowed war victims to claim compensation for both direct and indirect war losses, most Russian Jews proved too politically immature to submit claims. The relief organizations, Efroikin argued, concentrated solely on the philanthropic needs of the refugees in the present, rather than worrying about their reclaiming of property in the future. From the beginning, then, Efroikin criticized the Jewish relief organizations for not understanding the collective, national import of their work.[78]

By 1916, this mild criticism gave way to a scathing critique of EKOPO and its Petrograd Central Committee. Only through Jewish internal "spiritual destruction" and through external circumstances did Petrograd emerge as the center of Russian Jewish life. The Petrograd *kehile*, from which the Central Relief Committee emerged, served as an embarrassment to the historical *kehiles* in the Pale that united all Jews from richest to poorest. Tendentiously, he marked a division between the traditional, inherently democratic *kehile* of the Pale and the oligarchic *obshchina* in Petrograd, for which a payment of twenty-five rubles was required for membership. He described the oligarchic Petrograd *kehile* leadership in the following scathing words: "a heap of dry bones, which no spirit in the world would have the power to revive, a bunch of dried leaves, that long ago stopped drawing sustenance from the moist Jewish folk's tree—these are the *pani* of the Jewish *kehile* in Petrograd, our heads of the kahal."[79]

With their undemocratic spirit, argued Efroikin, the leaders of EKOPO remained out of touch with the needs of the masses that they purported to serve. If EKOPO had succeeded in mobilizing a massive grassroots relief effort, it was despite, not because of, its elitist leadership. These oligarchic leaders simply could not crush the democratic spirit of the relief workers in the field. As long as the leadership of EKOPO remained in the hands of this elite, it could at best function as a giant charity box *(tsdoke pushke)*, with all the self-help initiatives remaining in the hands of its subservient relief organizations. To add insult to injury, the democratic minority on the Petrograd Relief Committee, claimed Efroikin, had not adequately lobbied for the democratization of the institution. Efroikin further dismissed the recent reorganization of EKOPO to include a broader sample of Russian Jewry as inconsequential, since the majority of seats on the relief committee still went to members of the Petrograd *kehile*. This arrangement possessed the danger of retarding the progress of Russian Jewish democratization for years to come. The democratic minority, therefore, had to appeal to the Russian Jewish public for support in its struggle for the democratization of EKOPO and its Petrograd Committee. Progressive elements in Russian-Jewish society had to join the fight, realizing that relief work belonged to the entire nation. In his words:

> The time has come when the true Jewish democracy in the province and in Petrograd itself should actively intervene to organize a wide public protest movement here in Russia and to appeal to the Jewish community in America, which supports the Jewish relief work. It is time that this democracy ceases to look at the relief work with the disdain of superficial radicalism, which sees in it no more than philanthropy, rather than an important national matter, which will leave deep remnants in Jewish life of today

and of tomorrow. This must be stated loudly and in front of the community. And if Jewish democracy is alive and is life-capable, it now cannot be silent.[80]

This entire tirade reveals the extent to which Efroikin had transformed himself from a socialist autonomist to a folkist. It must be remembered that in 1907, he had disparaged Vitebsk's *kehile* as bourgeois, clerical, and tyrannical.[81] Now he romanticized the traditional *kehile* of the Pale as a representative national institution. This movement from socialism to democratic nationalism explains his insistence that progressive Jews not boycott EKOPO but rather transform it along populist lines. Efroikin thus represented exactly the kind of democratic (though in his case, no longer socialist) secular Yiddishist whom Ginzburg and the other elite leaders of EKOPO so feared. Yet at the same time, it was Efroikin's populist Diaspora nationalism that blinded him to the nationalizing potential of EKOPO. Rather than recognize EKOPO as an imperfect, not fully representative form of the Jewish self-government for which he longed, Efroikin only could reject it as an elitist organ of philanthropy. When it came to the democratizing of Jewish life, Efroikin seemed incapable of recognizing partial, incremental progress when it emerged from a source whose national credentials he dismissed.

Nor did Efroikin have a more positive view of Jewish relief efforts in Poland. Like other Diaspora nationalists, Efroikin looked toward the example of the Polish national movement as both inspiration and threat. Whereas he praised the Poles for having organized the citizens' committees, Efroikin criticized what he termed "the ruins of the Warsaw *gmine*" (community council often led by the acculturated wealthy elite) for producing a noneffective commission to help victims of the war. Rather than receive crumbs from the Polish citizens' committees, he urged, the Jews should form their own national committee, for which the *kehiles* could serve as building blocks. The present leadership of the *kehiles* in the hands of the assimilationists and the Orthodox, however, would thwart this goal. Although the Zionists currently functioned as the only national group with the power to effectuate change, they had severed themselves from the folk masses through their failure to support mass organizations. A new Polish Jewish leadership would have to emerge that would unite with the progressive, secularizing elements of the Jewish folk masses. Efroikin in effect called on Polonized Jewish intellectuals to "go to the nation," by uniting with "*folkstimlekhe* circles" in the same way that Russified intellectuals had done several decades earlier. The crisis of war, he argued, must lead to Jewish national unity. Because the conditions of war had discredited both the assimilationists and the Zionists, democratic nationalists could assume the leadership of Polish Jewry. By joining forces with Polish democrats, these Jewish democrats could help forge a bright national future for the Jews in a Poland that would recognize the national rights of all its minorities.[82]

If Efroikin did not see shades of gray when it came to the democratization of Jewish relief organizations, he applied an incremental approach to Jewish participation in all-Russian politics. Efroikin noted that the usually friendly Kadets had cautioned the Jews to table the issue of equal rights until after the war. This call, however, dare not lull the Jews into political apathy. Rather, he argued for Jews to recognize all the signs of political support wherever they existed. Efroikin therefore applauded the resolution passed by the Smolensk city duma calling for the abolition of the Pale. Given the refugee crisis, it was now in the interests of city governments both inside and outside the Pale to agitate on behalf of the abolition of Jewish residence restrictions. Russian Jews, explained Efroikin, therefore had to lobby these institutions, even if results would not come until the war's end. The cultivation of Jewish political consciousness and the forging of political alliances with progressive Russian forces served as the most pressing task during the war.[83]

Efroikin also maintained interest in the fourth Duma, despite its refusal to address the plight of the Jews. In a heavily censored article from February 1915, he expressed his consternation that whereas all the Duma deputies praised the Poles for their patriotic sacrifices, they had remained deafeningly silent regarding Jewish persecution, which had reached medieval proportions. As in his prewar articles, Efroikin singled out the Jewish Duma deputies for the greatest censure for not more forcefully articulating Jewish demands. The articulation by the Jewish Duma representatives of a vision of the Jews' place in the empire following the war's end, far from disloyalty, would have reinforced a sense of Jewish belonging in Russia. The following statement re-veals both the limitations that the tsarist censor placed on Efroikin's critique as well as Efroikin's genuine hopes for a Jewish national fu-ture in Russia:

> And in the meantime . . . until the "blessed hour" arrives, let us gather all of our material and strength in order to, together with all the peoples, defend the country of our future, the country that after victory must re-new and revive itself and we will yet see our best and most beautiful hopes realized. We do not have a few heroes and martyrs to display to the coun-try and the world; we have not brought a few sacrifices. Let us bring the last and highest sacrifice that a nation has the potential to give—our own heart, which bleeds from pain and sorrow.[84]

Left unsaid in this statement was Efroikin's deep conviction that Jew-ish national renewal would occur together with a thorough demo-cratization of the empire. Still, he no doubt sincerely believed that the Jewish national future depended on a Russian victory in the war.

Even as the silence of the Kadets toward Jewish suffering continued to irk him, Efroikin nonetheless continued to look to the Duma as the source of incremental improvement of the Jewish political plight. The tsar's replacement of the reactionary interior minister, Ivan Goremykin, with a slightly less reactionary minister who vowed to work with the Duma, signaled to Efroikin the regime's growing acceptance of par-liamentarism. Efroikin also applied this positive approach to the for-mation of the Progressive Bloc, despite the presence of anti-Semitic deputies in its ranks. A Jewish boycott of the Progressive Bloc only would play into the hands of reactionary forces, which sought to cripple the Duma's ability to act. The true radical position, unlike that adopted by politically immature left-leaning Jews, concluded Efroi-kin, consisted of supporting the Progressive Bloc in its struggle against tsarist reaction. True, conceded Efroikin, the bloc's statement regard-ing Jewish rights remained vague and tepid. Yet the fact that the right-wing members of the bloc agreed to its inclusion into their plat-form at all was cause for hope. If Russian Jewry constantly petitioned the Duma for an amelioration of its rights, perhaps it could yield tangible results.[85]

In Efroikin's autonomist vision, the Jewish attainment of personal and national rights could occur only within the context of an alliance with the progressive forces in general Russian politics. Even if these alliances would yield no fruit during the war, they would prepare the way for success in the postwar era. Efroikin demonstrated this perspective most dramatically during the circulars affair. During the war, he served as a member of an executive committee, comprising members of those Jewish political parties and groups that remained loyal to Russian liberalism (the Folkspartey, the Folksgrupe, moderate Zionists, and socialists). When the circular affairs occurred, the executive committee had the difficult task of advising the Jewish Duma members whether or not to leave the Kadet faction of the Progressive Bloc. The Russian Jewish liberal Sliozberg argued against such a move on the grounds that the Kadets still remained the Jews' best hope for amelioration of their legal status. Efroikin argued against secession from the Kadet faction of the bloc based on his unique combination of Diaspora nationalism and liberal politics:

> If Jewish deputies don't have the right to remain in the faction, then others don't have the right to stay in the party. Genrikh Borisovich [Sliozberg] arrives at this [same position] from another side. I fear this other side which is why I express opposition against exiting this faction. Each Jew can be in the party which suits his convictions. You see in all of these questions only the Jewish perspective and you forget all the rest. You repudiate the general political struggle. Where is the basis for independent Jewish politics? As long as we live in someone else's government, we will have no possibility for independent politics. I understand your yearning for independence, but it still isn't, it can't be independent politics.[86]

Efroikin's cautioning against the executive committee's imposition of its will upon the Jewish Duma members revealed his populist, democratic ideology. It was not the role of Russian Jewish notables and intellectuals to dictate the party loyalties of other Jews.[87] More deeply, however, this statement makes sense only within the context of Efroikin's own unique perspective on the connection between Jewish involvement in all-Russian politics and the formation of a national Jewish politics. A true national Jewish politics, implied Efroikin, did not entail a retreat from general Russian politics but rather an embrace of them. Efroikin thus reiterated his prewar position that a true Jewish politics entailed transcending a narrow Jewish perspective when it came to the general Russian struggle for democratization. Far from demonstrating national weakness, this participation as equals in the struggle for the future of Russian liberation would demonstrate the interconnectedness of Jewish and Russian destinies. As before the war, Efroikin preached an incremental approach, in which Jewish participation in the all-Russian struggle would lead inexorably to an independent national Jewish politics.

In a recent work, Jeffrey Veidlinger argued that the Jewish public culture that emerged in inter-revolutionary Russia exemplified Russian Jewry's embrace of "this world" *(oylem haze)*. Rather than engage in the rigors of religious observance in the hopes of attaining life in the world to come *(oylem habe)*, increasing numbers of Russian Jews sought aesthetic, cultural, and social fulfillment in this world. The paradoxical results of the Revolution of 1905, in which the suppression of revolutionary activity coincided with the preservation of freedom of the press and assembly, fueled this worldly cultural and social activity. Having transferred the religious messianism of their youths into revolutionary activity, young Russian Jewish revolutionaries had agitated for the revolutionary transformation of the empire. With the onset of political reaction, they turned toward the incremental work of building a Jewish culture, public society, and national economy.[88] Tcherikower, Efroikin, and Kalmanovitch all underwent this transformation from revolutionary to incremental Diaspora nationalism and Yiddishism. Yet Veidlinger noted that World War I brought with it a struggle between the forces of "this world" and the "next." Whereas relief workers of EKOPO and its constituent organizations embraced the "this-worldly" task of relief, many revolutionaries, diplomats, and Jewish nationalists engaged in a utopian otherworldliness, in which they imagined the crucible of the war as culminating in full-scale Jewish national liberation. On the ruins of their destroyed world, East European Jews would experience new life.[89]

Veidlinger's metaphor of the battle between this world and the world to come proves a useful one for understanding the activities of Tcherikower, Efroikin, and Kalmanovitch during the years 1914–1917. An examination of their activities and writings during this time demonstrates that worldliness and utopianism coexisted in the hearts and minds of the same people. This contradiction emerged as still another result of the "paradoxical politics of marginality." The very historical processes that forced these men to be practical also fueled their dream that the war would culminate with Jewish national renaissance and liberation. It was the refugee crisis and the government's failure to ameliorate it that led EKOPO and other relief organizations to assume the role of an internal Jewish national self-government. The *kassa* movement, begun before the war, now understood its task as nothing less than the rebuilding of the Jewish economy.

All three men, each in very different ways, engaged in practical work to save Russian Jewry: Tcherikower as a propagandist abroad, Efroikin as a leader of the cooperative movement and a political commentator and adviser, and Kalmanovitch as an editor and cultural producer. All three acutely followed news of the war and sought to help their readers find their place within the crisis. Yet this heightened activity created a perception of the inevitability of the triumph of Diaspora nationalism, which in turn led to utopianism. All three believed strongly that the war would accelerate the internal process of the transformation of Russian Jewry into a modern, secular, democratic, and autonomist nation. In the crucible of war, Russian Jewry also would rise to new heights in Yiddish cultural productivity. Also paradoxically, the war if anything only heightened these men's attachment to Russia as the country of Jewish national renaissance. The seeds of the political and cultural activities begun during the war would bear fruit at the war's culmination.

In these dreams, Tcherikower, Efroikin, and Kalmanovitch were not alone. As the carnage of the war continued, diplomats and intellectuals on all sides embraced a utopian vision of a better future, whether in the form of national liberation or socialist revolution.[90] For Diaspora nationalists, realism and utopianism always had coexisted in uneasy tension. With the February Revolution, the scales tipped largely in the direction of utopianism. Tcherikower, Efroikin, and Kalmanovitch joined with nearly all other Diaspora nationalists and Yiddishists in believing that the hour of national redemption had come. The years 1917–1921 would raise these expectations to new heights but also dash them as never before.

CHAPTER THREE

Losing Russia as a Base

THE YEARS 1917 through 1921 brought unparalleled upheaval to the Jews of Eastern Europe. In the midst of World War I, prospects for the immediate future of East European Jewry seemed dim. Yet suddenly, in February 1917, the entire situation of Russian Jewry changed forever. Jews greeted the news of the abdication of the hated Nicholas II with jubilation. In April, the new Provisional Government granted Russian Jews what its leaders futilely had demanded from successive tsarist regimes for decades: full civil rights as citizens and abolition of the hated Pale of Settlement. Although in its nine-month period of rule the Provisional Government did not officially recognize Jewish rights to national autonomy, it did indicate that it would look favorably upon this principle. In the course of twelve months, Russian Jewry voted in three separate democratic elections: for local modernized, democratic *kehiles,* for an All-Russian Jewish Congress, and for the All-Russian Constituent Assembly. In the months following the February Revolution, Jewish national culture in Hebrew and Yiddish flourished. Moreover, in November 1917, the majority of Russian Jews greeted news of the Balfour Declaration, the British promise of a national home in Palestine, with jubilation.[1]

In the imagination of the vast majority of Russian Jewry, 1917 loomed as a messianic year, in which national redemption appeared imminent, both in Russia and in Palestine. This messianic excitement, however, did not last long. In late October 1917, the Bolsheviks, led by Vladimir Lenin, successfully executed a coup d'état that toppled the Provisional Government. Although the Bolshevik regime allowed for elections to the Constituent Assembly in November 1917, it disbanded this democratic institution after it met just once in January 1918. Soon, Russia fell into a state of anarchy and civil war. Recognizing that the Bolsheviks would disrupt Jewish religious, economic, and cultural life, the vast majority of Russian Jews initially opposed them. Promising the Jews broad-sweeping national autonomy, Ukrainian nationalists received the warm support of Jewish leaders in their bid for territorial autonomy and reluctant support for the Ukraine's full-fledged independence.[2]

As the civil war between the Bolsheviks (the Reds), an anti-Bolshevik coalition (the Whites), and Ukrainian nationalists raged, tens of thousands of Jews fell victim to murderous pogroms in the Ukraine, initially promulgated by all three armies. In time the Bolshevik forces granted the Jews a measure of protection against the armies of the Whites and the Ukrainian nationalists. Faced with the choice of death at the hands of the anti-Bolshevik forces, or life coupled with religious, cultural, and economic dislocation under Communist rule, most Jews chose the latter as the lesser of two evils.[3] Within a three-year period, however, the initial euphoria of most Russian Jews had turned first to despair and then, at best, to a sober realism.

In the meantime, however, by 1921, half of the Jews formerly under tsarist rule found themselves living outside the Soviet Union, in such successor states as the newly independent Poland, Lithuania, Latvia, and Romania. To a greater or lesser extent, all these countries officially promised their Jewish populations national autonomy. Whereas Poland demonstrated its unwillingness to comply with the Minorities' Treaty from the very beginning, Lithuania and Latvia at first made good on their promises. As emerging nation-states, however, these countries largely rescinded these promises by the middle 1920s. Within the interwar period, the political, cultural, and economic destinies of the Jewish communities in the successor states that once had been part of the Russian Empire would greatly diverge from one another and from that of those Jews remaining under Soviet rule.[4]

Diaspora nationalists and Yiddishists experienced the trajectory of euphoria to despair to a greater extent than Jewish intellectuals to their ideological right and left. To their right, the Zionists, though instrumental in the struggle for Jewish national autonomy in Russia and the successor states, placed their greatest hopes, at least in principle, in the future of the *Yishuv* in Palestine. Members of the Bund, Poale Zion, and the United Jewish Socialist Labor Party (Fareynikte) at least initially did not react with utter despair to the Bolshevik Revolution, since as socialists they looked to the new regime for support of their proletarian vision of Jewish national culture. In the immediate years following the revolution, these parties split between those who went underground to maintain their political independence and those who joined the Communist Party, eventually manning the Evsektsiia, the Jewish sections of the Communist Party.[5] It was thus only the non-socialist Diaspora nationalists and Yiddishists who understood the Bolshevik Revolution as completely having shattered their great hopes for a Jewish national future in Russia.

Tcherikower, Efroikin, and Kalmanovitch all participated in the political and cultural renaissance that occurred in Petrograd in 1917. They similarly all moved to Kiev following the Bolshevik Revolution, where they attempted to salvage their autonomist and Yiddishist dreams.

Expectations of the Revolution

Tcherikower articulated the ecstatic euphoria and newfound hope for Jewish national rebirth in Russia that many Russian Jews, particularly autonomists, experienced upon hearing news of the February Revolution. Living in New York at the time, he wrote:

> Our dreams were so presumptuous and daring—and yet, one lucky caprice of fortune, one elementary gesture of history, and reality surpassed all the most daring fantasies.
>
> Even the most daring fantasy: "A *republic* in Russia," and "all boundaries against Jews are abolished." *The revolutionary regime proclaimed full rights for Jews.*
>
> I go from the editorial office to a café, from the café to our political circles, look around and listen to our writers, activists and doers—they suddenly became strong supporters of Russia. *"Velikaia Rassiia"* [Great

Russia], they cry with excitement and specifically in Russian—the great Russia, we always believed in Russia, the best land, the most beautiful people; a fountain of patriotism actually sprouts from them.[6]

Also representative of the Jewish socialist and nationalist response was Tcherikower's congratulatory attempt to credit Jewish revolutionaries with creating conditions that led to the revolution. Even Dubnov, always careful in his historiography to depict the majority of Russian Jews as loyal to the tsarist regime despite their oppression, now argued polemically that Jewish sacrifices in the revolutionary movement made them deserving of equal personal and national rights.[7] In a historical essay published in March 1917, Tcherikower echoed Dubnov in his portrayal of Jewish history under the Romanovs as a line of almost uninterrupted suffering, which "rose higher and higher until the current March days of the year 1917, when the line was suddenly interrupted and cut down, to the fortune and triumph of all of Russia and of the Jews." At the end of the article, Tcherikower tellingly contrasted religious Jews, who felt compelled to recite a prayer for the welfare of the tsarist government, to the Jewish revolutionaries who contributed to the storm that finally toppled this despotic dynasty.[8] In this nod to Jewish revolutionaries, Tcherikower also no doubt invoked the memory of his own initiation into revolutionary politics during the Revolution of 1905. In general, veterans of the Russian Jewish socialist and nationalist movements experienced the events of 1917 through the prism of their nostalgia for their youthful revolutionary activity that had occurred twelve years earlier.

Following their expressions of euphoria, Diaspora nationalists and Yiddishists began to articulate their vision of the future of a liberated Russian Jewry. Like all other Jewish nationalists, Tcherikower warned that civic emancipation in the absence of national rights would lead to West European–style assimilation. He reminded his readers that Russian Jewry had won negative freedom—namely, the freedom from oppression—but had yet to win its positive freedom, which meant national rights and the creation of national institutions. Yet Tcherikower also shared in the autonomist conviction that Russian Jewry, through its desire for national self-determination, had learned from the historical mistakes of its Western counter-parts.[9] He therefore greeted such first steps toward Russian Jewish national autonomy as the Conference of Jewish Parties and Organizations, held in Petrograd immediately following the revolution, as "perhaps the most beautiful moment of the last several decades since the new Jewry was born." Similarly, he interpreted the plans for a Russian Jewish Congress as a sign of national health.[10]

As another symbol of this national health, Tcherikower pointed to Jewish refugees exiled during the war to the Russian interior. Reversing his previous pessimistic assessments, Tcherikower argued that dispersion beyond the Pale had not led to the diffusion of Jewish national energy. Rather, the refugees had chosen to settle in Jewish communities both within and outside of the Pale.[11] Moreover, they had adjusted well to their new surroundings, where they experienced little anti-Semitism from their neighbors. Tcherikower's verdict was clear: the experience of the refugees proved that it was possible for Russian Jews to maintain their national identity beyond the traditional community of the shtetl. Several years earlier, Tcherikower had used the image of the war refugee to incorporate the suffering of Russian Jewry into the collective memory of Jewish martyrdom. Following the February Revolution, Tcherikower refashioned the image of the refugees once again, this time into the vanguard of Russian Jewry, which proved its readiness to experience a synthesis of civic and national emancipation.[12]

In order to achieve this task of national emancipation, Efroikin and other autonomist political activists and intellectuals revived Dubnov's Folkspartey originally founded in 1906. In April 1917, Efroikin joined with Dubnov and Perel'man to create a "National Group" and in June formed the Jewish Democratic Union. The new Folkspartey emerged as an umbrella organization of these and similar groups. In this effort, Efroikin joined with other leading Russian Jewish intellectuals, such as Wolf Latski-Bertoldi, Yoysef Chernikhov, and Shtif, who, in such periodicals as *Evreiskii mir* and *Di yudishe velt,* had advanced the non-Bundist variants of autonomism and Yiddishism that would form the ideological basis of the Folkspartey.[13]

Although these men earlier had combined their Diaspora nationalism with socialism, by 1917 they had largely eschewed class conflict in favor of national autonomy for all strata within Jewish society. As evidenced from its name, the Jewish Democratic Union and then the Folkspartey emphasized the value of democracy. Through this term, this group indicated its belief that it spoke on behalf of average Jews whom it sought to involve in the political process. Democracy also meant the creation of representative forms of internal Jewish government, led by a nationalist intelligentsia that rejected the assimilationist goals of Jewish plutocrats. The Jewish Democratic Union, then, embodied in its platform Efroikin's transformation during the inter-revolutionary years from a socialist to a populist. Like Efroikin, the Union and then the Folkspartey believed that through its narrow concentration on the Jewish proletariat rather than artisans and petty merchants, Jewish socialism had ignored the needs of the majority of Russian Jews. The founders of the Folkspartey hoped to form a broad party for the majority of Russian Jews unrepresented by older, established parties. In the election campaigns of 1917, Folkspartey flyers repeatedly stressed that the Zionists worried about Palestine, the Orthodox sought to use religion to maintain power, and the socialists concentrated narrowly upon the proletariat. Only the Folkspartey represented the needs of the average Jewish artisan and small shopkeeper.[14]

The Folkspartey thus advertised itself as a populist party of the entire Jewish people, which would pay special attention to the "common man." Seeking to woo voters from the ranks of this population, the Folkspartey spoke of fighting for credit for small businessmen as well as agronomical help for Jewish farmers. These intellectuals believed that a large-scale education campaign would persuade the "Jewish masses" to join with the nationalist intelligentsia in "tak[ing] their fate in their hands."[15]

Even more central to the Folkspartey than its calls for democracy was its advancement of a positive, maximally Diaspora nationalist political program. The bedrock of personal-national autonomy would be the newly elected democratic *kehiles* (in Russian, *obshchiny*), which were to assume cultural, social, and political functions. Culturally, the *kehiles* would build and support kindergartens, schools, evening courses, folk universities, libraries, and professional educational institutions. Socially, they would strengthen such self-help organizations as cooperatives, better the situation of Jewish artisans, regulate emigration, and ameliorate the suffering of war refugees. Similarly, the *kehiles* would have to run nursing homes, hospitals, and sanatoriums, as well as register births and deaths. Politically, the *kehiles* would represent and defend the Jewish population to the organs of local government. The Jewish population would elect members of the *v'a'ad* (board) of the *kehiles* through the secret ballot and direct elections. Although the state and local Russian governments would provide the *kehiles* with some funds, the *kehiles* would raise the remaining money through the imposition of a progressive income tax upon the local Jewish population.[16]

In short, the Petrograd-based Folkspartey adopted the model of the modernized *kehile* that Dubnov first had proposed over a decade earlier in his *Pis'ma o starom i novom evreistve*.[17] The party's platform also represented the consensus that had emerged from a decade of debate among Diaspora nationalists over the scope and nature of the *kehile's* autonomy. Parting with Dubnov's original view, the ideologues of the new Folkspartey called for the complete exclusion of religion, which they viewed as a private affair, from the supervisory role of the *kehile*. Not seeking to alienate traditionalist voters, however, the party emphasized that it would remain neutral in religious matters. Another departure from Dubnov's original position was the party's adoption of the unabashedly Yiddishist demand that Yiddish serve as the language of instruction in the Jewish schools. The party not only declared Yiddish as the official language of the future *kehiles* but also demanded that Russian Jews have the right to address the parliament and the courts in their native tongue. These demands epitomized the merger of Diaspora nationalism with Yiddishism, which had occurred during the inter-revolutionary years.[18]

Those who championed this maximally autonomist vision, whether or not they joined the Folkspartey, viewed the Bund, with its refusal to work for national goals across class divisions, as an impediment to the realization of their vision. As the largest Jewish nationalist party, it fell to the Zionists to argue over the scope of autonomy, the attitude of the future All-Russian Jewish Congress toward Palestine, and the right of this representative body to support national rights for Jews outside of Russia. The Bund, in contrast, hewed to its party ideology in refusing to recognize a worldwide Jewish people and in understanding itself as the representative only of the Jewish workers in Russia. It therefore understood even its very participation in the All-Russian Jewish Congress, which would include representatives of bourgeois parties, as a compromise. Unlike the Zionists and the folkists, the Bund thus sought to limit the role of the congress to that of advisory council alone, arguing that only the future All-Russian Constituent Assembly could make binding decisions about Jewish autonomy. In the end, the folkist Meir Kreinin brokered a compromise that led the Bundists and the Zionists to sit together at the preliminary conference for the congress. The Zionists agreed to de-emphasize Palestine, and in exchange, the Bundists agreed that the congress would discuss the plight of Jews in other lands.[19]

Still in New York, Tcherikower expressed his disgust over the refusal of the Bund to view the Jewish people as a unified nation. Now that Lithuanian and Polish Jewries no longer belonged to Russia, he argued, the Russian Bund would no longer discuss their plight. It went without saying, he stated with disgust, that the fate of the Jews of Palestine did not concern them.[20] Upon his return to Russia, Tcherikower reported with dismay what he understood as the Bund's ambivalent and limited conception of national autonomy. The extension of the concept of autonomy by nationally inclined Bundists, argued Tcherikower, limited itself to institutions of social welfare and would not lead to a change in Bundist ideology and practice. Similarly, he dismissed the proposal advanced by Bundist leader Moyshe Rafes to join the Bund with the Fareynikte as a ploy designed to fight the nationalistically inclined Jewish socialist parties. After the Bolshevik coup d'état, Tcherikower also criticized what he perceived as the Bund's movement away from its historical alliance with the Mensheviks, in favor of the Bolsheviks, at the very moment when this latter group's "insanity has poisoned the workers' street."[21]

A far greater impediment than internal political squabbles to the establishment of Jewish national autonomy in Russia was the political turmoil that accompanied the Provisional Government's rule from the start. In April and again in July 1917, the Bolsheviks attempted a coup d'état. Between March and August 1917, the Alexander Kerensky-led provisional government, a coalition of liberals and socialists, governed in an uneasy cooperation with the exclusively socialist Committee of Soviets. Autonomists looked favorably upon Kerensky's Provisional Government, since they believed that its vision of a multiparty system would prove beneficial to the implementation of national rights. Not surprisingly, Tcherikower hailed Kerensky as the hero of the revolution whose combination of strong statesmanship and leadership of the people earned him the right to run the Provisional Government. In contrast, Lenin, with his "political tactlessness and blind fanaticism," was the Provisional Government's nemesis who threatened to destroy Russian society through a separate peace with Germany and a dictatorship of the proletariat.[22]

Given Tcherikower's previous disenchantment with European socialists for their support of the war, his opposition to a separate peace demonstrates the extent to which Russian patriotism and Jewish nationalism merged in his consciousness in the aftermath of the February Revolution. A self-described *heyser khosid* (passionate admirer) of the new government in Petrograd, Tcherikower defended its opposition to a separate peace by arguing that such a move would grant a posthumous victory to the historical monarchical alliance between tsar and kaiser. More significantly, Tcherikower argued that a separate peace with Germany would contradict revolutionary Russia's best interests by unduly strengthening Germany and weakening the Allies, who had helped to make the revolution possible. Another major reason that Tcherikower opposed a separate peace with Germany was that he did not want the large percentage of Russian Jewry that lived in the Vilna, Kovno, and Bialystok regions, then under German occupation, to fall permanently outside of Russian rule. In an effort to reconcile his stance with his former pacifism, Tcherikower explained that he only opposed a separate peace between Russia and Germany, not a general peace between the Allies and Germany and Austria.[23]

Efroikin had his opportunity to support the policies of the Provisional Government and to oppose a separate peace in a speech to the Democratic Conference, which occurred in July 1917. The Democratic Conference resulted from the crisis that gripped Russian coalition politics during the summer of 1917. Largely because of Marxist orthodoxy, the Mensheviks refused to heed their radicalized constituents, who increasingly called for an all-socialist government with the

slogan, "All power to the Soviets." Although non-Marxist, the Socialist Revolutionaries followed in the path of the other socialist parties
in this regard. By the summer, however, these parties were ready to
entertain the possibility of a socialist coalition that would exclude the
Kadets. Although convened to solve the question of the nature of coalition government, the conference ended inconclusively.[24]

As a representative of the Folkspartey, Efroikin argued that only an
inclusion of democratic elements of bourgeois society in the government could save the country internally from chaos and counterrevolution and externally from the Germans, whom Efroikin also believed
Russia should continue to fight. To his Yiddish readership, he later
explained that only a union of all classes could produce the sacrifices
needed for the success of Russian democracy. Sharply censuring the
Bolsheviks for inciting the selfish interests of the workers, soldiers,
and peasant masses, Efroikin argued that the demand of these groups
for instant gratification would lead to civil war.[25] At the conference
itself, he championed the continued division of power between the
Provisional Government and the Committee of Soviets. The fledgling
experiment in democracy in Russia, argued Efroikin, required shap-
ing by the intellectual elite. In his words: "Destiny desired to give serious responsibility for the fate of the revolution to the development of
organic higher culture generally, political intellect specifically, and by
this we must especially understand democracy."[26] Efroikin, like Tcherikower, clearly believed that the interests of all-Russian and Jewish
politics converged. He thus spoke about the need for a coalition between bourgeois and proletarian elements of Russian society in the
same manner that the Folkspartey preached a supra-class Jewish politics. Like Tcherikower, Efroikin believed that Kerensky, whom he
hailed as "one of the great spirits of the revolution," could lead the
forces of Russian democracy to victory. Efroikin in fact emphasized
Jewish loyalty to the democratic cause, arguing that Jews well understood that a failure of the revolution would spell the end of Jewish
rights.[27]

As Russian Jewry prepared to vote for representatives to the All-
Russian Constituent Assembly, members of the Folkspartey joined
"national blocs," largely dominated by Zionists that supported maximal demands for national autonomy. Although the Folkspartey itself

received only a tiny minority of votes, a combination of the Zionist ticket and the national blocs won over 80 percent of all Jewish votes cast for Jewish parties. Thus, despite their own partisan failures, leaders of the Folkspartey rightfully could argue that their political vision of national autonomy had won a majority of votes. It is interesting, then, that Efroikin, who had argued for nonpartisanship in all-Russian politics, opposed the formation of the national blocs. At a convention of Volynian communities held to prepare for the elections to the Constituent Assembly, he argued that the Folkspartey could not support a "national bloc" that included Zionists and liberals. To Efroikin, both the Zionists and the Kadets compromised the principles of autonomy for their larger ideologies. When the convention supported the Zionist dominated national bloc by referring to it as the "Jewish national" ticket, Efroikin demanded that this bloc be called by its true name.[28]

Like other Diaspora nationalists, who had envisioned the new Russian republic as existing within the same borders of the former tsarist empire, Efroikin reacted with alarm to demands for territorial autonomy by the various nationalities among whom the Jews lived. At the Democratic Convention, he argued for the territorial integrity of the newly reconstituted Russia, taking aim at the Bolshevik concept of the "international" in the process. In his words:

> The path to world-international, the real path, not in words, is not that great Russia should break down into small little countries, so-called independent [countries]. Just the opposite! The correct path is that Russia should remain whole and strong, and that internally in the country, the peoples who occupy the country should develop themselves, and they should live peacefully among themselves. We believe that our fatherland will prove able to embody in itself the ideal of the best people of our time, the ideal of the working people in all lands.
>
> So that the peoples in Russia can freely develop themselves and so that the country can remain united, it must be that they are given national-territorial and national-personal autonomy. All Jewish parties are unanimous [in the belief] that the Jewish people must receive national-personal autonomy.[29]

To this end, Efroikin called upon the provisional government to create a Parliament of National Affairs, in which all nationalities would receive representation, so that the demands of various nationalities would not clash with one another. This demand probably reflected

Efroikin's and the party's realization that the demands of territorial nationalities such as the Ukrainians and Belorussians would clash with the national interests of the Jews living in those regions. Similarly, Efroikin called on the Provisional Government to immediately recognize the legality of the democratically elected *kehiles* and to legitimate the right of these communities to impose an income tax upon their constituents. He also demanded that the government accord Yiddish the same rights in public and state life as all other officially recognized languages.[30]

Tcherikower similarly viewed territorial autonomy as a threat to the non-territorial Jewish nation. He explicitly stated that the Jews would fare better in a large, centralized state than in a federation of smaller states, in which nationalism and anti-Semitism could thrive. He therefore proposed that at the coming All-Russian Jewish Congress, Jews assert their right to a national autonomy that would not depend on location or territory. This preference for non-territorial autonomy placed both Tcherikower and Efroikin in allegiance with the Socialist Revolutionaries and in opposition to the Bolsheviks, who favored national concessions to territorial but not to non-territorial nations.[31]

Reaction to the Bolshevik Revolution

Longing to participate in his long-deferred dream of a revolution in Russia, Tcherikower left New York in the summer of 1917 and returned to Petrograd. There he became a correspondent for Petrograd's *Undzer togblat*. By the end of October, his worst-case scenario occurred: the Bolsheviks seized power, overthrew the Kerensky Provisional Government, and began to establish one-party rule. As the Bolsheviks strengthened their grip, Tcherikower found himself increasingly despairing of the present, and therefore of the future, in Russia. In a three-part series of articles on the relationship of the German Social Democrats to Bolshevism, Tcherikower depicted the Bolsheviks as lying and conspiratorial in their deliberately distorted prediction of impending social revolution in Germany. The Bolsheviks, surmised Tcherikower, promulgated this lie in an attempt to muster domestic support for the Treaty of Brest-Litovsk.[32]

Tcherikower's disgust with the new regime reached new heights following the Bolshevik reaction to the Left Socialist Revolutionary (SR) revolt against the regime that occurred on July 6, 1918. Close allies with the Bolsheviks in the months following the October Revolution, the Left SRs considered the Treaty of Brest-Litovsk with Germany a betrayal of the revolution. Similarly, as members of a party that represented the peasantry, the Left SRs resented the government's policy of sending workers into the countryside to demand food from villagers. The Left SRs planned a revolt to correspond to the convening of the Fifth Congress of the Soviets in Moscow. Increasingly unpopular, the Bolsheviks already had banned the Mensheviks and the mainstream Socialist Revolutionary Party from participating in elections to the Soviets, in fear that these parties would command a majority. However, having been allowed to participate in the elections, the Left SRs held 40 percent of the seats at the Congress of Soviets. Members of this party hoped to use this forum to announce the abrogation of the Brest-Litovsk Treaty and to express their lack of confidence in the government.

When the Bolsheviks defeated this motion, the Left SRs resorted to a terrorist plot that they believed would push the Germans to go to war with Russia. On July 6, two Left SRs posing as representatives of the Cheka, the Soviet secret police, entered the German embassy and assassinated the German ambassador to the Soviet Union, Count Wilhelm von Mirbach. Following the assassination, the Left SRs briefly succeeded in winning over the majority of the troops stationed in Moscow and took several Bolshevik leaders hostage. Although the Left SRs could have overthrown the Bolshevik government, they floundered. The next day, troops loyal to the Bolsheviks arrested the Left SR leadership and restored Bolshevik control. Initially, the government arrested hundreds of Left SR members, including the delegates to the Soviet Congress. In the days that followed, however, the Bolsheviks released most of the prisoners and dealt very leniently with the leaders of the plot. At the time, plagued by civil war, anarchy, and growing unpopularity, the Bolsheviks feared to antagonize the popular Left Socialist Revolutionaries. However, during the Red Terror of the coming several years, the Bolsheviks exacted their revenge.[33]

Having traveled to Moscow to cover this story for *Undzer togblat,* Tcherikower understood the banishment of the Left SR representatives from the Fifth Congress of Soviets as the ultimate symbol of the establishment of one-party rule in Soviet Russia. He also described what he perceived as the environment of government lies and intimidation through which the Bolsheviks ruled:

> A lock was hung on the mouth of the entire press; who knows why and who knows for how long. . . . The style and the language of the official reports about the events are such that you have to be a Communist to understand them. A simple person of flesh and blood cannot chew such a Turkish language. And the usual psalm of victory reigns above all. A third of the Soviet Congress was arrested. . . . There is no opposition; one part of the opposition previously had been banished and the new stormy opposition, which had too much courage, was brought to its grave today, first stripped and afterward buried, as is done. Quietly and smoothly . . .—very commonplace.[34]

Tcherikower's despair in part stemmed from the fact that, as a longtime opponent of Bolshevism, he did not underestimate the calculations of Lenin. He recounted a chance encounter with a Bolshevik acquaintance in the immediate aftermath of the October Revolution. When Tcherikower asked his friend how he thought that the Bolsheviks, a minority party, would retain power, the man referred Tcherikower to a treatise that Lenin had written on the topic just one month before his coup d'état. On all major issues, ranging from the future of the Constituent Assembly to the rights of national minorities to the future economy under Bolshevik rule to a separate peace, Lenin, concluded Tcherikower, had deliberately misrepresented the truth.[35]

A year after expressing great pride in the Russian people for having liberated themselves from tsarism, Tcherikower now expressed his disgust over what he deemed the passive, non-patriotic reaction of Russian civil society to the loss of its hard-earned freedom. Tcherikower related how, during the political renaissance that followed the February Revolution, Jewish intellectuals joked that they would form a new party with the initials *i.i.,* to stand for *ibergeshrokene inteligentn* (fearful intellectuals). This joke, lamented Tcherikower, had assumed tragic proportions at a time when many anti-Bolsheviks yearned for a

German invasion of Russia that would topple the Bolsheviks. As seen in the following passage, Tcherikower understood this dream as morally no superior to Bolshevism: "The entire organism of Russia is infected with laziness, with a sickly passivity. Bolshevism is the expression of neglect in one circle. The dream about the German, as in general the passive waiting for a redeemer from the side—is the expression of the same sickness in the other circles. Only the psychology of despair of the all-Russian decadence could give birth to such still-born children."[36]

Efroikin similarly reacted with growing despair to the Bolshevik seizure of power. As the editors of *Di yidishe folksblat*, the Folkspartey's weekly journal, Efroikin and Shtif condemned the October Revolution as a coup d'état seeking to rob the Russian people of their great victory of voting for representatives to the Constituent Assembly. They only hoped that Bolshevik isolation on the morning after revolution would doom their rule. Yet, as the Bolsheviks censored the press and drove the moderate political center underground, Efroikin increasingly doubted that the Constituent Assembly could rescue the country from disintegration. If the people managed to elect democratic representatives to the Constituent Assembly, however, they might still have the opportunity to "rebuild the ruined center of the country, unify it, and renew it."[37]

As this last shred of hope gave way to sober reality, Efroikin also mourned the breakup of Russia into independent successor states as spelling the death of a unified Russian Jewry. From the late eighteenth century until World War I, Lithuanian, Polish, and Ukrainian Jews had comprised a united Russian Jewry that experienced modernization together through such movements and processes as Haskalah, Zionism, and the rise of Yiddish culture. Now, however, Russian Jews would face the future as minorities in emerging nation-states. Similarly, those Jews who remained within Russia's borders would face the "internal destruction and external slavery" wrought by the Bolshevik Revolution, reduced in size and political power.[38]

In a prescient assessment, Efroikin predicted a dark future for Jewish national autonomy in the successor states. Although the successor states might guarantee personal emancipation and national autonomy, he argued, the small size of these fragmented Jewish communities would preclude autonomy's implementation. The peasant nationalities that would lead most of these successor states, moreover, would force the Jews from their traditional economic role in commerce and industry. Echoing the Yiddishist call for a synthesis between Jewish and European cultures, Efroikin feared that the low cultural level of these peasant nationalities would negatively affect the development of secular Yiddish culture. Despite the concrete and pessimistic nature of his assessments, Efroikin offered grandiose and utopian solutions. Transforming his mood, Efroikin wrote that the Jewish people, no less than the rest of the world, stood at the brink of a new era. He called for the Jews to engage in reconstruction just as had the other nations that endured World War I.[39] The contemporary historical moment, he argued, would determine the fate of nationalities for the coming centuries. In this charged atmosphere, the Jews would have to organize so that they could adequately represent themselves as a nation at the coming Peace Conference. Invoking the rhetoric of all proponents of the "new Jewish politics," Efroikin called for the replacement of "a politics for Jews" conducted by *shtadlonim* (intercessors) behind closed doors, with a true "Jewish politics," forged by the people themselves. With the following dramatic words, Efroikin unveiled his plan: "The *klal yisroel* that until now was only a unity in potential must become a unity in actuality."[40]

The breakup of the Russian Empire, he argued, demanded the creation of an international Jewish World Association run by a *klal yisroel v'a'ad* (Jewish People's Assembly). The American, Russian, Polish, and other Jewish congresses would elect representatives to this parliamentary body. This international assembly, funded from taxes on the international Jewish community, would help to regulate Jewish emigration and to establish Jewish cultural institutions. Most importantly, however, the *klal yisroel v'a'ad* would achieve legal recognition as the official representative of the Jewish nation and would lead the battle for the implementation of Jewish national rights throughout the world.[41]

Underlying this grandiose scheme was Efroikin's belief that the world stood at the threshold of a new era, when the international community would redefine the concept of "the nation" as a personal-cultural association rather than as a territory-based group. In his words:

As for all peoples, the time also has come for us when we should be accepted as members of the modern family of cultural nations. And perhaps it is precisely we Jews, who always charted new paths, always were an example of a pure nation, stripped of all external signs with which nations sometimes identify themselves such as state, land etc., perhaps it is precisely we who are destined to lay the foundation stone for national rights in the relationship between nations. . . .

The idea regarding the nation, as a personal culture-association, which sounded so strange to the nationalities that sit upon their own land, morally now has won. The same sooner or later will occur with the idea regarding the national association, which stands above the boundaries of the state.[42]

The jarring contrast between Efroikin's levelheaded assessments of the dangers posed to Russian Jewry by the dissolution of the empire and his utopian solution points once again to Frankel's "paradoxical politics of marginality." Despite relative political powerlessness, at the end of World War I Jewish leaders envisioned themselves as at the cusp of a new era in which their national dreams would reach fruition. It was the immediate context of the Bolshevik Revolution and the dissolution of the Russian Empire that prompted Efroikin to apply Dubnov's vision of Jewish autonomism within Russia to the international arena. Yet his conception of Jewish nationhood as an international "personal culture-association" actually shared much in common with the beliefs of several Zionist thinkers, such as the British Sir Alfred Zimmern and the American Horace Kallen. These Jewish nationalist intellectuals rejected the principle of territorial national determination, championed by America at the Paris Peace Conference, as both impractical and unethical. Kallen wrote, "Sovereignty is international anarchy."[43]

Instead of territorial sovereignty, Kallen, Zimmern, and others envisioned the creation of an international Jewish national community that promoted both Jewish national rights and the creation of a worldwide Jewish culture. Although they arrived at their visions from very different backgrounds, the similarity of the perspective of Zimmern, Kallen, and Efroikin demonstrates the attractiveness of non-territorial nationalism to Jewish nationalists of all stripes in the immediate aftermath of World War I. Believing that national chauvinism had led to World War I, Zimmern and Kallen would have agreed with Efroikin that the

Jews could serve as a model of a non-statist nationalism that would blend the universal with the particular, and the international with the national. Although they may not have realized it, these counter-statist Zionists owed their vision of the Jews as trailblazers of ethical, extra-territorial nationalism to Dubnov. Within the context of the aftermath of World War I, this belief not only invested the Jews with a sense of mission but also sought to transform the normative definition of nationhood to match the Jews' own status as a stateless nation.[44]

Diaspora Nationalists React to the Balfour Declaration

Events of the fall of 1917 were not kind to the political vision of the autonomists. Just before the Bolshevik coup, Diaspora nationalism had to react to the challenge of England's issuance of the Balfour Declaration, which the majority of Russian Jews greeted with great joy. In the aftermath of the October Revolution, the Zionists, buoyed by their first major diplomatic victory, went on the offensive by arguing that the Balfour Declaration would allow for the creation of a healthy national life in Palestine.[45] Diaspora nationalists such as Dubnov and Efroikin, to whom territorial nationalism proved anathema, had to refute this claim.

Dubnov explained the messianic fervor with which Russian Jewry greeted the Balfour Declaration as stemming from the fact that Russian Jews understood the war as the apocalyptic battle of Gog and Magog, the eschatological struggle that the Bible predicted would precede Israel's redemption. Not completely dismissive of the Balfour Declaration's potential, Dubnov predicted that the political chaos and the growing anti-Semitism in the successor states of Poland and Romania might well lead to a major Jewish emigration to Palestine. There, an increased Jewish population could achieve full national autonomy under British or international control. Given the fact that the Arabs constituted a majority in Palestine, the Jewish community there could achieve autonomy but not an independent Jewish state. Comparing the Zionist quest for statehood to Sabbateanism, Dubnov argued that the Zionists' inevitable failure would lead to Jewish disenchantment as profound as that experienced after Sabbatai Ṣevi's conversion. As a *klal yisroel* ideologue, Dubnov stated that he opposed both the socialists and assimilationists who denigrated the millennia-old Jewish dream of the land of Israel, and the Zionists, who proved ready to turn their backs on the nine-tenths of the Jewish people that would remain in the Diaspora. Despite this polemic against Zionism, Dubnov had in fact embraced a position regarding the relationship between Jewish autonomy in the Diaspora and in Palestine that many Zionists had come to espouse in the aftermath of World War I. Whereas in Palestine both Jews and Arabs would enjoy national autonomy, Jews would continue to struggle for their collective national rights in the East European Diaspora. During the interwar era, the difference between Dubnov and his Zionist rivals became increasingly one of emphasis, not of substance.[46]

In his response to the Balfour Declaration, Efroikin emerged as more Dubnovian than Dubnov himself. First, he attacked the Zionist goal of creating a Jewish state in Palestine on practical grounds, arguing that the Balfour Declaration did not promise statehood, that the Jewish community of Palestine had not built a national economy, and that the Arabs constituted the majority. More centrally, Efroikin polemicized against the creation of a Jewish state on ideological grounds. Throughout its history, argued Efroikin, the Jewish people consciously chose to remain in the Diaspora, banishing the dream of the return to Zion to the messianic future. Sh. Rozenfeld, another contributor to *Di yidishe folksblat,* criticized Efroikin for his alleged double standard in emphasizing historical Jewish apathy toward settling in Palestine while ignoring the fact that the majority of contemporary Jews did not demand cultural autonomy and Yiddish schools. Efroikin responded with the somewhat disingenuous argument that the fact that the common people sent their children to kheyder, whose language of instruction was Yiddish, proved their desire for Yiddish education. Whenever given the opportunity, argued Efroikin further, Jews always had created organs of autonomy.[47]

Efroikin then invoked Dubnov's argument that Jewish autonomy in the premodern era would serve as a model for modern national identity both for Jews and non-Jews. In Efroikin's words:

> The people established a unique spiritual world, which had no equal. A wonder for the world, almost a legend, was the entire people, which liberated its existence from the reign of a piece of land. Now, we already know

that this "exile-idea," the nation, as a spiritual collective, is destined to outlive states, that the future belongs to it. The medieval Jewish thought is becoming now the most modern, the basis of the current nation in general, which uproots itself more and more from territory, which parts from its "own land." Jews are, as apparently Shimon Dubnov said somewhere, not a nation but rather the nation, the preview, of the example of contemporary nations generally. . . .

Together with all oppressed and persecuted nations, we have to annul the idea itself of one's own and someone else's regarding land, which various nationalities populate. The Zionists, oppositely, want to strengthen this feeling for property, taken from the gentiles, and therein rests the greatest contradiction to their ideology, to that which our people worked out through its thousand-year experience, through its wisdom of life.[48]

Efroikin proved typical of Yiddishist Diaspora nationalist ideologues in his revulsion for the Zionist ideology of *shelilat ha-golah,* or negation of the exile, which dismissed Jewish culture in the Diaspora as debased. Copying from Dubnov, Efroikin reinvested the Jews with chosenness through their mission to spread non-territorial nationalism throughout the world. Efroikin's praise of Jewish achievements in the Diaspora, moreover, typically illustrated the romantic manner in which many Yiddishists and Diaspora nationalists glorified Jewish popular culture, especially that which was produced in Yiddish. At the same time, Efroikin's critique of Zionism for its alleged desire to retreat from world culture echoed the Yiddishist belief that modern Yiddish culture in the Diaspora would emerge as a synthesis of the uniquely Jewish with the European. Yet, in his uniform depiction of all Zionists as having negated the Diaspora, Efroikin perhaps unknowingly overlooked voices such as those of Zimmern and Kallen in the Zionist camp who shared his critique of territorial nationalism and who celebrated Jewish statelessness.[49]

Like Efroikin, Kalmanovitch reacted negatively to the Balfour Declaration with its promise of territorial sovereignty in Palestine. In particular, Kalmanovitch argued that the promised Jewish national home would prove no more than a tool in the hands of British imperialism, which sought a buffer to separate the Arabs of Syria from those in Egypt, thereby protecting British control of the Suez Canal. With the Balfour Declaration having granted them civic and religious but not political rights, the Arabs of Palestine would turn to nationalism to successfully destroy this Jewish buffer. Just as the Chmielnicki massacres had resulted from the Poles' use of the Jews as tools to oppress the Ukrainians, so too would this British imperial scheme end in disaster for Palestine's Jews. Like Efroikin, Kalmanovitch also warned against the rule in Palestine of a Jewish minority over an Arab majority.[50]

Participation in the Cultural Renaissance of Russian Jewry

It is no surprise that Tcherikower and Efroikin, always politically conscious, focused on politics rather than culture in the aftermath of the February Revolution. In 1917, even autonomists and Yiddishists who previously had engaged almost solely in cultural activity turned to politics. Politically, Kalmanovitch shared Efroikin's folkist political convictions. A resident of Petrograd since the German occupation of Vilna in 1915, he actively participated in the intellectual life of a folkist circle that included Efroikin, Shtif, Niger, and Yudl Mark.[51] All members of this circle, especially Efroikin, looked to Kalmanovitch for intellectual acumen and encyclopedic knowledge. Mark, twelve years Kalmanovitch's junior, recalled that he and his contemporaries looked to Kalmanovitch for guidance in their search for national identity upon realizing that they "were fiery nationalists and that they weren't Zionists and also not Bundists." Kalmanovitch joined the reconstituted Folkspartey because of his conviction that the parties that had combined socialism with maximal Jewish nationalism such as the Seymists and then the Fareynikte had remained parties of the intelligentsia, which had not addressed themselves to the needs of the broad Jewish masses.[52]

In the politically charged environment following the revolution, Kalmanovitch argued for the supremacy of culture over politics. He bemoaned that Yiddishists had not taken advantage of their newfound freedom to create schools, cultural institutions, and literary journals because they had allowed politics to divert them. In particular, Kalmanovitch chided folkists both in Petrograd and in the Ukraine for debating the fine points of national autonomy rather than creating an actual Yiddish school system. This failure to translate the political quest for autonomy into concrete cultural activity could doom the entire autonomist experiment to failure.[53]

Although cultural activity may not have sprouted as quickly as Kalmanovitch would have liked, both Hebraists and Yiddishists succeeded in initiating a renaissance of Jewish culture in Russia in 1917, which the Bolsheviks did not immediately crush. In the aftermath of the February Revolution, Hebraists and Yiddishists alike organized societies and published journals with a freedom that had eluded them throughout the tsarist period. Hebraists in Moscow formed a populist cultural network, Tarbut, whose professed goal was the modernization of East European Jewry through Hebrew culture. Hebrew publishing houses and journals similarly blossomed. In the first months following the February Revolution, Yiddish culture lagged behind its Hebrew counterpart. Initially, only two Yiddish newspapers were founded, one of which, *Undzer togblat,* had Hebraist leanings. *Di yidishe folksblat,* in contrast, reflected the Folkspartey's autonomist, Yiddishist ideology. Although a party organ, *Di yidishe folksblat* consistently argued for the independence of Yiddish culture from politics.[54] As both Yiddish and Hebrew writers produced both belles lettres and translations of European literature, the debate between national-romantics and cultural radicals in both camps came to a head.

On the eve of World War I, Jewish national romantics had turned to folklore as a repository of Jewish national values. Just as fifteen years earlier Dubnov had argued that Jewish historical sources needed to be rescued from oblivion, so too did An-sky, Peretz, and Bialik approach the collection of folklore with the same sense of urgency. In 1912–1914, An-sky went on an ethnographic expedition in the Ukraine in an effort to collect remnants of Jewish material and spiritual folk culture. The destruction of the war and revolution added a heightened measure of urgency to this task. In a November 1918 address, An-sky called for the creation of a Jewish ethnographic society. In the crucible of war, he discovered an ethical mission in Jewish folklore through its emphasis on spiritual struggle rather than physical power. This unique ethical sensibility could animate Jewish national culture, folklore's modern substitute.[55]

In his final years, Peretz, too, expressed frustration with his disciples for what he deemed their blind imitation of European aesthetics instead of linking Yiddish literature to the "golden chain" of Jewish tradition. To Peretz no less than to An-sky, the heart of that tradition was Jewish folklore. Like An-sky, Peretz emphasized the moral superiority of Yiddish folktales to their European equivalents. In his growing frustration with his disciples, the secularist Peretz even argued that until it reached maturity, modern Yiddish culture would have to seek inspiration from its religious predecessor, whose living Orthodox representatives still preserved the folk's authentic values and way of life.[56]

In the Hebraist camp, Bialik called for a similar rescue of traditional values in classical Jewish texts. In *Sefer Ha-Aggadah* (which he coedited with Y. H. Ravnitsky), Bialik sought to reintroduce the modern national Jew to the treasures of religious texts, stripped of their theological underpinnings and presented as the literary canon of the Jewish nation.[57] In his call to his fellow Hebraists to engage in *kinus* (gathering), Bialik hoped that they would cull religious texts for values and literary formulations that would inspire modern Hebrew literature. According to Bialik, the broad, sweeping changes wrought by the Zionist revolution necessitated the preservation of the essence of the Jewish historical experience in the Diaspora. *Kinus* thus would deliver the remnants of the Jewish past to the new national culture. At the same time, the very choice of material to gather aided in this process of transformation from religious to national identity. The crowning achievement of *kinus, Ha-sefer ha-ʿivri* (the Hebrew book) would consist of the best Hebrew works throughout history and achieve canonical status as a bible for secular national Jews. Like Peretz, Bialik grew frustrated with his fellow Hebrew writers for not rooting their new culture sufficiently in traditional sources. This criticism was the subject of his seminal essay, "Halakhah ve-aggadah," which appeared in 1917 and sought to rehabilitate halakhah, Jewish law, as a source of inspiration for national Jews. In the life of the religious Jew, argued Bialik, the halakhah concretized the values expressed in the aggadah, the lore, through rituals and religious behaviors. In the same fashion, modern national Jews would have to concretize their commitment to national Jewish culture in their lifestyles. Bialik also used the term "halakhah" as a metaphor for ethnography. The new national culture and literature would succeed only if they could learn from folk customs and rituals in addition to folklore.[58]

During the heightened cultural production in the aftermath of the February Revolution, however, it became clear that many members of the next generation of both Yiddish and Hebrew writers had no desire to heed their masters' call. Rather, they chose instead to give free expression to their individuality through experimentation with the latest European literary trends. To these intellectuals, modern Jewish culture needed to transcend the parochial boundaries of its traditional canon in order fully to develop a literature worthy of a modern nation. In an effort to de-parochialize modern Jewish culture, participants in Russian Jewry's cultural renaissance translated large quantities of European literature into Hebrew and Yiddish. Their firm belief that the new Jewish culture, though unfettered to specific Jewish content, had to be expressed wholly in a Jewish language marked these men as cultural nationalists. The free development of an aesthetic culture in either Hebrew or Yiddish itself would prove a great contribution to the nation.[59]

Despite this shift toward cultural radicalism, most Hebrew and Yiddish writers during the revolutionary period still veered between national romanticism and radicalism, depending on their mood or the particular circumstance. Perhaps the fact that they were not aesthetes but rather scholars led Tcherikower and Kalmanovitch to express their preference for cultural preservation over de-parochialization. These men's implicit conviction that scholarship functioned as the new national culture's greatest asset placed them in conflict with the majority of Russian Jewish cultural nationalists of the period, whose emphasis was decidedly literature and the arts.[60] Their search for values for modern Jewish culture in the collective past also made them receptive to the preservationist call of An-sky, Peretz, and Bialik.

Kalmanovitch therefore used *Di yidishe folksblat* as an arena to advance his expansive vision of Yiddish culture, which he believed should incorporate the entire historical legacy of the Jewish people. In a positive book review, Kalmanovitch heralded *Biblishe literatur* (Biblical literature), written by Chaim Shoys and introduced by Zhitlovsky, as the first work of modern biblical studies to appear in Yiddish. Alienated from the Bible because of its traditional inseparability from rabbinic interpretation, secular national Jews did not know how to recover biblical values for their children or how to reconcile the Bible with modern science. For this reason, Kalmanovitch praised

Shoys both for his work's historical-literary perspective and its accessibility to the "broadest reading circles." Here again, Kalmanovitch valued both scholarship and popularization. Kalmanovitch's embrace of the Bible, cleansed of rabbinic interpretation, as a source of inspiration for modern Yiddish culture also proved typical for Yiddishists of this era. At the time of the February Revolution, Kalmanovitch thus remained a disciple both of Dubnov and Zhitlovsky, in his vision of modern Jewish culture incorporating scholarship on all periods of Jewish history, including the biblical and ancient periods.[61]

On the heels of his political disillusionment, Tcherikower combined his long-held interest in historiography with a belief in the national merits of ethnography. It was symptomatic of his Yiddishist identity that he now combined Dubnov's historicism with the populism of Peretz and An-sky. Tcherikower thus wrote an article for the new journal He-'avar (The past) that sought to rescue disappearing traditional Jewish values for national Jews. The editors of He-'avar, founded in Petrograd during the heat of the stormy events of 1918, expressed their conviction that Russian Jews needed the past as a guide. Viewing history neither as a cemetery nor as a museum, the editors of He-'avar sought to guide its readers in the search for "a usable past." To that end, they encouraged their readers to send them material on Jewish history, folklore, and ethnography. They stressed that the scholarly work of the journal would remain nonpartisan.[62]

He-'avar thus merged Dubnov's national mission for Jewish history with Peretz's, An-sky's, and Bialik's elevation of folklore as a repository of national creativity. In the same year, 1918, Bialik and several other folklorists began to publish Reshumot, a Hebrew-language journal that explored the folklore and ethnography of Jews both in Eastern Europe and throughout the world. The fact that Hebraists turned to the study of the Russian Jewish past in He-'avar demonstrates, moreover, the extent to which even Hebraist Zionists concentrated their efforts upon the building of autonomous politics and culture in the aftermath of the February Revolution.[63] It is very understandable that the historical mission of He-'avar attracted the Yiddishist Tcherikower. Not a Hebrew writer, Tcherikower probably wrote his contributions in Yiddish or Russian and had them translated into Hebrew for the journal.

In his article "Me-yerushat mishpahah patriarkhalit" (From the inheritance of a patriarchal family), Tcherikower mirrored the journal's combination of historiography with ethnography. The article mined the will of a Jewish Warsaw merchant, Hirsh Tsintsimer, who lived at the turn of the nineteenth century, as a source of national ethics rooted in Jewish tradition. In his introduction, Tcherikower echoed the urgency of An-sky's recent ethnographic expedition in his call to preserve traditional values from the rapid erosion of time:

> Daily, the color of traditional Judaism increasingly fades; the patriarchal nature of the Jewish family of that entire environment continues to disappear, and also the ideology, which sprouted on the ground of that life, continues to sink into the abyss of the past. The old concepts and opinions, all the laws of patriarchal ethics that ruled in Jewish family circles and were the rule are being forgotten. The stream of life is erasing the old colors and mercilessly destroys without a trace all remembrance of the forms of life that once were. This loss requires searching after. It is necessary to save from the sleep of forgetfulness the old forms of life and their colors and to renew in our memories their patriarchy—if only for knowledge's sake.[64]

Like Bialik in his "Halakhah ve-aggadah," Tcherikower thus articulated an appreciation for Jewish law as an embodiment of Jewish ethics. The traditional Jewish "patriarchy" emerges in this article as a foil to contemporary secular egalitarian society. Yet Tcherikower expressed nostalgia and even reverence for the values of the traditional Jewish past. Especially intriguing was Tcherikower's favorable depiction of Tsintsimer's dispersal of funds for charity, since socialists rejected charity as a retrograde institution that legitimated the persistence of poverty. To some extent, this veneration resulted from Tcherikower's long-standing penchant to bifurcate his socialist and Jewish nationalist identities.[65] On a deeper level, however, this respectful portrait conjured the image of an idyllic premodern Jewish ethic that tempered the social ills accompanying the accumulation of wealth with the dedication to the religious obligation of social justice. However imperfect, traditional social justice must have appeared attractive to Tcherikower in 1918, after his having witnessed the beginning of Bolshevik terror and expropriations.

In this respectful depiction, Tcherikower invoked a short story by Peretz. Peretz designed his story, "Fir doyres, fir tsavoes" (Four generations, four wills) as four successive wills of four successive generations of Polish Jews. Whereas the wills of the first and second generation expressed strong religious sensibilities, the third will reflected the loss of traditional values and the crass materialism that accompanied the twin processes of acculturation and European-style embourgeoisement. The last will assumed the role of a suicide note of the materially privileged but morally starved fourth-generation son. The similarities between Tsintsimer's historical will and the second will in Peretz's story led Tcherikower to surmise that Peretz had modeled his on that of Tsintsimer.[66]

By blaming acculturation for the ethical decline of the Jewish bourgeoisie, Peretz left himself room to rehabilitate and appropriate the values of the premodern Jewish business class. Although elsewhere he leveled blistering attacks against the Jewish bourgeoisie for its exploitation of the poor, here Peretz demonstrated a respect for the fictional author of the second will, R. Binyomin, who understood his wealth as ephemeral and felt a religious responsibility to give charity. Through this veneration, Peretz sought to instill in his readers a sense of irony that contrasted religious dedication to social justice among the premodern business class with the absence of a similar ethic among purportedly egalitarian secular Jews. Deeply ambivalent, Peretz did not desire a return to traditional Jewish society, which he saw in some ways as primitive, but rather an incorporation of the best of its values into its modern national substitute. Tcherikower's judgment that the morals of the earlier religious generation proved superior to that of the contemporary, materialistic one shared in Peretz's ambivalence:

> And, however we relate . . . to the hardened spirit of patriarchal Jewry, still, from an ethical-aesthetic vantage point, they are still higher than the types of the later generations. And the reason is that in them dwells God in whom they believe, for they possess a religious-ethical idea that concentrates all the forces of their souls to one point. . . .
>
> From where is the strength of the patriarchal stance in old Judaism that is strong and powerful in its spirit? Upon this, the will of R. Hirsh Tsintsimer gives us the answer in his short, pithy advice to his children: "Always, my children, be amongst the persecuted and not the persecutors."[67]

On the one hand, "patriarchal Jewry" possessed a "hardened spirit." Yet its belief in God led to the development of an all-encompassing "religious-ethical idea." Whereas traditional Judaism was doomed to oblivion, implied Tcherikower, impassioned study of Jewish historiography and ethnography could lead to the survival of the best of its values in secular form.[68] To Tcherikower, Tsintsimer's quotation of a Talmudic dictum calling for identification with the victim over the aggressor pointed toward the humanistic ethical imperative that animated traditional Judaism. Like Peretz and An-sky, moreover, Tcherikower elevated Jewish passivity in the face of persecution to the level of a national value. When searching for a foundation of Jewish national survival in the modern age, Tcherikower, after all, had turned to martyrdom.

After leaving Petrograd in 1918, Tcherikower continued his cultural activities in Kiev. In 1917–1918, Kiev emerged as a center of highbrow Yiddishism. A group of Yiddishists associated with the Fareynikte party, such as Moyshe Litvakov, Moyshe Katz, and Moyshe Zilberfarb, joined forces with young Yiddish writers and literary critics such as Dovid Bergelson, Nakhmen Mayzel, and Pinkhes Kahanovitsh (Der Nister) to create their own publishing house, the Kiever Farlag. Kenneth Moss described the ideology of this group and its publishing house as the creation of "an entirely secular, national-radical, and monolingual Yiddish literary culture that would . . . incorporate the best of European and the older Jewish culture (including Hebrew literature) through translation."[69]

Even more impressive were the cultural ambitions of the newly founded Kultur-Lige. The Kultur-Lige sought to establish a broad network of Yiddishist cultural organizations. Touting the slogan "to make our masses *inteligent*," it both supported high culture and sought to make it accessible to the masses. Establishing sections for literature, theater, the visual arts, and music, the Kultur-Lige similarly formed its own press that produced textbooks and original literature in Yiddish and in translation. Its large and impressive bookstore cornered the Yiddish book market.[70] At the same time, it created a network of Yiddish public elementary schools throughout the Ukraine as well as folk universities, in which adult learners could study at night. The Kultur Lige declared for itself the following goal: "developing and disseminating to the people Yiddish secular culture in all spheres of human creativity, such as literature, art, music, theater and others as well as aiding in the construction of the modern Yiddish democratic school and other educational institutions."[71] Although members of the Jewish socialist parties dominated the Kultur-Lige, its activists took seriously the separation of culture from politics. As a result, non-socialist Yiddishists and even Zionists such as Ben-Zion Dinaburg (Dinur) taught in the Kultur-Lige's folk university and published historical anthologies for its schools.[72] Both Tcherikower and Kalmanovitch also taught in the folk university.

By late October 1918, folkists who had arrived to Kiev from Petrograd opened their own publishing house, the Folks-Farlag, which in many ways served as a continuation of Efroikin and Shtif's *Di yidishe folksblat*. This press reflected an expansive vision of Yiddish culture through its translations of Hebrew and European literature and biblical and rabbinic literature as well as its production of Jewish scholarship. The Folks-Farlag's staff demonstrated the extent of its nonpartisanship through its employment of radicals, folkists, and even Hebraist-Zionists. For instance, Dinaburg, a Hebraist, headed the history and Jewish studies section together with Kalmanovitch.[73]

In Kiev no less than in Petrograd, Tcherikower revealed how he attempted to wed ethnographic methodologies to historiography. As a Yiddishist and Diaspora nationalist, Tcherikower believed in the application of Bialik's *kinus* to historiography but differed with its Hebraist, Zionist focus. He revealed this different focus in two separate reviews of two historical textbooks written by Dinaburg, one a compilation of primary sources surveying all of Jewish history and the other a textbook of Jewish history. Dinaburg's "chrestomathy" of sources served as his application of Bialik's genre of *kinus* to historiography. Published by Bikher-velt, a prominent Yiddishist press, this source collection demonstrated the level of nonpartisanship that existed in Kiev at the time. Yet Tcherikower's review revealed the inextricable link between politics and scholarship even in this atmosphere of cultural freedom. Despite lofty declarations of the independence of culture from politics, Yiddishists in Kiev had little use for conventional Zionism, with its emphasis on Palestine and on Hebrew. Whereas producers of belles lettres often ignored this divide, Tcherikower as a historian had no such luxury. He revealed his Yiddishist, autonomist perspective through his criticism of Dinaburg for concentrating too much on the political historical narrative of the Bible and not enough on the Bible's cultural-historical values, a popular theme with many Yiddishists.[74]

In his review of Dinaburg's Jewish history program for Yiddish schools, Tcherikower criticized him similarly for concentrating too much on the history of ancient Israel and not enough upon Jewish history in the Diaspora. In particular, Tcherikower noticed the lack of mention of such important ancient Diaspora figures as Philo and Josephus. Similarly, he complained that the richest and least well-known period in Jewish history, the Middle Ages, received the least attention in the book. This criticism reflected Tcherikower's Dubnovian conception of Jewish history, which recognized the Middle Ages as an era of Jewish national autonomy. In contrast, Dinaburg, like many other Zionist historians, concentrated in his curriculum more on the history of the Jewish people in its own land in antiquity than on later periods in the Diaspora. Despite the book's many shortcomings, Tcherikower still managed to greet this work as a "first attempt" and to praise Dinaburg for his professionalism as a Jewish historian and educator.[75]

Efroikin, too, turned to cultural activity after he no longer could involve himself in Russian politics. No doubt his shred of hope for the Russian Constituent Assembly faded forever when the Bolsheviks dispersed this institution in January 1918. Initially deciding to remain in Petrograd, he continued his work as a folkist, only now in the realm of culture. In *Di yidishe folksblat,* Efroikin and Shtif had argued that if high Yiddish culture were to serve as a tool of nation building, it would have to remain free from political allegiance. Since the Bolsheviks did not immediately repress Yiddish culture, Efroikin continued to attempt to realize this cultural vision by heading the Petrograd branch of the Folks-Farlag. Through his association with the Folks-Farlag, he now had a connection both to Kalmanovitch and to Tcherikower, both involved in its activities. From Petrograd, Efroikin, together with Yoysef Yashinski, also led the "I. L. Peretz Literary Association," which proposed the writing of a Jewish encyclopedia in Yiddish. Confident that the Folks-Farlag would undertake this project, Efroikin asked

Dinaburg to join the editorial staff, which consisted of Kalmanovitch, Latski-Bertoldi, and Lestschinsky.[76]

By the summer of 1918, the Bolsheviks had tightened their grip on Jewish cultural life in Petrograd. Kalmanovitch joined the stream of Yiddishist intellectuals who moved to Kiev. In fact, as early as 1917, the former Seymist, Shimen Duben, now active as a Yiddishist in Kiev, enthusiastically asked Kalmanovitch to throw in his lot with the Kiev Yiddishist project, imploring him "to listen to the voice of history."[77] Although Kalmanovitch long had dreamed of a time when a state government would support Yiddish culture, he reacted to the burgeoning Yiddishist cultural life in Kiev with skepticism.[78] Kalmanovitch feared that the environment of internal Jewish political fractiousness would sacrifice Yiddishist cultural goals. For instance, in letters to Niger and Vayter, Kalmanovitch warned that the work of Kiev Yiddishists, although promising, remained in its infancy. In particular, Kalmanovitch leveled a critique regarding what he deemed the dangerous mixture of politics and culture at the Kultur Lige and its institutions. When Litvakov attacked the nationalist ideology of the Jewish bourgeoisie upon the opening of the *folks-universitet,* Kalmanovitch loudly criticized his words as a "caricature of scholarship," which desecrated the institution that just had been dedicated.[79] Not surprisingly, Kalmanovitch also complained to Niger that extracurricular political and cultural activities lowered the quality of the *folkuniversitet*'s teachers.[80] Following the ascendancy of the conservative Hetmanate regime in the Ukraine, Kalmanovitch wrote to Vayter that the socialist political agitation of Kultur-Lige activists could lead to the closure of the entire institution as "a nest of revolution."[81] In an environment of external political turmoil and internal political contention, Kalmanovitch feared that the Yiddish renaissance embodied by the Kultur Lige would not survive.[82] Quite tellingly, he expressed his preference for Vilna, then under German occupation, over Kiev.[83] In essence, he did not take the Kultur-Lige's leaders, mostly representative of the Fareynikte party, at their word when they promised to separate their socialist politics from their cultural work.[84]

Despite his skepticism and anxiety, Kalmanovitch taught classes in Jewish history, Yiddish literature, and philology both in the Kultur-Lige's *folks-universitet* and in its teacher training seminar.[85] In his work for the Folks-Farlag, he collaborated with Dinaburg in composing a long list of works in Jewish studies, written in European languages, that the publishing house hoped to translate into Yiddish.[86] At the Folks-Farlag, Kalmanovitch also continued his translation of scholarship in European languages into Yiddish, translated part of Dubnov's five-volume *History of the Jewish People,* and worked on a comprehensive Yiddish dictionary, a project that he never finished.[87]

Participation in Jewish National Autonomy in the Ukraine

In their bid first for autonomy and then for independence from Russia, Ukrainian nationalists promised Jews broad-sweeping national autonomy. Moyshe Zilberfarb, a leader of the Fareynikte, served as the first minister of Jewish affairs of the newly independent Ukraine. Another organ of Jewish autonomy was the National Council (Natsional-rat), which served as the ministry's advisory board. In the midst of a chaotic civil war and the successive rise and fall of several Ukrainian governments, Jewish political factionalism seriously hampered the autonomous experiment. The Bund, Fareynikte, and Poale Zion initially dominated the Natsional-rat, leading the Zionists to boycott this institution. When the conservative Hetmanate regime came to power, the socialists found themselves on the defensive and had to share power with the Zionists. At the same time, the socialist leadership allowed for direct elections both to local *kehiles* and to a Provisional Jewish Constituent Assembly. Although voter turnout was low, the election granted a mandate to the Zionist-Orthodox bloc.[88]

Meeting for the first time in November 1918, the pre-parliament to this assembly appointed a twelve-member executive committee, known as the Nationality Secretariat, which the Bund refused to join. Tcherikower served as the Nationality Secretariat's head. When, in December 1918, the socialist-leaning Ukrainian Directory overthrew the conservative Hetmanate, it reinstituted the Jewish Ministry, appointing the Poale Zionist Avraham Revutsky as minister. Viewing this move as undemocratic, the Nationality Secretariat refused to accept his authority. In February 1919, Bolshevik troops conquered Kiev, ending the activities of the Nationality Secretariat.

At first glance, it may appear strange that Tcherikower, a non-Zionist who in the past had allied himself with Poale Zion, would serve as the manager of the Nationality Secretariat despite its overwhelming Zionist character and its battle with Revutsky. Just as in the All-Russian Jewish Congress a year before, however, it was the Zionists who represented the largest mass political party to endorse full Jewish national autonomy. Like the folkists of Petrograd, Tcherikower no doubt decided to join in a coalition with the Zionists to achieve this larger goal. The fact that Latski-Bertoldi, an active member first of the Russian Folkspartey and then of its Ukrainian successor, also joined the Nationality Secretariat bolsters this argument. Tcherikower also probably now supported a separate peace between the Ukraine and Germany, something that Poale Zion opposed. Reversing his stand on this issue, Tcherikower no doubt hoped that such a separate peace between Ukraine and Germany could save Ukrainian Jews from Bolshevik dictatorship. In allying himself with the Zionists, Tcherikower also may have expressed his protest against members of the socialist parties, who had begun to switch their loyalties away from the Ukrainians toward the Soviets.[89] In the chaotic last months of 1918 and first months of 1919, Tcherikower still believed that Ukrainian independence functioned as the last chance for a significant percentage of Russian Jewry to enjoy national autonomy. Soon, however, the eruption of widespread murderous pogroms in the Ukraine, political chaos in Kiev, and the entrance of the Soviets would rob Tcherikower of this cultural vision as well.

The combination of repression and anarchy in Petrograd and the allure of national autonomy in the Ukraine led Efroikin to settle in Kiev as well. Seemingly undaunted, he ran again on the Folkspartey ticket, this time in October 1918 as a candidate for the Ukrainian Jewish Constituent Assembly. An election flyer that offered brief biographies of the Folkspartey candidates described Efroikin as a political activist and writer who first participated in SERP before leaving socialism behind for a purely nationalist ideology. Efroikin's foray into Ukrainian Jewish politics might at first appear surprising, given his vociferous arguments against Ukrainian secession just a year earlier. Like many of his fellow folkists, however, Efroikin must have convinced himself that his dream for Jewish national autonomy could achieve fruition in the Ukraine. Efroikin, however, had no more success in this election than in his previous one in Russia. As they had a year earlier, the Zionists received a mandate, and the Folkspartey received just 3 percent of the vote.[90] When the Ukraine fell to the Soviets in 1920, Efroikin left Russian soil forever, immigrating to Paris.

The wave of murderous pogroms that engulfed Ukrainian Jewry in 1919–1920, often perpetrated by Ukrainian forces, soon overshadowed both the implementation of Jewish national autonomy and the Jewish cultural renaissance in Kiev. Kiev's Yiddish-writing literati turned away from their impressionistic experimentation to prose and poetry that eulogized the victims of the pogroms.[91] Given the centrality of martyrology to Tcherikower's Jewish nationalism, it is not surprising that he quickly abandoned his other political and cultural activities to become the chief chronicler of the contemporary apocalypse. In May 1919, as word of the scale of the pogroms reached Kiev, the Jewish National Secretariat, which Tcherikower headed, joined with the Folks-Farlag and the Central Committee of Kiev for Relief of Pogrom Victims to create the "Editorial Board for Gathering and Researching Materials regarding the Pogroms in the Ukraine." Immediately, the editorial board issued the following call to the Jewish population, which it printed in the Yiddish press:

Jews!
A terrible pogrom curse has befallen Jewish cities and towns, and the world does not know; we ourselves do not know, or know very little. It must not be silenced! Everything must be told and recorded.
It is an obligation upon every Jew who comes from the unfortunate Jewish cities, to report everything that he has seen, so that the news should not be lost.
We implore [you] to report to the commission that gathers and researches all the news regarding the pogroms.[92]

The editorial board sought documentation in order to inform the world of the atrocities, intending to publish documentary evidence of the pogroms in Yiddish, Russian, English, and perhaps in French or German. Funded by various Russian Jewish organizations such as EKOPO, ORT, and OZE, the editorial board attracted such public intellectuals and activists as Dubnov, Zilberfarb, Lestschinsky, Kreinin, P. Dubinsky, and N. Mirkin. Although officially Shtif was editor and

Tcherikower secretary, the day-to-day work fell upon Tcherikower. As the de facto head of the board, Tcherikower collected documents, eyewitness accounts, and photographs of the pogroms, transmitted the information to other Jewish organizations, and meticulously copied each document twice to preserve the material in case of the loss of the original. On July 29, the board accepted Tcherikower's proposal that it immediately prepare a book that would document the most important pogroms "in order to familiarize the world with what is occurring in the Ukraine." To meet this goal, Tcherikower proposed that the book appear in Yiddish, Russian, and one foreign language.[93] Because of the pace of political upheaval in Kiev, Tcherikower and the board did not succeed in publishing such a book.

In a matter of months, Tcherikower had succeeded in collecting and meticulously organizing an impressive archive of pogrom material. As Kiev continued to change hands, the various regimes sought to confiscate the archive. The Directory led by Semon Petliura, for instance, sought to suppress news of the atrocities that its legions had committed. In contrast, the Soviets sought access to the archive in order to smear the name of the Ukrainian nationalists. The Folks-Farlag remained the chief sponsor of the editorial board's mission, after the Secretariat of Jewish Affairs and the Central Kiev Relief Committee ceased to exist.[94]

Once the Soviets established permanent control over Kiev in 1921, the Evsektsiia (Jewish sections of the Communist Party) eventually communized the Kultur-Lige's publishing house under state sponsorship. In such an atmosphere, activists from the Folks-Farlag decided to escape from the Soviet Union. In a private correspondence, Kalmanovitch, himself part of this group, described how the majority of this group fled to Minsk and Bobruysk, where they spent the winter, before crossing into independent Lithuania in the spring. Elias and Riva Tcherikower, however, headed to Moscow together with the pogrom archive, where they clandestinely established contacts with members of the Folks-Farlag, other Jewish organizations, and Lithuanian diplomats. From Moscow, they smuggled the archive to Berlin.[95] Upon arriving in Berlin, Tcherikower wrote to a colleague in New York: "Blessed is He who revives the dead! Several months ago, I uprooted myself from the Ukraine and Russia and ceased to be dead. . . . The united Jewish social organizations in Moscow and Kiev (EKOPO etc.) commandeered us together with the archive abroad, in order to publish it here."[96]

Even in Germany, however, Tcherikower met with little success in publishing his history of the pogroms. In Germany, the editorial board changed its name to the Historical Archive of Eastern Jewry. It planned the publication of seven volumes based on the archive, which would analyze different aspects of the pogroms. The planned authors of these volumes were Tcherikower, Shtif, Lestschinsky, and Yoysef Shekhtman. From these seven volumes, only one appeared in 1923, written by Tcherikower and titled *Antisemitizm un pogromen in ukrayne in di yorn 1917–1918 (tsu der geshikhte fun ukraynish-yidishe batsihungen)* (Anti-Semitism and pogroms in the Ukraine in the years 1917–1918: The period of the Central Rada and the Hetman).[97]

Whereas originally Tcherikower sought to influence world opinion through his historiography, after the Soviet victory he concentrated upon commemoration. Indeed, Tcherikower's other works in the immediate postwar years testify to his goal to create a memorial to the Russian Jewish experience of euphoria and despair during the revolutionary years of 1917–1921. In fact, even before leaving the Soviet Union, Tcherikower coedited a book of historical documents titled *Di idishe avtonomiye un der natsionaler secretariat in ukrayine: Materialn un dokumentn* (Jewish national autonomy and the National Secretariat in the Ukraine: Materials and documents). In the introduction, Tcherikower and the other coeditors envisioned this book as a memorial to the brief, lost epoch of Jewish autonomy in the Ukraine. Speaking of the pogrom-devastated, Soviet-occupied Ukraine of 1920, Tcherikower and the other editors described the purpose of the book as rescuing "one of the most characteristic periods in the development of Jewish autonomy" from historical oblivion. "The martyrology of the book itself" symbolized the fate of its subject.[98]

Four years later in Berlin, Tcherikower memorialized the revolution by editing a book that he intended to serve as the first in a series, titled *In der tkufe fun revolutsiye (memyarn, materialn, dokumentn)* (In the period of revolution—memoirs, materials, documents).[99] In the introduction, Tcherikower bemoaned the fact that seven years after the revolution, the Jews had produced no historiography analyzing the objective historical influence of these tumultuous years upon the Jewish people. Momentarily, however, Tcherikower abandoned the objective stance of a historian to emotionally describe the impact that the revolution had upon Russian Jewry:

> And who has the right to record these events in history more than the Jews? The revolution did not elicit such dramatic experiences from anyone else more than us. It brought us the greatest political joy and the greatest excitement, hope and enthusiasm; it brought new rights, and opened new doors. It, however, became the source of the most horrific afflictions that ever befell our destiny. . . .
>
> It is therefore a great surprise that the strong political experiences and catastrophes have hardly yet enriched Jewish literature at all with any material, and have left our soul and memory plain and fruitless.[100]

Tcherikower here expressed his own experience of the revolutionary years, from their euphoric beginning to their catastrophic end. It is interesting that Tcherikower emphasized that not publicistic newspaper articles, but rather only historiography, could capture the true meaning of these events. Perhaps unwittingly, he offered his explanation here for why he himself turned away from publicistic political writing toward historiography. Only historiography, he argued, proved ripe for the task of preserving all the details of Jewish suffering for future generations. Tcherikower realized that the tsarist expulsions of the Jews from the front in 1915, which he mourned so much at the time, remained a fading, undocumented memory. Similarly, without historical documentation, he feared that the pogroms of 1919 would eclipse all memory of the heady days of 1917. Despite his call to his readers to send contributions for further issues, no future volumes appeared.[101]

Reactions to the Sovietization of Yiddish Culture in the Ukraine

When the Soviets occupied Kiev in 1919, Yiddish culture became radicalized. Having experienced the negative reaction of the Hetmanate regime to Jewish ambitions for autonomy, many members of the Yiddishist elite looked to the Soviet regime for state support of Yiddish culture. As throughout Soviet territory, members of the Bund and Fareynikte in Kiev had to choose between maintaining their unique political identities and joining the Ukrainian Jewish Communist Alliance (the Komfarband). At its May 1919 convention, a vocal minority of Kultur-Lige members signaled their organization's radicalization by heatedly arguing for the exclusion of non-socialists from its ranks. Regarding aesthetic culture, Rafes, a Bundist now turned Communist, shocked other Yiddishists with his declaration that he planned to sweep Mendele, Peretz, Sholem Aleichem, and "your whole petit-bourgeois culture" off the Jewish street. Although he resisted joining the Komfarband, the Bundist A. Litvak also contributed to the erosion of the distinction between culture and politics by calling on Yiddish writers to depict the revolutionary struggle rather than recycle themes regarding the shtetl. Indeed, the literary journal that Litvak edited, *Baginen,* featured both realistic and impressionist prose that championed the theme of revolution.[102]

In response to such attacks, the Yiddish novelist Dovid Bergelson published an essay, "Dikhtung un gezelshaftlekhkeyt" (Art-literature and the revolutionary public), in which he argued for the separation of the political and cultural realms. According to Bergelson, the goals of revolutionary politics and of art were mutually exclusive. Whereas the revolution sought to create a new society from scratch, art had to draw on the collective past for inspiration. Even as he declared political loyalty to the new order, Bergelson argued that the revolution could not look to literature as a tool.[103] Even though such leaders of the revolution as Trotsky shared this view of the bifurcation of revolutionary politics from aesthetic culture, those who sought to engage in cultural work divorced from a political agenda found themselves increasingly on the defensive.

As a cultural nationalist with an antipathy toward the Bolsheviks, Kalmanovitch reacted to this political encroachment upon Yiddish culture with horror. Writing to Niger after the Polish army temporarily had expelled the Soviets from Kiev, Kalmanovitch assumed a tone of passive, religious resignation in describing his experience of "famine, sword, and pestilence." Indeed, Kalmanovitch invoked the biblical imagery of the *tokhakhah,* the passages of rebuke found both in Leviticus 26 and Deuteronomy 28, to convey the sense of physical and spiritual devastation that he had witnessed as a result of the civil war, the pogroms, and the Soviet conquest. In discussing the fate of his old mother who endured the ravages of the civil war in another area in the Ukraine, Kalmanovitch ironically mused, "The kosher soul! Granted we sinned, [by] wanting a revolution, so what do you expect? But they, the elderly, those who are happy with their lot, why do they deserve this, Master of the Universe? For the sins of the children?" Desperate for material support, he both implored Niger to help him and his wife's family financially and to contact his siblings in Chicago, with whom he had had no contact for nearly a decade.[104]

Kalmanovitch's main crisis, however, was not material but rather spiritual. He simply could not stand Jewish cultural life under the Soviets:

> I will speak briefly, perhaps you'll understand; the fact that they are the only material basis for Yiddish cultural work makes this cultural work loathsome to me—against my will I write, against my will I teach my students, against my will I take part in various undertakings to which I am recruited. I regard this [material] source as stinking, bloody, and thus I am certain that a culture which has these people as its supporters is impure at its root. At any rate, all the others here are differently oriented or pretend that they are satisfied, and there is such a whoredom of conscience and spirit, that those who we were accustomed to see as virtually paragons of virtue now seem in my eyes as though they were bathed in the lake of Hell to which "that man" [Jesus of Nazareth] was condemned. [The smell] carries, it seems to me, for a mile. And when the *gedoylim* [the big ones—the Bolsheviks] are here, everything Jewish which is not on their side, just like every other aspect of culture, is buried. They destroyed the Jewish soul more than all the pogroms here. For me personally, there is only one salvation, if it is not too late, and that is to get out of here.[105]

As early as 1920, Kalmanovitch thus had developed what would become an obsessive hatred of official Soviet Yiddish culture. Placing the welfare of Jewish culture above the physical safety of Jews, he rejected the consensus of most Jews in the Ukraine, even nationalists, who preferred life and relative physical safety under the Soviets to death and turmoil under the Whites and Ukrainian forces. His greatest disappointment was the perceived betrayal of the Yiddish literati, who professed allegiance to the Soviet regime as soon as it established its power in Kiev in 1919. Reporting on the May 1919 convention of the Kultur-Lige, Kalmanovitch blamed Bergelson for setting the tone of capitulation to the Soviet regime, which the other Yiddish literati followed. In his words:

> Instead of standing firm against these boors, who would, as could be foreseen, trample everything, they kissed their uncouth boots. Instead of saying: I am for Yiddish culture and the Kultur-Lige, where there is talent and knowledge, a Jew such as Bergelson prostrated himself completely to demonstrate that he created, creates, and will create "proletarian culture." . . . I, however, will never forgive him and never will forget the shame that Yiddish literature kissed up to and flattered the few score of party men, who with superficial smiles listened as the great Bergelson chattered something about . . . "revolution," "proletariat," which they knew all by heart and they could formulate better than him. . . . And here was the beginning of the descent, which pulled and continues to pull the entire contemporary generation of Yiddish literature into the abyss.[106]

Given Bergelson's defense of non-revolutionary literature in his "Dikhtung un gezelshaftlekhkeyt," it is interesting that Kalmanovitch singled him out for capitulation to Soviet standards for Yiddish literature. Clearly at the Kultur-Lige convention, Bergelson indeed, quite tendentiously, had declared the proletarian nature of his fiction, even as his novella *Opgang*, published that same year, portrayed the decaying world of the pre-revolutionary petty-bourgeois youth of the shtetl. Indeed, Kalmanovitch surmised that, Bergelson's protestations notwithstanding, the famed author had declared literary allegiance to the revolution in hopes of material gain. Similarly, Kalmanovitch accused those Yiddishists who helped the Communists dissolve the Kultur Lige as motivated by a desire for gain. Moss explained Kalmanovitch's disillusionment as follows: "In Kalmanovitch's view, what happened was not merely the 'conquest of culture by politics' but the Yiddishist intelligentsia's complicity in the diminution of its own dream of a new Jewish culture."[107]

Kalmanovitch's hatred of Soviet Yiddish culture led not only to his dream of escaping Soviet territory but also to growing despair about the future of Yiddish culture throughout the world. In 1921, after having left the Soviet Union, Kalmanovitch confided to Niger his fear that Yiddish culture in all of Europe would fall under the sway of the Soviets. According to Kalmanovitch's assessment, no Yiddishist, neither in the Soviet Union nor elsewhere, had exposed what he considered the false propaganda regarding a Yiddish cultural renaissance in the Soviet Union. Kalmanovitch extended his pessimism to Yiddish culture in independent Lithuania, Poland, and even to his beloved Vilna. Kalmanovitch arrived at a historical schema in which Yiddish culture had followed its working-class carriers into the Communist camp, where the two both lost their identities. As the political parties that represented the Jewish working class drew closer and then merged with the Communists, Kalmanovitch, a nationalist to the core, thus recognized the ultimate incompatibility between an allegiance to Moscow and the continued separate existence of a Jewish working class—the potential civil society that would receive and mold Yiddish culture.[108]

In the spring of 1920, Kalmanovitch even dreamed of abandoning Eastern Europe altogether by settling in America. His wife's pregnancy and his resistance to leaving the Old Country (di alte heym) prevented him from acting on this desire. Still, in the fall of 1920, he joined a group of Yiddishist autonomists, including Tcherikower, in leaving Kiev. Because of fear of the Soviet authorities, these intellectuals and their families decided to spend the winter in Bobruysk and Minsk. Nearly penniless in Bobruysk, Kalmanovitch supported himself through lectures to the Minsk Teachers' Seminary regarding Yiddish grammar and on its proper instruction in Yiddish schools. This Soviet-sponsored institution then published these lectures, together with an introduction by Kalmanovitch, in the phoneticized Soviet Yiddish orthography that he so despised. Finally, in the spring of 1921, the destitute Kalmanovitch family made its way to Kaunas. Initially pessimistic about prospects for Jewish national autonomy in Lithuania, Kalmanovitch hoped to proceed to Berlin to work for the Folks-Farlag. Only after he found work more easily in Kaunas than he expected to in Berlin did he decide to stay in Lithuania and to fight for the creation of a national Yiddish culture there.[109]

Russian Jewry reacted to the dramatic events of 1917 with messianic fervor. Dubnov captured the pulse of many Russian Jews, secularizing though still steeped in tradition, when he argued that they interpreted World War I as the apocalyptic war of Gog and Magog and the events of 1917 as its messianic culmination.[110] As Russia descended into Bolshevik terror, anarchy, civil war, and pogroms, this messianic fervor proved short-lived for most Russian Jews. The socialist national-ist Russian Jewish intelligentsia, however, remained so invested in the events of 1917 that they refused to allow the messianic fervor to die even as reality often contradicted their dreams. These "true believers" in the potential of the revolution acted in a similar way to the minor-ity of faithful followers of Sabbatai Ṣevi who continued to believe in him as the messiah even following his conversion in 1666.[111]

In his classic work, *Prophecy and Politics,* Jonathan Frankel de-scribed the various socialist and nationalist movements that emerged in Eastern Europe at the end of the nineteenth century as examples of secular messianism. Consequently, he understood the ideological fer-vor that gripped Jewish socialists and nationalists following 1881 as a continuation of the tradition of Jewish messianic movements that punctuated all of Jewish history. According to Frankel, the fact that most of Russian Jewry passed directly from a traditional religious identity to that of a secularizing national group, without a prolonged intermediary stage of acculturation and assimilation, explained this leap from a passive religious to an active secular messianism.[112] Whereas Central and West European Jewries experienced several gen-erations of emancipationist and integrationist ideology before turning to Jewish nationalism, Russian Jewish intellectuals, Zionist, Diaspora nationalist, and socialist alike, moved from Jewish traditionalism to integrationism to nationalism and Jewish radicalism all in the con-densed span of ten to twenty years. Consequently, when they em-braced a Jewish national identity, these intellectuals could rely on a deep familiarity with Jewish traditional texts for inspiration.

Several conclusions emerge from Frankel's thesis. First, it was the secularism of these intellectuals that unleashed the messianic poten-tial that had long lain dormant in the religious tradition. Traditional religious Jews subscribed to a passive theology, waiting for God to bring the redemption at the end of days. Secularizing national Jews rejected this theology even as they continued to believe in the unique historical destiny of the Jewish people. This combination of contin-ued deep-rootedness in the tradition and estrangement from its God-centeredness released the messianic fervor of these first and second generations of Jewish radicals and nationalists. Second, the secular nature of this messianism removed the messianic ideal from a distant supernatural future and sought its attainment in the present. Zionists, Diaspora nationalists, and socialists all worked tirelessly for the imminent redemption, though they differed with one another as to its place and nature.

When the February Revolution arrived, Jewish nationalists and socialists of all stripes believed that the era of redemption had dawned. Unlike their traditional counterparts, they understood their newfound freedom not as the product of divine intervention, but rather as the culmination of their years of struggle.[113] Precisely for this reason, members of this elite persisted in their messianism even as reality contradicted it. When the Bolshevik Revolution ended the dreams of the vast majority of this intelligentsia for a democratic, parliamentary Russia in which Jews would enjoy autonomy, few of them completely despaired. As we have seen, many members of the Bund and the Fareynikte initially remained optimistic that the Soviet regime would support their vision of the creation of a new proletarian, but still thoroughly national, Jewish identity. By joining the Evsektsiia, some of these intellectuals hoped to realize their dream of the transformation of the Jewish people into a secular, proletarian, Yiddish nation through the decrees of the Soviet state. When the Bolsheviks repressed Zionist and Hebraist activities, Russian Zionists, now buoyed by the diplomatic coup of the Balfour Declaration, transferred the messianic euphoria of 1917 to the political and cultural life of the *Yishuv*.

Although the Bolshevik Revolution dealt their dreams of national autonomy a severe blow, Diaspora nationalists and Yiddishists such as Tcherikower, Efroikin, and Kalmanovitch also refused to succumb to despair. Even as they consciously recognized that Bolshevism and the disintegration of the Russian Empire doomed their autonomist dream, they attempted to salvage it by switching its implementation to the Ukraine or the international arena. Their pursuit of a Yiddish-language-based national autonomy in the Ukraine, the successor states, and then in the international arena stemmed, of course, from practical considerations in addition to utopianism. Simon Rabinovitch has argued that in the politically contentious environment of revolutionary Russia prior to Bolshevization, autonomism emerged as one of the few political ideologies and platforms that united almost all Jewish parties. The very creation of an All-Russian Jewish Congress and a democratic Petrograd *kehile* demonstrated that Russian Jewry viewed itself as an extraterritorial nation in need of autonomy. In elections to the congress, the *kehile,* and to the All-Russian Constituent Assembly, Russian Jews granted a mandate to those national parties that demanded maximal Jewish national autonomy. The fact that the Zionists rather than the Folkspartey, which remained a marginal party of intellectuals, emerged as the leaders of these demands, did not dampen the folkists' sense of success.[114]

Even though the Bolshevik Revolution dealt the autonomist dream a mortal blow in its native Russia, Tcherikower, Efroikin, and Kalmanovitch had reason to believe that its popularity among Jews, no less than governmental promises, would lead to its success in the Ukraine and Lithuania. Still, as reality demonstrated that their dreams could not survive the disintegration of the multinational Russian Empire into nationalizing nation states, these men's ideological persistence assumed a level of utopianism. All three men were convinced that the revolution had inaugurated an era in which the Jews would be born anew as a proud, secular nation that could contribute to the world's moral regeneration. In this regard, they interpreted the revolutionary period and its aftermath as a prolonged messianic experience.

CHAPTER FOUR

At the Crossroads

W ITH THE FOLLOWING WORDS, Tcherikower and Efroikin introduced their new journal, *Oyfn sheydveg:*

The entire surrounding world stands now at the crossroads, lives in great
unrest, and is undergoing a deep sociopolitical and ideological crisis. The
world will one way or another emerge from the crisis. However, we Jews,
if we will not find true support, a path, new strength in ourselves in order
to further preserve our survival as a people, we can be crushed under the
wheels of history. We live in a time of the painful liquidation of the age of
emancipation with its humanitarian and democratic principles. We are
becoming transformed into a people of refugees. . . .

There is no wise man like the tested man. From our bitter trials we must
learn. And above all we must set ourselves honestly and seriously to revise
our old ideological baggage and to leave only that which can help maintain the fallen Jewish mood and to revive the frozen national energy—a
revision not merely for the sake of criticism but rather in order to find
new methods for the fight for Jewish existence. Searching such paths—
that is the goal of our publication.[1]

By April 1939, when the first issue of this journal appeared, all of
the political and cultural ideologies that Tcherikower, Efroikin, and
Kalmanovitch embraced had proven themselves unable to alter the
frightful plight of a European Jewry caught in Nazi Germany's ever-
widening net. In the final months before the advent of World War II,

these three men abandoned the last vestiges of their faith in Diaspora nationalism and Yiddishism. Central to both these ideologies was a belief in the ability to synthesize European and Jewish politics and culture. The failure of the successor states to implement Jewish national autonomy during the interwar period weakened this belief. The *Anschluss*, the Munich Pact, and the Evian Conference of 1938 shattered this hope inalterably. In the aftermath of these events, Tcherikower and Efroikin, like most of the contributors to the journal, understood their generation as living "at the crossroads" *(oyfn sheydveg)* between eras of emancipation and the repeal of emancipation, which they labeled counter-emancipation. They, moreover, conceived of their journal as an organ to create an ideology of Jewish survival for a new age in which the fate of the Jewish people and European civilization no longer converged. Abandoned by Europe, the Jews had to shift their gaze inward if they were to survive.

By then a wealthy businessman, Efroikin donated a huge sum of money for the publication of the journal and then invited Tcherikower to join him as editor. When creating their journal, Tcherikower and Efroikin invited many Jewish intellectuals, Yiddish-writing and otherwise, to contribute essays. The German-writing Jewish intellectuals Max Brod and Stefan Zweig, for instance, both contributed articles addressing the question of whether Jews should involve themselves in European politics.[2] However, most of the contributors to this journal emerged from the ranks of current and former Diaspora nationalists and Yiddishists. Many of the contributors, such as Latski-Bertoldi and Niger, were former members of the Russian Folkspartey who had collaborated politically and culturally with Tcherikower, Efroikin, and Kalmanovitch since the days of the publication of *Di yudishe velt* during the years of Russian reaction. Significantly, most of these men, with the exception of Kalmanovitch, had followed Tcherikower and Efroikin's path in leaving Eastern Europe following the victory of the Soviets in the Russian Civil War.

The following argument emerges from the essays of the contributors to the journal: The entire European world, both the Fascist regimes and the democracies, have abandoned the Jews. Without support, the Jews should instead retreat from politics and turn inward to strengthen their cultural life. One hundred and fifty years of the Jews' attempts at assimilation into a European society that would ultimately betray them had significantly depleted the reserve of strength needed to cope with the Nazi onslaught. Collapsing all of modern Jewish history, these writers blamed emancipation and Haskalah as the cause of this degeneration. Emancipation had led to a selfish individualism that condemned all experiments at secular Jewish identity to failure. In contrast to the Jews of the modern age, those living before the emancipation had lived exemplary communal lives, sacrificing for the common good and providing religious meaning in their lives. Indeed, the official end of emancipation could paradoxically free the Jews to return to the internal sources of their strength. Some, like Tcherikower, even joined other Yiddishist intellectuals in calling for a return to the ghetto.

It is only within the context of the failed political and cultural experiments of the interwar era as well as the crisis of Nazism in the 1930s that we can understand the ideological revision expressed in the pages of *Oyfn sheydveg*. We thus turn to a brief overview of the political and cultural careers of Tcherikower, Efroikin, and Kalmanovitch during the interwar era.

The Interwar Period

Throughout the interwar era, Tcherikower, Efroikin, and Kalmanovitch continued to attempt to implement Diaspora nationalism, now outside of Russia. At the end of the Russian Civil War, Tcherikower and Efroikin abandoned Eastern Europe permanently, settling, respectively, in Berlin and Paris. Kalmanovitch, on the other hand, remained in Eastern Europe, living in the successor states of Lithuania, Latvia, and Poland. In both cases, however, these men had to come to terms with the loss of Russia as the arena for the implementation of their political and cultural ideologies.

For Tcherikower and Efroikin, they did so by seeking to implement their Diaspora nationalist vision on the international arena. In the 1920s, both men became involved in Emigdirekt, an immigrant aid organization that understood emigration as a collective Jewish national concern. In its refusal to send emigrants only to Palestine and its insistence on serving all sectors of the Jewish economy, not only the workers, Emigdirekt sought to implement Diaspora nationalist emigration plans.[3] Tcherikower served as the secretary of Emigdirekt, and Efroikin regularly attended its meetings as a representative from France. During the 1920s in Paris, Efroikin forged connections with South American government embassy officials and with ship companies in his efforts to direct the emigration of Jewish refugees to areas in the New World where they were likely to succeed economically. Eventually, these connections led to the founding of his own travel agency, Oceana. Efroikin used his newfound wealth to become a patron of Yiddish culture and to involve himself in communal leadership. After Sholem Schwartzbard assassinated Semon Petliura in retaliation for his alleged leading role in the wave of pogroms perpetrated by Ukrainian forces under his control during the Russian Civil War, Tcherikower became involved in Schwartzbard's defense. During the trial, which lasted from 1926 through 1927 and ended in an acquittal, Tcherikower provided Schwartzbard's lawyers with documentation from his pogrom archive of the atrocities committed by Petliura's forces. Because of his wealth and his communal involvement, Efroikin also served as a member of Schwartzbard's defense committee.[4]

During the 1930s, Tcherikower and Efroikin continued their attempt at the international implementation of Diaspora nationalism through their participation in the World Jewish Congress movement. By this point, however, this attempt at national consolidation occurred in the shadow of the rise of Nazi Germany and its increasing persecution of German Jewry. Tcherikower and Efroikin brought with them the same goals to the World Jewish Congress movement as they had to earlier political projects: the mobilization of the worldwide Jewish people against anti-Semitism, the purposeful organization of the Jewish economy, and the control of Jewish emigration. In pursuing these goals, they had to concede to the fact that it was the Zionists who led the congress movement and who championed their vision of Jewish national unity. Under this influence as well as the specter of Nazism, Tcherikower and Efroikin began to despair of Diaspora politics as fraught with dissension and internal weakness. As such, at least unconsciously, they moved closer to Zionism.[5]

Between 1932 and 1936, Efroikin sought to implement his Diaspora nationalist vision as the president of the Federation of Jewish

Societies, the non-socialist, non-Zionist organization of East European Jewish immigrants in Paris. As its head, Efroikin sought to implement many of the goals of the Russian Folkspartey, now on a local level. Under the federation banner, he organized a system of secular afternoon Yiddish schools and even sought to unify the native French Jewish and the East European immigrant communities through the creation of a Parisian *kehile*. This plan failed, largely because of the apathy of the native French Jews and the internal division among the East European immigrants between leftists and nationalists. As his autonomist vision failed, Efroikin found himself increasingly attracted to socialist Zionism, the movement that he had rejected in his youth. Following the Zionist Congress in Lucerne, Switzerland in 1935, Efroikin told leaders of Poale Zion that although he originally had disparaged their party as "too bourgeois," he now realized that their actions had proven them "the true radicals."[6]

In response to this ideological transformation as well as to the increasingly anti-Semitic environment of the 1930s, Efroikin despaired of Jewish involvement in general politics. A firm believer of Jewish involvement in political struggle in late tsarist Russia, Efroikin now argued that Jews should comport themselves as they had done in the Middle Ages—by involving themselves solely in their own internal affairs. In 1938, Efroikin visited Palestine and returned to Paris an admirer and supporter of the Labor Zionist leadership of the *Yishuv*.[7]

During the interwar era, Kalmanovitch's political path deviated from that of Tcherikower and Efroikin. In 1921, when they headed west, he escaped from the Soviet Union to the successor state of Lithuania. In an effort to win Jewish support for its fledgling state as well as for its bid for control of the contested city of Vilna, the Lithuanian government initially offered the Jews broad, sweeping Jewish national autonomy. Between 1921 and 1925, Lithuanian Jewry possessed a Ministry of Jewish Affairs, a National Parliament, and democratically elected *kehiles*. The internal divisions among Lithuanian Jews, divided between Zionist-Hebraists, autonomist-Yiddishists, leftist Yiddishists, and the Orthodox, severely impeded the implementation of Jewish national autonomy. Within this fractious environment, Kalmanovitch forcefully made the case for the autonomist Yiddishists, who sought to use government funds to create a unified Jewish school system with Yiddish as the language of instruction. In his battle with Hebraists, the Orthodox, and internationalist Yiddishists, Kalmanovitch championed the de-parochialization of Yiddish culture, arguing against a set Jewish content for the curriculum of the school system. At the same time, however, he believed, as he had before World War I, in the redemptive religious potential of Yiddish culture, in whose name the stifling rituals of the religious tradition needed to be overcome. When the Lithuanian government shut down its institutions of national autonomy in 1925, Kalmanovitch left for nearby Latvia, which still offered its Jewish population autonomy. There he edited a Yiddishist folkist newspaper, *Di letste nays*. In Latvia, however, with its mixture of Russian-speaking, German-speaking, and Yiddish-speaking Jews, his ideology of Yiddishist autonomism proved even more ill-suited than in Lithuania. When the newspaper failed, Kalmanovitch left Riga for Lithuania, where he eked out a living as a teacher, ironically in a Hebrew-speaking Tarbut school.[8]

Despite these political failures, all three men experienced success in their cultural dream of creating an institution of higher Yiddish learning, YIVO. The brainchild of Nokhem Shtif, YIVO was created in Berlin in 1925. From the beginning, Tcherikower served as one of its founders and as the head of its historical division. Efroikin supported YIVO financially. Having moved to Vilna soon after its founding, YIVO invited Kalmanovitch in 1929 to serve as one of its administrators and as a leader of its philological section. YIVO represented the implementation of the Diaspora nationalist, Yiddishist dream in the absence of government support. Recently, Cecile Kuznitz has demonstrated how, to Yiddishists, YIVO became the national academy of the stateless Yiddish-speaking nation. From the distance of Berlin, Tcherikower oversaw the various studies of the historical section and edited its journal, *Historishe shriftn* (Historical writings). Having moved to Vilna, Kalmanovitch involved himself in all the details of the running of the institution. After his flight to Paris following the Nazi rise to power, Tcherikower still maintained faith that YIVO would sustain the Jews culturally and spiritually during dark times.[9]

Kalmanovitch, however, entertained deep doubts about the viability of Yiddish culture. In 1931, he published a major essay in which he analyzed the phenomenon of the seeming success of antinationalist Soviet Yiddish culture. Deeply perturbed by Shtif's defection to the Soviet Union, Kalmanovitch came to the extreme conclusion that Soviet Yiddishists forced Jewish students to attend their antinationalist, antireligious, anti-Hebraist schools in order to more quickly murder the next generation's connection to the Yiddish language. Soviet Yiddishists, argued Kalmanovitch, sought to eradicate the *loshn koydesh* (Hebrew-Aramaic) component of the language so as to more quickly kill the language and pave the way for Soviet Jewry's Russification. In this article, Kalmanovitch rejected the long-held Yiddishist assumption that East European Jews loved their language. Instead, he began to envision Jews as filled with self-hatred and a penchant toward national self-destruction. Jewish linguistic acculturation in Poland and in the other successor states only increased this conviction. Following Hitler's rise to power, Kalmanovitch abandoned Diaspora nationalism in favor of territorialism. In particular, he joined Frayland, the territorialist organization founded by I. N. Steinberg that sought to settle East European Jews in a territory other than Palestine. Not threatened by linguistic acculturation, the Jews in this territory, envisioned Kalmanovitch, would create the kind of Yiddish culture that had eluded them in the Diaspora.[10]

By the late 1930s, all three men thus had largely despaired of the ideologies to which they had dedicated most of their careers. The crisis of 1938, with the Munich Pact, the *Anschluss,* and *Kristallnacht,* transformed this ideological despair into a commitment to ideological revision. It is to this political crisis, the culmination of a half decade of increasing extrusion of the Jews from the European body politic, that we now turn.

The Political Plight of European Jewry in the 1930s

By April 1939, when the first issue of *Oyfn sheydveg* appeared, all the political ideologies of European Jewry had revealed their ineffectiveness. To integrationists, the 1930s could not have proven more devastating. The Nuremberg Laws, passed in 1935, exemplified the Nazi assault on the gains of emancipation by banning Jews from German universities and from the medical profession, by legislating the expropriation of Jewish property, and prohibiting intermarriage between Jews and Aryans. In March 1938, Hitler's troops invaded Austria, bringing its Jews under Nazi rule. On the night of November 8 - 9, 1938, the Nazi SA (*Sturmabteiling*—storm detachment) murdered thirty-six Jews, deported tens of thousands to concentration camps, and destroyed Jewish property in supposed retaliation for the assassination of a German diplomat by a Polish Jew, Hershel Grynspan, in Paris.[11]

If the fate of German Jewry in the 1930s revealed the bankruptcy of integrationism, then events in Poland and the Baltic states pointed to the final collapse of the dream of Diaspora nationalism. In 1919, Poland had reluctantly signed the Minorities' Treaty, which promised the Jews government funding for Jewish schools and exemption from work on the Sabbath. From the beginning, however, the Polish Republic indicated its refusal to abide by this agreement, consolidating instead ethnic Polish political, economic, and cultural hegemony to the detriment of other ethnic minorities. Plagued by economic depression in the mid-1930s, all elements of Polish society turned on the Jews, with pogroms erupting in small towns. Universities introduced a system of "ghetto benches," in which Jewish students had to sit segregated from other students. By the late 1930s, the far right manifested its enamorment with Nazi treatment of the Jews. The government tacitly supported economic boycotts against the Jews that led to the growing pauperization of the Jewish population. Although later amended, the Sejm's prohibition of *shehitah* (ritual slaughter) in 1936 demonstrated the absurdity of the dream of national autonomy in a country that even sought to repudiate the religious freedom that served as a foundation of emancipation. The ban on *shehitah* also proved a blow to the accommodationist Agudas Yisroel, the anti-Zionist, anti-Bundist Orthodox political party, which had believed that if only Jews would profess allegiance to the Polish government and not meddle in Polish affairs, they would receive religious freedom.[12]

The failure of the "new Jewish politics," which called for assertions of national pride to replace traditional Jewish appeasement policies, revealed Jewish political powerlessness in interwar Poland. Without practical success, the various adherents of Jewish political ideologies could only fight among themselves, with the growth of extremes on the political spectrum: the Bund, the illegal Polish Communist Party, and revisionist Zionism all gained adherents because of the varied radical solutions that they offered for the present crisis. Throughout the 1930s, Lithuanian and Latvian Jewry experienced a similar process of extrusion. Following the collapse of Jewish national autonomy in the mid-1920s, Lithuanian Jews found themselves excluded more and more from government positions. In the late 1930s, Lithuanian students introduced ghetto benches for Jews in universities, learning from their Polish neighbors to the south. In Latvia, the semi-Fascist regime that assumed power in 1934 eliminated Jews from the civil service as well as from other public areas of life.[13]

Proponents of Jewish national autonomy could claim only slightly greater success in the area of culture. Even as interwar Poland could boast of TsISHO and Tarbut, the impressive Yiddish- and Hebrew-language school systems, more children attended the religious schools of Agudas Yisroel than these two secular school networks combined. The fact that 60 percent of Jewish students studied in Polish state schools, moreover, contributed to a process of linguistic acculturation of Polish Jewish youth in the interwar period. Despite anti-Semitism and the nationalist leanings of Jewish youth, Polonization thus made dramatic inroads, especially in Congress Poland and Galicia. The ultimate dream of autonomists—universal education of the youth in secular, Yiddish-language schools—thus failed to materialize in interwar Poland. The concomitant processes of secularization and Polonization undergone by what many called "a generation without a future" help explain the popularity of the youth movements in interwar Poland. An increase in suicides among Polish Jews reveals that many, alienated from both Jewish tradition and Polish society, succumbed to despair. In Lithuania and Latvia, TsISHO and Tarbut fared better than in Poland. However, only in small Latvia did more Jewish students attend Yiddish than Hebrew schools.[14]

Thinking of interwar Polish Jewry when forming their ideology, the contributors to *Oyfn sheydveg* recognized all the attributes that they bemoaned: political contentiousness despite powerlessness, acculturation despite anti-Semitism, and despair, rather than rejuvenation, accompanying the process of secularization. Despite this bleak assessment, in reality, the modernization of Polish Jewry led most often to nationalism and limited acculturation. Still, these contributors' language-based nationalism nonetheless led them to misinterpret the statistics on linguistic Polonization as evidence of a process of assimilation similar to that which had allegedly occurred in Western Europe. Although Lithuanian and Latvian Jewry acculturated to a lesser extent than did Jews in Poland, contributors to *Oyfn sheydveg* such as Kalmanovitch had firsthand experience with the internal and external failures of Diaspora nationalism and Yiddishism in these small successor states.

The contributors to *Oyfn sheydveg* could take even less comfort in the fate of Yiddish culture in the Soviet Union. Even in the 1920s, nationalist Yiddishists such as Tcherikower and Kalmanovitch had frowned on Soviet Yiddish culture's lack of Jewish content, a reality that reflected the official ideology of socialist content and national form. Indeed, the 1920s and 1930s witnessed a process of voluntary Jewish Russification, with young Jews abandoning Yiddish language and culture in exchange for unprecedented opportunities for educational and career advancement in Russian society. By 1939, the intermarriage rate of Soviet Jews had risen to nearly 30 percent, with 55 percent of Russian Jews declaring Russian as their mother tongue. The Stalinist purges combined with Russian Jewish acculturation had significantly weakened Yiddish culture in the Soviet Union even as the dream of establishing a Jewish autonomist region in Birobidzhan ended in failure.[15]

Nor could the Jews turn toward the Western democracies for support. The policy of appeasement pursued by the Western democracies in the late 1930s sacrificed Jewish refugees and brought Zionism to its nadir. In the aftermath of the Arab Riots of 1936, the British, in hope of Arab support, declared their promise of the Balfour Declaration fulfilled. The White Paper of May 1939 locked the doors of Palestine to the majority of European Jews by limiting immigration to fifteen thousand Jews per year until 1944, when it would cease completely. At that time, the British mandate would end, to be replaced by an Arab state in Palestine. All Jewish attempts to legally reverse the effects of the White Paper proved futile. The Evian Conference, convened on July 6, 1938, at President Franklin Roosevelt's orders, revealed the

Western democracies' unwillingness to alleviate the plight of European Jewry. Despite their purported humanitarian aims, all delegations arrived at the conference with instructions from their governments not to ease immigration restrictions in their countries. Unwilling to criticize Nazi Germany, the Evian Conference thus symbolized a repudiation of Jewish emancipation, with all parties tacitly approving Jewish political powerlessness. A further capitulation of the democracies came in early October 1938 with the Munich Pact, in which England promised not to attack Germany for its invasion of Czechoslovakia in exchange for a promise of no further expansion. In the democracies' realpolitik, designed to avoid war at all costs, no consideration remained for the hapless Jews caught in Hitler's ever-widening net.[16]

With the Jews never as powerless in modern times as in the late 1930s, it seemed that the end of the emancipation era indeed had arrived. The fact that this repeal of emancipation coincided with the 150th anniversary of the Declaration of the Rights of Man made matters all the more poignant. In the meantime, all the ideologies advanced to ameliorate the plight of European Jews had failed miserably. The time thus proved ripe for the appearance of a journal such as *Oyfn sheydveg,* which sought to forge a new Jewish politics and culture to accommodate the conditions of counter-emancipation. Having themselves once participated in the "new Jewish politics" in Eastern Europe, these intellectuals emerged as natural candidates to assume this task.

The Rhetoric of Return to the Ghetto, 1938

Oyfn sheydveg emerged as the most dramatic expression of a transnational ideological revision that had begun among Yiddishist intellectuals during the stormy events of 1938. At that time, several leading Yiddish writers both in New York and Paris expressed a desire to "return to the ghetto," as a metaphor for their desire for an inward retreat and for feelings of betrayal toward European civilization. In April 1938, following the *Anschluss,* the New York–based Yiddish poet Jacob Glatstein published what was destined to become his most famous and controversial poem, "A gute nakht, velt" (Good night, world), in which he expressed his disgust with Western civilization. Writing that he would willingly return to the ghetto with its yellow stars, traditional garb, and Talmudic singsong, Glatstein employed these images as a metaphor for a retreat from the modern world that had betrayed the Jews. A month later, Glatstein published an essay in which he argued against the opinion that cultural isolation in a forced ghetto would weaken Jewish creativity. Rather, Glatstein argued that Yiddish literature itself served as the product of a cultural ghetto.[17]

Other American Yiddish and Hebrew writers soon joined Glatstein in his call for a return to the ghetto. The researcher Shmuel Feigin and the former socialist-turned-religious-penitent Chaim Lieberman used the term "ghetto" to signify a Jewish retreat from politics and a return to the internal sources of Jewish creativity. Jews, they argued, now had to recover the spiritual strength that had sustained them throughout the Middle Ages. In this retreat from the outside world, Feigin criticized the Jewish community for its faults, whereas Lieberman hurled invectives at the non-Jewish world for its immorality and violence. Other Yiddishist intellectuals, such as H. Leivick, Yoysef Opatoshu, and Niger, rejected this call for retreat, agreeing that Jews should return to their internal cultural resources but maintaining that they should continue to link their fate to that of all humanity.[18]

In July 1938, talk of a return to the ghetto manifested itself in the Yiddish press in Paris, with different Yiddish writers understanding this concept differently. For instance, in the daily *Parizer haynt,* the Zionist writer A. M. Fuchs argued that the Jewish people had proven willing to sacrifice its own identity in order to provide Europe with humanism. This sacrifice, however, had proven a *"brokhe levatole,"* a blessing in vain, since Germany had destroyed this humanistic culture in less than twenty-four hours. The Jews, he argued, needed to create their own national humanism that would benefit themselves and not just an unreceptive outside world.[19] The French Yiddish journalist A. Kremer agreed with the call "back to the ghetto," defining it as follows: "Let us sincerely take a look at where we stand in the world; let us see if we should engage ourselves upon other paths than those which we have traveled until now."[20]

On December 18, 1938, East European Jewish emigrés gathered in the Paris Alboius Theater to listen to the leading intellectuals of their community debate the issue of Jewish retreat into the ghetto. The participants included Tcherikower and Efroikin. Among the other participants were future *Oyfn sheydveg* contributors Avrom Menes and Aaron Steinberg.[21] Tcherikower began his address with a review of the recent literature that spoke of a return to the ghetto. Despite popular belief, explained Tcherikower, Jews first chose to live in ghettos, and only later did the authorities impose these living quarters upon the Jews. Even in America and France, he argued, many Jews still lived voluntarily in compact masses in ghettos. Because he understood all Jewish creation as stemming from the ghetto, Tcherikower interpreted the call to return to the ghetto not as a desire to lock Jews out of the world but rather as "a feeling of returning to oneself, to strengthen the national discipline." He welcomed this call to ideological revision as an appropriate response to the shocking events of 1938. This inner turmoil hopefully would transform itself into "a new national revival, a new path, which we must search."[22]

Efroikin, similarly, embraced the call of return to the ghetto by calling upon Jews to live among themselves and not act as missionaries to the rest of the world. Rejecting a universalism that "sees only the distant and overlooks the close," Efroikin argued that the Jews could redeem the world only after first redeeming themselves. Stating that he rejected passivity, Efroikin argued that the Jews should rebuild their lives, not waiting for the kindness of others. He also stated that he believed that the Jews needed their own land, which he identified as "the land of Israel." Still, he called on Jews throughout the Diaspora to reject assimilation and to live a Jewish life. On the eve of World War II, Efroikin thus embraced the very ideology of cultural consolidation coupled with political retreat that he had rejected during the years of tsarist reaction. Whereas in the late Russian period Efroikin raged against those who persisted in the mentality of the ghetto Jew, now he embraced the call to return to the ghetto as "a feeling of coming to oneself." Perhaps even more significantly, influenced by his recent trip to Palestine, Efroikin now undermined his Diaspora nationalism by referring to Palestine as the site of a future Jewish national home.[23]

Historical context provides insight into why Paris emerged as a center of this ideological crisis. In the eyes of *klal yisroel* nationalists such as Tcherikower and Efroikin, Paris served as a paradigm for a Jewish community too dedicated to its individual interests to demonstrate much concern for refugees from Nazi-occupied lands. Indeed, the representative organizations of the native French Jewish community served as models for these Diaspora nationalists' depiction of a plutocratic assimilationist Jewish leadership concerned only with its own interests. The Central Consistory of the Jews of France and the Alliance Israélite Universelle, the two leading organizations of native French Jewry, for instance, blamed the rise of right-wing French anti-Semitism on the political activity of East European Jews. Consequently, these organizations refused to lobby on behalf of Jewish refugees, and avoided condemning the Nuremberg Laws in language that the French might deem too particularistic.

With French rightists accusing Jews of warmongering in the aftermath of the signing of the Munich Pact, Julien Weill, chief rabbi of Paris, stated that he stood unwilling to make "the least contribution" to the rescue of German Jewry, since such a move would prove contrary to French foreign policy.[24] Viewing Grynspan's assassination of Ernst von Rath at the German embassy in Paris as a provocation, representatives of native French Jewry published a letter addressed to von Rath's mother expressing their sorrow for the murder of this Nazi secretary.[25] The editors of *Oyfn sheydveg* thus found themselves confronted with a French emancipationist ideology transformed into what they deemed a caricature of itself. Tcherikower and Efroikin's criticism of the selfishness of Jewish communities in democratic lands, and their call for an internal consolidation, moreover, came in the aftermath of a failed attempt by immigrant groups to unify the Paris Jewish community into a *kehile* system.[26] When this plan failed, *Oyfn sheydveg* functioned as an attempt to achieve the same goal from a purely cultural perspective.

The reality of native French Jewish opinion was only slightly more nuanced than the editors of *Oyfn sheydveg* believed. From 1933 through 1939, most French Jewish publicists emphasized the French legacy of emancipation, oftentimes ignoring the contested nature of this historical process in French circles. Most often, native French Jewish journalists and intellectuals comforted themselves by arguing that the repudiation of Jewish emancipation to their east owed itself to the nature of the German people and to unique historical circumstances in Germany. Such an essentialist argument inoculated these French Jews against the fear that the extrusion of the Jews occurring in Germany could repeat itself in France. In addition, native French Jews emphasized Jewish rootedness in France, minimizing or ignoring the impact of the fourteenth-century expulsions. In 1939, on the 150th anniversary of the French Revolution, leading French Jewish publicists continued to emphasize the commitment of the French people to Jewish equality as part of the sacred union, contrasting French civilization with German barbarity. Still, some native French Jewish intellectuals called for a deepening of Jewish collective ties, criticizing the individualistic excesses of emancipation. The Paris Yiddish press, in contrast, approached current events from a more pan-European perspective than its French equivalent. Although it carried articles from those calling for retreat into the ghetto, the French Yiddish press also revealed the extent to which East European Jewish immigrants to France had imbibed the native French Jewish community's belief in French exceptionalism as a bastion of liberty.[27]

In the French Jewish press, it was only a small group of young native French Jews and the children of immigrants who reacted critically to this persistence of emancipationist ideology. In the pages of the newspaper *Samedi,* these young French Jews criticized both the French government and native French Jewish leadership for their disdain of Jewish refugees. *Samedi* writers also pointed to the divergence between Jewish and French interests in regard to a policy of appeasement and understood the Germans as having willingly embraced Nazism rather than having suffered its imposition from above. A group of young, native French Jewish intellectuals called for an even bolder revision of their community's assimilationist leadership in their weekly journal *Affirmation,* which first appeared in January 1939, two months before the appearance of *Oyfn sheydveg.* These intellectuals, like their Yiddishist counterparts, responded to the rise of Hitlerism and French anti-Semitism by disentangling the connection between French liberal values and Judaism and by arguing that the Jews could rely only on themselves. Beyond calling for Jewish pride and unity, the contributors to *Affirmation* offered little concrete advice.[28]

The appearance of *Affirmation* just two months before *Oyfn sheydveg* reveals the unique prism through which Tcherikower, Efroikin, and Kalmanovitch understood their creation of a counter-emancipationist ideology. While perhaps not directly influenced by opinions stated in *Affirmation*, the editors of *Oyfn sheydveg* did take note of this journal, as evidenced by the inclusion of its review by Jacques Jefroykin, Efroikin's nephew. Arguing that the *Affirmation* contributors who had abandoned assimilation in response to Nazism proved too ignorant of Judaism to propose anything else except Jewish pride, this review emphasized the positive, if not condescending, reception that Yiddishist intellectuals accorded this French Jewish journal. Unlike these French-writing intellectuals, argued Jefroykin, Yiddishist intellectuals should "connect [themselves] with the spiritual values that we have to protect" rather than merely uniting against a common enemy.[29]

Like the writers in *Affirmation*, the contributors to *Oyfn sheydveg* felt compelled to react to what they considered the perfidy of the assimilationist leaders of native French Jewry. At the same time, however, because these Yiddishists had witnessed the failure of their dream of the creation of a secular Jewish identity, they also turned to the traditional Judaism of their pre-radical youths in order to discover the values that would inform their new conservative ideology of national consolidation. This difference in perspective also led contributors to *Affirmation* to champion self-defense even as *Oyfn sheydveg* contributors disparaged it. Whereas *Affirmation* writers embraced an activist policy as a natural component of their rebellion against their parents' emancipationist ideology, the contributors to *Oyfn sheydveg* already had participated in revolutionary activity in their youths and had despaired of it. No other political policy remained for Tcherikower, Efroikin, and Kalmanovitch except for retreat. This despair of politics ironically led these intellectuals to embrace the same type of quietism as that endorsed by the emancipationists in the name of political accommodation.

Retreat from Politics

Throughout the articles of *Oyfn sheydveg*, the opinion prevailed that Nazism functioned as an enduring rather than as a passing phenomenon. In his article "Di tragediye fun a shvakhn dor" (The tragedy of a weak generation), Tcherikower called for ideological revision by arguing that the tragedies that had befallen the Jewish people in the six years since Hitler's rise warranted a questioning in the belief in democracies and rationalism.[30] In his article "Vu haltn mir in der hayntiker velt?" (Where do we stand in the contemporary world?), Efroikin similarly rejected the assessment that Hitler and Mussolini imposed Fascism upon unwilling populations. If whole societies chose the leadership of boors and rogues, then "such can happen only in a human society that was morally sick and that didn't have the spiritual strength to fight the noxious microbes that sucked out their marrow and souls."[31]

In the wake of the Evian Conference, these writers cautioned against relying on the democratic lands and on the socialist parties for redemption. Understanding the difference between democratic and Fascist regimes as one of degree rather than kind, Efroikin cautioned against relying on the democracies for support. Efroikin understood the Munich Pact as the democracies' "capitulation to robbers." This pursuit of realpolitik had led to the democracies' refusal to provide refuge to persecuted Jews and to England's support of the Arabs in their attempt to block Jewish emigration to Palestine. Socialism, moreover, revealed its moral bankruptcy when members of German and Italian socialist parties proved willing to abdicate their ideology's long-term goal of international brotherhood for the short-term economic prosperity that Fascism offered. According to Kalmanovitch, the democracies could save only Jewish individuals and not the Jewish people, which disappeared under conditions of freedom. This disenchantment with democracy led these thinkers to an embrace of Jewish isolationism. Efroikin, for instance, argued that in the event of war, the Jews would have no obligation to fight for England, which expected Jewish support despite its policies in Palestine.[32] Feeling betrayed by the government of France, he embraced the politics of interest that thirty years earlier he had rejected as the hallmark of the ghetto mentality.

The warning of the *Oyfn sheydveg* contributors against Jewish involvement in European politics also stemmed from these intellectuals' disgust at the extent to which the European moral crisis had penetrated the Jewish community. Tcherikower spoke for them all when he stated:

> The tragedy of our generation does not consist in the amount of afflictions that have befallen our lot, but rather in that the generation has lost the old beliefs and has despaired of the new. Through and through individualistic, skeptical, and rationalistic, our generation is devoured by assimilation— right or left—and has lost its past strength. It stands now empty, expelled, without the innocence of a believer and without the primitive strength of a fighter—without any consolation in its afflictions.[33]

Having despaired of most ideological programs for Jewish survival, the *Oyfn sheydveg* editors and contributors hoped to create a new rhetoric for an age of counter-emancipation from the language of the pre-secular past. By invoking a traditionalist tone and content, these thinkers could best express an ideology of antimodernism. They hoped that this ideology would serve to rearm the Jewish people with "the innocence of a believer" and the "primitive strength of a fighter." With the fiery tone of traditional Jewish preachers, these writers exposed to their readers the extent of Jewish assimilation, which prevented European Jewry from responding adequately to the rise of Nazism. Then they employed a rhetoric of restoration of religious and traditional values in order to lead their readers to their new ideology of national retreat and cultural consolidation. In reality, these writers envisioned more a creation of a self-sufficient, self-validating Jewish culture than they did a literal return to the lifestyle of the Middle Ages. In an age when external conditions conjured images of medieval persecution and marginalization, these intellectuals naturally turned to the medieval Jewish experience as a usable past from which they could draw inspiration for the re-creation of internal Jewish social and cultural life.

Tcherikower, Efroikin, and Kalmanovitch first depicted the victims of Nazism as thoroughly assimilated. Living in Germany or France at the time of Hitler's rise to power, they judged German Jewish reaction to the rise of Hitler against their East European nationalist sensibilities. So assimilated was German Jewry, argued Tcherikower, that it blamed Nazi hatred on its inability to rid itself of its last vestiges of Jewish identity and on the persistent presence of *Ostjuden*. Moreover, stated Tcherikower, German Jews reacted to the Nuremberg Laws not with righteous indignation but rather with shame. Whereas premodern Jews would have chosen martyrdom over apostasy, now many Jews in Nazi-occupied Austria and Czechoslovakia converted to Christianity in the vain hope that conversion would save them from racial anti-Semitism. Tcherikower and Kalmanovitch also disparaged as empty rhetoric the German Jewish slogan to wear the yellow badge with pride. Accusing his generation of sordid selfishness, Tcherikower blamed Jews living in democratic lands with breaking the economic boycott against Germany and not contributing financially to the refugees. Efroikin similarly observed that "Save yourself, whoever can" proved the only ideal of individual Jews who had lost their sense of belonging to the Jewish people because of assimilation.[34]

It was the ideology of emancipation that these intellectuals blamed for the weakening of collective bonds between Jews. Tcherikower and Kalmanovitch both argued that emancipation and Haskalah continued to greatly influence Jewish life despite these ideologies' supposed obsolescence. Assimilation, argued Tcherikower, emerged as the product both of West European Reform Judaism and of Soviet Yiddishization.[35] Despite a minority's recognition that Reform Judaism had contributed to the loss of Jewish identity, most German Jews still "clamored after the old god of emancipation."[36]

Tcherikower attacked not just the Reform movement, but also the Haskalah, which he believed had weakened Jewish national solidarity in the East European heartland. In a series of popular historical articles that he published contemporaneously with *Oyfn sheydveg*, Tcherikower criticized the legacy of the Russian Haskalah for what he considered its adherents' betrayal of the Jewish masses. Just when Russian Jewry needed an intelligentsia to direct its protest against the oppressive policies of Nicholas I, the *maskilim* betrayed their own people by allying themselves with this despot, whom they hailed a liberator. From turning a blind eye to the suffering of the Cantonists to successfully petitioning the government to create modernized schools and to ban Jewish dress, the Russian *maskilim* consistently sought to undermine the Jewish masses.[37] The mid-nineteenth-century Russian *maskil* no doubt served as a perfect analogue in Tcherikower's imagination for the Evsektsiia and the Soviet Yiddish elite, which also initiated government persecution of the traditional

Jewish masses. A direct line linked the maskilic "informers" to their *Evsek* great-grandchildren.

Returning to *Oyfn sheydveg*, Tcherikower stated openly in his essay that the assimilation of Soviet Jews confirmed his disillusionment with radical Yiddishism. In a country where Yiddish achieved the status of a recognized language, the Jews still abandoned it in favor of Russian. Quoting statistics on the closing of Soviet Yiddish schools and cultural centers as well as on the high percentage of intermarriage, Tcherikower understood Soviet Jewry as in the process of "death by the kiss" of assimilation. Tcherikower also railed against Soviet newspaper reports that children in the Yiddish schools of Shklov and Kapulye, two *shtetlekh* in the old Pale of Settlement, celebrated Christmas in the presence of Christmas trees. Through this example, Tcherikower conjured the image of apostasy having penetrated the former bastions of traditional Judaism.[38] Soviet Yiddish culture failed to prevent this "ugliest death for a nation" because it could not answer the following fundamental paradox: "Why specifically Yiddish? If there is no national, historical or, dare we say, religious feeling of connection with the collective then why be a Jew in a country where you can freely partake of the general rich culture? Why send the children to a Yiddish school when the general ones prepare them much better for practical life?"[39] Kalmanovitch, who had posed this question as early as 1931, now ironically referred to Soviet Jews as "dead free people" *(mesim ḥofshim)*, a religious term indicating that death releases the individual from the obligation to observe the commandments. So, too, implied Kalmanovitch, assimilation had freed individual Soviet Jews from their responsibilities as members of the Jewish people.[40]

Kalmanovitch did not need any convincing to join with Tcherikower and Efroikin in this portrayal of the disintegration of the Jewish national collective. The crisis of 1938 only had heightened the despair that he felt over the future of secular Yiddish culture in the Diaspora. In the summer of 1938, Lucy Dawidowicz (then Schildkret) traveled from her native New York to Vilna to serve as an *aspirantur* (graduate student) in YIVO. During her year in Vilna, she became very close to Zelig and Riva Kalmanovitch, who adopted her as a surrogate daughter. Throughout Schildkret's time in Vilna, Kalmanovitch impressed upon her his view of Yiddishism as a bankrupt ideology. Decades later, Dawidowicz, an acclaimed historian of the Holocaust, recorded Kalmanovitch's reflections about the defects of Yiddishism as an ideology:

> He was contemptuous of Yiddishism as an ideology that proposed a solution to the anomalies of Jewish existence. "It's bankrupt. What kind of a movement can it be whose program is to read a Yiddish book and to go to the Yiddish theater once in a while?" He mocked it as a movement whose appeal could be only to people with a literary bent. Besides, Yiddishism had as its unarticulated premise the acceptance of bilingualism. Jews had to know the language of the country. "They need to buy bread and repair their shoes and work; they need to do it in the language of the country in which they live," he would argue. Then he would conclude triumphantly, with his sweet, shy smile: "The only solution is for Jews to have their own country, where they can live a normal life."[41]

As Kalmanovitch had stated to Dawidowicz, his goal remained Jewish normalization as a nation, not a reversion to a premodern conception of Jewish religious exceptionalism. Although radical secular Yiddish culture severed from its connection to Hebrew and the religious tradition angered him, he did not at this point preach a return to religious tradition. In fact, Dawidowicz recalled Kalmanovitch dismissing her yearning for an authentic religious experience in synagogue on the High Holidays as unrealistic. In the heart of Vilna, still populated by thousands of traditionalist Jews and their religious institutions, Kalmanovitch informed Dawidowicz that what she was looking for no longer existed.[42] In a letter to her mentor, the New York Yiddishist and educator Leibush Lehrer, Dawidowicz wrote that Kalmanovitch maintained a strictly secular lifestyle. "For Kalmanovitch, my kind of Jewishness has absolutely no value. He doesn't need Jewish holidays and festivals, in fact he works on Yom Kippur, but not in the same spirit as the Bundists."[43] Kalmanovitch confirmed this judgment by reacting with disdain to Hillel Tsaytlin's *Oyfn sheydveg* essay, which had argued that the current catastrophe needed to remind the Jews that they had not fulfilled their mission as God's chosen people:

> It would truly be a fortunate thing for the world, if indeed the sixteen million Jews would become moral people, thought only about *mitsves* and good deeds and began to teach the world the ethics of Judaism. What,

however, did God do? He actually gave forth a fine Torah, which is suitable for everybody: "And you shall live by them." And he made it that Jews—the millions of Jews—not know from this Torah and search for everything, both physical and spiritual, somewhere else. I must say against my will that this must be according to His will, as it were. If not? He would then punish the Jews and annihilate them. Perhaps He would choose another nation as the carriers of His Torah. Jews are no longer appropriate for it. . . . Either they will be a nation like all others, without the Torah—the seventy nations, Babylonians, Persians, Amorites, or they will not be at all. The Torah and *mitsves* are no longer a panacea for Jews. They already will pass it up [*zaynen shoyn moykhl*].[44]

Thus, Kalmanovitch's call inward in the pages of *Oyfn sheydveg* should not be read as a call to the Jewish religious tradition but rather to a national cohesion that he believed had existed in the premodern era. In search of national normalization for the future, Kalmanovitch continued to actively participate in Frayland, often speaking at its meetings regarding the bankruptcy of Yiddish and the need for an independent territory in order to realize a modern Jewish national culture. Throughout her year in Vilna, Dawidowicz attended Frayland meetings with Kalmanovitch, who enraptured his audience with speeches in favor of territorialism. In this search for national normalization through territorial concentration, Kalmanovitch had returned to his roots in Syrkin's Ḥerut.[45] However, darker thoughts regarding the compatibility of Jewish national renaissance with democracy began to overwhelm him. In Dawidowicz's words:

He showed that the survival of Yiddish was absolutely not at all connected with politics. . . , that the survival of Yiddish and the struggle to maintain Yiddish is not the same thing as the struggle for democracy and against fascism. He showed that political freedom weakened the drive to Yiddish and facilitated the path to assimilation, and that precisely in such periods and such places where Jews were persecuted Jewish culture flourished. Therefore, the struggle for Yiddish is not a partner with the struggle against fascism. He stopped there, perhaps because the logical development would lead to dangerous conclusions. As it was, people didn't understand him and began to protest: Kalmanovitch is a fascist.[46]

By this time, in fact, Kalmanovitch had come to believe that the process of modernity itself had destroyed the unity of the Jewish people. He poured out his frustration, often bordering on rage, in a letter to his friend and fellow Yiddish philologist Yudl Mark. The arbiters of modern Yiddish culture, Kalmanovitch complained, possessed absolutely no standards. Rather, a false allegiance to unity and to the attribute of mercy *(rakhmones)* compelled them to pass off mediocrities and worse for highbrow Yiddish literature. This misguided application of mercy served as a both a cause and a symptom of the downfall of modern Yiddish culture. The highbrow literary journal *Literarishe bleter* had become worthless. Noah Prylucki, whom Kalmanovitch labeled a "graphomaniac," had ruined YIVO's popular philological journal, *Yidish far ale* (Yiddish for all) with his professional incompetence and egoism. Lurking behind this tirade was the ever-present bogeyman of sympathy for Soviet Yiddish culture. The fact that his revered mentor, Zhitlovsky, had turned from critic to defender of the Soviet Union proved the final straw for Kalmanovitch. In his words:

> Look at Zhitlovsky. A destruction has become of him. In old age he has become the Red Oppressor's servant! What is this? Is he so naïve that he believes that it can be imagined that from the non-kosher source the redemption for *mame loshn* will come? *That from this impurity of assimilation the sparks of national renaissance will emerge?* The result is the opposite: He who lowers himself into that pit—even if it is with the intention of releasing the "sparks"—will lose his own sparks and will only take on impurity. This is true and tested. So it is with pain that we must part with a mentor [*rebe*]. What he says and what he said are no longer interesting—he has lost both worlds.[47]

This explosive statement brims with religious imagery that illuminates the deep sense of spiritual betrayal that Kalmanovitch felt. The term "the Red Oppressor's servant" (der tsoyrer haedoyms a meshores) functions as a play on words that conjures the image of Esau and the Roman Empire (Edom—the Red One), depicted in classical Jewish sources as the implacable foe of Jacob and the Jewish people. The Soviet Union for Kalmanovitch had assumed this typological level of evil. Kalmanovitch's reference to Zhitlovsky's attempt to release holy sparks from impurity referred to Sabbatai Ṣevi, the seventeenth-century false messiah, and his followers. In order to justify Sabbatai Ṣevi's antinomian acts, Nathan of Gaza, his prophet, declared that through sin, he was releasing sparks of holiness from their impure shells. According to the teachings of Lurianic Kabbalah, from which Sabbateans drew inspiration, the physical world's creation had trapped the sparks of divine holiness in impure shells. Subsequent generations of Sabbateans used this theology of redemption through sin to justify their abrogation of Torah law and, in the case of the Doenmeh in Turkey and the Frankists in Poland, their collective apostasy.[48] Given that Kalmanovitch had invested modern Yiddish culture with religious significance, it is not surprising that he reflexively invoked the religious terminology of irredeemable sin and false messiahs to describe his loss of faith. Zhitlovsky, whom Kalmanovitch had depicted in the past as a redeemer of Jewish culture for a secular age, had turned out to be a false messiah, reenacting the perfidy of Sabbatai Ṣevi.

This sense of betrayal led Kalmanovitch to the grim conclusion that modernity had destroyed the collective Jewish nation. His essay for *Oyfn sheydveg*, Kalmanovitch declared to Mark, finally would strip Yiddish culture of mercy by declaring this truth. In his words:

> I, however, don't pose the question as to whether or not we have "American Jewry," "Polish Jewry," "world Jewry," but rather if something exists at all that we call "Jewry." It seems to me that "the emperor has no clothes." It is not the arguments amongst the Yiddishists and Yiddish cliques that are the impediment; rather it touches upon something more essential, in the very existence of a Jewish life today. And already from the facts that I bring, the question of "this or that way Yiddish" is no more than froth over glazed water.[49]

The essay to which Kalmanovitch was referring was "Untern hamer fun der geshikhte" (Under the hammer of history), which appeared in the first issue of *Oyfn sheydveg*. In this article, he argued that assimilation resulted from the historical process of modernity itself. In the Middle Ages, he argued, Jewish individuals had lived as members of the Jewish community. Capitalism, however, had granted these individuals the opportunity to seek their fortunes in non-Jewish society. Unlike in the case of European societies where the achievements of individuals benefited their own nation, the success of individual Jews benefited their host nation, rather than the Jewish people. Emancipation, argued Kalmanovitch, served as the movement to legalize this reality even as Haskalah emerged as the ideology to justify it. Capitalism, thus, operated as the hammer of history that shattered the Jewish people, "with Haskalah its symbol and assimilation its blade."[50] Given this bleak view, Kalmanovitch could not envision national salvation as emerging from the ultimate victory of the democracies over the Nazis. Rather, he observed that the Nazi extrusion of the Jews from civic life had forced Jewish individuals to return to their collective Jewish identity. The most noteworthy example of this phenomenon, argued Kalmanovitch, was the benefit that German Jewish refugees brought to the *Yishuv* in Palestine. Only in that society did he recognize the first signs of national regeneration.[51]

Even as Kalmanovitch offered a historical explanation for the disintegration of Jewish peoplehood, he framed his discussion in meta-historic and religious language. For instance, he prefaced his article with a quotation from Pushkin that stated that the hammer both broke glass and forged iron. Returning to this image at the end of the essay, Kalmanovitch attempted to bracket the entire modern Jewish era between the two blows of the hammer of history: the blow of capitalism at the time of the French Revolution, which led to the shattering of the Jewish people like glass, and the blow of Nazism, which had the potential to reforge the Jewish people like iron.[52]

Indeed, Tcherikower, Efroikin, and Kalmanovitch all viewed Nazism as a potential catalyst for the reconstitution of Jewish communal consciousness. Tcherikower even recognized a positive side to the rise of Nazism:

> And who knows, perhaps the Jewries in the Fascist and half-Fascist lands would have been devoured internally if not for Jewish historical providence, which imparted to the contemporary Hamans the idea to build the anti-Semitic movement on principles not of religion but rather of race. And from this standpoint, it is perhaps true that "the Holy One Blessed Be He made a blessing for Israel" that this illogical [racial] theory has rendered apostasy purposeless. What would become of these Jews, if they would be able to save their lives and property through conversion?[53]

Through such pronouncements, these writers forged a historiosophy of the ensuing persecutions steeped in religious tradition. With Tcherikower referring to the force of "Jewish historical providence" and Efroikin speaking of current events as manifestations of "God's whip," these writers revealed their antimodern rhetoric. Tcherikower,

Efroikin, and Kalmanovitch all invoked the traditional beliefs that the Jews suffered as a result of sin and that their persecutors served as divine agents of this punishment. Kalmanovitch, for instance, provided his essay with transcendent religious meaning by prefacing it with a quote from the Talmud that stated that, for the messiah to come, an evil tyrant would have to pass decrees that would lead the Jewish people back to God.[54] All three writers also articulated their belief that given the internally destructive nature of emancipation, Nazism served as the negation of a negation, from which a positive might result. Returning to the image of the hammer as breaking glass and forging iron, Kalmanovitch ended his essay as follows:

> The hammer of history smashed the Jewish people of the Middle Ages. The connection between its parts did not withstand the severe blows. Now, it [the hammer of history] beats again, meeting individuals. It finds them torn from their roots. It finds them relying on themselves alone, rambling in an empty world. What are they, these broken pieces of the Jewish people: are they glass or are they steel? Will the blow from the heavy hammer break them once and for all, or will it forge them together into a new unity?[55]

Parting Ideologically with Dubnov

It is not surprising that these writers' ideological crisis met with the resistance of their mentor, Dubnov. As Dubnov heard about the ideological revision in the pages of *Oyfn sheydveg*, he grew increasingly anxious about the contents of the forthcoming journal. In his correspondence with Tcherikower, he stressed that just as he had rejected the call backward (*nazad* in Russian) following the pogroms of 1881, so too did he reject this call now. He further warned Tcherikower: "If we *now* should fall apart from fighting, we are lost people and *kaddish* will have to be recited after our generation. No—'I shall not die, but live!' [Psalms 108:17]."[56] Dubnov decided that he could not let this ideological revision go unanswered. Dubnov decided that he would state his disagreement with the journal's contents in a letter to the editor.[57] In this letter, which appeared at the front of the second issue of *Oyfn sheydveg*, Dubnov expressed his continued belief in emancipation, Diaspora nationalism, and the common cause of the

Jewish struggle with that of the democracies. Recognizing that the contributors to *Oyfn sheydveg* despaired of European civilization, Dubnov began his letter by reminding them that 1937 had marked the two thousandth anniversary of the entry of the first Jews upon European soil. Detailing the magnitude of Jewish suffering during what he referred to as "Haman's times," Dubnov disapproved of the fact that the contributors to *Oyfn sheydveg* believed that they stood "at the crossroads" of ideological revision rather than upon "the battlefield" in the fight against the Nazis. Only after the Jews had helped the democracies to defeat Nazi Germany and then found homes for the Jewish refugees could they afford the luxury of ideological contemplation.[58]

Dubnov reserved his harshest critique, however, for his disciples' belief that emancipation had led only to assimilation and that the Jewish entry into the world of European politics had not benefited the Jews at all. In his words:

> In our epoch of counter-emancipation we dare not pose the ironic question: "Well, what has emancipation brought us?" True, it brought assimilation, but also freedom and human dignity. It revived the free person in the Jew. The task of our great national movement in the past fifty years consisted of the struggle for emancipation *without* assimilation, for both civic and national rights. We succeeded in winning such liberty after World War I, but only in a juridic sense, in the treaties of the League of Nations with the east European states. Hardly had this total emancipation been realized, when the Hitlerite plague came upon the scene to poison the minds of the people in those countries in which there were large Jewish centers. Does this mean that we were deceived by emancipation? We must fight against the spirit of counter-emancipation, against the vicious plans of "emancipating" millions of Jews from the countries which Jews helped to build up for many centuries together with the Christian population [. . .]. We stand or fall with the progress or regress of entire mankind as a whole, and not with a few of its degenerate parts.[59]

In response, Tcherikower respectfully declared Dubnov's theories outdated, arguing that only by standing at the "crossroads" of ideological revision could the Jews fight "on the battlefield" with the democracies as their proud equals. Tcherikower began by expressing consternation that Dubnov, of all people, did not recognize the need for an ideological reevaluation. Moreover, the great ideological revisions among *maskilim*-turned-nationalists, such as Peretz Smolenskin and Moshe Leib Lilienblum, had occurred during turbulent times. Tcherikower then asked Dubnov to recall the unsettled historical climate in the late 1880s when he first began to articulate his theory of Diaspora nationalism. Then, Tcherikower further questioned Dubnov's assumption that the Jews should join the enemies of Fascism in their battle against Hitler without qualifications. Even though the wrongs committed by the democracies against the Jews paled in comparison to those of Germany, these grievances still warranted that the Jews qualify their support of these countries. Why, asked Tcherikower, should the Jews support the democracies without qualification, when other national minorities made demands of their governments in exchange for support? Through this argument, Tcherikower sought to refute Dubnov's charge that he and the other contributors to *Oyfn sheydveg* had succumbed to political resignation. In reality, argued Tcherikower, an ideological reassessment would help to transform the Jews into a true factor in the war against Hitler.[60]

Despite his arguments to the contrary, Tcherikower's position was indeed one of political retreat. He revealed this truth in his criticism of Dubnov for referring to the upcoming 150th anniversary of the first French emancipation as *zman ḥerutenu* (the season of our freedom), the Jewish liturgy's traditional name for the holiday of Passover.[61] Again, Tcherikower pointed to Dubnov's own previous assessment of the gains of emancipation, in which Dubnov had argued that the individualism inherent in emancipation had destroyed the Jewish collective. The darkness of the Nazi era, however, now had blinded Dubnov to the fact that the successor states of Central and Eastern Europe had failed to deliver on their promises of Jewish national autonomy. In contrast to Dubnov's conviction that national autonomy still could join forces with civic emancipation, Tcherikower argued that assimilation served as emancipation's only twin. Tcherikower ended his letter on a wistful note, explaining that he and his colleagues had exchanged their teacher's optimistic theories, rooted in Haskalah and positivism, for pessimism, influenced by the neo-romanticism of their own youths. In Tcherikower's words:

> Perhaps your optimistic prognosis is correct and not our skeptical one, with warnings and conditions. In yours is felt the certainty of the rationalist generation, to which you belong, and the wholeness and epic nature of

your environment. We envy you. Your youthful temperament, that "I shall not move from my place" notwithstanding all Jewish failures, impresses us greatly. We, however, belong to another generation, a generation with a restless and discontented mood, of searching and longing for a repairing for our agitated souls. You can label this revision, soul searching, repentance, or spiritual crossroads. However, I assure you that this is not despair and it is certainly not resignation.[62]

Tcherikower's public repudiation of Dubnov's ideology must have caused both men emotional pain. The ideological divergence between teacher and students occurred as a result of the different intellectual climates in which these men matured. Dubnov, born in 1860, belonged to the last generation to make the transition from tradition to modernity through the direct medium of Haskalah. Dubnov's letter to the editors of *Oyfn sheydveg* reveals his lifelong insistence on the progress of liberalism and emancipation despite doubts precipitated by the Russian revolutions, the Russian Civil War, the rise of Fascism, and even the approach of the Second World War. Still, this image of Dubnov as an intellectual refugee from the nineteenth century who had lived too far into the twentieth requires some modification. The gap between his perception of the reality in the 1930s and that of his students, despite their rhetoric, was not that far apart. Dubnov, after all, fully admitted that world Jewry was living through "Haman's times." Moreover, four years earlier, Dubnov had admitted in a publicistic article that the twentieth century was emerging as the antithesis of the nineteenth. At no time during the long nineteenth century, argued Dubnov, had political reaction succeeded in completely stifling freedom of speech. It was the combination of twentieth-century technology with dictatorship that had given rise to the totalitarian regime, which succeeded where all previous regimes had failed. Through political terror and indoctrination, Stalin had created a new generation of automatons that did not possess even the instinct for freedom that the older generation had to suppress in itself if it sought to avoid prison. The leaders of Fascist Italy and Nazi Germany had learned from the Soviet model, applying it to rightist politics. Still worse, a bestial nationalism with its division of humanity into superior and inferior races completely had eclipsed the liberal nationalism of the nineteenth century.[63]

What distinguished Dubnov's vision from that of his disciples was thus not his view on the nature of contemporary events but rather his belief that ultimately the forces of liberalism and humanism would prevail. In his 1935 article, Dubnov sought to comfort his readers by invoking a rabbinic aggadah that depicted Adam as frightened upon the first nightfall that dawn would never come. The aggadah, explained Dubnov, ended with Adam realizing upon daybreak that the universe operates according to natural laws. Dubnov assured his readers that in similar fashion the night of Fascism and communism would come to an end and humanism would ultimately triumph.[64]

A Turn Inward

The contributors to *Oyfn sheydveg* proposed a return to the internal sources of Jewish cultural strength in an age of counter-emancipation. Although sometimes not agreeing over the exact nature of Jewish internal values, all contributors believed that modeling Jewish life after medieval Jewish separatism could allow the contemporary generation to draw spiritual strength from these reserves. Consequently, these intellectuals engaged in a romanticization of the pre-emancipation era, depicting its Jews as living in harmony with the Jewish collective and its spiritual values. In their call for a return to the ghetto, these intellectuals' rhetoric for an ideology of counter-emancipation reached its climax. Nearly all the contributors to *Oyfn sheydveg* emerged united in their belief that Jews must restore their national character through a rejection of external influences and through a turn inward. It was Efroikin who, at the end of his essay, established the connection between national restoration and internal consolidation:

> The foremost criterion for our behavior must be the survival of the nation, the preservation of our spiritual character. If the nations, notwithstanding that we openly and honestly proclaim our distinctiveness, give us full rights—all the better. If they, however, demand from us the remuneration that we morally and spiritually mix with them and lose our distinctiveness, it is then better for us to be half citizens as long as we remain complete Jews.
>
> The struggle for our existence amongst the nations and for our human rights will only then be a reality and not a mimicked phrase, when we

shall once again find the path toward ourselves, and to our own source. In ourselves alone lies still a treasure of spiritual strengths; we only must discover them, gather them, and with them resist, endure—until the wrath passes.[65]

This passage encapsulates the entire enterprise of *Oyfn sheydveg*. Whereas emancipationist ideology offered the promise of individual rights in exchange for regeneration, Efroikin reversed this condition by offering the promise of national regeneration in exchange for the repudiation of individual rights. Efroikin spoke for the other contributors when he urged Jews to use this time of external persecution to effectuate an internal national consolidation.

In his *Oyfn sheydveg* article, Tcherikower conceived of the return to the ghetto as a process of national consolidation, in which the intelligentsia would return to the masses. To Tcherikower, the ghetto symbolized cultural and literary productivity:

> We desire to return to the ghetto, or more precisely, if we remain in that crooked Jewish land then we do so willingly and not forcibly. World culture belongs to all and it also will knock on the closed doors [of the ghetto]. As Bialik once said in a private conversation, "Better that my tree stand next to me in the garden and the golden apples of my tree fall to the other side of the fence, than the tree stand on the other side and the golden apples fall into my garden already ripe." Historically, we already walked this path until assimilation led us astray from it.[66]

This passage reveals the nature of Tcherikower's rhetorical use of the term "ghetto" for his ideology of counter-emancipation. If the external world pushed the Jews back into the ghetto, then at least the Jews should understand segregation as culturally beneficial. For instance, he argued that the ghetto served as a cultural haven in which Yiddish language, literature, and theater evolved. A return to the ghetto, moreover, would secure a return to the natural state of Jewish history. In his historical schema, Tcherikower ironically inverted the maskilic and *Wissenschaft des Judentums* conception of a golden age in antiquity, degeneration in the Middle Ages, and restoration through emancipation. Tcherikower's restorative historical conception, in contrast, envisioned the Middle Ages as the lost golden age and emancipation as the source of degeneration. As part of this restoration, Tcherikower called for Jews not to concentrate on the outside world's shortcomings but rather to engage "in an accounting with ourselves, our own sins against Jewish collective interests and also to a certain extent our sins against the world."[67] Tcherikower thus sided with those who conceived of a return to the ghetto as an opportunity for internal reflection rather than attribution of external blame.

With this ideology of return to the ghetto came a tempering of Tcherikower's commitment to secular Yiddishism, which he still had articulated as late as early 1938.[68] Secularism, Tcherikower maintained, had led not to the creation of a new Jewish identity as promised by Yiddishism but rather to assimilation. Moreover, he concluded that no form of secular Jewish identity, including nationalism, could serve as a substitute for religion in motivating the Jewish people toward self-sacrifice and martyrdom. It was no accident, then, that long submerged religious feelings arose to the surface precisely at the time of great external persecution. Nonetheless, Tcherikower ultimately dismissed an actual return to traditional observance as unrealistic:

> We know that the call backward is in vain. The old sources of religious faith are very dried up, even among the common people themselves. Our generation is too far gone in skepticism, indifference, and criticism to be able to once again bind itself with *tfiln* straps. We long ago lost the past simplicity of religious faith, and no one has the strength to once again pour old wine into old vessels. But we also do not have the strength to free ourselves from the need for *yontev*, and from envy of the harmonious religious world of previous generations. We are tired of gray, rationalistic commonplaces. This is a tragedy of the generation that conducts a struggle with itself, a struggle between modernism and its own inheritance.[69]

Underlying Tcherikower's despair in the secular experiment was his conviction that the current crisis of Nazism, in contrast to past persecutions, had not led to a cultural renaissance. In his 1939 essay, Tcherikower repeated his assertion, first articulated during World War I, that throughout Jewish history, martyrdom had served as a catalyst for cultural renaissance:

> Nobody in our sober age of our rational generation expected the once-upon-a-time free-will *"akeydes,"* the *Kiddush Hashem* with the proud words of *"Alenu le-shabeaḥ"* upon the lips, *selikhes* [penitential liturgical poems] of revenge such as "God, do not be silent to my blood," and no avengers such as Simḥah Kohen in Worms in 1096. However, we could expect a deep shaking up of the soul and crisis in thinking and action. Our

generation, however, remained loyal [to its previous ideologies] and no revolutions in Jewish spiritual life have occurred in the last terrible years.[70]

Now that the intimate connection between oppression and cultural renaissance had been severed, however, he saw little hope for the future of Yiddish culture.

On Emancipation and Autonomy

After the eruption of World War II, Dubnov and his students persisted in their debate about emancipation in the pages of the third issue of *Oyfn sheydveg*, which, because of Germany's invasion of France, was never published. Among the manuscripts gathered for the third *Oyfn sheydveg* was Dubnov's polemical "*Inter-arma* (1940): Gedanken fun a historiker vegen di tsilen fun krig un friden" (*Inter-arma* (1940): Thoughts of a Jewish historian on the goals of war and peace). Kalmanovitch similarly prepared an essay, "Bay vos haltn yidn haynt?" (Where do Jews stand today?), which he succeeded in publishing in the Lithuanian Yiddish periodical *Ringen*. Although he did not write a direct response to Dubnov, Tcherikower persisted in his ideological revision in a diary that he penned in a transit camp in the South of France, to which he had fled after the fall of Paris. Arriving in America, he also addressed the issue more indirectly in an article on the relationship between martyrology and Jewish historiography. Efroikin too did not record his responses to the outbreak of World War II and the fall of France in essay form. However, his actions as a communal leader in the unoccupied zone of France during this period attested to his persistence in the ideological revision begun in the pages of *Oyfn sheydveg*. A comparison of the writings and activities of Dubnov, Tcherikower, Kalmanovitch, and Efroikin reveals the extent to which the aged historian and his disciples reacted differently to the Jewish plight during the brief two-year period between the advent of war and the onset of genocide.

Dubnov's faith in the democracies, which he had expressed so fervently on the eve of the war, wavered in his article for the third, wartime *Oyfn sheydveg*. Now the German invasion of Eastern Europe, which he had dismissed in his previous letter to the editor as unlikely, had transpired. Even as he persisted in his conviction that the Jews must unite behind the Allies, he entertained growing doubts about his previous assertion that a liberated Europe automatically would lead to a liberated Jewry. In a private letter, Dubnov wrote of his desire to publish a series of articles in the American press to articulate the Jewish expectations from the Allies during and after the war. Dubnov decided to give this new series of articles the same name as a series of articles he had written during World War I, "*Inter-arma*," to define Jewish demands to the victors. It is clear, then, that this article for the third *Oyfn sheydveg* was meant to serve as the first installment in this series, which would later appear in English translation. The fact that Dubnov intended this article for a non-Jewish British and American audience explains its blatantly polemical style.[71]

At the beginning of his article, Dubnov expressed his desire to minimize the distance between his roles as historian and publicist. He argued that whereas World War I had begun as a "meaningless, bloody war," it only later received meaning through the fight for national minorities' rights. World War II, in contrast, began as the just battle to free Europe from Hitler's barbaric yoke. Dubnov then continued by commenting that the democracies had initially reacted only with silence to the Nazi assault on the Jews, the first victims of the war. Dubnov addressed himself to the Allied leaders, stating that their continued silence was unforgivable.[72] In vivid prose, he detailed the Nazi persecution of the Jews who "have been wandering for some years over sea and land, searching for an asylum for the night" and who seldom had experienced in their history "such a tragic moment, such a terrible catastrophe."[73] The moral cowardice of the Allies emerged in this article in sharp contradistinction to the tragic suffering of the Jews. In fact, Dubnov condemned the Allied leaders for their refusal to list the Jews as victims of Hitler's aggression along with the Czechs, Austrians, and Poles. In order to reverse this disturbing trend, Dubnov invoked a moral argument that sought to equate the Allies' war goals with the rescue of the Jewish people. In his words:

> And you, the fighters for a "new Europe," have passed over this very tragic moment in world history in silence! What a fine gesture it would be, if you, going into the holy war, would extend your hand to the Jewish people and say: "Upon you is befallen an evil and barbaric enemy, the like of which

was never in your history since the Persian Haman. We are going into the war to protect all of Europe from barbarism, and also you, after seven years of torture and humiliation. We want to protect the children of that ancient people, who three thousand years ago proclaimed the first moral laws to the world, those very laws that the neo-barbarians have now abolished and trample with their feet." Such a *word* would be the greatest historical *act* of our time.[74]

In contrast to his hopefully defiant mood in 1939, Dubnov began to fear that the Allies' ultimate triumph in the war might come too late to save the Jews. Reversing his prewar position, he responded to those Allied leaders who made the argument that the liberation of the free world would also liberate the Jews with the counterclaim that "if the war will last long, very few of them [the Jews] will remain."[75]

But Dubnov did more than rely merely on moral arguments. He also hoped to move the British to action by appealing to their self-interest. Indeed, he ended his essay with a call to the Allies to solve the Jewish problem now, before the betrayed Jews would overwhelm them with their demands at a future peace conference:

> Now, you want to pass over the Jewish problem in silence, but right after the war it will arise before your eyes in its full magnitude, in its world import. To the future peace conference will come Jewish representatives from every country throughout the world and will demand justice from the "New Europe" for the people, which suffered more than anyone from Hitler's terror. They will come from Central and Eastern Europe and demand guarantees for the remnant of the ruined Jewish centers in Germany, Austria, Czechoslovakia, and Poland to ensure that the new Poland will not deceive the world with its wild anti-Semitism as it did before the Versailles Peace. They will come from America and raise the question about organizing hundreds of thousands of immigrants, who knock at the closed gates of the "new world." They will come from Jewish Palestine and pose the difficult question: Why did you not admit hordes of refugees that escaped from the European murderer into their own borders and forbid Jews to buy land in a great portion of the land of Israel in the full heat of the current war? They will also raise the question of the weakened, and spiritually persecuted Jews in Soviet Russia, where more than a million Jews from occupied Poland recently arrived.[76]

This passage reveals both Dubnov's growing realization of the democratic world's abandonment of the Jews and his response to it. Now that the war had begun, Dubnov partially succumbed to the same pessimistic convictions that plagued his students regarding the democracies' relationship to the Jews. Yet, unlike them, he did not argue for political retreat but rather for public engagement. Despite his disenchantment with the Allies, Dubnov still no doubt maintained that the Jews stood on the "battlefield," the metaphor that he employed in his letter in the second issue of *Oyfn sheydveg*. Now, however, this image represented the fight for public opinion in which the Jews had to join. Far from representing a true ideological transformation, this fiery polemic reveals how Dubnov sought to rescue his lifelong optimistic vision from the ruins of his collapsing world. At other key moments of admittedly lesser crisis, such as 1905 and during the Bolshevik Revolution, Dubnov had asserted his optimism in the ultimate triumph of liberalism, despite his pessimistic distrust of European liberals, whom he suspected of betraying the interests of the Jewish people.[77]

Tcherikower, in contrast to Dubnov, experienced the first year of war in France. The first effects of the war that Tcherikower felt were economic, with the disappearance of all his sources of livelihood.[78] More deeply, however, the war only heightened the ideological revision that he had begun on the war's eve. As he reflected in his diary, recorded after having fled Paris from the invading Nazis:

> The year 1939 (after Munich and the destruction of Czechoslovakia) and especially since the beginning of the war, when the Jewish moment in the struggle with the enemy was, even by the democrats, relegated into a corner not to be mentioned, was a time for me of a certain crisis in mood. . . . Are the old formulas, in which our thought is so steeped truly absolute? Certainly we all believe in political democracy, it is our entire support, without it we too are broken. But the democratic world itself is living through a deep moral crisis, it is lacking its past juices and past proud security, one can feel in it a sign of sadness and even sometimes a sign of old age. And we see this [phenomenon] the best in its relationship to the Jews, the touchstone of history.
>
> It is no surprise that people begin to contemplate, begin to reevaluate.[79]

On the eve of the war, recalled Tcherikower, this mood had fueled the entire *Oyfn sheydveg* project, as well as his academic articles about the Russian *maskilim* and a piece regarding the early Jewish revolutionary movement in Russia. In the nine months between the outbreak of war and the fall of France, this restless mood only had increased. During that time, Tcherikower had turned to new historical themes that reflected his despair with enlightenment, rationalism, and the legacy of emancipation. For instance, he planned a study of the Orthodox reaction to French emancipation, to Napoleon's Sanhedrin, and to Napoleon's export of emancipation to Central and Eastern Europe. The Orthodox world, which Tcherikower claimed had comprised the vast majority of the Jewish people at the turn of the nineteenth century, had reacted to emancipation with a wariness that demonstrated its national health. This Orthodox reaction to emancipation, misrepresented in the official historiography, begged a fresh historical analysis. This contrast of the national credentials of the Orthodox with the national betrayal of the modern intelligentsia served as a sharp departure in Tcherikower's thinking. Continuing in this theme, Tcherikower also planned a study about the war waged by the early Jewish anarchists and socialists against "the Master of the Universe," through their Yom Kippur balls and antireligious propaganda. This antireligious stance, claimed Tcherikower, had led the early Jewish radicals, including Zhitlovsky, to embrace anti-Semitic stereotypes about the Jewish role in the economy. In his diary, Tcherikower candidly sought the psychological causes of this ideological revision. Perhaps, he surmised, it resulted from his sublimation and redirecting of his deep despair over the fall of Polish Jewry into Nazi hands. More concretely, Tcherikower surmised that these new interests, which included reading about themes of ancient Jewish history, resulted from the greater amount of time that he now had on his hands.[80]

Whatever the cause, Tcherikower rejected the notion that this ideological revision smacked of defeatism but rather argued that it proved appropriate for the new historical era in which the Jews were now living. Echoing the words of his response to Dubnov in the pages of *Oyfn sheydveg*, Tcherikower wrote that such an ideological revision proved appropriate "after the great Jewish misfortune of the last years, when all our hopes lie in ruins." The current catastrophe made it impossible to persist in the "the *elevated* spirit, pride, the bygone belief in the strength of humanity and emancipation. *There is no wise man like the tested man* [Ein ḥoḥom ke-b'a'al ha-nisayon]."[81] Tcherikower described a process of national consolidation that he had experienced during his seven years in Paris, in which he came to feel more purely "Jewish nationalist" rather than simply Yiddishist. Now, the entire Jewish historical spirit, the historical traditions, old Hebrew literature, and the secret of Jewish survival interested him. This re-embrace of the entirety of the Jewish experience in the crucible of suffering acted as a homecoming of sorts, which enacted in his personal life Tcherikower's longtime interest in the connection between Jewish suffering and identity. In his words:

> When I left Paris four weeks ago in a new exile, without thinking, I took with me from all my books one book—my grandfather's Bible and with it a miniature, printed *Sefer Torah* (Torah scroll), which I accidentally discovered in my archive. Is this an accident, an intention, a feeling of patrimony? . . .
>
> The last years broke many old routines and accepted truths. The great Jewish misfortune and the misfortune of the world had its influence. My natural identity emerged, the strong Jewish feeling, the strong inclination to live Jewishly amongst Jews. "Be-sokh 'ami ani yoshev." "I dwell amongst my people." But where is it, that "amongst my people"?[82]

Tcherikower certainly had reason to feel depressed. The nine months from the outbreak of war until the invasion of France in June 1940 witnessed a renewed tension between native French Jewry and East European Jewish immigrants. As a wave of patriotism enveloped both communities, native French Jews urged the immigrant community to maintain a low profile, fearing an anti-Semitic backlash. When the Germans invaded on June 10, 1940, nearly one hundred thousand French Jews, including tens of thousands of East European immigrants, sought escape from northern France to the unoccupied south by car, train, and foot. The Tcherikowers participated in this exodus, leaving their Paris apartment at 6:30 a.m. on June 11, the morning after the invasion. Symbolically, Tcherikower enacted the liturgical experience of exile, which he had romantically depicted two years before at the dedication of the French branch of YIVO. The Tcherikowers traveled for a week from Paris to Vichy and then on to a transit camp on the border of the Pyrenees Mountains. Throughout much of the diary, Tcherikower sought to come to terms with his newfound refugee status. He and Riva had arrived in the camp "bare and naked," with hardly any food and clothing. During their stay in the camp, he complained about the lack of basic foodstuffs such as eggs, butter, and sugar. Their whole life, he complained, had devolved into a struggle for physical survival. He explained that he felt like a hunted animal that seeks nothing more than escape from the hunter.[83]

Far more unsettling was his anxiety about the future. With his back to the Pyrenees, all Tcherikower could dream about was escape from Europe. Although he yearned for Palestine, he dismissed this dream as unrealistic in the aftermath of the British White Paper and during wartime. His first hope, therefore, was escape to Santo Domingo in the Dominican Republic. Although this escape route appeared unfeasible, an opportunity for emigration to America eventually emerged. The American branch of YIVO, Amopteyl, procured a visa for Tcherikower, thereby restoring his faith in his "YIVO family."[84]

Relieved about his personal salvation, Tcherikower spent the remainder of his time in the transit camp mourning the ensuing catastrophe of European Jewry as well as worrying about his future in America. For years, reflected Tcherikower, the memories of his difficulties in earning a living during his sojourn in America twenty-five years earlier had prevented him from returning there. With its apathy toward Yiddish culture and its competitive nature, the American Jewish community would prove a difficult environment in which to spend the next period of his life.[85] More deeply, however, Tcherikower felt intense anxiety about leaving Europe, even though it had sunk into chaos. In his words:

> Yet—Europe, the unfortunate old Europe with all its darkness, unease and insanity, we love so much, are used to it, lived in it. Now, go uproot the connection and throw yourself, nearly in your old age, in the American boiling kettle of ambitions. Running and outrunning, of . . . nouveau riche, of eternal haste! Yet, Europe has become too insane and sick, heading itself to its destruction. Should we be there undeservingly and remain waiting upon its ruins?[86]

Boarding a ship to New York in September 1940, Tcherikower consoled himself that he and Riva would begin life anew in New York. Yet the collective tragedy remained. In time, he tried to convince himself, a scab would form over the wound, and he, together with the Jewish people, would move on. Yet he immediately contradicted this hopeful prediction with the following question: "However, can there be ascents in our generation of people and activists with so many poisoned dreams?"[87]

Throughout his diary, Tcherikower persisted in the theme of his *Oyfn sheydveg* essay by expressing deep pessimism over the future of European Jewry and decrying the lack of Jewish national solidarity in the present generation. When he received a letter from his close friend, the Yiddish poet Daniel Tsharni, describing in idyllic terms conditions in occupied Paris, Tcherikower reacted with anger. "There is no going back to such a city, which betrayed in such a way, which smiles to everyone that tramples it violently."[88] Parisian Jewry, moreover, had left Hershel Grynspan, whom Tcherikower hailed as an idealist, behind in Paris to meet his inevitable fate at the hands of the Nazis. The French had begun to adopt anti-Semitism from their conquerors. French Jewry, which did not possess the cohesion of Polish, or even German and Austrian Jewries, now would experience the unmasking of its hidden Jewish identity. This statement belied the tensions between East European immigrants and native French Jews, who persisted in their emancipationist ideology throughout the 1930s and into the early 1940s. Even as immigrant leaders continued to attempt unification of the two communities, their native French counterparts refused to associate themselves with a group that could make them look foreign in the eyes of Frenchmen.[89]

Tcherikower also deeply worried about the future of YIVO, which he knew had fallen into Soviet hands. He pondered ruefully: "An end to so many years of all of our hard work, of so much effort, of so many successes? Was all this the devil's work—literally the work for the demon's path? And what will happen with our people, with the political and cultural activists?"[90] On several occasions, Tcherikower questioned whether with his work for YIVO he had done nothing more than rocked a "stillborn child."[91] In particular, Tcherikower worried about the fate of his old friend, Dubnov. When he received a letter from Kalmanovitch detailing how the Soviets had sidelined him and overtaken YIVO, Tcherikower further despaired that all his cultural work had been for naught. His hatred for the Soviet Union and its denationalized Yiddish culture rivaled that of Kalmanovitch. In particular, he fulminated against news that Soviet Yiddish activists prepared a celebration of the eight hundredth anniversary of the birth of the medieval Spanish Hebrew poet Yehuda Ha-Levi. What a joke, remarked Tcherikower, that the country that banned the use of

Hebrew and Jewish nationalism would celebrate the birthday of the poet who penned odes to Zion. Surely, the Soviet Yiddishists involved must have had ulterior motives, he concluded, such as imitating the celebration by Russians of their famous writers or winning over the Jews of such newly acquired territories as Bialystok and Bessarabia.[92]

In his diary, Tcherikower also persisted in the themes of his 1939 essay by venting his rage against the leadership of Jewish relief organizations for abandoning their fellow Jews once the war had erupted. The representatives of HICEM, the emigration association for which Tcherikower had once worked, had left France for the safety of America. Angrily, he compared them to the proverbial mice that jump off a sinking ship. Nor did Tcherikower have any kinder words for the Joint Distribution Committee or the representatives of the Federation of Jewish Societies. It was for Efroikin as a communal leader, however, that Tcherikower reserved his harshest words. Apparently having heard a rumor that Efroikin was hiding in Nice, Tcherikower angrily accused him of relying on his wealth to absolve himself of all communal responsibilities during the war. In this accusation, Tcherikower betrayed his disdain, and perhaps also his jealousy, for Efroikin's nouveau riche status.[93] As it turns out, Efroikin was not hiding but engaged in communal activities in the South of France.

All that remained for Tcherikower was to read the current catastrophe into liturgical collective memory. Throughout the diary, he referred to the current era as one enveloped "in the darkness of Egypt."[94] The refugee crisis of French Jews became "the exodus from France."[95] The tragedy, he concluded, had assumed huge proportions because European Jewry had failed to heed the warnings of history. Having tragically misread European civilization's attitude toward the Jews, the refugees still oftentimes refused to take their sober assessments to their logical conclusion. The end of the Diaspora period in Jewish history was dawning, since there were no more diasporic lands to which the Jews could flee.[96] Reflecting on the war between England and Germany, Tcherikower recognized that its outcome would determine the fate of Europe for generations to come:

> We have a strong belief that England will win. But what, God forbid, if not? How many times in the last years did our faith deceive us? Faith is blind. Blind, we simply are afraid to see black, to lead our pessimistic

thought to its conclusion, to its brutal conclusion. And therefore the tragedy comes to us so unexpectedly, so psychologically unprepared. Herein lies the kernel of the catastrophe, which we are all enduring personally. If we had not been afraid to look into our pessimistic thought to the end, we and thousands and thousands others would have abandoned Europe long ago. However, not in a wild running, by foot, without possessions, chased and exhausted; however it would have been a normal exodus from Egypt—an exodus from Poland, an exodus from France etc. And also I would not be standing as now bare and naked, without all the material gathered throughout decades, archives, books, intimately dear things, an empty and expelled person, with a deep brokenness in my heart that I left ownerless and perhaps handed over to the executioner a piece of my embodied soul, years and years of collection, there in the rooms of my abandoned Paris dwelling? And even now, when we are already beaten dogs, our thought still does not want to allow a pessimistic outcome and it grabs hold of the faith that the world cannot go under, Hitler cannot vanquish the world, the best ideals of humanity cannot be trampled by tanks, no matter how great in number they are. However, how often the poisonous fly of pessimism and despair penetrates: And what if he does? What then will be with the world, with the Jews, with all of us? Or [maybe] the world is stronger, humanity's better ideals will not allow themselves to be entirely trampled by the executioner's feet, and they will once again in the darkness and in the sufferings begin to weave anew their eternal web, to gather strength, to elevate the mood, until history will erase from the world the black dark chapter of Hitler and throw it in the wide garbage bag of broken idols, madmen and heroes for a time![97]

Although not overtly Zionist, Tcherikower's vision of an orderly exodus from Europe echoed Herzl's vision in *Der Judenstaat*. In that classic work, Herzl envisioned the creation of a Society of Jews and a Jewish Company that would provide the bureaucratic infrastructure for the orderly evacuation of the Jews from Europe.[98] Tcherikower, however, envisioned European Jewry as not having heeded history's warning and therefore having to evacuate Europe in haste and pandemonium. It is also instructive to compare for a moment the balance of pessimism and optimism in this passage to that in Dubnov's piece. Dubnov, no less than Tcherikower, recognized that the democracies had abandoned the Jews. Despite his misgivings, however, he believed that the Jews had no choice but to join the battle and remind the Allies of their obligations toward the Jews. Sooner or later, the Allies would emerge triumphant, and with victory, the badly battered Jewish people would rise to new life together with a liberated humanity.

Tcherikower, however, based his assumptions on an opposite premise. Logic dictated that a long, dark epoch was dawning. It was doubtful whether the Allies would win the war. With the doors of most countries slammed to them, the Jews had nowhere to go. Although he hoped against hope that the forces of liberalism and civilization would emerge triumphant, he believed that a far grimmer outcome proved far more likely.

Upon settling in America, Tcherikower vacillated between some of the same emotions that he expressed in his diary: despair over the fate of European Jewry, hope for a brighter future in America, and solace in the ability to return to his scholarly work. Added to these emotions, however, was now a strong sense of survivors' guilt. At a gathering of recently arrived refugee Yiddishist intellectuals in New York, Tcherikower ruminated, "Why did I specifically merit to be saved from Hitler's clutches? What will be with the others?" His eyes filling with tears, Tcherikower's face only calmed when he declared his intention to persist in his work for YIVO, especially as editor of *Historishe shriftn,* and as a producer of the *Algemeyne entsiklopedye in yidish* (General Encyclopedia in Yiddish). He consoled himself with the fact that he found himself among family and friends. The following statement reveals the poles of despair and determination around which his mood swung: "Everything was lost. The entire archive. Thousands of volumes. Rare historical collections. Thousands of volumes for the encyclopedia. However, we will republish it. We will re-create it. We must."[99]

After having settled in America, Tcherikower addressed the relationship of the current catastrophe to his scholarship by penning a historiographical reflection, "Yidishe martirologiye un yidishe historiografiye" (Jewish martyrology and Jewish historiography). By reflecting on the divide between the liturgical collective memory of martyrology and the academic discipline of Jewish historiography, Tcherikower obliquely addressed the chasm between secular Yiddish culture and the Jewish religious tradition. In the article, he discussed the striking absence of historiography during most periods of Jewish history, which he attributed to the hegemony of rabbinic Judaism. Faced with a harsh reality of ongoing persecutions, the rabbis chose to escape into the ahistorical world of halakhah and aggadah rather than to attempt to record all their woes.[100]

In his survey of the relatively rare manifestations of Jewish historiography during the medieval and early modern periods, Tcherikower granted primacy to martyrology in all its forms. Returning to one of his common themes, he argued that persecution and the experience of martyrdom awakened the Jewish people's deadened historical consciousness. The chronicles, *selikhes*, and *kines* (dirges) that expressed this consciousness gained popularity with the masses over the rabbis' objections.[101] Tcherikower emphasized the gap between these premodern works of commemoration and modern Jewish historiography:

> Jewish misery gave rise to a philosophy of suffering. One has to suffer for Jewishness—"The Torah is acquired only in pain," wrote the Gaon of Vilna. The pious Jew viewed his suffering as a punishment for his sins by God, and occasionally he came before God as plaintiff. The traditional Jewish historical literature is also permeated with the spirit of religious naïveté.
>
> Our modern scientific study of history has set out upon an entirely different path. It is no longer instigated by surrounding catastrophes. However, without the old historical primitives we should never fully understand the Jewish past and the innermost experiences of the people, and would soon lose our historical bearings.[102]

In conceiving of a chasm between premodern Jewish martyrology and modern Jewish historiography, Tcherikower anticipated by four decades Yosef Yerushalmi's argument that modern Jewish historiography advanced an opposite and often inimical goal to that of premodern Jewish works of martyrology and commemoration. The professional historian, argued Yerushalmi, understood his or her task as exposing the realities behind the collective memories that Jews often employed as means to strengthen their religious and national identities.[103] Unlike the professional historians that Yerushalmi described, Tcherikower belonged to the East European model of the political activist turned scholar/publicist. It is not surprising, then, that a closer look reveals that Tcherikower's article itself, as well as his entire career, belies this neat bifurcation between collective memory and historiography. Given the fusion of martyrology and historiography throughout Tcherikower's works, what begs explanation is his insistence in this article of the absolute separation of these spheres.

Underlying the entire article is its martyrological tone and content. Of all works of sixteenth-century Jewish historiography, Tcherikower deemed 'Emek Ha-bakhah (The Valley of Tears), Joseph Ha-Kohen's account of persecutions, as the most important. Particularly telling was Tcherikower's source for much of his information on martyrology: Shimon Bernfeld's Sefer Ha-dem 'aot (Book of tears), an anthology of Hebrew chronicles and liturgical poems that detail acts of martyrdom. Bernfeld, a historian and anthologist, understood all Jewish history in the Diaspora as one of uninterrupted suffering.[104] At key moments, Tcherikower even left the realm of historiography to express a martyrological flourish. For instance, after quoting a passage from the sixteenth-century Marrano chronicler Samuel Usque that described all of Europe as an "inferno on earth," Tcherikower commented, "Do not these words sound as if written today?"[105] Tcherikower, moreover, ended the article with a quotation from Solomon ibn Verga's Shevet Yehudah, which deliberately blurred the boundaries between martyrology and historiography:

> The author of Shebet [sic] Yehudah draws a portrait of Jewish martyrology and poses the question: "Why are the Jews persecuted so much?" "Jewishness"—he says in response—"is a malady for which there is no healing." And he goes on: "Jews are like a lighted torch that burns and is consumed in fire, but illuminates the way for others." This light is revealed unto us in Jewish history.[106]

Jewish suffering and identity thus proved at once ineluctable and redemptive.

Tcherikower's despair regarding the ability of contemporary secular Jews to respond to the persecution of Nazism with national renaissance led to his insistence on the divide between Jewish martyrology and historiography. As long as Tcherikower had argued that modern Yiddish culture could serve the same role as traditional Torah study, he also believed that historiography could fill the role of traditional martyrology. This belief had sustained Tcherikower during World War I, the Russian Civil War, and during the turbulence of the interwar period. Once, however, he despaired of this vision, cultural disruption and decline replaced renaissance. Losing belief in cultural renaissance at the beginning of World War II, he also abandoned his faith in the national purpose of historiography. During World War I, he had followed Dubnov's path in weaving the current tragedy into the seamless web of suffering. If Tcherikower would accomplish this task now, it would be on a personal level and not in his role as a historian.

Still, in "Yidishe martirologiye un yidishe historiografiye," Tcherikower wrote, "without the old historical primitives we should never fully understand the Jewish past and the innermost experiences of the people, and would soon lose our historical bearings."[107] What Tcherikower expressed here was a wistful desire to escape from context back to the text. Yet, as a modern historian, he judged the traditional martyrological texts as "old historical primitives." Once again, Tcherikower thus expressed the dilemma that he had first articulated in the pages of *Oyfn sheydveg*: although modern national culture had failed to sustain Jewish loyalty, the religious tradition proved irretrievable. The best for which a modern national intellectual could hope was inspiration from the unsullied collective memories of the past.

If the cord between Jewish suffering and the religious tradition had been severed, Tcherikower concluded that the Jewish radicals of the late nineteenth and early twentieth centuries proved largely responsible. Upon arriving in America in 1940, Tcherikower had the opportunity to realize his study of the struggle of Jewish anarchists and socialists against Judaism, which he termed "the war against the Jewish God." Tcherikower's goal in writing this article was clearly polemical. He began and ended the article with a condemnation of those New York Yiddishist educators and activists who objected to the introduction of the study of Bible into the curriculum of the secular Yiddish schools. These people, together with Soviet Yiddishists, needed to know their lineage. For that purpose, Tcherikower described the antireligious demonstrations of the anarchists and socialists in London and on New York's Lower East Side as the coarse expression of a nihilistic rationalism. In essence, Tcherikower argued that Jewish radicalism had been born in the original sin of antireligiosity that bordered on anti-Semitism. Sensationally, Tcherikower reported the extent of these radicals' provocation of the sentiments of religious Jews: the publication of satires that parodied traditional High Holiday prayers, and the Yom Kippur balls and public celebrations. The motivation behind these attacks, concluded Tcherikower, was a deep hatred for Jewish tradition and all things Jewish. It was not any wonder, then, that many of these same radicals embraced anti-Semitic arguments about the parasitical role of the Jews in the economy. Although many of these anarchists later repented and became nationalists, their damage remained indelible. Their attack of Judaism deeply estranged them from the masses that they could have served. More profoundly, they left behind heirs who continued in this struggle against the Jewish national spirit.[108]

This article thus further expressed Tcherikower's disillusionment in the Enlightenment as a force that had devolved among Jews into a tool to attack traditional Judaism and its practitioners. A direct line linked the radical Haskalah of the 1870s to the anarchists of the 1880s and 1890s to the Soviet Yiddish culture of the interwar era. Like Kalmanovitch, Tcherikower had become convinced that the Jewish secular revolution had failed because of its founders' disdain for the Jewish masses and their culture. The specter of the Evsektsiia, with its show trials against the kheyder and zealous persecution of all aspects of Jewish religious life, also lurked behind this depiction of the Jewish anarchists. Tcherikower thus sought to create an ignominious patrimony for the Soviet Yiddish intelligentsia and its supporters. No doubt perturbed by the Soviet sympathies of many American Yiddish activists, Tcherikower sought to inform them of their tainted ancestry.

Kalmanovitch in Vilna

When the Soviets occupied Vilna on September 1, 1939, Kalmanovitch fled northward into Lithuania, first to Kaunas and then to Ponevezh. There, he made plans with Amopteyl to travel to America to join the administration of YIVO in New York. However, in October, the Soviet Union issued an ultimatum to Lithuania, allowing it to retain its independence in exchange for the presence of Soviet military bases and troops on Lithuanian soil. To make the deal look not completely one-sided, the Soviets handed Vilna over to the Lithuanians as a gift. Lithuanian rule of Vilna, now renamed Vilnius, lasted from the end of October 1939 through mid-June 1940. With plans for YIVO to resume its activities under the Lithuanians, Kalmanovitch decided to travel back to Vilna. The outbreak of the war, however, had brought profound changes to YIVO's administration. In Copenhagen en route to an academic conference when the war began, the head of YIVO's philological section and one of its principal leaders, Max Weinreich could not return to Vilna. The arrest and subsequent execution of Rejzen by the Soviets left YIVO still further bereft of leadership. Kalmanovitch, therefore, felt a special responsibility as the only remaining representative of the original YIVO administration to return to Vilna. Another factor that changed the face of YIVO was the presence of members of the Warsaw Yiddishist intelligentsia, who had fled the Nazi occupation for Vilna.[109]

With the establishment of Lithuanian rule over Vilna, these refugees, together with some native leaders, proved anxious to resume YIVO's activities. In fact, many of YIVO's leaders, including Weinreich, reacted with optimism to Lithuanian rule, hoping that the Lithuanians would grant YIVO and the secular Yiddish school system the state support that Poland had denied it.[110] Kalmanovitch too initially expressed this hope, arguing that Lithuanian rule would prove the antidote to linguistic Polonization, which had spread like "psoriasis" among Vilna Jewry during the interwar period. As Kalmanovitch wrote to Niger: "Today, there is no country in which Yiddish rules as Lithuania ... I can very peacefully declare the verdict: The Yiddish potential of one quarter million Jews in Lithuania is much more than ten times stronger than the Yiddish potential in the former Poland." The fact that Kalmanovitch, despite his ideological revision, could express such optimistic sentiments reveals the extent of the allure to even disillusioned Yiddishists of Lithuanian rule, with its promise of state support for Jewish national education and its potential to return Polish-speaking Jews to Yiddish. Yet Kalmanovitch remained skeptical about the future of YIVO, given his fear that the Soviets or the Germans would soon conquer the city.[111] And after he lived several months under Lithuanian rule, Kalmanovitch's despair returned in full force. Deeply saddened by the disappearance and suspected murder of Rejzen by the Soviets, he did not believe that YIVO had any future as long as the war lasted. This depression led him to fight with his colleagues at YIVO over the activities of the institution during the war and over plans to create a chair for Yiddish at Vilnius University.

Fueling Kalmanovitch's despair was his discovery of the extent of Soviet sympathies among many of the young Vilna Yiddishists associated with YIVO. Given the stark alternatives between persecution at the hands of the Nazis or physical safety coupled with economic, religious, and cultural dislocation at the hands of the Soviets, most Vilna Jews chose the later as the lesser of two evils. Whereas many did not seriously espouse Communist ideology, still others assumed leadership roles during the brief Soviet rule in September and October 1940.[112] Some proponents of Yiddish culture believed that Soviet government support, despite its imposition of ideological limitations, would prove preferable to the open disdain of the Polish government. Because of his obsessive hatred of the Soviet Union, however, Kalmanovitch could not see these nuances. Rather, these pro-Soviet sympathies served for him as a damning indictment of Vilna Jewry and the secular Yiddish culture for which it was famous. In a letter to Naftoli Feinerman, the head of Amopteyl, he wrote:

> In general, this episode in the history of Vilna displayed in full brightness the status of Yiddish culture generally, and specifically it functioned as a reflection upon the elements grouped around YIVO. It pulled almost everyone there [toward the Soviet left], like the wolf in the forest, according to the Gentile proverb. Those who awaited this for a long time had their dreams realized, and others quickly broke their old gods and began serving the new master. . . . However, [after the Lithuanians took the city from the Soviets] some remained whose hearts were and remained in the east. And that especially eats at me. I cannot forgive that after the murder of Zalman Rejzen, these people still have the gall to sit amongst us, as if nothing happened. I told this to one of them . . . to his face. Such a commotion ensued that I nearly threw away the whole affair, and wanted to go look for work somewhere else. However, because of good friends, I bowed and remain sitting guarding the little that belongs to me.[113]

At the meetings of YIVO during this time, Kalmanovitch assumed a pessimistic and belligerent stance. YIVO created a temporary administration that included both veteran Vilna activists and refugee Yiddishist intellectuals. On December 8 and 9, 1939, an intense debate ensued at this administration's meeting over the scope of YIVO's activities under Lithuanian rule. Kalmanovitch began the meeting by calling for a moment of silence for the catastrophe that had befallen Polish Jewry and for the arrest of Rejzen. When several of the participants suggested the expansion of YIVO's activities to include support for the Yiddish school system and the production of popular academic material for a broad audience, Kalmanovitch responded with an unequivocal no. Moreover, Kalmanovitch already had made plans to transfer the publication of *YIVO bleter,* YIVO's main academic journal, to New York. He also refused to take any new plans upon himself, including plans for a twenty-fifth anniversary of the death of Peretz.[114]

As a reason for the end of all these activities he cited the loss of communication with the Jews of Poland and America because of the war, as well as lack of funds. All that YIVO should undertake during the war, he insisted, was to finish cataloging its inventory. To this suggestion, David Kaplan-Kaplansky accused Kalmanovitch of planning to sabotage the board's plans. Kalmanovitch denied the charge of sabotage, explaining his decision by referring to Rejzen's disappearance: "The head and the heart of YIVO has left us. How can YIVO live without him?"[115] Nearly all others present at the meeting vociferously disagreed with Kalmanovitch's decision to transfer *YIVO bleter* to New York, seeing it as a symbolic admission of the destruction of the East European center of Yiddish culture.[116] At a meeting in March 1940, Kalmanovitch went still farther. Prylucki, who had arrived from Warsaw, commented on the irony that whereas he, a penniless refugee, was filled with optimism, Kalmanovitch, a local who had not lost anything, saw the present and future in the bleakest colors. To this charge, Kalmanovitch shocked his audience with the following words: "As long as the war endures, we can say that the prewar YIVO no longer exists. In wartime, there can be no work that we won't have to tear [in the middle]. Mr. Prylucki provoked me and I will allow myself to be provoked: I would contend that we should shut down YIVO until after the war; however, there are people here and we have to support them."[117]

This statement led to calls for Kalmanovitch's resignation as the chair of the temporary administration. Shloyme Mendelssohn, a Bundist educator, for instance, argued that Kalmanovitch wronged the institution with such words, which were tantamount to liquidation and defeatism. Instead, Mendelssohn pointed to the experience of World War I, when the German occupation brought the opportunity to create Yiddish schools. Another, M. Kahanovitch, a Vilna activist, came to Kalmanovitch's defense by arguing that, given his moody temperament, Kalmanovitch had exaggerated his point in the heat of argument. Kalmanovitch, for his turn, retorted that he had meant exactly what he had said. "It has to be understood what is mood and what is fact. Rejzen was optimistic, he remained and was arrested; I was pessimistic, I fled and I am standing here now. I in fact do not believe in Jewish life here, yet I work and want there to be a Jewish life. There can be no work, since nobody is working; it is war-time."[118] Sh. Galinsky responded to Kalmanovitch's outburst by urging the committee to remove Kalmanovitch as its chair and to limit his role in YIVO to purely academic matters. During such a time, he argued, YIVO could not trust the implementation of its plans to such a pessimist. Later that day, Kalmanovitch obliged. He announced his resignation as chair of the temporary administration and stated that he would offer a press release explaining the reason for his departure. Before walking out of the meeting, he assured those present that he would continue in his work for the institute.[119]

Kalmanovitch proved equally as combative when it came to the issue of the establishment of a chair of Yiddish studies at Vilnius University. In this instance, Kalmanovitch's opposition arose from both his pessimism over the future of Yiddish culture in the Diaspora and from his personal animosity toward the originator of the proposal, Prylucki. Upon his arrival in Vilna, Prylucki had proposed his idea of a Yiddish chair to Professor Mykolas Biržiška, a liberal, pro-Jewish historian of Lithuanian history and culture, who in 1940 was elected rector of the Great University in Kaunas. Given his pro-Jewish sympathies and Lithuania's desire to win over Vilna Jewry, it is not surprising that this professor reacted positively to the proposal and proved ready to help implement the plan. YIVO's temporary administration reacted angrily to what they considered Prylucki's usurpation of their prerogative in negotiating this position.[120] From the beginning, Kalmanovitch expressed his skepticism that the Lithuanian government would establish such a chair, arguing that the best for which YIVO could hope was a lector. In January 1940, Kalmanovitch joined Pinkhas Kohn and Vladimir Kaplan-Kaplansky as an official delegation to meet with Biržiška. When members of YIVO's philological section nominated Kalmanovitch for the university chair, he categorically refused to accept the nomination. After Kalmanovitch refused the offer, Weinreich nominated himself.[121]

At the March meeting of the temporary administration, Prylucki expressed his anger over the fact that the YIVO leaders had both excluded him from the process and refused to nominate him for the position. To this charge, Kalmanovitch did not conceal his hostility to Prylucki. Prylucki, he countered, was nothing more than an autodidact without the "minimum academic qualifications" for the post. Kalmanovitch blamed Prylucki for ruining YIVO's popular academic journal, *Yidish far ale* and consequently expressed his desire to remove Prylucki as editor. At the meeting, Kalmanovitch, in his refusal to accept the nomination himself, allowed his personal animosity for Prylucki to launch him into an attack against the entire Yiddishist enterprise: "I thought on my own that I am not appropriate. Yiddish did not apply to me nor did the institute. I implemented what the Yiddishists demanded of me with outstanding loyalty." He then referred to his recent visit of his son, Sholem, in Palestine, where he had been offered a position with the National Libratry: "I could have received a spectacular position in the land of Israel, and could have remained near my only son yet I didn't remain there, because I gave my word that I would return."[122]

In addition to expressing their anger that Kalmanovitch had personally attacked Prylucki, the other members of the temporary administration would not let his attack on Yiddish culture go unanswered. Kaplan-Kaplansky stated, "If we heard before such opinions that there is no Jewish people and that Yiddish does not exist, we then knew that Mr. Weinreich and Rejzen reined in Kalmanovitch's pessimism. Now it is not possible that Kalmanovitch should lead YIVO."[123] Another time, Kaplan-Kaplansky rejected Kalmanovitch's candidacy for the chair of Yiddish studies, citing Kalmanovitch's opinion that the Jews are not a people and that Yiddish would not survive. Clearly, Kalmanovitch had repeated the assertions that he had articulated in the pages of *Oyfn sheydveg* to his YIVO colleagues. After a sharp exchange with Kaplan-Kaplansky, Kalmanovitch stormed out of the meeting.[124]

Kalmanovitch's seemingly erratic behavior stemmed from the profound psychological distress engendered by his conclusion that he had dedicated his life to a cause that he now considered misguided and futile. The outbreak of war and Vilna's brief occupation by the Soviets had only confirmed the conclusion at which he arrived in the 1930s: Jewish national life, and indeed Jewish life itself, had no future in the Diaspora. He therefore had spent his life fighting for the wrong ideal. Even now, when he belatedly could have joined his son in the Zionist renaissance in Palestine, a sense of duty had brought him back to the quicksand of Vilna. If Kalmanovitch vented these feelings at YIVO meetings, he articulated them in a more polished manner in his essay for the third *Oyfn sheydveg,* later published in *Ringen.* Almost point by point, this article repudiated the stance that Dubnov had taken in his article "*Inter-arma* II." Although Kalmanovitch had not read the article, he repudiated what he knew to be the stance of his former mentor.

Much more pessimistic than Dubnov, Kalmanovitch began his essay by stating that even though Jewish sufferings may have reached their height in quality, that in quantity, the destruction had just begun. Unlike Dubnov, who envisioned Polish Jews streaming to a future peace conference to demand their rights, Kalmanovitch assumed the permanent destruction of the Polish Jewish community. In fact, he referred to those few Jews who would survive the war as the *she'eris ha-pletoh*—a liturgical phrase meaning "the surviving remnant." Whereas Dubnov looked externally to the Allies for help, Kalmanovitch asked his readers to turn their gaze inward to understand the cause of their current plight. Unlike Dubnov, who blamed the Allies for their indifference, Kalmanovitch blamed the Jews themselves for their failure to comprehend their true situation before it was too late.[125]

In prophetic style, Kalmanovitch stated that Isaiah's vision had come true in which God had declared that he would close the people's eyes, ears, and heart to the truth. Referring to the founders of the Zionist movement as "wise Jews and Jews with love for their people," Kalmanovitch explained that they had predicted the possibility of such a catastrophe as early as two generations ago. Although a majority of East European Jews had paid lip service to Zionism, they behaved as if they felt at home in Eastern Europe.[126] This article thus signaled the completion of his transformation from Diaspora nationalist to territorialist to Zionist.

Rather than listening to the warnings of the Zionists, Jews rather attempted to convince their neighbors that they should attain equal rights in their lands of residence. In Kalmanovitch's words:

In practical life, all the warnings of the wise Jews and the lovers of Israel had no value; we even did not notice the lightning, which would illuminate for the whole world from time to time the situation of an eternal people in exile that has no strength to die and no will to live. Those lightning strikes burned wounds into our flesh in the years when the elemental forces of the nations in Eastern Europe raged in fury in 1905, 1917. Later, clawing with our nails, we isolated ourselves in the cities where we sat, in the "positions," which we supposedly occupied, in the "culture," which we supposedly created in our places of residence. We convinced ourselves . . . that the situation can be imagined when we would win the war for our right to live in exile, amongst strangers, who cannot tolerate us, who perhaps do not have to [tolerate us], since they are only flesh and blood and not angels. They are living practical people who must satisfy their material and spiritual needs in a world of struggle for existence, and not philosophers and theoreticians of humanism.[127]

Whereas Dubnov argued that the Jews must convince their European neighbors of the Jews' contributions to society, Kalmanovitch argued that such a reminder would prove futile. Rather, he argued that the Jews must divorce themselves from European culture, economic life, and politics. Addressing the political implications of the Jews' misguided striving for emancipation, Kalmanovitch ironically described how East European Jews had attempted to prove their worthiness of equal rights "with signs and wonders."[128]

In the remainder of the essay, Kalmanovitch excoriated Polish Jewry for its political activism in the face of its worsening plight in the late 1930s. Typical for Kalmanovitch, he blamed the entire Polish Jewish society for its fatal blindness. Even as the Polish boycott of Jewish businesses in the second half of the 1930s had ruined the Jews financially, Jewish businessmen considered themselves heroes if they remained in business. Moreover, Kalmanovitch indicated, even *Haynt*, a Zionist newspaper, urged its readers to fight for their rights. Especially irksome to Kalmanovitch was the Bund's victories in *kehile* and municipal elections in 1939. To Kalmanovitch, the Bund represented the opposite of his current ideology. Like Dubnov, he blamed the Bund for furthering the destruction of the unity of the Jewish people through its emphasis on class. Unlike Dubnov, however, Kalmanovitch took issue with the Bund's central ideology of *doikeyt* (hereness), which preached that the Jews must defiantly fight for their rights in their lands of residence. Because of his now anti–Diaspora nationalist bent, Kalmanovitch understood Polish Jewry's turn to the Bund as evidence of its feeling at home in Poland. As Kalmanovitch himself admitted, though, no meaningful possibility of emigration existed for the vast majority of Polish Jewry. Having no other choice than to remain in Poland, the majority of Polish Jews decided to fight against their extrusion from the economic and political life of the country. According to many historians, Polish Jews turned to the Bund because they believed it was the Jewish political party with the most ties to the world of Polish politics. Kalmanovitch, however, dismissed this search for allies among the Polish working class as futile.[129]

Unlike Dubnov, Kalmanovitch did not believe that the Jews should lobby the Allies to rebuild the Polish Jewish community. Whereas the democratic countries had promised the Polish leadership in exile to rebuild Poland upon the war's end, they made no such promises to the Jews regarding Polish Jewish life. Similarly, the Soviets, who had occupied eastern Poland, made no specific mention of the Jews in their midst. The fate of the war would determine the fate of the Jews, without the need for the Allies to consult them or to ask for their help. Unlike Dubnov, who named the American Jewish Congress and the World Jewish Congress as the future representatives of the Jewish people at a peace conference, Kalmanovitch argued that the Jews had no effective representative organization that could demand favors from the Allies in exchange for Jewish support of the war effort.[130]

In the eerily prescient conclusion to the essay, Kalmanovitch argued that the Jews could not save themselves from the coming slaughter. Those left alive at the end of the war only could save themselves and the Jewish people by evacuating the Diaspora. In his words:

> An essential transformation in the Jewish situation in the world only can occur when Jews become active. That can only happen when the concept that they are in exile will become just as alive within them as the concept that they are human beings. Jews, however, demand human rights for themselves even if they are in exile. This is a contradiction similar to cold fire: in exile, Jews can have no human rights. In exile, they cannot be active. The current catastrophe of the great, rooted, and creative Jewish collective came through no fault of its own, completely without its participation. It is

a result of its being in exile. It had no choice in the misfortune; it cannot rescue itself. . . . The Polish-Jewish collective only could hold out its neck to the knife of the butcher: "Here, slaughter!" And the slaughter only will cease when the other's hand grows tired, dangling without strength.

When will Jews begin truly to see and to hear and to feel? The time that the prophet pointed out indeed has already arrived:

> Until cities will be desolate without inhabitants,
> and houses without people,
> and the earth will become desolate in a desolation . . .

We will have the sign, if we will survive, that Jews will become truly active and begin to tear themselves from exile.[131]

Despite his complete despair with Jewish life in the Diaspora and with Yiddish culture, Kalmanovitch remained at his position in YIVO until the Soviet reoccupation of Vilna in mid-June 1940. In the days before the Soviet reconquest, Kalmanovitch informed Niger that he was writing for "the last time in a long, long time, maybe forever." Both missing his son and imagining Jewish national life in the *Yishuv,* Kalmanovitch informed Niger that he was attempting to secure a certificate for immigration to Palestine. He also recognized that a Soviet occupation would mean the end of his work for YIVO. With resignation and an attempt at humor, he wrote that if the Jewish Communists forced him to leave YIVO, he would "sit down and learn a page of Talmud." As the political noose tightened, Kalmanovitch's previous despair gave way to resignation and even resolve to survive the war. As he wrote Niger, "We must fill ourselves with faith and belief that we will still live to see with our own eyes how peace will once again come and the world will still remain in place."[132]

Once the Soviets reentered Vilna, they immediately fired Kalmanovitch as curator of YIVO, replacing him with Moyshe Lerer, an archivist with Soviet sympathies. During the summer of 1940, the Soviet authorities together with pro-Soviet Yiddishists purged YIVO of the Bundists, folkists, and Zionists who had once worked for it. In an editorial, the now Communist Vilna *Togblat* boasted that YIVO had finally been liberated from its oligarchic clique of academic leaders and returned to the masses to which it belonged. In particular, the editorial singled out "one of the chief schemers from the Yiddish Scientific Institute [who] traveled around preaching the dark purpose of

Yiddish."[133] Clearly, the editorial writer had Kalmanovitch in mind. From mid-June 1940 until a year later when the Nazis invaded, Kalmanovitch earned a meager livelihood as a copyeditor of Yiddish, Russian, and Lithuanian books.[134] In January 1941, the Soviets appointed Kalmanovitch's nemesis, Prylucki, as director of YIVO. Soon, they renamed YIVO "The Institute for Jewish Culture" and incorporated it into the Scholarly Academy of the Soviet Lithuanian Republic.[135] Although struggling to eke out a living, Kalmanovitch seemed relieved to no longer be responsible for an institution in whose mission he no longer believed. Although deeply saddened by the many personal losses around him, Kalmanovitch no longer expressed feelings of depression in his letters, only resignation and a deepening religious faith. In the words of his last letter to Niger, from April 1941:

> Regarding YIVO, I am trying to forget. (By the way, here we can consider it completely a dweller in the dust). . . . I think that you are generally taking this into consideration, and the Amopteyl now is stepping forth as the entire YIVO. And I want to understand . . . that you are having some success. I wish you with my whole heart for still more. Maybe I will yet have the opportunity to work together with you. If not, I will take pleasure from afar; I will also be satisfied.[136]

His worse predictions for YIVO having reached fruition, Kalmanovitch only could sit on the sidelines and watch events unfold. But he would not stay on the sidelines for long. With the Nazi invasion of Vilna two months later, the last and most dramatic chapter of his life as a public intellectual began.

In April and August 1939, the contributors to *Oyfn sheydveg* could not have realized that European Jewry stood "at the crossroads" not just between emancipation and counter-emancipation but also between life and death. As David Roskies so aptly suggested, *No Exit* would have proved a more appropriate title than *Oyfn sheydveg*, since the fate of both West and East European Jewries would finally converge on the trains that led to the death camps.[137] Despite this bleak reality, the historian must not understand the enterprise of *Oyfn sheydveg* as one of unmitigated despair. Efroikin spoke for all the contributors when he wrote that the Jews should retreat from politics and concentrate on their own internal culture "until the wrath passes."[138] These intellectuals may have despaired of all contemporary ideologies, political movements, and governments, but they did not despair of the Jewish future. Indeed, the very act of articulating a new ideology for an age of counter-emancipation conveyed these writers' belief that the Jews needed to prepare for the future.

In 1939, at the very moment when no escape seemed possible for European Jews, a group of Yiddishist intellectuals sought refuge in the realm of ideology. Because these men had all experienced the opposites of tradition and modernity, Eastern Europe and the West, and idealism and disillusionment, they offered a strikingly uniform diagnosis of the Jewish plight. True, much of their counter-emancipationist ideology emerged as a reaction to political events of the late 1930s. Yet, far from merely reactive, these intellectuals actively forged an ideology that both accurately assessed the frightful plight of European Jewry and, more importantly, provided it with hope by calling for an internal consolidation.

In 1940, when the last of the articles had been written for the third issue of *Oyfn sheydveg,* East European Jewry, though badly battered, still could conceive of a collective future. In this brief moment between the outbreak of war and the eruption of genocide, Dubnov, Tcherikower, and Kalmanovitch approached the cataclysm of World War II through the ideological visions that they had articulated fully on the eve of the catastrophe. Whereas these men once had subscribed to the same ideology, Dubnov no longer shared the same language of discourse with Tcherikower or Kalmanovitch. In his letter to the editor in the second issue of *Oyfn sheydveg,* Dubnov rightly recognized this journal as his students' ideological repudiation of his political and cultural vision.

In one overriding respect, the articles of all the *Oyfn sheydveg* contributors discussed here, both Dubnov and his students, exhibited a striking similarity, despite all their manifest differences. They revealed the final, most bitter irony regarding the fate of Diaspora nationalism and Yiddishism: these ideologies had failed according to their own terms. Four decades earlier, Dubnov had conceived of Diaspora nationalism as a political means for the Jewish community to itself shape the nature and effects of emancipation. Rather than settling for the personal emancipation offered them by governments, the Jews would retain their collective identity by demanding national autonomy. Four decades later, however, Dubnov could only salvage his vision for the future by raging against the Western powers in a futile attempt to remind them of their obligations to the Jews. In addressing his words to the democracies, Dubnov admitted, unwillingly and perhaps unknowingly, to current Jewish political powerlessness.

At the end of a life committed to the study of Jewish history, Dubnov found himself living through that history's nadir. Even as the world collapsed around him, he refused to relinquish his belief in the ultimate attainment of equal civil and national rights by the Jews of Eastern Europe. Yet several of his most committed students no longer shared in his optimism. In the final two years of his life, Dubnov must have felt a double sense of betrayal—both from the outside world and from his former students. And his students must have felt a sense of loss as well. At the moment when they needed guidance the most, however, they found no comfort in their mentor's words. These men thus parted from one another ideologically just as the same fate enveloped them together with all of European Jewry.

Elias Tcherikower, age
twenty-two. Poltava, Russia,
1903.
*(Archives of the YIVO Institute
for Jewish Research, New York)*

I. L. Peretz, 1908.
*(Archives of the YIVO
Institute for Jewish Research,
New York)*

Back row, second and third from left: Elias Tcherikower and Riva Teplitsky (Tcherikower). St. Petersburg, 1908.
(Archives of the YIVO Institute for Jewish Research, New York)

Catherine Breshkovsky (a veteran Russian revolutionary and founder of the Socialist Revolutionary Party) and Chaim Zhitlovsky.
(Archives of the YIVO Institute for Jewish Research, New York)

Front row (from left): Moyshe Zilberg, Dovid Einhorn. Second row (from left): Zelig Kalmanovitch, Dan Kaplanovitch, Mendele Moykher Sforim (Sholem Yankev Abramovitch), A. Litvak, Falk Halpern. Top row: Ben Eliezer (M. Lazerson), Lipman Levin, Yankev Zerubabel, Dvoyre Baron. Vilna, 1910.
(Courtesy of Yuval Luria)

Front row, farthest right: Riva Tcherikower. Back row, farthest left: Elias Tcherikower. Alexandria, Egypt, 1915.
(Archives of the YIVO Institute for Jewish Research, New York)

Elias and Riva Tcherikower, circa 1915.
(Archives of the YIVO Institute for Jewish Research, New York)

Back row, left to right: Baal Makhshoves (Isadore Eliashiv), Elias Tcherikower, Nokhem Shtif, Zelig Kalmanovitch, Dovid Bergelson, Wolf Latski-Bertoldi.
(Archives of the YIVO Institute for Jewish Research, New York)

Zelig, Rivele, and Sholem
Kalmanovitch. Minsk, 1920.
(Courtesy of Yuval Luria)

Front row, starting second from left: wife of Dovid Bergelson, Nokhem
Shtif, Jakob Lestschinsky, Zelig Kalmanovitch, Dovid Bergelson and son,
Baal Makhshoves. Lithuania, circa 1920.
(Archives of the YIVO Institute for Jewish Research, New York)

The defense committee of Sholem Schwartzbard. Back row, left to right: Yisroel Efroikin, Elias Tcherikower. Front row starting from second to left, left to right: Sholem Schwartzbard, Leo Motzkin, Sholem Asch. Paris, 1926 or 1927.
(Archives of the YIVO Institute for Jewish Research, New York)

Party to celebrate Sholem Schwartzbard's acquittal. Far front, farthest to the right: Yisroel Efroikin. Second row (seated), third from left: Sholem Schwartzbard. Third row (standing), third from left, Sholem Asch; fourth from left: Riva Tcherikower; seventh from left: Elias Tcherikower. Paris, 1927.
(Archives of the YIVO Institute for Jewish Research, New York)

Left to right: Rivele, Sholem, and Zelig Kalmanovitch. Vilna, 1937.
(Archives of the YIVO Institute for Jewish Research, New York)

Simon Dubnov. Riga, 1937.
(Archives of the YIVO Institute for Jewish Research, New York)

Back row, far left: Elias Tcherikower; Second from right: Jakob Lestschinsky.
Far right: Riva Tcherikower. Front row; left: Ida Dubnov; Second from left:
Simon Dubnov.
(Archives of the YIVO Institute for Jewish Research, New York)

Official portrait of Yisroel
Efroikin.
*(Mémorial de la Shoah/CDJC/Coll.
MJP)*

CHAPTER FIVE

The Holocaust

DURING THE HEIGHT of World War II, Tcherikower, Efroikin, and Kalmanovitch found themselves on different continents under very different conditions. In September 1940, Tcherikower arrived in New York, where, until his sudden death in 1943, he managed to return to his historical studies. Efroikin, in contrast, lingered in the South of France until 1942, after which he found refuge for the rest of the war in Montevideo, Uruguay. At the beginning of Efroikin's sojourn in Montevideo, he found himself in a state of great anxiety, fearing that his only child, Jules, and his daughter-in-law had not made it safely out of Vichy France. Refusing to attend public meetings, Efroikin withdrew into himself and into his own research. Once he heard that his son had safely escaped the Nazis, he published articles and even a book, returning to his role as a public intellectual, which he had abandoned upon leaving Russia over two decades earlier. Kalmanovitch, who turned down a visa sent by Amopteyl in New York, remained in Vilna, first under the Soviets and then under the Nazis. Incarcerated in the Vilna ghetto, Kalmanovitch was forced by the Nazis to select books to ship to Germany, for their planned museum to the extinct Jewish race. He perished in the work camps of Estonia in early 1944.[1]

Yet, despite their very different circumstances, all three of these men deepened the ideological revision in which they had been engaged on the eve of the war. In New York, Tcherikower realized his project of writing a history of the Jews of France during the time of the French Revolution. From a historical perspective, he undermined the legacy of emancipation by arguing that it had contributed to Jewish marginality rather than power. Efroikin, first in France and then in Uruguay, continued to call for a return to the ghetto and a retreat from the modern world. Kalmanovitch, in the meantime, wrote a ghetto diary in which he turned to the Jewish religious tradition for a meta-historical explanation of the catastrophe, imagining the ensuing genocide as hastening the process of a national consolidation and the creation of a future in Palestine. Each in his own way, these men despaired of their former ideologies even as they sought ways to implement them in extremis. It is to Tcherikower's reimagining of the dawn of modern Jewish history that we now turn.

Tcherikower on the French Revolution and the Jews

As an immigrant from Nazi-occupied France in New York, Tcherikower had the presence of mind to return to his historical studies by addressing some of the themes about which he wrote in his 1940 diary. In particular, he realized, at least in part, his study of the French Revolution's effect upon French Jewry. In reality, as he had confided in his diary, this study proved a scholarly continuation of his despair in the failure of emancipation. Tcherikower incorporated his study in a two-volume collection of articles, titled *Yidn in frankraykh* (Jews in France), which he himself edited. Published in 1942 by the historical section of YIVO in New York, the book originated as a project of the Paris section of YIVO. Nearly all the contributors to the volume, including Tcherikower, Avrom Menes, and Zosa Szajkowski, had functioned as YIVO activists in Paris. Ready for publication at the time of the Nazi invasion of France, the book had to wait two more years to be published in New York. In the introduction, Tcherikower stated openly that YIVO found it impossible to publish a collective work about Jews in France in such a time from a purely academic standpoint. Rather, the reader would detect a common historiographical perspective in all the articles, which traced "a line from ascent to descent" of French Jewry from the rise of emancipation in the late eighteenth century to its repeal and French Jewry's present destruction. In the process, the studies would concentrate on the everyday lives of non-elite French Jews, first those in Alsace-Lorraine and then the East European Jewish immigrants in Paris. Touting his book as the first study of French Jewry in Yiddish, Tcherikower noted the tragedy that some of the volume's contributors currently were still trapped in transit camps in the South of France.[2]

Tcherikower intended his study as a revision of the historiographical tradition that lauded the French Revolution as the inauguration of an era of Jewish liberation first in France and then in all of Europe. In order to make his contemporary message clear, Tcherikower subtitled his first essay "One Hundred Fifty Years after the Jewish Emancipation." Tcherikower's essay argued that a fresh look at the French emancipation would reveal its dark legacy. The first sentence set the tone for the entire work: "Jewish history, which at the end of the eighteenth century turned sharply from its old traditional path to a completely new one, chose for its experiment the Jewish community of France, which was small, weak, internally divided, and played no role in the life of general Jewry."[3] Despite this reality, Tcherikower continued, nearly all Jewish historians of the revolution, from Graetz to Dubnov, described the historical significance of the revolution with the same "pathetic" words of praise used by the Jewish participants in the events themselves. Tcherikower noted the irony that French Jewry had continued to praise the legacy of the French Revolution without qualification even on the eve of emancipation's liquidation. Now that the era of emancipation had ended, argued Tcherikower, historians could more objectively assess its legacy. Instead of celebrating the external victories of emancipation, argued Tcherikower, he would analyze the internal contradictions and ambiguities of the process.[4]

What emerged from this investigation is a portrait of emancipation far different from that presented in previous historiography: the debate over Jewish emancipation in French political and social circles at the time of the revolution, far from demonstrating greater acceptance of the Jews, highlighted their precarious and marginal status. Anticipating many of Arthur Hertzberg's arguments by several decades, Tcherikower argued that racial anti-Semitism had its origins in the French Enlightenment and the revolution.[5] Anti-Semites, moreover, used the newly established freedom of the press and assembly to agitate for pogroms. Unlike previous historical accounts, Tcherikower's investigation stressed the prolonged nature of the Jewish struggle for emancipation, which came for the Jews of Alsace-Lorraine after all other groups had achieved their rights. The French demand that the Jews had to choose between emancipation and internal autonomy, moreover, met with the resistance of the traditional Jews of Alsace-Lorraine. Their leaders, insisted Tcherikower, made every effort to obtain emancipation alongside the continued existence of autonomous *kehiles,* before they finally had to bow to the pressure of the revolutionaries. In short, the story of the emancipation of French Jewry was not one of triumph but rather of tragedy.

Tcherikower's revision of the story of French Jewry had its villains and heroes. His villains consisted externally of both those French statesmen and thinkers who sought to deny emancipation to the Jews and those who begrudgingly offered it to them in exchange for the abolition of their corporate identity. Internally, Tcherikower's villains were the Portuguese Jews of the South of France and the acculturated Jews of Paris who attempted to distance themselves from the Jews of Alsace-Lorraine in order to attain emancipation. His internal heroes, in contrast, were the Jews of Alsace-Lorraine themselves, who doggedly insisted on emancipation together with the persistence of communal autonomy. In Tcherikower's imagination, the Portuguese and Parisian Jewish communities served as analogues for West European Jewry, with its penchant for assimilation and hatred of traditional Jews. The Jews of Alsace-Lorraine, in contrast, were analogues for East European Jewry, with its desire for a synthesis of personal and communal rights. Tcherikower even went as far as to declare the Jewish masses of Alsace-Lorraine an "eastern" Ashkenazic Jewry that functioned as France's *Ostjuden.*[6]

He thus created a counter-genealogy of Jewish modernity that wistfully mourned a lost opportunity. Had the East European model, here projected backward upon Alsatian Jewry, emerged victorious, emancipation would have come hand in hand with Jewish national autonomy. However, non-Jewish pressure and internal Jewish betrayal assured the victory of emancipation at the price of that autonomy's destruction. Instructive of the mood pervading this vision is the fact that Tcherikower imagined no heroes as existing in this story on the non-Jewish side, which ultimately determined the outcome of the struggle. Rather, even proponents of the emancipation of Jewish individuals insisted on Jewish abdication of all forms of corporate status.

Jewish nationalist historians, insisted Tcherikower, had erred in envisioning French Jewry as immediately ceding its rights to communal autonomy in exchange for emancipation. Rather, from the time that the Jewries of Alsace-Lorraine first presented their petitions to Louis XVI in February 1789, they requested the liberalization of state policy toward the Jews coupled with assurances of collective autonomy. It was the acculturated Jews of the South of France and Paris, in contrast, who petitioned the king for individual rights and for separation from the same legal category as the benighted Jews of Alsace-Lorraine. This tragic division in the Jewish community in the name of elitism contradicted the revolutionary spirit and thus met with the resistance of revolutionaries such as Abbé Grégoire. Tcherikower also emphasized that the Jewries of Alsace-Lorraine similarly petitioned the National Assembly in December 1789 for both civil and political equality and for the continued jurisdiction of their communal authorities. Only when the entire French political spectrum, from royalists to Jacobin revolutionaries, rejected this demand did these Jewries half-heartedly abandon their demand for Jewish national autonomy.[7]

To Tcherikower, the intellectual voices of the Jewries of Alsace-Lorraine, Yeshaya Ber Bing, Serf Ber, and Ber Isaac Ber, served as an alternative model of the Haskalah that, if successful, could have achieved a modernity that combined personal and national emancipation. The Berlin *maskilim*, wrote Tcherikower, "would have not thought for a minute about happily giving up the old forms of Judaism with all its 'privileges' for the price of becoming Germans." In contrast, the more moderate *maskilim* of Alsace-Lorraine tempered their battle for political rights with a strong sense of Jewish national pride. Bing, for instance, wrote a petition to the National Assembly in which he bravely accused the Christian French world of oppressing the proud Jewish nation for centuries.[8] In their petition to the National Assembly in August 1789, these leaders insisted on the right of the Jews to maintain autonomy by bravely stating, "and the national assembly certainly will not take away from us in the moment of freedom that which the previous regime granted us in a moment of oppression."[9] In response to an attack from the bishop of Nance demanding that the Jews abandon their internal autonomy, one of the Jewish leaders in the struggle for emancipation penned a brochure in which he wrote: "Better death with its horrors, than the old disgrace of humiliation."[10]

Thus, initially the leaders of the Jewries of Alsace-Lorraine offered a third way between the conservatism of Orthodoxy and the assimilatory tendencies of Berlin Haskalah. Had their vision won, implied Tcherikower, modernity would have led to Jewish national rebirth rather than to degeneration. A combination of external anti-Semitism and the internal perfidy of the Jews of the South and Paris, however, undermined their position. Citing its objections to continued Jewish autonomy, the National Assembly voted to table the vote on Jewish emancipation. Only after confronting this reality as well as the granting of emancipation to the Portuguese Jews of the South did the leadership of the Jewries of Alsace-Lorraine reluctantly agree to relinquish their demand for autonomy.[11]

Ultimately, Tcherikower blamed not other Jews but the leaders of the revolution for the failure of the Jews to achieve national rights together with their personal emancipation. In his words:

> A second, more tragic feature was that according to the ruling "philosophy" of the revolution, it was difficult to grasp the needs and demands of the Jews as a *collective,* as a unique collective. Jews then had enough friends amongst the "philosophes" and "patriots," yet none of them could grasp exactly what the Jews wanted: to leave the ghetto—and nonetheless to remain a collective on its own? They were ready to give full rights to Jews, but on the condition that they become Frenchmen "like everyone else," to renounce their historical uniqueness of a community and only observe, if they so desire, their religion, to which the "philosophes" were apathetic and later even adversarial. One group of Jews accepted this condition with joy, but the second, a larger one, agreed with a heavy heart and with the secret hope that life would annul this condition.[12]

It was the revolutionaries' deliberate lack of empathy for the nature of Jewish identity, then, that created the tragic gulf between the good of Jewish individuals and the collective that Tcherikower had bemoaned openly in his publicistic article in *Oyfn sheydveg*. A misinterpretation of the nature of Jewish communal autonomy motivated the Jews' seeming friends such as Abbé Grégoire and Clermont-Tonnerre to equate it with the privileges of such estates as the nobility and the church. Clermont-Tonnerre's famous statement, "We must deny everything to the Jews as a nation; we must give them everything as individuals," concluded with the ominous warning that if the Jews would not renounce corporate identity, France would have to expel them. This "either or" proposition united both the right and left in French political circles. The revolutionaries embraced this perspective, argued Tcherikower, because their zeal for the philosophy of natural rights and the freedom of the individual led them to seek to equalize all members of society through the abolition of privilege. Seeking to create a unified French citizenry, the leaders of the revolution could not understand that the Jewish demand for autonomy lacked any threat of political separatism. With the communal life of traditional Jewry equated with "privilege," Jewish identity became reduced to the realm of religious confession. Yet any institutional embodiment of this religion became synonymous with the hated church, against which the revolutionaries fought. With the term "nation" equated with a body politic, the leaders of the revolution thus rejected all forms of Jewish autonomy as a "state within a state." In Tcherikower's words:

> And herein lies the tragedy of that Jewish generation, that the revolutionary epoch could not grasp the unique phenomenon of Jews, who, from one side sincerely want to be French citizens, and from the other want to preserve something of an intimate second life as *Jews*. This appeared to them as a wild contradiction to the revolution, to its spirit and "philosophy,"—and the condition was presented to the Jews—either-or. Specifically this contradiction the revolution could not bear, even though it [the revolution] itself was a chain of internal contradictions, much more serious than this one.[13]

Twenty-five years earlier, in the midst of World War I, Tcherikower had expressed his despair over the one-sided nature of the Jewish love affair with European civilization. The Jews understood other cultures, he had concluded, far better than those cultures had understood the Jews. Now, in the midst of World War II, he returned to this dark conclusion to argue that this misunderstanding rested at the heart of what he considered the tragedy of Jewish modernity. To Tcherikower, the French failure to understand the Jewish demand for autonomy foreshadowed twentieth-century Europe's rejection of Diaspora nationalism. Diaspora nationalists, as I have argued, predicated their ideology on the belief in the goodwill of dominant national groups and political entities in recognizing the Jews as a national minority. Once they despaired of this goodwill, it was difficult if not impossible for Diaspora nationalists to maintain faith in their ideology. Through his emphasis on the failure of the French to understand the Jewish desire for a synthesis of personal and national rights, Tcherikower indicated his conclusion that Diaspora nationalism had no supporters in the non-Jewish world. During World War I, despite his doubts, Tcherikower still championed a linear view of the history of Jewish emancipation: the personal rights won through the French Revolution led inexorably to the demand for national rights by Russian Jewry a century later. In this vision, he followed Dubnov's lead. Now, however, Tcherikower traced the origins of the failure of Diaspora nationalism to the events of the French Revolution itself. By imagining Alsace-Lorraine at the end of the eighteenth century as an analogue for the Russian Pale of Settlement at the beginning of the twentieth century, Tcherikower could invoke historical precedent in his judgment of Diaspora nationalism as a stillborn project.[14]

If he had formerly drawn a triumphant line between the personal emancipation of the late eighteenth century and the anticipated national liberation of the twentieth, Tcherikower now collapsed the processes of emancipation and auto-emancipation into a united story of failure. In so doing, he continued in his historiography what he had begun publicistically in *Oyfn sheydveg*: the collapsing of the entire 150-year period from 1789 to 1939 as a tragic era that internally weakened the Jewish collective in the name of an ephemeral political emancipation. The National Assembly's emancipation of French Jewry in September 1791, concluded Tcherikower, "was surrounded with such reservations, which had to sting the feeling of citizenship of the newly liberated."[15] Tcherikower emphasized how the demand of the National Assembly that the Jews take an oath of loyalty before their naturalization set them apart from the rest of the French citizenry.

Rather than treating the Jews according to the principles of the French Constitution and the Declaration of the Rights of Man and of the Citizen, the National Assembly related to them as it had to members of the church from whom it had demanded a loyalty oath. Given the church's power and its counterrevolutionary politics, demanding a loyalty oath from its members made sense. By applying this standard to the Jews, however, the National Assembly identified them as a potential fifth column. Of course, most disturbing to Tcherikower was the demand that in exchange for emancipation the Jews relinquish all former privileges, meaning autonomy. He fulminated against all previous Jewish historians who praised this clause as not damaging to Jewish religious identity. The National Assembly, moreover, further narrowed the act of emancipation by concurrently limiting the amount of debts that the Jews could collect from Christians.[16]

Characteristic for this work, Tcherikower gave the final voice not to those Jewish leaders who hailed the declaration of emancipation as a messianic act but rather to the embattled Jews of Alsace-Lorraine, who interpreted their loss of communal autonomy as an evil decree. During the revolutionary years, stated Tcherikower, the government began to refer to the emancipated Jews as "former Jews," unable to reconcile even Jewish religious identity with the concept of French citizenship. As part of this study, Tcherikower proved unable to include his desired detailed study of the reaction of Orthodox Jewry to emancipation. However, he did leave his readers with a sense of the extent of persecution that religious Jews experienced under Jacobin rule, with its cult of reason and suppression of religion. "The religious Jews consider this time as one considers the time of an evil decree [gzeyre]: they hid together with their religious quorums in the cellars, as of old, or they fled and experienced exile."[17]

This image of the religious Jews of Alsace-Loraine as Marranos at once beckoned backward to medieval Spain and forward to the Soviet Union of the interwar era. Through this image, Tcherikower erased the dichotomy between medieval oppression and modern liberation that long had served as a hallmark of modern Jewish historiography. Rather, he implied, the centralization of the state through the French Revolution only strengthened its power to crush the Jews' internal life. Lurking behind this image was the reality of the revolution in Tcherikower's native Russia, which also had begun with the emancipation of the Jews but had continued to destroy all forms of Jewish religious and national culture and politics. The straight line from the French to the Russian revolutions thus led not, as he previously had believed, from personal to national emancipation but rather from medieval religious to modern state-controlled anti-Semitism. It was through the emancipation of Jewish individuals, implied Tcherikower, that the state had successfully destroyed the Jewish collective.

Tcherikower's completion of this major historical essay during the war, as a new immigrant in New York, proved a major accomplishment. In what turned out to be the last year of his life, Tcherikower once again channeled his grief and despair into scholarship, retreating from the world of publicistics. The fact that it took a generation before this study appeared in print in a non-Jewish language naturally limited its impact on French Jewish historiography. Still, it broke new ground in its use of primary sources to demonstrate the extent of French anti-Semitism and the prolonged nature of the emancipation process. Although Tcherikower's conception of the nature of Alsatian Jewry's communal autonomy proved somewhat anachronistic, he nonetheless exposed the previous historiography's assessment of French Jewry's quick surrender of corporate identity as a fallacy. Tcherikower's conclusion that anti-Semitism as a mass phenomenon originated in the same democratization process that led to emancipation anticipated the findings of the next generation of Jewish historians, living in the United States and Israel during the second half of the twentieth century. Writing from the perspective of World War II, Tcherikower went still farther than his successors, arguing that the emancipation process itself reflected this process of anti-Semitism.[18]

In his three years in America, Tcherikower deeply mourned the fate of European Jewry. Having personally experienced the other great tragedies of twentieth-century East European Jewry such as the Russian Revolution, the Russian Civil War, and the pogroms, he felt uncomfortably distant from the battlefield in the safety of America. Perhaps it was this sense of disconnection together with his despair over the future of European Jewry that led Tcherikower, the lifelong Diaspora nationalist, to increasingly long for Palestine. Yet it would be wrong to characterize Tcherikower's final years as ones of isolation and depression. Quite the contrary: Tcherikower became an integral member of the Yiddish cultural scene and of the Yiddishist group that centered around YIVO. In Amopteyl, he found solace in the continuity both of his scholarship and of the scholarly mission of YIVO. His final years in New York also proved very productive ones. In addition to *Yidn in frankraykh,* he also edited the large two-volume *Geshikhte fun der yidisher arbeter-bavegung in di fareynikte shtatn* (History of the Jewish labor movement in the United States), writing many of its chapters himself. Through these studies, Tcherikower returned to the theme that had interested him since his debut as a Yiddish writer during World War I. He also continued in his roles as head of YIVO's historical division and as editor of *Historishe shriftn.* As during World War I and the Russian Civil War, Tcherikower thus channeled his grief over his people's fate into his scholarship.[19] In the morning hours of August 28, 1943, "the Angel of Death," as his friend Daniel Tsharni put it, "so unexpectedly tore Tcherikower from his overloaded writers' desk." Tcherikower had died of a heart attack at the age of sixty-two.[20]

Shriftn, Oyfn sheydveg's Ideological Successor

The journal that during the war most perpetuated the ideology expressed in *Oyfn sheydveg* appeared on the other side of the world in Buenos Aires. Titled *Shriftn* (Writings), this journal explained its mission in its subtitle, "An Anthology of the Treasures of Old and New Jewishness." Although the reference to old and new Jewishness originated with Dubnov, Tsvi Schwartz, the initial editor of the journal, had something entirely different in mind. Rather than promoting a political ideology, Schwartz sought to advance a cultural nationalist vision that sanctified the entire millennia-old Jewish tradition. *Shriftn* serves as an example of the cultural retrenchment for which the Yiddishist intellectuals in *Oyfn sheydveg* called as a response to Nazism. The journal made its ideological statement first primarily through the editor's selection and translation of both classical Jewish sources and modern articles and fiction. Later, the journal published original work as well. Efroikin became involved with *Shriftn* not only because of its cultural orientation but also because of his personal friendship with

Schwartz. Attracted to its expansive vision of Yiddish culture, Efroikin helped Schwartz shape the journal and the ideology of *integrale yidishkeyt* (integral Jewishness) that it came to espouse. Through his correspondence with Avrom Golomb, Efroikin attracted him to the journal as well. Following Schwartz's death in early 1945, Efroikin and Golomb assumed the journal's editorship. At that time, they added to the journal the significant subtitle "A Journal of Integral Jewishness."[21]

Taken as a whole, the journal accentuated the following themes: it presented all layers of Jewish culture, religious and secular, Hebrew and Yiddish, as nationally sacred; it offered a spiritual response to Nazism by emphasizing the moral superiority of classical Judaism to contemporary European culture; it perpetuated the counter-emancipationist ideology of *Oyfn sheydveg* by accentuating the need for Jewish culture to divorce itself from its morally inferior European and American counterparts; and it accomplished this task against the background of growing mourning over the recent news of the Nazi destruction of Polish Jewry.

The central feature of *Shriftn* was its elevation of all layers of Jewish culture to a level of national sanctity. In response to the catastrophe befalling East European Jewish civilization, East European Jewish nationalist intellectuals reacted by sacralizing every aspect of the disappearing civilization. Suddenly, the bitter rivalries between the Jewish religious tradition and its secular substitutes, Zionism and Diaspora nationalism, Hebraism and Yiddishism, faded into the background as adherents of all these ideologies faced the same tragic fate. As early as June 1940, the aged secular communal leader of Vilna Jewry, Dr. Jakub Wygodzki, expressed this sense of solidarity at the funeral of Rabbi Chaim Ozer Grodzenski, the leader of the Vilna Orthodox community. Just days after the Soviet conquest of Vilna, Wygodzki told the crowd of thousands gathered that this funeral marked the end of the rivalries between the various religious and secular ideologies. Now, Vilna Jews would have to struggle for their individual survival as they observed the disintegration of their beloved community.[22] *Shriftn* demonstrated that this cultural retrenchment proved a near universal reaction of Yiddishist intellectuals to the catastrophe, even those living in conditions of freedom.

These intellectuals sought to understand the unprecedented nature of the tragedy precisely by reading it into the timeless web of Jewish tradition.

Soon after officially assuming the editorship of *Shriftn*, Efroikin and Golomb wrote a statement of purpose that described the evolving ideology of the journal. The journal, they argued, came to express the ideology of *integrale yidishkeyt* that represented all Jewish values and that gave the Jews the "weapons for faith, perseverance, and permanent internal striving." In a time of persecution, the editors of *Shriftn* sought to connect their readers to Jewish eternality. In their words:

> *Shriftn* sought to awaken in the Jew's consciousness that he is the son of a great people, an eternal people—an *am oylom*, a people which cannot be destroyed through all the persecutions and all the barbarities.
>
> Through that consciousness, *Shriftn* wanted to elevate the personal importance of each Jew and to bind him both to the glory of his grandfathers in the past and to the forces of freedom and justice that certainly will rule the future.
>
> *Shriftn* sought to implant in hearts that unique strength, that holy courage and that fiery national sense of importance that our spiritual heroes and martyrs possessed.[23]

For this purpose, stated the editors, the journal concentrated on the nature of Jewishness in all its manifestations: wisdom, culture, morals, tradition, Jewish holidays, Jewish history, Jewish psychology and character.[24] *Shriftn* thus embodied Jewish cultural nationalism's move from fluidity to essentialism in its definition of Jewish national identity. Just like other integral nationalists, the writers in *Shriftn* posited an essentialist national identity that set apart their national group from all others. Like their non-Jewish counterparts, they envisioned their nation, in this case the Jews, as possessing a unique set of national characteristics that transcended time and space. Yet whereas German and East Central European integral nationalists emphasized racial, physical, and military superiority, proponents of *integrale yidishkeyt* argued that the secret of Jewish superiority rested precisely in the rejection of those values in exchange for spiritual and moral perfection. Inheriting this essentialist nationalist vision from Peretz, his disciples no longer believed as he had that other European nations would follow the Jews in pursuing this transcendent vision. Rather, in the midst of World War II, his disciples concluded that the Jews remained alone in their spiritual striving in the midst of a Europe that had sunken into the depths of barbarity.

Efroikin's Counter-Emancipationist Ideology during the Holocaust

In 1944, Efroikin published *In kholem un oyf der vor* (In dream and in reality) in which he articulated his reaction to World War II and to reports of the genocide of European Jewry. At 369 pages, this long-winded work was Efroikin's first book. It also represented the culmination of his return to the literary world of publicistics. In many ways, the book represented the culmination of Efroikin's ideology of counter-emancipation. This ideology led in several opposing, even counterintuitive directions. As in the pages of *Oyfn sheydveg,* he articulated his deep disgust with the democracies for the abandonment of the Jews. In the pages of *In kholem un oyf der vor,* Efroikin expanded this disillusionment to a general critique of the nonrepresentative nature of democratic governments. Together with a critique of democracy, however, also came a rejection of capitalism and praise for socialism. In this manner, Efroikin thus returned to an ideology that he had first espoused and then rejected three and a half decades earlier. His simultaneous critique of capitalism and embrace of socialism, moreover, led him to an economic explanation of the rise of Fascism.

His combined disdain for democracy and enamorment with socialism led him to a newfound admiration for Stalin and for the Soviet Union. This ideological shift is the most surprising of all, given both Efroikin's previous vehement anti-Bolshevism and his continued commitment to Jewish nationalism. Another manner in which Efroikin strongly departed from his former ideological position was through his embrace of belief in territorial nationalism. A lifelong advocate of non-territorial cultural autonomy, Efroikin now argued that the only solution of the nationalities question rested with the creation of nation-states.

In his evaluation of the predicament of the "Jews among the Nations," Efroikin displayed this same balance between change and continuity in ideology. The era of counter-emancipation, he argued, would lead to the inexorable extrusion of the Jews from the politics, society, and culture of all the Diaspora countries in which they dwelled. On the one hand, this despair led him to embrace Zionism with its territorial solution to the Jewish national question. On the other hand, his ideology of "return to the ghetto," which reached a rhetorical crescendo in this book, breathed new life into his dream for Jewish national autonomy in the Diaspora. Extruded from general society, those Jews who chose to remain in the Diaspora would have to build powerful institutions of local and supra-communal autonomy. Efroikin's ideology of counter-emancipation thus allowed him to envision the implementation of his autonomist vision divorced from its original liberal basis. Now committed to an illiberal politics that saw the desires of the Jewish individual as standing in opposition to that of the national collective, Efroikin envisioned organs of Jewish national autonomy as organizing all aspects of the lives of Jewish individuals. Perhaps it was this very shift away from liberalism that led Efroikin to his positive assessment of Jewish life in the Soviet Union. It was the planned nature of Jewish cultural, economic, and social life there that impressed him. Written from the distance of the Americas, the book displayed Efroikin's lack of consistency as a thinker. Faced with news of the destruction of East European Jewry, Efroikin reacted in a self-contradictory manner. Like Kalmanovitch and like the writers of *Shriftn,* Efroikin venerated all layers of Jewish national culture and politics. Unlike the others, however, Efroikin looked increasingly to the Soviet Union for salvation, propelled in that direction by his disillusionment with the democracies.

In the book's introduction, Efroikin stated that a major purpose of his book was to break Jews of their false illusions. In an ironic paraphrase of a rabbinic dictum, Efroikin stated that of the ten measures of illusions that descended upon the world, contemporary Jewry had grabbed nine of them. Principal among the illusions, argued Efroikin, was that an Allied victory would spell a brighter future for the Jews. The depth of the Jewish tragedy, however, belied that facile assumption. Efroikin repeated his assertion, first stated in his *Oyfn sheydveg* article, that the difference between Nazi Germany and the democracies was one of historical circumstance and degree, not one of kind.

Demonstrating his awareness of the genocide, Efroikin asserted that Hitler had decided to turn Jewish bodies into "soap and fertilizer" only after the Allies demonstrated their unwillingness during the first two years of the war to accept any Jewish refugees into their midst. Even with news of the genocide, argued Efroikin, the Allies refused to do more than issue empty proclamations of condemnation. The contemporary generation of Jews, unlike their traditional counterparts, bestowed the title "righteous Gentile" so promiscuously that they fawned over those who never backed their empty words of support for the Jews with action. The Allies' abandonment of the Jews, argued Efroikin, called into question the naïve belief that the war pitted the forces of altruistic Christendom against evil neo-paganism. The Allies fought in defense of their homelands, not for any higher ideals. The war would usher in not a new era of peace but rather a simple realignment of power. As in the past when victors assumed the ideology of the vanquished, the Allies might well adopt racist policies toward Jews and people of color even after the Nazis' downfall. The war thus would end on a distinctly anti-messianic note.[25]

This pessimism contrasted with the meta-historical utopianism with which Efroikin had looked to the end of World War I. The ensuing catastrophe during World War II led many other nationalist thinkers in both directions of meta-historical optimism and historical pessimism. In the Warsaw ghetto, the majority of intellectuals who responded to a questionnaire composed by the historian and communal activist Emanuel Ringelblum and his *Oyneg Shabes* archive to commemorate two and a half years of ghetto life envisioned a bleak future for Jews in a Europe liberated by the Allies. Having reaped the benefits of the Nazi extrusion of the Jews from society, they predicted, the Poles would not allow for the reinstatement of Jewish rights. Intellectuals such as Hillel Tsaytlin also voiced a bleak prognosis for the future of the Jews of Palestine, where, he believed, the British would never allow for the creation of a Jewish state. For intellectuals surveyed such as Shia Perle, the famed interwar Yiddish novelist, the only ray of light came from the Soviet Union. In order to survive, these intellectuals concluded, the Jews would have to break their penchant for assimilation and return to their religious and national traditions.[26] Efroikin's predictions thus were in line with those of many other Yiddishist intellectuals both living under Nazi occupation and abroad. In fact, by arguing for an inexorable process of Jewish extrusion, Efroikin offered himself refuge in a meta-historical flight of fancy despite his pessimism. This process of extrusion would lead to the reestablishment of a premodern form of Jewish national autonomy and to the creation of a Jewish state in Palestine that would, in turn, lead to Jewish national survival.

Efroikin's disillusionment with the democracies brought with it an accompanying rejection of capitalism, which he understood as in its last throes. The sordid selfishness of the European bourgeoisie had led to its selling out the various European nations in the name of profit. The democracies, moreover, had become the tools of the bourgeoisie, disenfranchising the poor and racial minorities. Only an implementation of socialism, stated Efroikin, would eliminate this disparity and allow democracy to fulfill its ideals. Yet, in order for that to occur, socialism would have to sever its connections to the capitalist system, into which it had imbricated itself. The refusal of the majority of socialists to part with private property, he argued further, both led to the failure of socialism and paved the way for the rise of Fascism. Understanding Fascism as the middle ground between capitalism and communism, Efroikin argued that its success emerged from its nationalization of the economy without abolishing private property. Elevating the nation over class as the central aspect of human identity, Fascism demanded that both capitalists and workers make their economic interests subservient to the needs of the state. Expanding on an argument that he first had advanced in *Oyfn sheydveg,* Efroikin stated that Fascism had gained popularity by realizing many of the goals of socialism. In fact, he did not blame the masses for choosing bread over freedom. Fascism proved dangerous, he asserted, not because of its economic restructuring of the state but rather because of its primitive, immoral political philosophy that divided all of humanity between the racially superior and inferior. Fascists similarly did not see society as the sum of its parts but rather as a metaphysical entity representing all past, present, and future generations. The combination of fascist economic policy and political ideology led invariably to the weakening of personal liberties.[27]

It is revealing that Efroikin, despite his overt disgust for Fascism, adopted many of its features in his vision of postwar Jewish construction. In all matters ranging from emigration to residency rights to economic roles, Efroikin argued that postwar Jewry would have to renounce many individual liberties. Also, Efroikin's conception of "integral Jewishness" matched his definition of the Fascist conception of the nation as an irrational bond that united all past, present, and future generations. His belief in territorial nationalism and the dangers posed by the presence of ethnic minorities also perhaps originated from this influence. Perhaps this anxiety of influence helps to explain Efroikin's counterintuitive embrace of the Soviet Union. Unable to admit to an influence from Fascism, Efroikin turned to the other great representative of authoritarianism, the Soviet Union, in his search for an appropriate model. The fact that the Soviet Union also fought for the liberation of Europe from the Nazis contributed to this psychological process. An embrace of the Soviet Union also allowed Efroikin to return to his socialist roots, now in a very different form.

Having despaired of the democracies, Efroikin reserved his praise for the Soviet Union. He even went as far as to compare it to the Jews, another victim of lies and false propaganda. Defending the Soviet Union against its Western detractors, Efroikin rejected their comparison of it to Nazi Germany. Whereas Fascism saw only relative worth in human beings, communism subscribed to the humanistic belief in the sacredness of each individual. Despite the fact that the Soviet Union had not led to the withering of the state or to the disappearance of national and religious identities, it had produced the most egalitarian society in the world. A newfound apologist for Stalin, Efroikin argued against Leon Trotsky's contention that the Soviet system had created a new unequal order on the rubble of the old by making a division between a privileged bureaucracy and the ordinary workers. Western criticism proved particularly unfair, since in fighting for its survival, the Soviet Union also was helping to save the world. Efroikin also now believed that the Soviet Union possessed a more representative form of government than its democratic counterparts. Stalin, he argued with apparent sincerity, had been elected to all his positions. The one-party system and political terror proved only temporary measures used to fight counterrevolution. Whereas socialists had believed that the path to socialism ran through democracy, Russia inverted the order. A far truer religious spirit reigned in the officially godless Soviet Union, he argued, than in the hypocritical West, which worshipped the god of profit. Regarding Stalin's policy of "socialism in one land," Efroikin wrote: "There is no doubt, that the existence itself of one socialist country, and moreover such a rich and powerful country as the Soviet Union, is the greatest argument for socialism, much more convincing than the most beautiful and widespread propaganda under the still unrealistic slogan of social world-revolution."[28]

It was in its nationalities policy, argued Efroikin, that the Soviet Union had succeeded most. In this regard, Soviet reality proved superior to Communist doctrine. Whereas Stalin originally had imagined the policy of "nationalist in form, Soviet in content" as a transitory step toward the creation of an international Communist culture, the Soviet nationalities demonstrated vigorous staying power. Wisely, the Soviet Union created a system in which its various nationalities both could experience cultural self-determination and feel loyal to the Soviet state. Rather than forcing linguistic assimilation upon the nationalities, the Soviet Union created "a fraternity between peoples, races and languages." Rather than eliminating nationalism, the Soviet Union humanized it and thus created "a brotherhood of nationalities." Whereas most states treated territories in which ethnic minorities lived as colonies ripe for economic exploitation, the Soviet Union built industries in these areas. Seemingly forgetting the popular Russian anti-Semitism that he had combated decades earlier, Efroikin argued that this nationalities policy emerged from the generosity and good-heartedness of the Russian people. In romantic fashion, Efroikin described how the Soviet Union took care of its national minorities as "an older brother needs to worry about a younger and weaker brother."[29]

Turning to the predicament of the "Jews among the Nations," Efroikin displayed this same balance between ideological change and continuity. Although embracing Zionism, he argued that it must incorporate the best elements of folkism. This synthesis of two opposing ideologies demonstrates Efroikin's embrace of a belief in integral

Jewishness, which celebrated various and opposing strands of Jewish national politics and culture. At root, his rejection of Diaspora nationalism came from its unstated presupposition of waiting for redemption to come from the hands of non-Jewish allies. In order to avoid the consequences of this reality, he argued, modern Jews idealized the non-Jewish world and dismissed anti-Semitism as stemming from transient causes such as capitalism, despotism, and absolutism. In contrast, premodern Jews developed a much more realistic attitude toward the non-Jewish world precisely by rooting anti-Semitism in a religious conception of Jewish chosenness and exile. Its glorification and normalization of the exile had thus doomed autonomism to failure, despite this ideology's deep roots in the Jewish past and in Jewish tradition. In his words:

> It sought to divorce exile from redemption, the two motifs of Jewish feeling and thinking, which are bound together and do not allow themselves to be parted, as long as the exile exists and as long as the redemption has not come. No true, authentic Jewish folkism can be imagined that immortalizes the exile; certainly not if it glorifies it—a thought with which the folk did not and never will make peace. Folkism had chances to be accepted and to spread amongst the people only if it would have incorporated itself as part of the camp of Jewish liberation, the Zionist movement.[30]

Efroikin then stated that in his turn to Zionism, he joined in the company of other former leaders and ideologues of Russian Jewish folkism such as Wolf Latski-Bertoldi, Yoysef Tshernikhov, and Kalmanovitch. He even argued tendentiously that Dubnov himself had moved closer to Zionism in his old age.[31]

Efroikin repudiated both his former ideology and the arguments upon which it was based. Twenty-five years earlier, in the aftermath of the February Revolution, he had waxed poetic about the impending triumph of non-territorial nationalism, of which the Jews served as trailblazers. Now, in contrast, Efroikin reversed himself by criticizing the folkist argument that understood the Jews' status as a stateless nation as advantageous and avant-garde. By lacking territory and national property, the Jews, he argued, actually constituted the only truly proletarian nation in the world. The argument that the future belonged to Diaspora nations, argued Efroikin, failed to account for the anomalous situation of the Jews. Otto Bauer and Karl Renner had devised their conception of personal cultural autonomy for national minorities that possessed a homeland in which their ethnic group possessed a territorial majority. Those who argued that the Jewish future after the war rested with federations of nationalities possessing cultural rights also were fooling themselves, since the Jews, unlike these groups, possessed no territorial base. The Jews would possess no power until they had a territory.[32]

Non-territorial cultural autonomy, argued Efroikin, proved as much of a threat to national majorities as to the minorities. As an example, Efroikin pointed to interwar Czechoslovakia, in which the ethnic Germans of the Sudetenland undermined both the country and the peace of the entire European continent. The antidote to this instability would be the creation of nation-states with largely ethnically homogeneous populations. In order to achieve this homogeneity, Efroikin advocated population transfers of hostile ethnic minorities to states in which they themselves composed the majority. So, for instance, he argued for the repatriation of ethnic Germans from East Central Europe and the expulsion of the eight hundred thousand Arabs of Palestine to other Arab states.[33]

Underlying this dramatic repudiation of his previous ideology was Efroikin's move from liberal to integral nationalism. The Versailles system failed, he insisted, because it reduced national identity to culture and language rights rather than something more primordial. Repudiating his past in SERP and the Folkspartey, Efroikin now concurred with the Bolshevik position advocating a territorial, rather than a personal-national, solution to the nationalities question. Autonomists, including Efroikin, had defined the nation as a spiritual entity that eschewed loyalty to any one land.[34] Now, in contrast, Efroikin argued that nationalism was not principally about culture but rather an "*integral social unity*" not easily shed.[35] In his move away from spiritual toward integral nationalism, Efroikin now posited a deeply nonrationalistic connection between members of a group to one another and to their land.

Non-territorial autonomy, he argued, brought disastrous consequences not just upon European nationalities but also upon the Jewish nation. Like Kalmanovitch in his Vilna ghetto diary, Efroikin identified the historical Jewish sin as not returning sooner to the land of Israel. To Efroikin, this sin of Jewish complacency in the exile would lead to a postwar reality in which Diaspora Jewry would have to return to the ghetto:

> It is a punishment for a sin that has lasted too long, nearly two thousand years: for the sin of remaining in exile. . . . Our sins delay the redemption. The most just people in the world can be attacked by evil people and can, if they [the evil people] are stronger than they are, be enslaved to them. However, a just people never will make peace with its fate forever and will escape from prison to freedom, from slavery to freedom. If it does not do this, the world is justified to doubt its justness and even more so should it doubt itself. That is why all Jews, consciously or unconsciously, look toward the relatively small settlement in the land of Israel with so much love and with so much heart yearning. In this Jewish *avant-garde,* we see the *awakened Jewish conscience,* from it flows in all Jewish veins the belief that the Jews want and can truly *repent.* Liberation from exile means that the Jews will redeem themselves and at the same time atone for their sins, which they commit not only against their God but also against themselves every extra day that they remain under a foreign yoke in the lands of slavery.[36]

Paradoxically, however, Efroikin's belief in the ultimate futility of Jewish life in the Diaspora did not lead him to negate all the ideals of autonomism. Rather, in keeping with the principles of integral Jewishness, he hoped to synthesize the best of opposing Jewish political and cultural trends. The Zionists had erred significantly, argued Efroikin, in adopting an ideology of negation of the exile. Jews always had looked at the exile as a punishment and misfortune but not as an object of disdain and hatred. Rejecting the supernatural belief in an instant redemption, Efroikin rather argued that the Jewish people would redeem itself incrementally. This liberation would begin in the Diaspora itself, even as Jews concentrated their energies more and more on building the land of Israel. By negating the Diaspora entirely, however, the Zionists ignored the twin foundations of Jewish consciousness: exile and redemption. Only when Zionism embraced Diaspora culture, as preached by folkists, would it succeed it winning over the entire Jewish people to its side.[37] Here, Efroikin returned to his old critique of SERP and Poale Zion in which he had argued that the Jewish national renaissance would begin in the Diaspora and culminate in Palestine.

Yet, unlike in 1909–1910, Efroikin now believed that this national renaissance in the Diaspora would occur under bleak conditions. This assessment of the future of the Diaspora came from his conviction that the Jews, if they were to survive, would have to forge an ideology for an age of counter-emancipation. In a chapter titled "The end of a two-hundred-year mistake," which first appeared in *Shriftn,* Efroikin delved into the reasons for the failure of emancipation. Assimilation, he argued, was based on the false belief that the Jews could become members of a religious confession like all other religions. In reality, those Jews who had risen to positions of leadership such as Sir Herbert Samuel in Great Britain and Leon Blum in France hurt Jewish national interests in their futile attempts to demonstrate their loyalty to their home countries over that of their loyalty to the Jews. Dubnov had erred greatly in assuming that patriotism and Jewish national loyalty could go together.[38] It was "the rivers of Jewish blood . . . shed by a Christian people" that awoke Jewish plutocratic leaders to their tragic two-hundred-year mistake. Hitler proved the messenger of this bad tiding.[39] Hitlerism, moreover, had made anti-Semitism fashionable, even in the democracies. As a result, the extrusion of the Jews from political, economic, and social life spread from Central to Western Europe and even to America, whose Jewish community was in the process of social and economic ghettoization.[40]

Throughout the essay, Efroikin argued that two major factors led to the Jews' mistaken embrace of emancipation. First, European Jews tragically misread the conditions that Christian proponents of emancipation had offered in exchange for an entry ticket into European society. Whereas Christian thinkers expected the Jews to relinquish all national characteristics and to become members of a Jewish church, even the most assimilated of Jews were not prepared to comply. More viscerally, Efroikin argued that Jewish national distinctiveness rendered assimilation futile. At times, Efroikin's integral nationalist conception of Jewish identity drifted into a racialist conception of Jewish distinctiveness. Invoking the historian Cecil Roth, Efroikin described how Marranos in Spain and Portugal retained a separate identity even five hundred years after their conversions. On a visit to a Marrano village in Spain, Efroikin imagined himself as in the center of the old Jewish ghetto in Vilna. These loyal Catholics, he explained, possessed such "pure, typical Jewish faces, such deeply sad Jewish eyes." Those Jews who currently engaged in assimilation, argued Efroikin, would return to the Jewish fold against their will.[41]

As a reaction to the extreme hostility that assimilation had elicited, Efroikin advocated Jewish isolationism. In so doing, he furthered the rhetoric of return to the ghetto, which he first had espoused on the eve of World War II. Rather than having to endure "forced segregation," the Jews should engage in a process of "self-isolation," which would signify the Jews' desire not to overstep their bounds by penetrating the Gentile world. Although critics would be correct in equating this delineation of Jewish space with ghetto, argued Efroikin, such a solution proved superior to the complete extrusion from society that Jews currently were experiencing. If the civilized world contained any last ounce of decency, it would grant the Jews this minimal separate space as a *"onetime act of justice."*[42]

This statement revealed the extent to which Efroikin's call back to the ghetto represented simultaneously a deviation from his original autonomous vision and its fulfillment. As ideological systems, both Diaspora nationalism and Yiddishism sought to merge the particularly Jewish and the universally human. The ideology of "back to the ghetto" served as perhaps the greatest manifestation of despair in this synthesis; instead, this ideology sought to insulate Jewish culture from a European society that had brutalized it. Twenty-five years earlier, Efroikin had made the case for Diaspora nationalism based upon the argument of Jewish rootedness in Russia and in the Diaspora. Now he argued that Jewish alienation in the Diaspora led to the necessity of retreat into the ghetto. Autonomism, moreover, had emerged as one of several manifestations of "the new Jewish politics." This politics had envisioned the Jews actively demanding both personal and national rights. The call to the ghetto, however, emerged as a response to the perceived failure of these politics and consequently called for a Jewish return to premodern political quiescence.[43]

Efroikin's call for retreat to the ghetto also came with a great deal of ambivalence. Like Jacob Glatstein and other originators of the call to return to the ghetto, Efroikin recognized that a physical and cultural retreat would prove both liberating and suffocating. Only the ghetto, argued Efroikin, could grant the Jews true freedom and preserve Jewish identity from disintegration. Still, he did not discount the steep price that Jews would have to pay for national survival in the ghetto:

> But ghetto means material want and spiritual narrowness. Bitter days and dark times await us. Jews, separated from the wealth of the great world, will become once again, as they once were, a poor nation. *Kabtsansk* will once again emerge as the capital of the Jewish exile state. And the old Jewish pack, which we thought we could hide in a museum, will once again accompany us in our wanderings over the paths . . . of the world. Ghetto means always being dependent on the kindness of the nations, always fearing for the Jewish individual, for his life and existence, and for the fate of the community. Ghetto means also however—always breathing spiritually stale air. Limited to our four ells and surrounded on all sides . . . we must with good will renounce many freedoms. There is not full freedom in a besieged field. Let it only be that it does not go so far that if a Baruch Spinoza would appear amongst us that we would excommunicate him.
>
> Ghetto is a harsh punishment but an earned one and we must *accept it with love*.[44]

Efroikin genuinely mourned the negative aspects that came with a divorce of the Jews from European civilization. Yet his call for return to the ghetto also allowed him to imagine the fulfillment of his autonomist political and cultural vision, albeit under radically different circumstances. Throughout the book, Efroikin reiterated many of Dubnov's arguments that national autonomy functioned as the natural state of the Jewish people. The fact that autonomy had flourished for the Jews in all historical periods and not just in the Middle Ages, Efroikin argued, belied the assertion that the modern era could not support Jewish autonomous existence. The traditional *kahal*, he argued further, operated essentially as a secular national organ of communal control and discipline. Ultimately, it was external persecution and the internal despotism of the rabbis and wealthy that accounted for the traditional *kahal's* failures. Thus, Efroikin returned to Dubnov's ideology even when ostensibly rejecting it.[45]

Unlike Kalmanovitch, who in his 1939 essay blamed external historical factors for the disintegration of Jewish collective existence, Efroikin blamed the Jews themselves. It was the *Hofjuden* (the court Jews), in pursuit of their own financial gain, and the *maskilim*, in pursuit of Westernization, who joined forces in destroying Jewish national autonomy. Implicitly disagreeing with Tcherikower, Efroikin argued that French Jews could have maintained autonomous institutions after the French Revolution if they had so desired. Invoking the Zionist intellectual Jacob Klatzkin's terminology, Efroikin argued that history would judge the emancipation that accompanied the French Revolution as the "third destruction" in Jewish history, alongside the destruction of the first and second temples. In the name of emancipation, Jews turned against autonomy, the last fortress remaining for them, in the same manner that the French had stormed the Bastille. Although assimilation had seeped into the Jewish body politic, the folk masses that had remained healthily Jewish would save the Jewish people from this plague.[46]

Once a champion of both rights for the Jewish individual and for the Jewish collective, Efroikin now believed that the needs of the collective would have to severely limit individual freedom. Those who internally had destroyed Jewish autonomy at the dawn of emancipation, stated Efroikin, did so "in the name of the freedom and the right of the Jewish individual, a right to cowardice, a right to treason, a right to apostasy."[47] Efroikin thus elaborated upon the dichotomy between the collective and individual most forcefully argued by Kalmanovitch in the pages of *Oyfn sheydveg*. The failure of Jewish communal life, argued Efroikin, was that even Jewish national organizations fought for the rights of individuals to assimilate rather than to force them to live within their national group. Jewish organizations in the 1930s, for instance, had protested the *numerus clausus* in Hungary and the ghetto benches in Poland far more loudly than they struggled for state funding for national Jewish schools in these countries. In an extreme example, Efroikin argued that by protesting against the Nuremberg Laws, official Jewish organizations in reality were fighting for the right of Jews to apostasy. Given that Jewish law had banned sexual contact with Gentiles, Jewish national organizations should have rejoiced that the Nazis forbade it as well. Efroikin likened these nationalist organizations to stores that advertise kosher food in the window front but in reality sell non-kosher.[48]

With this retreat from individualism in favor of collectivism came a disparagement of the Jewish struggle for personal equality. In the modern era, argued Efroikin ironically, the struggle for individual equal rights assumed the status of a *mitsve* in Jewish political life that took precedence over all else. Even many proud national Jews such as Vladimir Ze'ev Jabotinsky had fallen into the trap of fighting for personal equality alongside national rights. At the Paris Peace Conference, stated Efroikin, defenders of Jewish national rights had to prove to their Jewish opponents that their demands would not harm the equal rights of the Jewish individual. The pursuit of equal rights, however, compromised the Jews both morally and politically. Morally, equal rights gave the Jews a share of responsibility for the "pillage and wars, murder and terror" practiced by Christian nations. The Jews, moreover, often experienced deterioration in their political situation with an embrace of equal rights and loss of corporate structures. Advocating Jewish self-segregation, Efroikin argued that the Jewish search for equal rights stemmed from an inferiority complex.[49]

It is not surprising, given Efroikin's illiberal conception of the damaging role of individual rights, that a major component of his new autonomous vision centered on the *kehile*'s power of coercion over the individual. The weakness of all previous party platforms demanding autonomy, he argued, was their lack of the power of coercion. Whenever granted government aid to create national schools in Hebrew or Yiddish, Jewish parents still preferred to send their children to general public schools. The modern *kehile* would thus have to reassert its muscle through the use of a modernized *ḥerem,* or excommunication. Efroikin thus envisioned Jewish national autonomy as controlling the Jewish individual and directing his or her political, economic, and residency choices. With the Jewish individual's rights in the larger state limited to basic civic and religious freedoms, he or she would have to find political fulfillment only within the *kehile.* The *kehile,* he argued, needed to prevent Jewish individuals from running for high political office and from mixing into non-Jewish political and religious affairs. In the grim postwar economy, predicted Efroikin, the only way for Jewish individuals to make a living could come through the *kehiles'* demanding a proportion of the national economic wealth in proportion to the number of Jews in the overall society. Although a *numerus clausus,* this system would prevent Jewish individuals from starving and at least provide them with some economic gains. Characteristically assuming both a reactionary and progressive stance, Efroikin argued that the *kehile* could apportion the funds allotted from governments in a socialist manner. The *Yishuv* in Palestine, he argued, served as an example of a socially just national control of the economy. As thirty years earlier, Efroikin called for directed emigration in the aftermath of the war. Unlike then, however, he hoped that the Jewish representative body in charge of this task would direct most Jewish immigrants to Palestine or another Jewish territory.[50]

Although in some ways Efroikin's vision of postwar autonomy continued his previous ideology, it broke with it dramatically in his praise for Jewish national life in the Soviet Union. He argued that with Yiddish as a recognized language in Belorussia and the Ukraine and the establishment of a Jewish national autonomous region in Birobidzhan, Jewish national autonomy had scored its greatest success in the Soviet Union. Efroikin praised the existence of Jewish soviets in areas with Jewish majorities as well as the presence of Jewish courts in which, he argued, a Jewish spirit reigned in their implementation of Soviet law. He even went as far as to compare the Jewish districts in the former Pale of Settlement with the early modern V'a'ad Arba' Aratsot (Council of the Four Lands) in Poland. The fact that Jews possessed a measure of self-rule in the Soviet Union was proof that autonomy could coexist with any political and economic regime.[51] Based on statistics from the 1920s, Efroikin painted a rosy picture of Jewish life in the Soviet Union, in which both religious life and the use of Yiddish flourished.

Still, Efroikin argued that Soviet Jewry needed to engage in self-segregation just like the rest of world Jewry in order to protect itself from mass assimilation and from the backlash that would come in its wake. The greatest threat of assimilation, argued Efroikin, was Jewish infiltration into Soviet areas and territories with few established Jewish communities. As an antidote to this threat, Efroikin pointed to the Soviet establishment of Birobidzhan as a Jewish autonomous region, which had so far failed only because of the Jewish penchant for assimilation. Jewish autonomous authorities in the Soviet Union, he argued, would have to limit the right of Jewish residence outside of areas of high Jewish concentration. The fact that a Jewish authority, rather than the Soviet authorities, would limit Jewish residency, argued Efroikin somewhat disingenuously, rendered comparisons to the hated Pale of Settlement spurious. It must be remembered that during World War I, Diaspora nationalists reacted to the disintegration of the Pale and the territorial diffusion of Russian Jewry with anxiety. Still, autonomists once had believed firmly in both personal freedom of residence and communal autonomy. Now, however, Efroikin believed that only a limitation of personal rights could assure national survival. Recognizing that "hundreds of thousands" of residents of the old Pale of Settlement had perished at the hands of the Germans, Efroikin argued that survivors should abandon these areas in favor of Birobidzhan.[52]

In the end, Efroikin even defended the Evsektsiia, arguing that its efforts at creating Yiddish schools belied its official antinationalist ideology. Although admitting to Lenin's fight with the Bund and with SERP as well as Stalin's denial of Jewish nationhood, Efroikin argued that the Soviet Union should be judged not by its beliefs but rather by its actions. Even as it had denied in principle Jewish claims of nationality, it had granted the Jews national rights. The major blame for the failures of Soviet Yiddish culture, therefore, rested not with Soviet authorities but rather with Jewish Communists themselves who had failed to launch a struggle against the ideology of national in form, Soviet in content. Through this explanation, Efroikin managed to criticize Soviet Yiddish culture while at the same time absolving Stalin from all responsibility for its failures. Yet Efroikin preached forgiveness for both the Evsektsiia for its excesses as well as for Jewish Communists abroad who had supported the Hitler-Stalin pact. In response to the demand of such anti-Communist Yiddishists as H. Leivick and Shmuel Niger that penitent Jewish Communists take a loyalty oath to the Jewish people, Efroikin argued that the Jewish nationalist camp should welcome them with open arms. Efroikin thus remained upbeat regarding the prospects of the Jewish national renaissance in the Soviet Union following the war. The end of the war, he argued naïvely, even would witness the fall of the wall that had separated Soviet Jews from the rest of world Jewry. The Soviet Union would recognize a Jewish state in Palestine, even as it engaged in a process of democratization at home.[53]

Whereas Efroikin praised the Soviet Union from afar, Kalmanovitch lived under its rule from the summer of 1940 through the German invasion in June 1941. There, he only deepened his hatred of the Soviets, whom he deemed the spiritual destroyers of Yiddish culture. Yet when the Germans invaded the Soviet Union, he soon faced the physical, not just the spiritual, destruction of his beloved Vilna Jewry.

The Nazi Destruction of Vilna Jewry

Soviet rule of Vilna came to an end on June 24, 1941, with the German invasion of the Soviet Union. In the days before the Nazi invasion, Heinrich Himmler assembled mobile killing squads, known as the *Einsatsgruppen,* and called upon them to murder the Jewish population of areas conquered from the Soviets. As early as July 1941, units of the *Einsatsgruppen* enlisted Lithuanian accomplices to kidnap Jewish men from the streets and from their homes and to murder them at Ponar, a wooded area to the south of the city. After the Nazis staged an alleged Jewish shooting at German soldiers (the work of Lithuanian accomplices), the Nazis arrested the thirty-seven hundred residents of the historical Jewish quarter of Vilna on August 31 and then murdered them at Ponar. Also in retaliation for this alleged shooting, known as the Great Provocation, the Nazis murdered all the members of the first *Judenrat,* which they had ordered formed during the summer. In September, the Nazis decreed that Vilna Jewry relocate into two ghettos, one large and one small, located in the now empty historical Jewish quarter of the city. By September, the word *Aktion* came to mean the forcible deportation of Jews out of the city to their deaths.[54]

After enduring the disappearance of loved ones and forced relocation, many Vilna Jews initially felt relieved upon entering the ghetto. Kalmanovitch expressed the sentiment of many upon meeting Mark Dworzecki, a Vilna doctor and intellectual, for the first time in the ghetto: "Abi tsivshn yidn . . . me darf hobn bitokhn" (As long as we are among Jews . . . we must have faith).[55] In the immediate aftermath of ghettoization, the Nazis demanded that the Jews form two new *Judenräte* for the ghettos. Since most of Vilna Jewry's traditional leadership already had been murdered, leadership devolved to neophytes and outsiders. A. Fried, an acculturated businessman with no prior leadership experience, became the head of the *Judenrat* of the larger ghetto. Jacob Gens, a businessman from Kaunas with a background in the Lithuanian army, became its chief of police.[56]

Despite initial feelings of relief, the first three months of the ghetto's existence brought unmitigated suffering to its inhabitants. The Nazis continued their *Aktionen* throughout September and October, now enlisting the help of the *Judenrat* and the Jewish police. October also brought the liquidation of the second, smaller ghetto and the murder of its inhabitants in Ponar. By the end of December, more than thirty-three thousand Jews out of an original population of fifty-seven thousand had been murdered. The Nazis thus succeeded in murdering the majority of Vilna Jewry within the first five months of their occupation of the city. Because of their subjugation to the terror of *Aktionen* and the trauma of dislocation to the ghetto, most Vilna Jews did not discover the true destination of those arrested until the majority of their community had perished.[57]

Between September and December 1941, the *Judenrat* and the ghetto police complied with the Nazi extermination policy in the hopes of sparing as many ghetto inhabitants as possible. Fried and Gens believed that the Germans' need for labor would lead them to spare at least the able-bodied ghetto inhabitants. By both turning over to the Germans the old and sick and finding jobs for those who remained, the leaders of the *Judenrat* and the Jewish police hoped to preserve the ghetto's existence. If the Jewish police would conduct the *Aktionen* themselves, argued Fried and Gens, they could minimize the number of victims. Fried and Gens were correct in surmising that at least some in the German administration did not want to murder all the Jews immediately. In fact, the SS argued with the Wehrmacht and German civil authorities over whether or not to exterminate all of the Jews in newly acquired Soviet territories or to have them work for the war effort. By the end of December, the latter opinion prevailed, and the mass murder came to a temporary halt.[58]

The ghetto's period of relative stability began in January 1942 and lasted until the spring of 1943. After a power struggle between the *Judenrat* and the Jewish police, the Nazis recognized Gens as the ultimate source of power within the ghetto. Once the *Aktionen* ceased, the majority of ghetto inhabitants came to believe in Gens's ideology of productivization, known as "work for life." This belief only increased after the Germans issued yellow passes to workers in the spring of 1942. In the meantime, Gens organized the ghetto, creating workshops within and sending others to work in German factories outside the ghetto. He also created an efficient bureaucratic administration within the ghetto to arrange for health, education, employment, social services, and cultural life. Gens also created a justice system, in which courts tried and sentenced criminals. After five Jewish criminals murdered a fellow ghetto inmate in the course of a robbery, Gens condemned all five plus another criminal to death. At the public hanging that followed, he spoke of the necessity of productivity and order so that the remnant of Vilna Jewry might survive. In addition, Gens also sponsored cultural activities such as literary contests, concerts, theater, literary evenings, and colloquia.[59]

At the height of the ghetto's period of stability, in the fall of 1942, Gens sent his police force to the small towns of Oszmiana and Swieciany at the behest of the Nazis to weed out "unproductive" elements of those ghettos and send them to their deaths. In a speech in the ghetto following these *Aktionen*, Gens defended his actions by arguing that by carrying out the Nazis' orders themselves, the police had strongly limited casualties. Whereas four hundred people had perished during the action, the Germans would have murdered more than a thousand had they implemented the plan themselves. Although Gens collaborated in these *Aktionen* in order to minimize casualties, many of the Jewish police engaged in acts of shameless opportunism, accepting bribes from those slated for death and helping themselves to the victims' property. Although they debated the propriety of Gens's decision to implement the *Aktion,* the majority of Vilna ghetto inhabitants believed that their ghetto remained safe.[60]

Not all ghetto inhabitants, however, believed that productivization would spare their lives. As soon as the stabilization period began, members of various youth movements formed the Fareynikte partizaner organizatsiye (United Partisans Organization, or FPO), which planned to take up arms against the Nazis. The leadership of the FPO consisted of representatives of youth groups across the political spectrum. Abba Kovner, a leader of the Marxist Zionist Hashomer Hatsair, was joined both by Joseph Glanzman, a Revisionist Zionist, and by Isaac Wittenberg, a Communist. In a public declaration made in

January 1942, Kovner implored the ghetto inhabitants to realize that all those taken away had perished in Ponar. A similar fate, he argued, awaited the rest of the ghetto inhabitants and indeed all of European Jewry. The only response to Nazi mass murder was self-defense in an effort to preserve Jewish honor. Invoking Isaiah 53:7, Kovner begged his fellow Vilna Jews not to go like sheep to the slaughter.[61]

During the period of stability, Gens agreed to look the other way as the FPO amassed weapons, on condition that the partisans would not initiate a revolt without his approval. This agreement ended in the summer of 1943, as partisan activity in the forests and work camps surrounding Vilna led the Nazis to pressure Gens to take measures against weapon smuggling into the ghetto. In July 1943, the Nazis demanded that Gens give them Wittenberg, after they had received his name from a captured Lithuanian Communist. Although Gens arrested Wittenberg, members of the FPO freed him. Afraid that the Nazis would use Wittenberg's escape as a pretext for the liquidation of the ghetto, the majority of the ghetto inhabitants demanded his surrender, going as far as to search for him themselves. In the end, the FPO persuaded Wittenberg to surrender himself to the Germans in order to avoid the liquidation of the ghetto.[62]

Beginning in the spring of 1943, Nazi actions slowly undermined the ghetto inhabitants' belief in Gens's ideology of "work for life." For instance, the Nazis tricked Gens by sending a transport of Jews in the Vilna ghetto not to Kaunas, as promised, but rather to Ponar. In June 1943, the SS leadership in Berlin issued a command to liquidate the ghettos in the East. In August, the transport of thousands of able-bodied Jews to work camps in Estonia made the ghetto inhabitants fear the approach of the ghetto's liquidation. In their desperation, many ghetto inhabitants believed rumors, fueled by Nazi defeats in Italy and in the Soviet Union, of the imminent collapse of Hitler. Panic only increased with the deportation of thousands more during the first days of September. The FPO, in the meantime, issued its call to revolt, arguing that liquidation of the ghetto meant its inhabitants' certain death. Although FPO members fired at the Nazis, the ghetto inhabitants did not heed the call to revolt. Rather, they preferred deportation to work camps in Estonia, which carried with it the possibility of survival, over certain death in an armed conflict with the

Nazis. When the FPO realized that armed revolt would not occur in the ghetto, it decided to send its members to the partisans in the forests. Executing Gens for his knowledge of the presence of arms in the ghetto, the Nazis deported the remaining ten thousand Jews of the Vilna ghetto to camps in Estonia and Latvia.[63]

Cultural Life in the Ghetto

On one level, the forms of Jewish cultural life in the Vilna ghetto demonstrated the extent of the secularization of East European Jewry by World War II. The majority of ghetto inhabitants chose to attend not religious services, study sessions, and sermons but rather theater, concerts, sports activities, and lectures. They composed mostly poetry, aesthetic prose, and diaries, rather than religious texts.[64] Vilna had earned its reputation as the "Jerusalem of Lithuania" in the eighteenth and first half of the nineteenth century for its traditional rabbinic culture. Yet by the interwar period many of its secular residents believed their city worthy of that title for its thriving modern Yiddish and Hebrew culture.

Yet, in the Vilna ghetto, secular intellectuals such as Kalmanovitch drew close to the Orthodox in ways that they would not have before the war. To a large extent, this rapprochement resulted from the narrowing of the social and cultural distance between varied groups that occurred in response to the extreme conditions of ghettoization. A comparison to the Warsaw ghetto proves instructive. There the staunchly secular Ringelblum, who before the war battled the Orthodox, now shared the podium with rabbis at an event organizing the ransom of Jews slated for public execution. This narrowing of social distance had its cultural analogue in the appreciation for Jewish tradition expressed by ghetto intellectuals. In Ringelblum's survey of ghetto life, some intellectuals in the Warsaw ghetto bemoaned what they perceived as Jewish linguistic acculturation during the war as well as national and moral degeneration. The respondents often blamed this state on Warsaw Jewry's loss of connection to religious tradition and called upon a religious return as a precondition for national rejuvenation.[65] In Vilna, known for its absence of a Polonized intellectual elite and for relative harmony between members of various classes and cultural orientations, this closing of ranks proved easier to accomplish than in Warsaw.

At a time of great peril to the future of East European Jewry, all aspects of its cultural legacy appeared precious. Members of the Vilna ghetto intelligentsia reacted to the extreme conditions in a manner similar to that of their ideological peers on the other side of the Atlantic who wrote for *Shriftn*. Like proponents of *integrale yidishkayt*, Kalmanovitch in the Vilna ghetto expressed an appreciation for the totality of Jewish cultural creation throughout history: the religious and the secular, and Hebrew and Yiddish all merged into one seamless web. Like the writers in *Shriftn*, Kalmanovitch too engaged in a delicate balance between a re-embrace of religious values and a continued belief in the values of humanism.

David Roskies has argued, moreover, that the intelligentsia of the Vilna ghetto reacted to the radical diminution of Jewish space caused by incarceration in the ghetto through a deepening of Jewish time. Given that the walls of the ghetto represented the end of the one-hundred-fifty-year dream of Jewish emancipation into European society and culture, Jewish intellectuals turned inward and mined the sources of the Jewish past to find meaning. One of the many commonalities of Yiddish culture in the Americas and in the ghettos during the war, moreover, was a preoccupation with the meaning of Jewish identity. Even as the editors of *Shriftn* gathered essays from religious and secular Jewish thinkers alike on the meaning of Jewish identity, the leading intellectuals of the Vilna ghetto debated this same issue.[66]

Even as the ghetto as a whole engaged in an active cultural life, Kalmanovitch helped to lead a small group of ghetto intellectuals in a mission of cultural rescue. Immediately upon entering Vilna, the Nazis sent in representatives of the Einsatzstab des Reichsleiter (special detail of Reich administrator) Alfred Rosenberg. The purpose of this special detail was to collect valuable Judaic books and documents, to be housed in Frankfurt at a future "Institut Zur Erforschung der Judenfrage" (Institute for the Study of the Jewish Question). Leading this work detail was Dr. Johannes Pohl, a Hebrew University trained scholar who coined the term "Judenforschung ohne Juden" (Jewish studies without Jews). Upon visiting Vilna in February 1942, Pohl appointed Kalmanovitch and Herman Kruk, a Warsaw Bundist activist and librarian, in charge of the task of selecting valuable Jewish books for shipment to Germany. At first, Kalmanovitch and Kruk headed a twelve-person team that performed this task outside the ghetto in the Vilna University library. Later, the Germans decided to operate a second sorting center in the former YIVO building and to expand the workforce to forty people. At this time, the two young Yiddish poets Avrom Sutzkever and Shmerke Kaczerginski joined the team. In the YIVO building, in which the group members would work for eight hours a day, they were treated somewhat more gently by their "intellectual" German bosses than those in regular work details. Still, the members of the work detail were allowed to eat and drink only during the several hours when their German masters went to lunch.

From the beginning, it became apparent that the Nazis wanted the team to ship only a minority of the material to Germany, condemning as much as 70 percent of the Jewish books and documents to destruction in paper mills. The Germans in charge of the operation, moreover, oftentimes chose to save books based upon fancy covers and bindings rather than their real worth. In order to spare as many of the books as possible from the paper mills, Kalmanovitch, Kruk, Sutzkever, and the others smuggled books from both the locations into the ghetto, where they hid them in walls and cellars of ghetto buildings. Eventually, the group hid material in an attic in the YIVO building itself. Incredulous that this group of men and women would risk their lives to smuggle books into the ghetto, the other ghetto inhabitants dubbed them "the Paper Brigade." In response to those who criticized this group for occupying themselves with paper at a time of life and death, Kalmanovitch simply stated, "Books don't grow on trees."[67]

Yet the extent to which Kalmanovitch believed in the ultimate success of the rescue effort is unclear. In fact, it seems that he believed that a far better way to ensure the books' survival was to convince the Germans of their worth. Once the books made it to Germany, Kalmanovitch concluded, they most likely would survive the war. Such a consideration was most likely behind an incident that confused and angered Kalmanovitch's colleagues. According to Kruk, one of the workers sorting books in YIVO came across a rare eighteenth-century

Yiddish book. Presumably, the members of the Paper Brigade planned to hide it. However, before they could do so, Kalmanovitch brought the book to Pohl, impressing him with its importance. To members of the Paper Brigade, this act appeared close to sabotage. Kruk reported that Sutzkever, when relating this story to him, "trembled with anger." For his turn, Kruk, no great fan of Kalmanovitch, attributed this act to the latter's "nervous confusion, absentmindedness, and helplessness vis-à-vis the powers that be."[68] According to Kruk, Kalmanovitch suffered from a debilitating nervousness in the presence of his Nazi captors that led him to divulge secrets to them. As another example, he pointed to Kalmanovitch's informing to Pohl of the permission that he had received from a lower-ranking Nazi to bring YIVO's card catalogs into the ghetto. Upon hearing the news, Pohl withdrew the permission.[69] Kalmanovitch's handing of the book to Pohl may have resulted from a sense of panic in the presence of his captors. More likely, however, was the explanation that he did so because he thought such an action could best ensure the book's survival.

Kalmanovitch's Continued Belief in Jewish National Culture

Despite his religious turn, Kalmanovitch did not totally retreat, either in word or deed, from his engagement with secular Jewish national culture. In fact, in the ghetto, Kalmanovitch functioned as a public intellectual to a greater extent than during most other periods of his life. The range of organizations that he headed, moreover, represented a continuity of his prewar activity. For instance, he helped to establish a Yiddish Literary Society and led a Culture House. In the Yiddish Literary Society as well as in the Teachers' Union, Workers' Lecture Hall, the Brit 'Ivrit (Hebrew covenant), and the Science Society, Kalmanovitch lectured on literary and national themes.[70] Whereas the day-to-day running of YIVO during the 1930s often detracted from Kalmanovitch's scholarship, in the ghetto he wrote several serious studies regarding Yiddish and Hebrew literary history. These studies revealed that Kalmanovitch persisted in most of the secular assumptions of Jewish cultural nationalism, even as he questioned their durability in the Diaspora.

Kalmanovitch's essay "Problemen fun literarisher geshikhte tsvishn yidn" (Problems of literary history among Jews) reveals that, despite his religious mood in the ghetto, Kalmanovitch still identified himself, at least at certain moments, as a secular Jewish nationalist. In this essay, he analyzed the methodologies of some of the leading Jewish literary historians of the first four decades of the twentieth century: Maks Erik, Israel Tsinberg, Ḥaim Naḥman Shapira, and Joseph Klausner. A major theme upon which Kalmanovitch focused was the extent to which these writers viewed modern Hebrew and Yiddish writings as manifestations of the same literature. Another major theme was one that had preoccupied Kalmanovitch throughout much of his career: the relationship of the "old" religious Jewish literary tradition to the new Hebrew and Yiddish literatures. Kalmanovitch, in fact, asserted a radical historical discontinuity between these two literary traditions. Everything from the Bible and the Talmud through the contemporary writing of Lithuanian rabbis, argued Kalmanovitch, could not be construed as literature in the modern sense of the word. Instead, it constituted part of a self-contained tradition that took for granted the divine authority of the Torah. Because of its dedication to the goal of demonstrating the unity and timelessness of the tradition, this writing lacked historical development.[71]

Yet Kalmanovitch argued that secular nationalist Jews, himself included, felt compelled to transform this religious heritage into literature, analyzing its literary worth and its genres. The question remained, however, whether a secular analysis of this premodern traditional literature would prove able to preserve both its unity and its connection to its modern counterpart. In his essay, Kalmanovitch engaged in a literary analysis of the Joseph story in the Book of Genesis from a secular critical perspective. Similarly, in a diary entry, Kalmanovitch referred to the material that he presented to the SS officer Willi Schaefer regarding biblical and rabbinic traditions about the life of Moses as "'agadat Mosheh rabenu"—the legend, or lore, of Moses our Teacher.[72] Although emotionally Kalmanovitch identified with the Torah and Jewish tradition on a meta-historical plane, on an intellectual level he still maintained a secular, critical orientation.

It is Kalmanovitch's essays on Aḥad Ha-ʿAm and Peretz, both written in the ghetto, that revealed the extent to which he still identified as a cultural nationalist. Both essays addressed the fact that both He-brew and Yiddish literatures developed far differently than their founders had intended. Whereas Aḥad Ha-'Am and Peretz both had envisioned a national literature with a particularistic Jewish content, their disciples veered from their vision. What is striking when com-paring Kalmanovitch's two essays is his different judgment regarding the same pattern of deviance of the students of both Aḥad Ha-'Am and Peretz. To Kalmanovitch, the fact that Peretz's students never se-riously attempted to imbue Yiddish literature with the spirit of the religious tradition of the Middle Ages served as proof of this modern culture's bankruptcy. Yet Kalmanovitch credited Aḥad Ha-'Am 's dis-ciples' turn to aesthetic culture unfettered to a particularistic Jewish content over their mentor's objections as leading to the full flowering of Hebrew culture in Palestine. This difference in perspective reveals that Kalmanovitch's despair over secular Yiddish culture resulted not from a rejection of national culture but rather from his despair with its implementation in the Diaspora. Since the old religious Jewish cul-ture gave way not to a thriving Yiddish culture but rather to linguistic acculturation, the Diaspora proved unfertile ground for national re-naissance. However, in Palestine, Hebrew culture could transcend spe-cific Jewish content in the aesthetic realm because of unique conditions in the *Yishuv.*

In this article, Kalmanovitch dealt with the rift between Aḥad Ha-'Am and his disciples over the role of aesthetic literature in the new Hebrew culture. From 1896 until his death over three decades later, Aḥad Ha-'Am opposed the creation of Hebrew belles lettres that would serve purely aesthetic purposes. Unable to reconcile himself to a Hebrew literature that did not address ultimate issues of Jewish identity, Aḥad Ha-'Am called upon those Jewish nationalists who desired aesthetic fulfillment to find it in the literatures of other lan-guages. This position elicited a rebellion from Aḥad Ha-'Am 's disci-ples, most notably Mikhah Yosef Berdyczewski. Berdyczewski rejected Aḥad Ha-'Am's notion of modern Hebrew culture as just as rigid and stifling to creativity as the rabbinic Judaism that it came to replace. To exclude aesthetic culture from the realm of Hebrew lit-erature, argued most of Aḥad Ha-'Am 's younger disciples, would prove tantamount to opening the door to linguistic acculturation. In particular, Kalmanovitch focused upon how Klausner, Aḥad Ha-'Am's loyal follower, nonetheless granted prominence of place to aesthetic literature upon his assumption of the editorship of his mentor's Hebrew journal, *Ha-Shiloaḥ*.[73]

Throughout the essay, Kalmanovitch viewed Aḥad Ha-'Am 's rejection of aesthetic literature as a result of the limitations of his cultural nationalist vision. Such a disparaging view of aesthetics, argued Kalmanovitch, befitted a middle-class East European Jew with a smattering of Haskalah, not one of the founders of a national cultural renaissance. Rather than predicting that the creation of a cultural center in Palestine would allow for the fusion of unique Jewish content with European aesthetic sensibilities, Aḥad Ha-'Am instead argued for the persistence of Jewish exceptionalism. Through his preference for analytical over emotional literature, Aḥad Ha-'Am perpetuated traditional Judaism's understanding of its own literature as possessing ultimate transcendent value. Because he represented the narrow historical era of the transition from Haskalah to the emergence of Jewish nationalism, Aḥad Ha-'Am could not transmit this attitude toward literature to his thoroughly nationalistic students. Once the Jewish national renaissance arrived in full force, the era of Aḥad Ha-'Am 's influence had ended and he became obsolete.[74]

In his preference for the vision of Klausner over that of Aḥad Ha-'Am, Kalmanovitch revealed that as late as the Vilna ghetto period, he still invoked his vision of a non-essentialist Jewish national culture, whose content would be determined in the course of cultural production itself. In Kalmanovitch's words:

> On the other hand, it [aesthetic culture] is more than a path, more than a source but it itself is a kind of solution to the question of national existence: if a Hebrew art exists, if creative Hebrew forces reveal themselves—it is a clear sign that the dew of our people has not dried up, and that there is permission to see in the very existence of belles lettres a hint of a national future.[75]

Here, Kalmanovitch articulated the ideological position of the Hebrew and Yiddish literati of early twentieth-century Russian Jewry and interwar Polish Jewry. These "culturists" had argued that an independent aesthetic culture not developing along strictly national lines was precisely what the modern Jewish nation needed. According to Kenneth Moss's apt metaphor, a national language functioned as a permeable membrane in protecting a national culture. Through a national language, a nation could explore all aspects of human identity, both the particular and the universal, without fear of losing its identity through assimilation. In the early 1920s, Kalmanovitch had expressed this non-essentialist view of national Jewish culture in his battle for the creation of a Yiddish school. In the ghetto, however, he tellingly concentrated upon the realization of this vision for Hebrew culture in Palestine.[76]

To Kalmanovitch, the ascendancy of aesthetic culture assured the arrival of a true Hebrew cultural renaissance. When Klausner filled *Ha-Shiloaḥ* with belles lettres, he did so in order to bridge the gap between what he termed "Hebrewness" *('ivriut)* and "generalness" *(klaliut)*. For this reason, Kalmanovitch understood the transition in *Ha-Shiloaḥ's* editorship as signifying the victory of a non-essentialist national culture.[77] Kalmanovitch ended his essay on a triumphal note regarding the present and future of Hebrew literature. Whereas Aḥad Ha-'Am's views were doomed to the past, Klausner merited to become "one of the builders of the renewed land of Israel, one the pillars of the rebuilt Jerusalem."[78]

Like his essay on Aḥad Ha-'Am, Kalmanovitch's essay on Peretz concentrated upon the failure of Peretz's disciples to realize his vision. Like Aḥad Ha-'Am, Peretz too envisioned a modern national literature that would serve as a continuation of the religious tradition. During the last decade of his life, Peretz articulated his vision of modern Jewish culture in a series of publicistic essays. According to Peretz, modern Yiddish culture needed to serve as a middle ground between what he deemed the atrophied world of religious Orthodoxy and the nationally suicidal path of assimilation. One by one, Peretz criticized the various ideological programs to which East European Jewry had turned to preserve Jewish identity in the modern age: Orthodoxy, political Zionism, and political Diaspora nationalism. If the former proved anachronistic, the latter two denied the unique spiritual qualities of the Jews. Although Peretz articulated his opposition to other ideologies far better than he proposed a concrete program of his own, he hoped to forge a Jewish national culture that would represent the unique Jewish spiritual tradition in modern form. In forging this culture, he argued, modern Jewish intellectuals had to both rebel against the religious tradition and draw from it. On the one hand, he heaped vitriol upon Tsaytlin and other penitent nationalist thinkers who sought a return to traditional Judaism. By freezing Judaism in the past, the Orthodox actually endangered Jewish survival. At the same time, Peretz called upon modern Yiddish writers to draw from the religious tradition preserved by the Orthodox when creating their new culture. Jewish traditional society could serve as an inspiration to the new culture until the latter achieved self-sufficiency.[79]

In his ghetto essay on Peretz, Kalmanovitch sought to understand Peretz's relationship to the Jewish religious tradition. Peretz, wrote Kalmanovitch, hoped that *yidishkayt*, "the ethical-religious spirit that unified the Jews into one closed community during the Middle Ages," would permeate modern Yiddish literature.[80] Regarding Peretz's paradoxical call to secular Jews to draw inspiration from the very Orthodox whom he blamed for alienating the youth, Kalmanovitch explained as follows:

> He [Peretz] considers the *modern* Yiddish intelligentsia, which allowed [him] to utter [on their behalf] the statements: "Dry are our souls," "Thirsty is our tongue etc." as even more fallen, even more empty, even more socially fruitless, than backward Orthodoxy. While the latter at least has content, albeit antiquated, the modern Yiddish intelligentsia, although externally appearing progressive, in reality possesses no spiritual content. If, let us suppose, the Orthodox recite their chapter of Psalms mechanically, without comprehension, without at the very least the original meaning of the Psalmist,—the chapter of Psalms nevertheless is an objective entity in itself, a universal worth, a source from which every human heart . . . finds rejuvenation and comfort. What, however, does the modern Jew have as a Jewish content? What can he offer the world from his own possessions?[81]

Kalmanovitch thus read into these passages by Peretz his own disillusionment with Yiddish culture.

Despite his praise of the Orthodox, Kalmanovitch in reality despaired not of the secularism of Yiddish culture but rather of its ability to be implemented in the Diaspora. Throughout the essay, Kalmanovitch emphasized that it was the *goles,* the exile, that doomed Peretz's vision for Yiddish culture. Because he functioned as the last great representative of *goles* Jewishness, Peretz's failure to reconcile the contradictions of his cultural vision doomed it to failure. Similarly, it was the abnormal conditions of exile that prevented Yiddish literature from accurately portraying Jewish life. For a normal nation (which to Kalmanovitch now meant a "territorial" nation), literature and creativity of the spirit mirrored real life. However, Yiddish literature found itself caught between the two contradictory tendencies of the Jewish religious tradition and acculturation into European society and culture. In order to establish its independence, modern Yiddish culture had to rebel against the religious heritage. Yet, as ever-increasing numbers of East European Jews engaged in a process of secularization, they found themselves drawn into the orbit of the "foreign" cultures that surrounded them.[82] A national Yiddish literature, then, could not reflect the aspirations of Jewish individuals as they abandoned the Jewish collective for surrounding cultures.

Echoing his argument from his 1939 essay "Untern hamer fun der geshikhte," Kalmanovitch argued that Peretz had failed to understand the destructive nature of the Diaspora. Whereas Aḥad Ha-'Am had tempered his spiritual nationalism with a call for a territorial center in Palestine, Peretz imagined the Jews as a Diaspora nation held together solely on the basis of culture. At the root of Peretz's cultural vision, argued Kalmanovitch, rested the ahistorical assumption that it was the power of the word that had bound the Jews into a collective unity during the Middle Ages. If Peretz had probed external factors that had contributed to Jewish collective identity in the premodern era, he would have realized that a spiritual culture itself remains an insufficient basis for national cohesion. In the modern era of national diffusion, modern Yiddish culture would prove no more successful than religion in sustaining Jewish collective identity. Ultimately, argued Kalmanovitch, Peretz's vision suffered from the fact that whereas it viewed the Jewish religion dynamically, it understood the Jewish people in static terms, as forever remaining a Diaspora people. The failure of Jewish secularism, then, was a problem of the Diaspora.[83]

Despite this verdict, Kalmanovitch battled for a Jewish nationalist education in the ghetto schools. In the ghetto schools, insisted Kalmanovitch, Jewish nationalist pride had to assume the highest priority. Kruk, a committed Bundist, reported disapprovingly of the following solipsistic statement that Kalmanovitch made to Gens regarding the education of Jewish children in the Vilna ghetto: "I don't want to know, I only know that I am first of all a Jew."[84] Kalmanovitch's belief in the future of Hebrew culture and his disgust at what he believed to be the Soviet-inspired radicalism of Vilna culture led him to rant against the by-then defunct Vilna Yiddish Real Gymnasium for its allegedly insufficiently Jewish curriculum. As Kruk derisively noted, "As usual, friend Kalmanowicz [sic] finds it necessary to shout that the spirit of the Jewish schools is not Jewish. Here of all places, in the ghetto, he wants to settle accounts with the former Vilna Academic Gymnasium for not teaching Hebrew."[85]

Despite this despair, Kalmanovitch's ghetto diary reveals traces of his secular-nationalist orientation. His emotional reliance upon God for deliverance did not mean that he lost all belief in the redemptive potential of humanity. Rather, he often tempered his historiosophical pronouncements about the divine meaning of the destruction of European Jewry with humanistic statements. Although he understood the Holocaust primarily as a catalyst to internal Jewish national consolidation, Kalmanovitch also believed that the memory of genocide would inspire humanity to righteousness. In a passage in which he inveighed against the FPO for its belief in an honorable death, Kalmanovitch merged a national with a universal vision of the redemptive meaning of the murder of European Jewry:

> The living Jewish people will always remember them in glory. Their death will be a monument to the crimes of their murderers. Their death is an atonement for the sins of the entire generation. Let all men the world over know how God's people were murdered innocently. All over the world they will be remembered and their memorial will remain a sign unto the coming generations. Whenever the spirit of tyranny arises again and seeks to spread its dominion over men, let it be remembered what the cruel tyrant did to the people of Israel, and men will brace themselves to suppress the evil spirit before it spreads. Glory and honor to the victims of the birth pangs of redemption![86]

Like the writers in *Shriftn,* Kalmanovitch turned to Jewish religious sources as repositories of the very humanistic values that he felt the Germans were trampling. Kalmanovitch's messianic vision owed as much to the humanistic tradition that informed his lifelong vision of Yiddish culture as it did to the traditional religious conception of the messiah. In this passage, Kalmanovitch merged the traditional belief in the "birth pangs of the messiah" with the humanist hope that the genocide of European Jewry could serve as a catalyst of a universal moral awakening. In other diary entries, Kalmanovitch envisioned a general human moral awakening at the end of the war. For instance, in a passage full of optimism over what he hoped was the impending end of the war, Kalmanovitch expressed hope for the return of "the same warm humanity we knew in our youth."[87]

This vision betrayed a positive evaluation of human nature despite Kalmanovitch's insistence upon the Jews' isolation and abandonment. Sometimes his very sense of isolation led Kalmanovitch to expressions of solidarity with humanity. For example, on December 31, 1942, he expressed his desire to celebrate New Year's Eve in his imagined future in Palestine. Given that the Germans sought to isolate the Jews from the rest of humanity, a celebration of the passage of universal time would prove a fitting form of resistance. Recalling scenes of drunken revelry in Berlin on New Year's Eve forty years earlier, Kalmanovitch expressed amazement at the fact that the same German people now had sunken so low. Despite the barbarity of the Germans, he nonetheless maintained hope that humanity as a whole would emerge intact following the war. In fact, even in the midst of the war, many non-Jews demonstrated their humanity in their relationship with the Jews. In his words:

> Man is still better than is generally assumed. The gentile woman in the market place that sells her goods cheaper to the Jewish woman buying from her clandestinely, for "she is wronged." Or the woman who meets Jews in the streets and exhorts them to return to God and comforts them: "Pray to Him, He will help." Wickedness has revealed its shame through its nakedness. It will have to crawl into hiding again and undoubtedly much deeper and farther than before. It will never be able to raise its head openly. Shall this be our comfort?[88]

As before the war, Kalmanovitch channeled this appreciation of human accomplishment into his cultural nationalism. Always a champion of the Jewish people, in the ghetto he venerated all Jewish activity, both secular and religious, as examples of spiritual resistance to the Nazis. In this sense, Kalmanovitch subscribed to the ideology of *Kiddush Ha-ḥayim,* or Sanctification of Life, which so many other Jews espoused in the Nazi ghettos. The traditional conception of *Kiddush Hashem* called upon Jews to sacrifice their lives rather than forfeit their religion. In contrast, advocates of *Kiddush Ha-Ḥayim* recognized that the greatest act of resistance to the Nazis' genocidal plan was to remain alive and to preserve their humanity.[89] Given that the Nazis attempted to strip the Jews of their humanity, Kalmanovitch deemed the continuance of normal human actions as heroic acts of national resistance.

Kalmanovitch articulated this ideology most fully in his essay "Der gayst fun geto" ("The Spirit of the Ghetto"), written just two weeks before his deportation to Estonia in September 1943. Written during a time of rumors and anxieties regarding the imminent liquidation of the ghetto, this essay sought to reflect upon the meaning of the ghetto's second anniversary. Unlike any other human society or institution, wrote Kalmanovitch, the ghetto inhabitants had absolutely no stake in the existence of the ghetto. Given that the ghetto symbolized extrusion from society and subhuman status, the ghetto inhabitants only could hope for liberation and for the ghetto's speedy demise. Cultural activity and the maintenance of normal life served as the greatest acts of resistance in the face of this attempt at dehumanization. The ghetto inhabitants thus had waged a successful battle to restore their lost humanity. Cultural activities thus attained sacred status as "the struggle for spirituality." The battle for normalcy also achieved this elevated status. As examples of cultural resistance and the struggle for normalcy, Kalmanovitch pointed toward "the children's homes . . . the children's library and reading room, the theater, the youth club . . . the generally satisfactory health conditions." Kalmanovitch ended the essay with the hope that this spiritual resistance would allow the Jews of the ghetto to survive until the "happy end."[90]

Another opportunity that he used to engage in nationalist rapture about the unique qualities of the Jewish people was the opening of a ghetto restaurant in June 1942:

> I was filled with a feeling of honor for the community of Israel [*kneset yisra'el*]. This flower bundle that all tread upon accepts its rebuke with love and smiles pleasantly with a very thin pain. Who are like you, O Children of Israel! I bow and prostrate myself before your will to live. From the depth of my heart I am filled with reverence and love for this wonderful nation. From the valley of death, a delicate flower sprouts forth and it will resurrect and straighten the oppressed.[91]

Here, Kalmanovitch worshipped not the God of Israel but rather the nation of Israel itself. He transmuted the religious conception of the *kneset yisra'el*, depicted in rabbinic sources as in communion with God, into a nationalist concept. Similarly, whereas the liturgy asked "Who is like Your people, Israel" within the context of praising God's unity and the unity of his name, here Kalmanovitch praised the nation alone. In a homily on a verse in the Song of Songs, Rabbi Eliezer taught that a Torah scholar should make himself into a "bundle of spices" that all tread upon so that his Torah knowledge endures. By association, Kalmanovitch granted a redemptive power to Vilna Jewry's acceptance of its suffering, linking it to the traditional image of the Jewish people as accepting its rebuke with love *(kabalat yisurin be-ahavah).*[92]

The ideology of *Kiddush Ha-Ḥayim* propelled Kalmanovitch to praise activities as national achievements that he either would have ignored or deemed an inappropriate waste of energy before the war. A major example is that of a sports field that the ghetto inhabitants built near the Vilna *shul hoyf* (synagogue courtyard), which possessed such buildings as the city's historic synagogue, traditional study houses, and the Strashun Library. Given that the *shul hoyf*'s buildings symbolized the best of Vilna's old and new Jewish culture, one might expect Kalmanovitch to judge the building of a sports field on their border as a sacrilegious act. However, within his ideology of *Kiddush Ha-Ḥayim,* the sports field acquired sacred status as a representation of the Vilna ghetto inhabitants' desire to live. In one diary entry, Kalmanovitch asserted that the unified work on the field by both old and young reasserted Vilna Jewry's national energy and prepared its youth for the building of a national homeland following the war's end.[93] Kalmanovitch articulated a more realistic assessment of the national worth of the sports field in a debate with ghetto intellectuals and with Gens over the propriety of erecting a monument to the ghetto. He rejected the argument that the erection of a monument was inappropriate given the uncertain future that awaited Vilna Jewry. In his words:

Tomorrow? Our strength will not create tomorrow, it will be created by others. The main thing for us is the present. We stood literally at the brink of the abyss—and yet we are living and creating. The artist must show the great strength of our hope to live—and the proof is the sports field. The children that play, the men and women . . . we live in the present. With our strength. We are active and not only passive.[94]

Kalmanovitch's conception of cultural resistance demonstrated the same central features as *Shriftn*'s *integrale yidishkayt* in its equal veneration of manifestations of secular and religious Jewishness. For instance, having attended a celebration commemorating the first anniversary of the Yiddish theater in the ghetto, Kalmanovitch commented that this event, which occurred on a Friday night, instilled "our people" with "courage and hope."[95] Such activities were necessary, argued Kalmanovitch, in order to keep the Jews alive until the liberation. All manifestations of Jewish culture had this life-preserving effect. When listing examples of the seething cultural life in the ghetto, Kalmanovitch pointed to the manifestly secular premier of a choir and a literary lecture titled "Shylock and Nathan." He then turned to the deeply religious *siyum,* the celebration of the completion of a Talmudic tractate, by members of the yeshiva named in memory of Rabbi Chaim Ozer Grodzenski. Turning once again to modern Jewish culture, he mentioned approvingly that the ghetto library was full of readers.[96]

In his actions, too, Kalmanovitch bridged the divide between what, across the ocean, *Shriftn* referred to as "old and new Judaism." In the ghetto, Kalmanovitch lectured widely on topics of Yiddish and Hebrew literature and on the meaning of Jewish nationalism. At the same time, however, he became a regular worshipper in Rabbi Shaulke's *kloyz,* or prayer house, where he studied Talmud with yeshiva students. Probably for this reason, Kalmanovitch received a personal invitation to their *siyum,* to which he alluded in his diary. Kalmanovitch also joined a *daf yomi* group, which studied a folio page of the Talmud daily. When the ghetto police sought to shut down this group and beat some of its participants, Kalmanovitch complained to Gens, thereby securing the study session's future.[97] Before the war, Kalmanovitch never would have imagined identifying with a yeshiva named for Rabbi Grodzenski nor seeking refuge in the world of the *besmedresh* that he had abandoned in his youth. Now, however, he studied Talmud together with the most conservative elements of Vilna Jewry, seemingly unfazed by the contradiction between their disapproval of modern Jewish culture and his involvement in it.

Kalmanovitch's Religious Turn

One of the most striking features of Kalmanovitch's diary is the extent of its religious tone and content. Kalmanovitch, the disillusioned Yiddishist, wrote his diary in a Hebrew that resonated with the cadences of biblical and rabbinic Hebrew. Moreover, Kalmanovitch often addressed his words in the diary to God, asking him to spare his people and to wreak his vengeance upon the Germans. In a few remarkable passages, Kalmanovitch recorded personal thoughts and sermons that he delivered in which he sought to uncover the hidden divine plan behind the destruction of East European Jewry. This religious tone and content, so novel for Kalmanovitch, came from two sources. First, his choice of Hebrew as the diary's language reflected his despair in the Diaspora and its modern Yiddish culture. Second, his usage of Hebrew led him to reflexively fall back on the biblical and rabbinic tone and content that had remained with him from his youth. Invoking a biblical and rabbinic cadence in the diary proved an effective psychological means of not only identifying with the roots of Jewish culture but also of writing the unprecedented catastrophe into the meta-historical narrative of Jewish survival. Under the extreme conditions of the ghetto, Kalmanovitch returned to some aspects of biblical and rabbinic faith and theodicy.

Through the tone and content of the diary, Kalmanovitch created a theological meta-history that left him with a shred of hope for survival even as he reconciled himself to his probable demise. Within this meta-history, the Jews of the ghetto were held captive in a cosmic battle between good and evil. As liquidation of the ghetto neared, he took refuge in the belief that God would reveal himself, deliver the Jews from harm, and turn the Germans' evil upon them. Within this meta-historical drama, the actual historical actors assumed typological identities. For instance, Kalmanovitch referred to the Soviets as the *gdoylim* (the great ones), the Nazis and Germans as respectively *ha-adonim* (the masters) and the *bene ha-gevirah* (children of the mistress), and such occupied nations as the Poles and the Lithuanians as *bene ha-shifḥah* (children of the handmaiden). Elsewhere, he referred to the Germans by the kabbalistic term used to describe the "dark forces," the *sitra aḥra*, and to Hitler as *sam*, or the devil. In associating the messianic redemption with the end of the war, Kalmanovitch implicitly identified the experience of the Holocaust with the traditional conceptions of *'ikveta de-meshiḥa,* the footsteps of the Messiah, and *ḥevle ha-mashiaḥ,* the birth pangs of the Messiah. The Talmud depicted this era as one of great tribulations and persecutions. In one entry, Kalmanovitch thus referred to the Nazis by the name Armilius, the evildoer who, according to the aggadah, would kill the Messiah son of Joseph before himself being killed by the Messiah son of David.[98]

When faced with fear of death, Kalmanovitch sought comfort in the words of the Bible and liturgy. He often ended his diary entries with quotations from the liturgy of supplications to God such as, "Master of the Universe, remember Thy compassion," and "Have compassion on Thy people, our Rock."[99] Upon hearing the news of a speech delivered by Hitler, Kalmanovitch commented, "The Power of Evil is still enthroned. The salvation of God [may come] instantaneously."[100] Religious Jews often invoked this last phrase, a colloquial expression of faith without a source in the Bible and rabbinic literature, to express their belief that God could redeem them in any moment. Still in other passages, Kalmanovitch called upon the ghetto inhabitants to recognize that their survival entirely depended on God's will.[101]

The more that Kalmanovitch began to doubt if Gens's program of productivization would save the ghetto, the more he poured out prayers of hope for redemption and for vengeance upon the Germans. Typical of such prayers is the following passage, strung together from quotations from the Book of Psalms: "The wicked man schemes against the righteous, and gnashes his teeth at him. The Lord laughs at him for [He knows that] his day will come. The wicked draw their swords [bend their bows], to slaughter [to bring down] the lowly and needy, to slaughter upright men. Their swords shall pierce their own hearts, and all their bones [their bows] shall be broken."[102]

In his memoirs of the Vilna ghetto, Kaczerginski described Kalmanovitch's great optimism that allowed him to believe in an immediate Allied victory even at the darkest moments. Yet Kalmanovitch's diary revealed that he often used this optimism as a mask for his fears. Oftentimes, Kalmanovitch expressed his fear that even if the liberation were near, the Nazis would seek to suppress evidence of their crimes by murdering all the Jews before their defeat. In one entry, he denied any personal fear of death, arguing instead that he hoped to survive to bear witness to the Nazi genocide of the Jews. During August 1943, the last month of the ghetto's existence, Kalmanovitch grew increasingly fearful that the deportation of thousands of Jews to Estonia signaled the liquidation of the ghetto. Echoing the words of the Book of Lamentations, Kalmanovitch wrote that with the productive workers gone, industry would wither and famine would ensue, a fate worse than the sword. Yet Kalmanovitch calmed his nerves by quoting Gens's assurances of the ghetto's survival.[103]

Caught in the ghetto population's terror of liquidation, Kalmanovitch also allowed himself to fall prey to false rumors of Nazi Germany's imminent collapse. He interpreted Nazi Germany's impending downfall as an example of the maxim recited by the late Second Temple sage, Hillel, when seeing a skull floating in the river: "Because you drowned others, you yourself were drowned."[104] Kalmanovitch refused to believe rumors that workers sent to Riga actually had met their deaths, quoting Psalms 37:13, "The Lord laughs at him, for He knows that his day will come."[105] In this verse, God laughs at Israel's enemies knowing that their downfall is imminent. Upon hearing rumors of Nazi Germany's imminent demise, Kalmanovitch initially experienced rapturous hope that God had listened to his prayers for deliverance. Ultimately, though, he had to admit to himself that the rumors were false.[106]

Kalmanovitch's religious mood sometimes moved him to deliver sermons and to ruminate in his diary over the theological meaning of the ensuing catastrophe. In his diary entry from October 11, 1942, for instance, he wrote how he celebrated the holiday of Simhat Torah in a ruined synagogue, now turned into a music school. Among the secular intelligentsia of the ghetto, Kalmanovitch was not alone in his attendance of this special event.[107] However, what made this visit unique was the fact that the rabbi honored Kalmanovitch with the first *hakafah*, the ritual of carrying the Torah scrolls around the synagogue. Before the ritual, Kalmanovitch offered the following words of theodicy to those gathered:

Our song and our dance are a form of worship. Our rejoicing is due to Him who decrees life and death. Here in the midst of this small congregation, in the poor and ruined synagogue, we are united with the whole house of Israel, not only with those who are here today and with the tens of thousands of the pure and saintly who have passed on to life eternal, but with all the generations of Jews who were before us. In our rejoicing today we give thanks too for the previous generations, the noble generations in which life was worthwhile. We feel that with our song today we sanctify the name of Heaven just as our ancestors did. And I, a straying Jewish soul, feel that my roots are here. And you, in your rejoicing atone for the aims [sins] of a generation that is perishing. I know that the Jewish people will live as it is written, 'As the days of the heaven upon the earth.' And even if we were the last generation, we should give thanks and say, 'Enough for us that we were privileged to be children of those!' And every day that the Holy One, blessed be He, in His mercy gives us is a gift, which we will accept with joy and give thanks to His holy name.[108]

Kalmanovitch's Simḥat Torah sermon emerged from his deep desire to identify with Jewish tradition and with all previous generations of Jews at a moment when East European Jewish civilization was coming to an end. What distinguished this sermon from other attempts at internal national consolidation was its deep meta-historical religious message. Perhaps it was his deep veneration for the Jewish past combined with the belief that Jewish behavior in the ghetto possessed transcendent religious and national value that led the ghetto inhabitants to hail Kalmanovitch as the "prophet of the ghetto."[109]

In his sermon, Kalmanovitch transformed this Simḥat Torah celebration into nothing less than a renewal of the theophany at Mount Sinai. By stating that the souls of past generations joined in their celebration, Kalmanovitch poignantly inverted a well-known midrash that stated that the souls of all future generations of Jews stood at Mount Sinai to accept the Torah. Whereas the original revelation at Mount Sinai stood as the symbol of the beginning of Jewish history, the Vilna ghetto represented this history's possible end. In the rabbinic tradition, Mount Sinai also symbolized the ultimate unity of the Jewish people. The ghetto Jews could honor the memory of those already murdered by the Nazis, atone for their generation's sins, and secure the survival of the Jewish people, implied Kalmanovitch, through their reconsecration to the Torah and to God. By uniting themselves with all past generations through their celebration of the Torah, the

Jews of the Vilna ghetto could contribute to the realization of the biblical promise of Jewish eternality.[110]

The superiority of the pious generations of the past to the contemporary secular one also served as a major theme of this sermon. By identifying those who had lived in the past as "the noble generations in which life was worthwhile," Kalmanovitch implied that Jewish life had lost its meaning in the present. As a "straying Jewish soul," Kalmanovitch had discovered his own roots in this "poor and ruined synagogue." On one level, this declaration signaled a national homecoming for Kalmanovitch, through which the modern secular nationalist intellectual felt comfortable again in the synagogue, worshipping with those who viewed the Torah as part of a timeless tradition. On a deeper level, however, this statement revealed Kalmanovitch's own process of religious, not just national, return. It was, after all, the piety and self-sacrifice of the previous generations that led Kalmanovitch to venerate them. The present secular generation, he implied, was incapable of acts of *Kiddush Hashem* without linking itself to the faith of its pious ancestors.

It was the memory of these pious ancestors that granted meaning to the present even if, despite Kalmanovitch's protestations to the contrary, no Jewish future might exist. By returning to tradition before their deaths, the Jews of the ghetto could link themselves to the age-old tradition of Jewish martyrdom and therefore give meaning to their current suffering. In his call for the ghetto Jews to express gratitude to God for their status as the descendants of the righteous, Kalmanovitch invoked the traditional conception of *zekhut avot,* or ancestral merit. The sermon's end in fact drew upon a statement in the first paragraph of the *shemoneh 'esreh,* or Eighteen Benedictions, the classical Jewish prayer: "Who will redeem their children's children for His Name's sake." Whereas the *shemoneh 'esreh* referred to the ancestral patriarchs Abraham, Isaac, and Jacob, here Kalmanovitch referred to past generations of East European Jews who had lived according to the Torah.

Six months later, on Passover 1943, Kalmanovitch deepened this religious message in a sermon that he delivered at a communal seder. In this speech, Kalmanovitch used the theme of Jewish identity for the purpose of encouraging his fellow Jews to engage in religious return.

Incarceration in the ghetto, began Kalmanovitch, made the majority of European Jews aware of the crisis of Jewish identity that had begun with the onset of modernity. Forced to live solely with other Jews, the ghetto inhabitants realized that they sometimes shared nothing in common with each other linguistically, culturally, and religiously. Unlike this multiplicity of identities during the modern era, Jewish identity in the premodern era had meant religious observance and a sense of belonging to *klal yisroel*. Clearly, Kalmanovitch here invoked his view of the modern era as one of Jewish national disintegration. At the end of his *Oyfn sheydveg* essay, Kalmanovitch had questioned whether or not Nazi persecution would reforge the Jewish collective. In this sermon, he answered that question in the affirmative. In the crucible of the ghetto, Jewish individuals were returning to the Jewish national collective.[111]

In a Polonized Jewish child studying a religious Jewish text in the ghetto, Kalmanovitch found a symbol of this return. When studying the Book of Genesis, the child expressed his hope that the ghetto Jews served as the descendants of the righteous Jacob, and the Nazis, those of the wicked Esau. In this seemingly innocent statement of a child, Kalmanovitch discovered the definition of contemporary Jewish identity. If, in a flight of fancy, a ghetto inhabitant would not want to switch places with his or her Nazi tormentors, then he or she was a true Jew. What determined Jewish identity psychologically, therefore, was the conscious choice to remain Jewish even in the face of persecution and annihilation. Kalmanovitch then used this definition of Jewish identity as the springboard to articulate a theological statement about the meaning of the destruction of East European Jewry:

> For a Jew is part of a sacred triad: Israel, Torah, and Holy One Blessed Be He. That means the Jewish people, the moral law, and the Creator of the Universe. This sacred triad runs through the whole of history. It is a reality that has been proved countless times. Our grandfathers clung to the triad, lived by its strength. And now, too, a Jew who does not cling to this triad is to be pitied. He wanders in a world of chaos, he suffers and finds no rationale for his suffering; he can be severed from his people, i.e. he can wish to change his self. But the Jew who clings to the triad need not be pitied. He is in a secure association. To be sure, this is a stormy period in history. A war is being waged against the Jew. But this war is not merely directed against one link in the triad but against the entire one: against the

Torah and God, against the moral law and the Creator of the Universe. Can anyone still doubt which side is stronger? In a war, it happens that one regiment is beaten, taken captive. Let the Jews consider themselves as such prisoners of war. But let them also remember that the army as a whole is not and cannot be beaten. The Passover of Egypt is a symbol of an ancient victory of the sacred triad. My wish is that all of us should live to see the Passover of the future.[112]

Kalmanovitch's search for the meaning of Jewish identity thus led him from his inherently secular cultural nationalist assumptions to a religious meta-historical perspective on the meaning of the destruction of European Jewry. Through identification with God, the Torah, and the people of Israel, the ghetto inhabitant could transcend the status of victim and become a combatant in a cosmic battle between the forces of good and evil. Only the Jew not bound to the Jewish tradition and to its divine author could see himself or herself as degraded. Kalmanovitch borrowed his belief in the triad of God, Torah, and Israel from Rabbi Moses Chaim Luzzatto, who stated, "The Holy One Blessed Be He, the Torah, and Israel are all one."[113] By linking themselves to God and to the Torah, the Jews too assured themselves of their eternity.

The concept of persecuted Jews as a captured regiment had its roots in a Talmudic statement that understood the benefit of the Diaspora as allowing for the survival of the entire Jewish people even when isolated communities suffered annihilation. Elsewhere in the diary, Kalmanovitch elaborated on this image of the Jews as a captured regiment in an attempt to provide a spiritual and psychological justification for Jewish suffering at the hands of the Nazis. Rather than concentrating on the barbarity of the Nazis who would receive their just divine punishment, Kalmanovitch argued that the ghetto Jews should turn their gaze inward. Far from an outside party, the Jews had agitated for the democracies to go to war against Hitler long before these countries were ready to do so. Once the war began, the Jews fell as the first and largest sacrifice to Hitler, who "at the moment holds 'us,' rules over us and does to us what his heart desires." Kalmanovitch ended on a triumphant note:

The meaning of the matter: "We" are not the lamb innocent of all guilt that the executioner slaughters. No. We are the vanquished camp, which fell victim, and perhaps fell victim until a certain moment. Behold today all of Europe is wallowing under the [oppressor's] high boot. Even the giant in the East surely fell. He is moving, and he apparently is arising from his slumber. And why cannot we guess that "we" will surely rise with all of the world? If you are only a lamb—the world is apt to have mercy on us, without doubt. But for a *nation* it is preferable that they consider it a dangerous enemy rather than having pity on it. Mercy is a complete destroyer. And especially for the Jewish people, for which it was possible to strangle and to lower, yet they surely know that *God* revealed Himself to it, that God emerges from it, in order to conquer the world.[114]

This statement, together with the previously recorded Passover sermon, reveals the extent to which Kalmanovitch's meta-historical perspective in the ghetto led him to retreat from the isolationist stance that he had articulated on the eve of the war. In the above-quoted passage, Kalmanovitch merged his nationalism with his religious conception of the godliness of the Jewish people. By ending his Passover sermon with the hope for the arrival of the "Passover of the future," Kalmanovitch invoked the classical belief in a future messianic redemption. The end of the war, intimated Kalmanovitch, would initiate a messianic era in which the Jews would return to the land of Israel.

If it was Kalmanovitch's cultural nationalism that largely led him to his religious return, then it is not surprising that his despair with the Diaspora loomed large in his evolving theodicy of the Holocaust. Significantly, he identified the sin of his generation that had condemned it to destruction as not the abandonment of traditional observance but rather failure to leave the Diaspora. Living in a volcanic part of the world that had devoured other nations in the past, East European Jews had failed to heed "the warning of the God of history" informing the Jews to "have eyes."[115] East European Jewry, he declared, received "the punishment it deserves" for trusting in the promises of Western civilization.[116] In another passage, Kalmanovitch repeated his condemnation of European Jewry for not leaving for Palestine, which he had first openly stated on the pages of *Ringen* in 1940.[117]

At times, Kalmanovitch merged this despair with the Diaspora with both his Zionist fervor regarding Jewish national renaissance and his veneration for the contemporary Orthodox. The following passage used these themes to attempt a meta-historical explanation of the destruction of Vilna Jewry. Because of the importance of this passage, I quote it nearly in its entirety:

> God's purpose in destroying the community of Vilna was perhaps to hasten the redemption, to alert whomsoever might still be alerted that there is neither refuge nor hope for life in the Exile. The Vilna community had served as a model and exemplar of a Jewish settlement in Exile with its own distinctive culture. Many, oh so many, did not perceive the net that lay hidden within this culture. And now the fortress of exilic Judaism has been breached, its temple has been destroyed forever.
>
> But if we take a hard look we can see that it was not necessary for the destruction to come from without. The fortress had already been destroyed and laid waste from within. Vilna had put up no resistance to the assimilation and obliteration of Jewish character, had not stood up to the spiritual destruction decreed by the Red conquerors.
>
> The death of Rabbi Chaim Oyzer Grodzenski on the very day that the Reds entered Vilna . . . can serve as a symbolic sign. The funeral . . . brought tens of thousands of Jews—one might have thought it was a veritable demonstration of Vilna Jewry behind the hearse of its most distinguished son, the Vilna Gaon's truest disciple, who displayed its honor and beauty for all the world to see; a last demonstration of Vilna's Jewish spirit [*yiddishkeit*], a vain attempt to prove that it still lived. But this proved to be its last manifestation.
>
> (I confess that it wasn't until I looked into Chaim Oyzer's archive that I apprehended a little something of his greatness). Our world of freethinkers, separated from him by 10,000 walls, also gained sustenance from his glory, and lived thanks to this cracked vessel, which is to say, the cracked vessel of traditional Judaism. And together we were all of us smashed, as it is written [Isaiah 31:3], "the helper shall trip and the helped one shall fall" ["Oyzer in Hebrew means "Helper"]. I do not know for certain, but I want so much to believe that somewhere, in the mystical recesses, somewhere in the depths of true believers, those spiritual giants, a hidden protest lay burning, and that they were yet contemplating to carry out acts of sanctification of God's name [*Kiddush Hashem*], [as it is written,] "The remnant of Israel shall do no wrong" [Zephania 3:13], save for those [of their number] who had succeeded in fleeing overseas. But from the outside—from the outside it appeared as if the Satanic Force had scored a complete and total victory, once and for all.
>
> And later, when the full evil was revealed and the decree of apostasy and [spiritual annihilation] were enacted in full—must we not admit that God, in His beneficence to the Jews of Vilna, reserved for them a beautiful death? [As David said to Gad,] "Let us fall into the hands of the Lord; and let me not fall into the hands of men" [2 Samuel 24:14]. A martyr's death is preferable to becoming degenerate. And if the Old Synagogue was laid waste, and all that remained was a heap of stones and bare walls, is that not a better fate than that young profligates appear who desecrate her sa-

cred objects and turn her into a theater or museum? For the very stone of those walls absorbed the prayers and sighs of our ancestors, their supplications for redemption, which ascend like an offering upon the altar. And we will be reminded of them whenever we long for the stones of our homeland, and we will take them into our hearts, and pass their memory on to our children and children's children in our liberated Zion. And these undesecrated stones will serve as a memorial to our Exile, for their merit was not to have been desecrated through the hands of their own children, by those who had once built the walls, but rather, through the hands of a savage nation, acting as the emissary of God. May their sacred memory serve to sweeten and soften our hearts, to recall and to guide the way for the children of Abraham.[118]

In this passage, Kalmanovitch combined his despair with the Diaspora, his Zionism, his hatred of the Soviets, and his newfound respect for the Orthodox in order to arrive at a theodicy of the destruction of Vilna Jewry. The destruction, he argued, had to come in two stages, a Soviet and a German, in order to preserve the collective national memory of Vilna as a holy community (kehilah kedoshah). What confirmed Vilna Jewry's national rot in Kalmanovitch's eyes was its lack of resistance to the Soviet occupation, something that had preoccupied Kalmanovitch since the first days of the war. Twenty years earlier, Kalmanovitch had voiced his preference for the pogroms of the Whites and Ukrainians over the Sovietization of Kiev. Now, he stated that Vilna Jewry's own collaboration in what he considered its national spiritual apostasy served as damning evidence of its moral degeneracy. God therefore chose the Germans, a barbarous nation, to destroy Vilna Jewry in order to protect its future collective memory. Kalmanovitch invoked the image of the Great Synagogue as a symbol of the best of Vilna's Jewish culture. According to Kalmanovitch's prophecy, the Nazis' impending reduction of the Great Synagogue into a heap of stones would inspire future generations to recommit themselves to Jewish tradition in the land of Israel, the only safe haven for Jewish national culture. According to Kalmanovitch's theodicy, God had sent the Nazis to destroy Vilna Jewry before it had time to desecrate its own tradition, turning it into a Soviet caricature of its former self.[119]

Kalmanovitch's praise of Rabbi Grodzenski also merged a nationalist critique of Vilna Jewry with genuine feelings of religious return.

Throughout most of Kalmanovitch's career and even in the ghetto, Rabbi Grodzenski represented that which Kalmanovitch opposed. In his half century as Vilna's spiritual leader, R. Grodzenski had battled the modernization and secularization of Vilna Jewry, which had paved the way for Vilna's emergence as a capital of Yiddish culture. As a leader of the Orthodox political party Agudas Yisroel, he also fought against Zionism, which Kalmanovitch so heartily embraced in the ghetto. Kalmanovitch, then, largely turned to R. Grodzenski's memory as a condemnation of his own fellow secular nationalist Jews. In declaring R. Grodzenski the true heir of the Vilna Gaon, Kalmanovitch jettisoned Vilna's entire modern Jewish cultural legacy. From *maskilim* to proponents of modern Yiddish culture, modern Vilna Jews traced their cultural and intellectual lineage back to this intellectual and spiritual giant. Through a word-play from the Book of Isaiah based upon R. Grodzenski's middle name, Ozer, or helper, Kalmanovitch argued that the merit of this great rabbi's dedication to Jewish tradition sustained secular Jewish culture as well. This statement drew upon the Talmudic belief that the righteous sustain the world.[120] It also mirrored Kalmanovitch's interpretation of Peretz's paradoxical attitude toward Orthodoxy as a source of inspiration for modern Yiddish culture despite its alleged backwardness. Kalmanovitch implied that R. Grodzenski's Orthodoxy, the true heir of Vilna's glorious traditional past, served as the "helper" and secular Yiddish culture as the "helped."

Ultimately, then, Kalmanovitch's newfound veneration of the Orthodox had more to do with his despair regarding the viability of Jewish national culture in the Diaspora than it did with an actual rejection of modernity itself. In this passage as well as throughout the diary, Kalmanovitch expressed his conviction that the Jewish religious tradition, although it had preserved Jewish national values to a greater extent than its secular counterpart, also was doomed to oblivion in the Diaspora. Kalmanovitch's conflation of the memories of R. Grodzenski's funeral and the Soviet conquest demonstrated his belief in the downfall of Vilna Jewry's traditional religious culture. In Vilna Jewry's demonstration of religious solidarity at the funeral, Kalmanovitch saw a false sign of hope that Vilna's religious Jews would resist the Soviet apostasy. Yet the lack of such spiritual resistance demonstrated, in Roskies's words, "that Satan had already triumphed, for even religious Jewry—schooled in the ideal of Kiddush Hashem and bearing witness to God's name through acts of martyrdom—had capitulated."[121]

Although he imagined it as stronger than its secular heir, Kalmanovitch still described traditional Judaism as a "cracked vessel." According to Lurianic Kabbalah, the primordial cracking of the vessels containing God's sparks created the physical universe. Just as Lurianic Kabbalah envisioned the sparks as ultimately returning to their divine source, so too did Kalmanovitch envision the essence of traditional Jewish culture as migrating to the land of Israel. Yet, as we have seen in his essay on Aḥad Ha-'Am, Kalmanovitch did not necessarily hope for the restoration of the religious tradition there. Rather, he hoped that the basic building blocks of the old religious culture, as symbolized by the synagogue's stones, would provide national Hebrew culture with roots.

Kalmanovitch's newfound appreciation for the Orthodox went beyond his veneration of the memory of Rabbi Grodzenski. When the Orthodox declared a public fast on May 31, 1942, Kalmanovitch attended the communal service, hoping that the religious would have the power to arouse the rest of the ghetto inhabitants to repentance. Although the rabbi's sermon impressed Kalmanovitch enough for him to summarize it in detail in his diary, he ultimately left the ceremony disillusioned. The fact that the event had not galvanized the ghetto inhabitants to repentance meant that all the ghetto inhabitants, including the Orthodox, had descended morally. Even as Kalmanovitch held out expectations for the redemption of Vilna Jewry based on the religious conception of repentance, he nonetheless concluded that the community, including the Orthodox, no longer could fulfill this religious value. In the stripped, naked Torah scrolls that Kalmanovitch discovered in the course of his work as a librarian for the Nazis, he saw a symbol of the descent and degradation of traditional Judaism. He brooded over the ultimate fate of even those few scrolls that he had managed to rescue, wondering if the "living spirit of these parchments" would rise once more.[122] Whereas earlier in his career Kalmanovitch had heralded the impending downfall of the Jewish religious tradition, now he mourned this historical process as a tragedy.

In another diary passage from the end of 1942, Kalmanovitch explained that East European Jewry would have disappeared even without a Nazi invasion. Yet if East European Jewry would have succumbed to Soviet assimilation, future generations would have blamed it with the cardinal sins of suicide and fratricide. Invoking the biblical story of Joseph, Kalmanovitch imagined Jacob's horror if Joseph's brothers had succeeded in their fratricidal plot. The brothers, however, had spared Jacob this agony by telling him the lie that a wild animal devoured Joseph. The analogy, though imperfect, is clear. The external destruction of East European Jewry by the Nazis redeemed its memory for future generations. In Kalmanovitch's words:

> There will be a page of history that will read: The grandchildren were not inferior to the grandfathers. Only fire and sword overcame them. A curse upon the murderer! Eternal glory to the innocent victim! But in this case, however, where comfort lures people into the camp of the mighty, it is of no interest to history. It will not condemn, but silence means condemnation. You are no longer. . . . History will cherish your memory, O inhabitants of the ghetto. Your most insignificant expressions will be studied, your battle for the individual will inspire poems, your impurity and moral decay will call and rouse to morality. Your murderers will stand in the pillory forever and ever. Humanity will look at them in horror and be afraid of itself and will endeavor to refrain from sin. . . . In this manner the catastrophe will find its way into world history. Extinction by means of a loving caress creates no sensation and means nothing to anyone. Eventually the Jewish people itself will forget this branch that was broken from it. . . . Refrain from sorrow! The nation will not be hurt. It will, we hope, come out fortified by these trials. This should fill the heart with joyous gratitude to the sovereign of history.[123]

Kalmanovitch, Gens, and the FPO

It was this elevation of the interests of the collective over that of the individual that led Kalmanovitch to his embrace of the policies of Gens. Despite the vast differences in their personalities, Kalmanovitch and Gens enjoyed a close relationship. Kalmanovitch fundamentally agreed with Gens's "work for life" ideology. The hope that at least a remnant of the ghetto inhabitants might remain alive if the ghetto remained productive permeated Kalmanovitch's diary. In one entry, for instance, Kalmanovitch wrote that for the ghetto inhabitants, work equaled life in a literal sense. He also often stated that when the Nazis witnessed Jewish productivity, they, like the biblical Balaam, were forced to bless the Jews against their will.[124]

He therefore praised Gens for his decision to publicly execute six Jewish criminals implicated in murder and robbery, arguing that their actions had endangered the ghetto's chances for survival. In his mix of extreme nationalism and religious fervor, Kalmanovitch understood this execution and its public nature as a fulfillment of the biblical commandment and justification for capital punishment, "so that they shall listen and see and not conspire [to sin]."[125] To the members of the police who carried out the execution, Kalmanovitch offered the following blessing: "And to those to whom the difficult task fell to serve as the vessel of wrath in the hands of the God of vengeance, my blessing is: 'May the God of Jacob protect you from such a task, and would that you merit to be the guardians of the walls in the dwellings in our land.'"[126] In a strange ideological twist, the ghetto police, widely reviled for their opportunism, became a symbol to Kalmanovitch of nation building.

This gap between popular perception and Kalmanovitch's evaluation reached its heights in Kalmanovitch's praise of Gens and of the ghetto police for their *Aktionen* during the fall of 1942. Kalmanovitch unequivocally agreed with Gens's speech following the actions, offering the following words of praise: "Praised be the God of Israel who has sent us this man."[127] Even two days later, when Kalmanovitch learned that, in contrast to Gens's report, the police had handed over women in addition to the elderly, Kalmanovitch maintained his words of praise. To Kalmanovitch, the ability to overcome pangs of conscience for the greater good served as the ultimate example of the subjugation of the needs of the individual to that of the community. As *Aktionen* proceeded, Kalmanovitch's convictions became firmer in this matter. Earlier in his ghetto experiences, Kalmanovitch approved of the policy of handing over victims to the Nazis in order to save the community but nonetheless maintained that the holy and pure refrain from involving themselves in such bloody tasks.[128] By the time of the *Aktionen* in Oszmiana and Swiecany, however, he argued that the police who actually carried out these actions were the holiest ghetto inhabitants of all:

In effect, we are as it is not innocent of Jewish blood. We have purchased our lives and our future with the death of tens of thousands. If we have decided that we must continue despite everything, then we must go through with it. And the forgiving God will forgive us. The old rabbi may serve as an example: "It is necessary to rescue all that can be rescued." This is the situation and we cannot change it. Of course, a noble soul cannot tolerate such deeds, but the protest of the soul has only psychological and no moral value. All are guilty, or better perhaps: all are innocent and holy, and above all, those who actually carry it through. They must control themselves, brace themselves, and master the sufferings of their souls. They liberate others and shield them from sorrow.[129]

It was this praise for Gens and the ghetto police that led many postwar readers of Kalmanovitch's diary to question his judgment. The Bundist Yitskhok Kharlash titled his article about Kalmanovitch's diary "An Approach That Can Drive You Insane." Kalmanovitch's old-fashioned religious faith, he argued, led him to despair of the world and of human action and instead to trust only in God. In contrast, members of the FPO put their faith in the progressive forces of humanity and in human action. Although hesitant to judge those in such a situation, Kharlash argued that resistance ultimately would have served Kalmanovitch's goal of creating a historical memorial for the victims more than passive resignation and support of Gens's collaboration. Shalom Luria, Kalmanovitch's son, later argued that it was his father's naïveté and ignorance of the Jewish police's abuses that had driven him to embrace this approach. In addition, Luria claimed that his father's lavish praise for the police resulted from a psychological process of reaction-formation, in which Kalmanovitch dealt with his disgust by turning it into unqualified support. Historian Dina Porat also suggested this possibility, arguing that Kalmanovitch's vociferous defense may have reflected the Vilna ghetto inhabitants' simultaneous acceptance of and repulsion by Gens's actions.[130]

Even had Kalmanovitch known the sordid details of the police's corruption, it is doubtful that he would have changed his assessment. It must be remembered that part of Kalmanovitch's theodicy was his elevation of almost all human acts of the ghetto inhabitants to a sacred status. Because he viewed the destruction of East European Jewry from a meta-historical perspective, Kalmanovitch often discounted the feelings and the motivations of individuals and judged decisions from a distant rather than immediate perspective. Just as he dismissed the mourning of ghetto inhabitants for their murdered relatives as a personal rather than a national tragedy, so too did he argue that the Jewish policemen's historical role outweighed their individual intent. Although the contemporary reader may question Kalmanovitch's judgment, he or she would be wrong to question his sanity based on this position. As seen in the above-quoted passage, Kalmanovitch's support of Gens's collaboration stemmed from a deep-seated hope that a large minority of the ghetto would survive until the liberation, if only it maintained its productivity. In addition to his religious belief, it was this belief in the endurance power of the ghetto inhabitants that allowed Kalmanovitch to maintain hope and sanity.

His support of Gens's collaboration in the *Aktionen* also demonstrates the extent to which Kalmanovitch subordinated his religious return to nationalist feeling. Despite Kalmanovitch's mention of a rabbi who had sided with Gens, the entire rabbinic tradition and the overwhelming majority of rabbinic authorities in the ghettos disapproved of collaborating in the murder of Jewish individuals in order to save the entire community. In fact, the Talmud ruled that, excepting certain limited circumstances, if a group of bandits demanded that a group of Jews hand over one of its members, the group should allow itself to be murdered rather than sacrifice an individual member. Kalmanovitch no doubt knew this tradition but rejected it because it conflicted with his nationalist vision of sacrificing the individual for the good of the collective.[131]

Another related and equally controversial position that Kalmanovitch took was his opposition to the FPO. On the surface, it appears that Kalmanovitch's condemnation of the FPO came from his mistaken impression that this organization was made up almost exclusively of members of the Revisionists. Kalmanovitch despised the Revisionists for what he considered their politics of disunity and what he deemed to be their Fascist tendencies.[132] Yet Kalmanovitch clearly knew that at least some of the leaders of the FPO, such as Kovner, were not Revisionists. When Kovner privately consulted with Kalmanovitch before issuing his call to arms, Kalmanovitch revealed his passive cultural nationalist ideology: "Against evil of such magnitude one cannot go with force. Our strength is our powerlessness. We are fated to be like all of Abraham's children." Kovner surprisingly later admitted that had he been ten years older, Kalmanovitch's invoking of the tradition of Jewish martyrology would have convinced him not to issue his call to arms.[133] This statement revealed Kalmanovitch's belief that the ultimate fate of the ghetto inhabitants rested in the hands of others: God, the Allies, and the Nazis. Kalmanovitch's only glimmer of hope lay in his belief that an orderly, productive ghetto might survive until the liberation. Acts of resistance threatened the ghetto with immediate liquidation. The futility of self-defense in the Vilna ghetto, wrote Kalmanovitch in his diary, barred any meaningful comparisons to self-defense units in late tsarist Russia, the Haggana in Palestine, or even the resistance in the Warsaw ghetto. Unlike the ancient zealots who waited to commit suicide until they had exhausted all other options, the FPO invited suicide through its call to arms. Selfish interests rather than a commitment to the nation thus motivated them. Given that the Allies eventually would defeat the Nazis, the Jewish individual in the ghetto best could serve the community by simply remaining alive.[134]

It was precisely the FPO's notion of an honorable death that Kalmanovitch rejected as emanating from a misguided allegiance to external European values. In his cultural nationalist ideology that valued the spirit over the physical, Kalmanovitch understood the FPO's notion of an honorable death as impugning the memory of those who had perished. In his words: "Self-defense is a false vision. It has no meaning or value and certainly no concrete significance. One dare not say that those who perished died the death of churls, although they went to their slaughter like lambs. The living Jewish people will always remember them in glory."[135] Kalmanovitch also intimated that the FPO's attempt to redeem Jewish honor sought to do so not in the eyes of traditional Judaism, which honored martyrdom, but rather in the eyes of emancipationist ideology, which looked externally for approval. Resistance, moreover, served as a hallmark of Polish culture, which increasing numbers of Polish Jews adopted during the interwar period despite their marginalization from Polish society.[136] When Kaczerginski asked Kalmanovitch how, after the war, Vilna Jews would be able to look their friends in the free world in the eyes if they did not resist, Kalmanovitch reacted with anger. He urged Kaczerginski to cease searching for external approval, assuring him that nobody would blame him for not resisting. Finally, indicative of his religious turn, Kalmanovitch reminded Kaczerginski of the promise of the world to come. "Here in front of you, you have this world," he commented wryly.[137]

In regard to his ideology of sacrificing individuals to save the community, Kalmanovitch practiced what he preached. According to Kaczerginski, as the liquidation of the ghetto neared, he and Sutzkever devised a plan to hide Kalmanovitch and other prominent ghetto intellectuals with Lithuanians. When that plan failed, they planned to take Kalmanovitch with them to the partisans in the forest. However, during an *Aktion* in September 1943 in which thousands of Jews were deported to Estonia, Kalmanovitch deliberately left his house and joined the throng of deportees on the street. According to Kaczerginski, Kalmanovitch approached Gens during the *Aktion* and said, "Mr. Commandant, are we going?" and walked toward the ghetto's gate.[138]

Kalmanovitch persisted in his ideology even in the camps of Estonia. In the Erdah camp he worked as a water carrier. His job cleaning the Narwa latrines of the refuse left by the dysentery- and typhus-infected camp inmates helped him to avoid hard physical labor. According to survivors, Kalmanovitch reacted to his work by stating, "I kiss the excrement of these holy Jews." Under conditions of annihilation, everything belonging to the Jews became holy, even their excrement. At least on the surface, Kalmanovitch persisted in his optimism, seeking to provide hope to his fellow inmates of an impending Allied victory. In December 1943, he addressed his fellow inmates at a clandestine Hanukkah celebration. In a postcard that he sent to Vilna from Narwa, he wrote simply, "I am lucky to find myself amongst the grandchildren of Abraham our Father." In Narwa, Kalmanovitch also reconciled with Moyshe Lerer, the Yiddishist who had replaced him as the head of YIVO at the time of the Soviet conquest. In the ghetto, Kalmanovitch would not forgive Lerer for his accommodation to the Soviets. Yet in Narwa, Kalmanovitch cared for Lerer when he became sick with dysentery, even sharing his food with him. When Lerer died, Kalmanovitch recited the *Kaddish* prayer for him. In the winter of 1944, Kalmanovitch finally succumbed to cold and hunger. Kalmanovitch's final words affirmed his belief in national renaissance in the land of Israel. According to survivors, Kalmanovitch went to his death addressing the following words to his German oppressors: "I laugh at you; I am not afraid of you! I have a son in the Land of Israel!"[139]

During the Holocaust, the fates of Tcherikower, Efroikin, and Kalmanovitch could not have diverged more. Yet, despite their vastly different circumstances, all three engaged in an attempt to further their ideologies of counter-emancipation. All three, moreover, mixed their realism and disillusionment with a meta-historical flight of fancy. In his historical essays on French Jewry, Tcherikower exposed the anti-Semitism inherent in the process of emancipation. Still, at the same time, he speculated about how Jewish modernity might have looked, if only the Jewries of Alsace-Lorraine had won their struggle for national as well as individual rights. By returning to the moment in which he believed European Jewish history had gone astray, Tcherikower perhaps hoped to point in a direction for the future. Efroikin, similarly, wrote with great bitterness about the future of the democracies and the Jews' place in them. Yet he, too, engaged in fantastic thinking by hoping that the extrusion of the Jews would pave the way for the reconstitution of Jewish corporate life, now directed above by the exclusionary, rather than the liberal, state. Although poor, persecuted, and numerically decimated, the Jews would emerge from the war with a state in Palestine and with national autonomy in the newly created ghettos in the democracies. That Efroikin, after three decades of anti-Soviet sentiment, would look for national salvation from the Soviet Union demonstrates both the extent of his disillusionment with the democracies and his hope for the imposition of Jewish national life from above. Kalmanovitch, unlike Efroikin, did not have to dream about ghettoization; he lived it. Yet, in the Vilna ghetto, Kalmanovitch transcended the grim daily struggle for existence by interpreting that very struggle as proof of Jewish eternality. Looking backward to his religious forebears, Kalmanovitch rejected the Yiddish secular experiment as a failure. The destruction of Vilna's Diaspora Yiddish culture would hasten Jewish national renaissance in the land of Israel. In their final years, Tcherikower, Efroikin, and Kalmano-vitch thus turned to a collectivist nationalism that repudiated their earlier liberalism. Yet, by ascribing meta-historical significance to the ensuing destruction, all three, each in his own way, attempted to rescue aspects of their ideologies for the future.

Conclusion

O NLY FIFTY YEARS separated the beginning from the end,"
wrote Samuel Kassow, referring to the rise and fall of
East European Jewish nationalist historiography, from Dubnov's first
call to gather historical material to Emanuel Ringelblum's documentation of life and death in the Warsaw ghetto.[1] This statement empha-
sizes the brief nature of the rise and fall of Jewish secular nationalism
in Eastern Europe. As disciples of Dubnov, Peretz, and Zhitlovsky, the
protagonists of this study attempted to create a secular Jewish national culture and politics as a substitute to the Jewish religious tradition that would sustain East European Jewry in the Diaspora. That
they did so against the background of revolution, world war, pogroms, and dislocation makes their effort all the more impressive. Yet,
by the eve of World War II, these three men joined other Diaspora
nationalists and Yiddishists in concluding that their experiment had
failed on its own terms. Rather than having become transformed into
a proud secular nation with nationally autonomous rights, East European Jewry remained deeply culturally divided and increasingly
politically marginalized. Secular Yiddish culture, these men concluded,
had failed to maintain Jewish identity in an era when increasing
numbers of Jews embraced the dominant nationalities' languages and
cultures. Most intriguing from a historical perspective is the fact that

the subjects of this study rendered this judgment on the eve of the Holocaust, not during it. In the words of Dan Diner, these men articulated a sense of "catastrophe before the Catastrophe."[2] The contingencies of history largely explain the failures of Diaspora nationalism and Yiddishism: the disintegration of the multinational tsarist and Habsburg empires, the rise of nationalizing successor states, the rise of Hitlerism and Stalinism. Yet it is still worth analyzing some of the inner tensions and dynamics within these movements to help explain the trajectory from hope to despair that these men experienced. Before doing so, however, it is worth reexamining the debate between Dubnov and his students from our vantage point, seventy years after World War II.

The break between Dubnov and his students on the eve of the Holocaust proves one of the most dramatic and tragic aspects of this book. Any discussion from hindsight regarding the propriety of the arguments of both sides risks ahistoricism. As late as 1940, none of these actors could have foreseen the demonic extent and nature of the genocide that the Nazis soon would unleash upon European Jewry. Similarly, given that Dubnov himself was murdered at the beginning of the genocide, it is impossible to surmise how he would have reacted to the reality of the Holocaust had he remained alive somewhat longer. Yet, from the historical perspective of seventy years later, it is possible to make some observations regarding which of these men's predictions were realized.

In their predictions, both Dubnov and his students proved correct in different ways. Thankfully, Dubnov was right about the ultimate triumph of European liberalism and democracy. Today, most of Europe lives in a post-totalitarian world: Nazi Germany fell some sixty-five years ago, and the Soviet Union, twenty years ago. Germany, once the fount of xenophobic nationalism and genocidal hatred, prospers as a unified, peaceful democracy. Russia, although far from completely democratic, has relinquished its hold over the former "Eastern bloc" nations and indeed upon its former republics, which look increasingly toward Western models of government and society for inspiration. Yet Tcherikower, Efroikin, and Kalmanovitch also were right in the sense that all these transformations came too late to save the millions of European Jews murdered by Nazi Germany and its accomplices. Themselves struggling for survival, the democracies proved too fragile and tainted by anti-Semitism to seriously intervene in the Nazi murder of European Jewry. Similarly, the Jewish communities in the democratic lands and in Palestine proved too politically weak and vulnerable to effectively change the Allies' position toward the plight of European Jewry. In terms of his long-term prediction regarding the emergence of two new hegemonic centers in America and Palestine, Dubnov proved prescient. Yet although the influence of Diaspora nationalist ideology and thought influenced American Jewry in profound ways, no American Jewish leaders ever seriously considered political organization along strict autonomous lines. The State of Israel has proven Kalmanovitch, Efroikin, and Tcherikower correct in assuming that if secular Jewish national politics and culture ever would be realized on a mass scale it would be in a future state in Palestine. Like mid-twentieth-century Zionists but unlike Dubnov, Kalmanovitch and Efroikin eventually envisioned this national renaissance as occurring in a territorial state, rather than in an autonomous multinational environment.[3]

Democracy versus Collectivism

From the beginning, Diaspora nationalists envisioned their ideology as the ideal synthesis of individualism and collective Jewish identity. Yet, in reality, the values of democratization and collectivism conflicted with one another. During the 1905 Revolution, the three protagonists of this study, each in his own way, ultimately rejected Marxist determinism to conclude that Russian Jewry itself would have to forge its own national renaissance. Much of their socialist zeal during and immediately following the revolution stemmed from their desire to liberate the Jewish masses from what they perceived as the dual oppression of the tsar and the existing Jewish elites. During the inter-revolutionary period, this impulse shed its revolutionary garb in favor of a liberal gradualism. Again and again, all three men argued that only a "democratic" transformation of East European Jewish society could create the political, economic, and cultural conditions for a Jewish national renaissance. This attempt at democratization reached its full expression during World War I and the February Revolution, which hastened the demise of the traditional Jewish community and culture and paved the way for the ascension of the new.

Yet, during the interwar era, Diaspora nationalists and Yiddishists often found the very process of democratization that they had championed used against them in the battle to remake Jewish society. In the experiment to implement Jewish national autonomy in Lithuania and Latvia, the Zionists and Orthodox consistently outflanked the Yiddishists and autonomists. Similarly, Tcherikower and Efroikin's attempts to implement the agenda of Diaspora nationalists on the international scale met with little success, with far more Jews espousing integrationism and Zionism than a vision of Diaspora nationalism. What recourse did a Diaspora nationalist and Yiddishist have when, to his or her horror, the majority of Polish Jewish parents chose, in the name of democratic principles, to educate their children secularly in Polish-language schools and religiously in Orthodox kheyders? Even more significantly, during the interwar era, Yiddishists watched as their fellow cultural activists to the east imposed an antinationalist Yiddishist cultural and educational program on a recalcitrant population. Their opposition to Soviet Yiddish culture did not stop Tcherikower, Efroikin, and Kalmanovitch from envying the Soviet Yiddishists' turn to state support and coercion.

Thus, it is not surprising that as the interwar years continued, these men became increasingly more illiberal and collectivist in their politics. Consistently, Dubnov proved more dedicated to the synthesis of liberalism with nationalism in his articulation of Diaspora nationalism than did his successors. On a conscious level, the most obvious force pushing Tcherikower, Efroikin, and Kalmanovitch away from democratic values toward collectivism was their deep disillusionment with democratic liberalism itself, which by the late 1930s appeared unable and unwilling to rescue European Jewry. Still, on an unconscious level, the general political and cultural trends of the entire era had their influence. The various larger ideologies to which these men wedded their political and cultural visions coincided with dominant trends in European politics and culture at the time: socialism during the 1905 Revolution, democracy and liberalism during World War I, and collectivism and a Jewish variant of integral nationalism during the late 1930s and into World War II.

In drawing this final comparison, I do not mean to draw any moral or even historical parallels between German and other Fascist integral nationalisms and the *integrale yidishkayt* that Efroikin expressed in the pages of *Shriftn*. The first promoted a xenophobia with genocidal consequences for Jews and other ethnic minorities. The second carried with it absolutely no political or social consequences for the Jewish treatment of non-Jews. In fact, Efroikin and Golomb built their vision of *integrale yidishkayt* as the mirror inverse of Nazism and European integral nationalism: in searching for a Jewish national essence, they looked to Jewish moral and spiritual qualities, not physical and military strength. This discussion of Jewish "blood" and racial characteristics harked back to Peretz. Yet there is no denying that their rejection of liberalism in favor of a collectivist national ideology that posited an essentialist difference between Jews and non-Jews drew from the search for organic, all-encompassing national identities around them. In a sense, this turn to collectivism served as much as an attempt to rescue their Diaspora nationalist vision as it did evidence of their despair of it. Ironically enough, having despaired of democracy and trying to make the best of a desperate situation, these men hoped that Nazism would prove the external force that would finally lead to the implementation of at least an attenuated version of their political vision. "Back to the ghetto" to these men thus meant the implementation of Jewish national autonomy, now in the absence of personal emancipation and through the oppressive, rather than the liberating, power of the state.

Cultural Radicalism versus Essentialism

Another tension than ran through the writings and activities of these three activists and writers was that between cultural radicalism and essentialism. Tcherikower, Efroikin, and Kalmanovitch all envisioned their political and cultural ideologies as superseding traditional religious Judaism in the hearts and minds of East European Jews. Yet, at the same time, they drew upon the past and its religious tradition to formulate the new culture. As we have seen, their conviction that their political and cultural work had transcendent value stemmed from the very religious tradition that they sought to uproot. Their inability to part with the notion of Jewish exceptionalism, even in their quest for national normalization, also originated in this source. Even as the living representatives of religious Orthodoxy posed a threat, our protagonists' political and cultural ideologies depended on many of the same meta-historical beliefs as the religious tradition, now transmuted into the humanistic realm.

In this regard, Tcherikower, Efroikin, and Kalmanovitch did not differ from other Central and East European nationalists of their era who sought to refashion ethnic identities largely rooted in religion into national ones. Yet, unlike Poles, Lithuanians, and other national groups, Diaspora nationalists and Yiddishists sought to accomplish this task in an environment of both extreme hostility and increasing linguistic acculturation. During the first half of the twentieth century, the average East European Jew simply was too involved in the battle for survival in an age of revolution, war, and chauvinistic nationalism to transfer the passion of his or her premodern religious culture (to the extent that he or she had shared in it) to the Yiddishist cultural experiment. Similarly, the realities of the interwar period led the majority of East European Jews to seek political solutions either far more minimal than that of Diaspora nationalism, such as the preservation of basic civil rights, or far more maximalist, such as communism and revisionist Zionism. All these factors led Tcherikower, Efroikin, and Kalmanovitch to despair of their political and cultural vision. Instead, they sought, in the words of David Roskies, to "drink from the well into which they once spat."[4] If they could not have Judaism in modernity, then they would have Judaism without modernity. Yet, for all their longing for the religious tradition and for the premodern ghetto, these men in reality could not return to the world of their parents and grandparents. Rather, each in his own way engaged in a process of negotiated return, which served as a last attempt to salvage their nationalist ideologies as much it did as an abandonment of them.

The trajectory of these three men from a mixture of cultural radicalism and neo-romanticism to essentialism proves telling about the history of East European Jewish cultural nationalism. Interestingly, the ideological direction of their journey contrasts sharply with that of Yiddish literati and aesthetes. For the novelists and poets whom

Kenneth Moss studied, the essentialist assumptions of their predecessors proved too stifling to their aesthetic revolution to maintain. To Tcherikower, Efroikin, and Kalmanovitch, the opposite proved true: ultimately, it was the cultural radicalism of the Yiddishist experiment that they came to reject. These men therefore went in the opposite direction from that of the "culturists" as the struggle with Orthodoxy and traditional East European Jewish culture faded: from greater emphasis on the individual and de-Judaization toward essentialism and collectivism. This divergence speaks to a fault line in Jewish cultural nationalism between aesthetic writers and their counterparts in the realm of scholarship and publicistics. This fault line increasingly divided the goals of the Yiddish literati from that of Yiddishist ideologues. To be sure, the Yiddishist ideologues shared the assumption with the literati that a national culture had to produce a literature of independent artistic merit. Yet the former, far more than the latter, depended on a set of symbols and ideas rooted in an essentialist cultural identity. This identity revolved around a mythologized image of a Yiddish-speaking nation, which naturally would choose the promotion of its own language and the survival of its group identity. The more that reality contradicted this image, the more essentialist and reactive the ideology became.

This disillusionment at least partially reacted to the very success of the aesthetic revolution, which had unfettered the individual literary psyche from that of the community. The aesthetic individualism of the literary cultural project ultimately clashed with the more collectivist, mythologizing tasks of producing a Yiddish historiography, founding an institution of higher Yiddish learning, and seeking the antecedents of Diaspora nationalism and Yiddishism in the past. Despite rhetoric to the contrary, Tcherikower, Efroikin, and Kalmanovitch increasingly obsessed about the Jewish content of Yiddish culture as they became more insecure about its ultimate survival. The divergence between the individual and collective that so bothered these three men thus had its roots in the cultural revolution itself. National folklorists, historians, and scholars wanted to impose an order—something that contradicted the liberated, individual ethos of the cultural revolution that they had helped to inaugurate. Ultimately, the subjects of this study came to believe that the de-Judaization of

Yiddish literature served as the first step of a process of cultural liquidation that would end with the abandonment of Yiddish itself.

To some extent, the disillusionment of the protagonists of this book emerged from the inability of the next generation of Yiddishists and Diaspora nationalists to replicate their own unique, angst-filled synthesis of traditional Judaism and secular national Jewish culture. In the end, such a synthesis proved a one-generation phenomenon. Only those steeped in the religious tradition that they had rejected could return to it time and again for inspiration for the creation of their new culture. Only those who left the *besmedresh* could miss it intensely and channel much of its passion for transcendence into the making of a new culture. For the next generation of both Yiddishists and Hebraists, traditional Jewish religious culture lost the immediate emotional force of a world of youth both rebelled against and then longed for. Instead, it became, to borrow Leslie Poles Hartley's famous characterization of the past, "a foreign country."[5] Tcherikower, Efroikin, and Kalmanovitch reacted to Orthodoxy as a tangible reminder of the identity that they sought to first supersede and then resurrect in an altered form.

In many ways, the ideological journey of Tcherikower, Efroikin, and Kalmanovitch anticipated a larger transformation in Yiddish culture, which manifested itself in the postwar era. After the crisis of humanism of the late 1930s, Yiddish culture would never be the same. Rather, many Yiddishists continued to preach either the negotiated return to religion or the incorporation of traditional values into Yiddish culture.

Following the war, for instance, Efroikin took some of his arguments that he had articulated during the Holocaust to their logical conclusion. In fact, Efroikin persisted in the two contradictory directions he had followed during the Holocaust. He both continued to forge an ideology for a protracted age of counter-emancipation and to attempt to realize his nationalist political goals. On the one hand, intellectually he took his counter-emancipationist ideology to its logical conclusion by declaring himself a religious penitent. In *A kheshbn hanefesh* (A soul searching), which he published in Paris in 1948, Efroikin argued that the secular rebellion against the religious tradition had amounted to no more than his generation's attempt to rid itself of its Jewish identity and to assimilate into European and American culture. The Jewish rejection of God had led not only to national disintegration but also to moral degeneration. Efroikin took this argument still further in his 1949 book *Kdushe un gvure bay yidn amol un haynt: gzeyres tov"shin- tov shin"hey* (Holiness and heroism among Jews in the past and today: the persecutions of 1940–1945). In this controversial book, Efroikin criticized East European Jewry for its alleged national and moral failings during the Holocaust. Whereas during the time of the Crusades Jews had chosen to die collectively *'al Kiddush Hashem,* in the latest catastrophe many Jews thought only of their individual survival. Efroikin contrasted what he deemed the immoral and opportunistic behavior of the acculturated Jews of the *Judenräte* and Jewish police with the much more exemplary behavior of those Jews who had remained loyal to the religious tradition. He thus applied his 1939 assertion, that acculturating Jews had allowed Europe's moral crisis to penetrate their inner lives, to those who had endured the Holocaust.[6]

Despite this radical repudiation of his previous ideology, Efroikin's actions during the last decade of his life demonstrated continuity with the past. His call to return to rabbinic tradition and religious observance should have led logically to his joining the Orthodox political party Agudas Yisroel. Instead, he became an active member in the Poale Zion–Hitahdut Party, the leading political party of the *Yishuv* and then of the fledgling State of Israel. Now in Zionist form, Efroikin thus continued to serve the twin ideologies of Jewish nationalism and socialism to which he had first committed himself four decades earlier. Using his travel agency, Oceania, as a front, he helped to finance and organize *Aliyah Bet,* the illegal emigration of Holocaust survivors to Palestine. The ships that he financed carried their passengers from Portugal to Palestine. This financial role in illegal immigration and his political involvement in Poale Zion led to Efroikin's close association with leaders of the State of Israel. Moreover, Efroikin continued to engage in Diaspora nationalist actions in practice even as he repudiated this ideology in theory. He thus participated actively in the rebuilding of Jewish communal life in Paris following the war. This activity led the newly formed *kehile* of East European Jews in Paris to elect Efroikin as their first head *(rosh ha-kahal).* Efroikin, however, would not serve in this role. In April 1954, he died at the age of seventy.[7]

Other Yiddishists, though not calling for active religious return, also persisted in the new directions forged in the late 1930s and during World War II. Until his death at the age of ninety-four in 1982, Avrom Golomb preached his vision of *integrale yidishkayt*, arguing for modern Yiddish culture to incorporate within it all elements from the Jewish past and from Jewish tradition. Leibush Lehrer, in his post-war writings, preached a similar vision of a secular Yiddish culture drawing influence from Jewish tradition. Through Lucy Dawidowicz, the ideological revision within Yiddishism reached a larger, English-reading American Jewish public. Through her intellectual exposure to Lehrer and to Kalmanovitch and through her nitty-gritty encounter with the depressing realities of Yiddish-speaking Vilna Jewry on the verge of its destruction, Dawidowicz despaired of Yiddishism as an ideology that could preserve Jewish identity. She thus spent her post-war career as a historian and public intellectual decrying the estrangement of modern Yiddish culture from its traditional religious roots. Instead, she sought to forge an American Jewish identity based upon both religious identification and support for Israel. Jewish secularism, she concluded, could only survive as long as traditional Jewish society provided it with human and cultural reserves. In this rejection of secular Jewish culture in the Diaspora and greater tolerance of it within Zionism and Israel, Dawidowicz followed in Kalmanovitch's and also, perhaps unwittingly, Efroikin's footsteps.[8]

This re-embrace of religion and tradition among Yiddishists demonstrates a seldom addressed paradox regarding modern Jewish identity, personified by this book's protagonists. All too often, modern Jewish historiography has championed a mono-directional line of progress from traditional Jewish religious identity to the triumph of secular nationalist substitutes. This book complicates this neat linear progress and indeed blurs many of the distinctions between the categories of the religious and the secular.[9] It demonstrates that in the first half of the twentieth century, people who cared passionately about the survival of the Jewish people often sought answers to Jewish identity consecutively in differing and often opposing camps. Members of different streams of the modern Jewish national movements borrowed from one another and even embraced each other's ideologies when they concluded that their opponents had been correct. As much as proponents of religious Orthodoxy and modern secular Jewish nationalism in all its varieties differed, both groups were united in their commitment to the survival of the Jews as a community that bore a unique culture and destiny. It is not surprising then that secular nationalists sought inspiration from the religious tradition and even sometimes sought to return to it.

Diaspora nationalism and Yiddishism as contemporary ideologies have passed from the scene. The issues of identity that their advocates raised, however, remain achingly relevant for Jews, and indeed for all members of religious and national minorities committed to preserving their identities in the modern (and some would argue the postmodern) world.

Notes

Introduction

1. Elias Tcherikower, "Di tragediye fun a shavkhn dor," *Oyfn sheydveg* 1 (April 1939): 10.
2. Yisroel Efroikin, "Vu haltn mir in der hayntiker velt," *Oyfn sheydveg* 2 (August 1939): 26.
3. Zelig Hirsh Kalmanovitch, "Untern hamer fun der geshikhte," *Oyfn sheydveg* 1 (April 1939): 29. This Talmudic passage comes from the Babylonian Talmud Sanhedrin 97b.
4. Ibid., 46.
5. Tcherikower, "Di tragediye," 28.
6. See for instance R. Elḥanan Bunem Wasserman, *Ma'amar 'ikveta de-meshiḥa u'ma'amar 'al ha-emunah: A balaykhtung fun der yetstiker tkufe* (Baranowicze, Poland: Ch. Wasserman, 1936).
7. Jose Casanova, *Public Religions in the Modern World* (Chicago: University of Chicago Press, 1994).
8. Benjamin Harshav, *Language in Time of Revolution* (Stanford, CA: Stanford University Press, 1999), 1–39, 57–62, 70–75. Harshav argues that the pogroms of 1881–1882 and subsequent tsarist anti-Semitic legislation directed this revolution in an "intrinsic" rather than an "extrinsic" direction. Jonathan Frankel's *Prophecy and Politics: Socialism, Nationalism and the Russian Jews, 1860–1917* (Cambridge: Cambridge University Press, 1981) remains the definitive study of Russian Jewry's embrace of Jewish nationalism and socialism in the decades following 1881. Frankel also explored how Russian Jews exported these ideologies to the United States and to Palestine. For a definition and discussion of the "cultural project," see Kenneth Moss,

Jewish Renaissance in the Russian Revolution (Cambridge, MA: Harvard University Press, 2009), 1–22.

9. Exceptions to this rule are David E. Fishman, *The Rise of Modern Yiddish Culture* (Pittsburgh: University of Pittsburgh Press, 2005), and Samuel Kassow, *Who Will Write Our History? Emanuel Ringelblum, the Warsaw Ghetto, and the Oyneg Shabes Archives* (Bloomington: University of Indiana Press, 2007).

10. Of course, this view of premodern cultural isolation itself was the product of modern Jewish historiography and collective memory. Recent studies have demonstrated the extent of Jewish-Christian cultural interaction during the medieval and early modern eras.

11. Jonathan Frankel, "S. M. Dubnov: Historian and Ideologist," in Sophie Dubnov Ehrlich, *The Life and Work of S. M. Dubnov* (Bloomington: Indiana University Press, 1991), 1–33. For Dubnov's call to Russian Jewry to study its own history as a means of promoting national self-consciousness, see Simon Dubnov, *Ob izuchenii istorii russkikh evreev i ob uchrezhdenii russko-evreiskogo istoricheskogo obshchestva* (St. Petersburg: A. E. Landau, 1891). For both Dubnov's historiographical vision and political conception of Jewish national autonomy, see Dubnov, *Pis'ma o starom i novom evreistvie (1897–1907)* (St. Petersburg: Obshchestvennaia Pol'za, 1907): 74–112, 313–315. In Yiddish, see Dubnov, *Briv vegn altn un nayem yidtntum* (Mexico City: Shloyme Mendelson fond, bay der gezelshaft far kultur un hilf, 1959): 93–113, 340–341. For a discussion of Dubnov's ideas within their historical context, see Simon Rabinovitch, "Alternative to Zion: The Jewish Autonomist Movement in Late Imperial and Revolutionary Russia" (PhD diss., Brandeis University, 2007), 22–65. For a discussion of Dubnov's vision of the modernized *kehile,* see Fishman, *Rise of Modern Yiddish Culture,* 67. For Zhitlovsky's synthesis of Jewish nationalism with socialism, see Zhitlovsky, "Tsionizm oder sotsiolizm," in *Gezamelte shriftn,* vol. 4 (New York: Dr. Hayim Zhitlovski Yubiley Komitet, 1917), 47–76. For a discussion of the content of his socialist autonomism and its historical importance, see Frankel, *Prophecy and Politics,* 258–287. For a discussion of Zhitlovsky's linguistically based conception of national autonomy, see Fishman, *Rise of Modern Yiddish Culture,* 18–31. The best discussions of Zhitlovsky's contribution to Diaspora nationalism are Frankel, *Prophecy and Politics,* 258–287, and Tony Michels, *A Fire in Their Hearts: Yiddish Socialists in New York* (Cambridge, MA: Harvard University Press, 2005), 125–178. The fact that Dubnov and Zhitlovsky both articulated Diaspora nationalist visions did not mean that they recognized each other's contributions to the creation of this ideology. See Rabinovitch, "Alternative to Zion," 39.

12. For the Bund's synthesis of socialism and nationalism and for its complicated relationship with the Russian Social Democratic Labor Party, see Frankel, *Prophecy and Politics,* 227–256, and Henry Tobias, *The Jewish Bund in Russia from Its Origins to 1905* (Palo Alto, CA: Stanford University Press, 1972).

13. Frankel, *Prophecy and Politics,* 279–282; Barry Trachtenberg, *The Revolutionary Roots of Modern Yiddish: 1903–1917* (Syracuse, NY: Syracuse University Press, 2008), 35–36; Rabinovitch, "Alternative to Zion," 37–44, 113–117.

14. Fishman, *Rise of Modern Yiddish Culture,* 68.

15. Joshua Shanes, *Diaspora Nationalism and Jewish Identity in Habsburg Galicia* (New York: Cambridge University Press, 2012); Simon Rabinovitch, "Alternative to Zion," 230–300; Noam Pianko, *Zionism and the Roads Not Taken: Rawidowicz, Kaplan, Kohn* (Bloomington: Indiana University Press, 2010), see esp. 1–59; David Shumsky, "Brith Shalom's Uniqueness Reconsidered: Hans Kohn and Autonomist Zionism," *Jewish History* 25 (2011): 339–353. Other scholars of interwar Zionism have contested the extent to which centrist and right-wing Zionists conceived of a future Jewish state in Palestine as a nationalities state. It also would be intriguing to know the extent to which the Zionist figures that Shumsky discussed were influenced by the writings and activities of Dubnov and other avowed Diaspora nationalists.

16. Fishman, *Rise of Modern Yiddish Culture,* 15, 101–102.

17. The best analysis of the conference in its proper historical and geographical context is Jess Olson, *Nathan Birnbaum and Jewish Modernity: Architect of Zionism, Yiddishism, and Orthodoxy* (Stanford, CA: Stanford University Press, 2013), 176–208. For a previous treatment, see Emanuel Goldsmith, *Modern Yiddish Culture: The Story of the Yiddish Language Movement* (New York: Fordham University Press, 1997), 183–219. For a study of the rise of Yiddish as a language of scholarship, see Trachtenberg, *Revolutionary Roots.*

18. For the work of more senior scholars in this field, see Fishman, *Rise of Modern Yiddish Culture;* Frankel, *Prophecy and Politics;* Frankel, "S. M. Dubnov"; Ezra Mendelsohn, *Zionism in Poland: The Formative Years, 1915–1926* (New Haven, CT: Yale University Press, 1981); Mendelsohn, *The Jews of East Central Europe between the Two World Wars* (Bloomington: Indiana University Press, 1983); Mendelsohn, *On Modern Jewish Politics* (New York: Oxford University Press, 1993); Goldsmith, *Modern Yiddish Culture.* For the more recent work of younger scholars, see Moss, *Jewish Renaissance;* Trachtenberg, *Revolutionary Roots;* Kalman Weiser, *Jewish People, Yiddish Nation: Noah Prylucki and the Folkists in Poland* (Toronto: University of Toronto Press, 2011); Cecile E. Kuznitz, *YIVO and the Making of Modern Jewish Scholarship* (New York: Cambridge University Press, forthcoming); David Shneer, *Yiddish and the Creation of Soviet Jewish Culture: 1918–1930* (New York: Cambridge University Press, 2004); Olson, *Nathan Birnbaum;* Shanes, *Diaspora Nationalism;* Rabinovitch, "Alternative to Zion." The two studies that follow their respective protagonists over the course of decades are Weiser, *Jewish People,* and Olson, *Nathan Birnbaum.*

19. Guy Miron, *The Waning of Emancipation: Jewish History, Memory, and the Rise of Fascism in Germany, France, and Hungary* (Detroit: Wayne State University Press, 2011).

20. Tcherikower, "Di tragediye," 6. I am grateful to one of the anonymous readers of this manuscript for suggesting that I more forcefully explicate in the introduction this "neither nor" position of my book's subjects.

21. This book focuses primarily on Tcherikower, Efroikin, and Kalmanovitch. In my forthcoming book, I analyze in greater depth the crisis of Yiddishist intellectuals on the eve of World War II in its wider context. See Joshua M. Karlip, *Oyfn Sheydveg: At the Crossroads: Jewish Intellectuals and the Crisis of 1939* (Göttingen: Vandenhoeck and Ruprecht, forthcoming).

22. David Engel, *Historians of the Jews and the Holocaust* (Stanford, CA: Stanford University Press, 2010), 1–42. Michael Bernstein coined the term "backshadowing" in referring to this process. He wrote, "backshadowing is a kind of retroactive foreshadowing in which the shared knowledge of the outcome of a series of events by narrator and listener is used to judge the participants in those events *as though they too should have known what was to come.*" Michael André Bernstein, *Foregone Conclusions: Against Apocalyptic History* (Berkeley: University of California Press, 1994), 16. Shneer used the term "backshadowing" to describe the process through which historians read the history of Soviet Yiddish culture through the prism of its tragic end in Stalinist purges. See Shneer, *Yiddish and the Creation of Soviet Jewish Culture*, 3. Here, I am applying this term to the process that Engel described in his work regarding the study of modern Jewish history and the Holocaust. The exception to the bifurcation of Holocaust history from its prewar context is Kassow, *Who Will Write Our History.*

23. Brian Porter, *When Nationalism Began to Hate: Imagining Modern Politics in Nineteenth-Century Poland* (Oxford: Oxford University Press, 2000); Miroslav Hroch, *Social Preconditions of National Revival in Europe: A Comparative Analysis of the Social Composition of Patriotic Groups among the Smaller European Nations* (New York: Columbia University Press, 2000), 86–97; for a discussion of other East European nationalist language movements, see Roland Sussex, "Lingua Nostra: The Nineteenth-Century Slavonic Language Revivals," in *Culture and Nationalism in Nineteenth-Century Eastern Europe,* ed. Roland Sussex and J. C. Eade (Columbus, OH: Slavica Publishers, 1983), 111–127; Ernst S. Dick, "The Folk and Their Culture," in *The Folk: Identity, Landscapes and Lores,* ed. Robert J. Smith and Jerry Stannard (Lawrence: University Press of Kansas, 1989), 11–28.

24. Theodore R. Weeks, *Nation and State in Late Imperial Russia: Nationalism and Russification on the Western Frontier, 1863–1914* (DeKalb: Northern Illinois University Press, 1996), 12–16, 112–121. Weeks's comparison between the Poles and Jews should not be stretched too far. Jews, unlike their Polish neighbors, had no history of militant opposition to tsarist rule.

25. Ibid., 123–125; Kuznitz, *YIVO,* introduction.

26. Hroch, *Social Preconditions,* 22–24; Weeks argued that the various nationalities in Russia's western provinces followed this pattern in the five decades from the Polish Insurrection of 1863 to the outbreak of World War I. See

Weeks, *Nation and State,* 111; Kuznitz, *YIVO,* introduction; Rabinovitch, "Alternative to Zion," 12–13.

27. Ernest Gellner, *Nations and Nationalism* (Ithaca, NY: Cornell University Press, 2006), 98–105. Gellner's model, however, possesses its own short-comings, such as his labeling Zionism, without irony, as a form of "diaspora nationalism" and his concentration on socioeconomic factors to the detriment of cultural ones in the rise of Jewish nationalism.

28. Anthony Smith, *National Identity: Ethnonationalism in Comparative Perspective* (Reno: University of Nevada Press, 1991), 8. Also see Pianko, *Zionism,* 31–32.

29. Smith, *National Identity,* 8. Also see Pianko, *Zionism,* 31–59. For Dubnov's vision of a merger of liberalism with ethnic nationalism, see Dubnov, *Pis'ma.* For a discussion of Zhitlovsky's turn toward racialist definitions of Jewish distinctiveness, see Matthew Hoffman, "From 'pintele yid' to 'Racenjude': Chaim Zhitlovsky and Racial Conceptions of Jewishness," *Jewish History* 19, no. 1 (2005): 65–78. For Peretz's racial formulation of Jewish identity as "pure blood" that nonetheless emphasized Jewish ethical superiority, see Y. L. Peretz, "Natsionalizm un tsionizm," in *Ale verk fun y.l. perets,* vol. 11, *Gedanken un ideen* (Vilna: Vilner farlag fun b. kletskin, 1925), 272–274.

30. I am indebted to Dr. David Engel, who, in his response to a conference paper that I presented, challenged my distinction between political and cultural nationalisms on the ground that cultural nationalists nearly always marshaled national culture for political goals. Regarding the insistence upon independence from politics in the new culture, see Moss, *Jewish Renaissance,* 281–285.

31. Fishman, *Rise of Modern Yiddish Culture,* 113; Talal Assad, *Formations of the Secular: Christianity, Islam, Modernity* (Stanford, CA: Stanford University Press, 2003); Casanova, *Public Religions.*

32. Fishman, *Rise of Modern Yiddish Culture,* 99; Kuznitz, *YIVO,* introduction; Kenneth Moss, "Jewish Culture between Renaissance and Decadence: *Di Literarishe Monatsshriftn* and Its Critical Reception," *Jewish Social Studies:* New Series 8, no. 1 (2001): 153–198.

33. Fishman, *Rise of Modern Yiddish Culture,* 101.

34. Harshav, *Language in Time of Revolution,* 14–41.

35. Ḥaim Greenberg, "Bor'ba za national'nuiu individual'nost," *Sborniki "Safrut,"* ed. Leib Jaffe (Moscow: Izd-vo "Safrut," 1917), 90. Here I use Moss's translation. See Moss, *Jewish Renaissance,* 280.

36. Fishman, *Rise of Modern Yiddish Culture,* 101–2. For Zhitlovsky's articulation of this radical Yiddishist ideology, see his "Yid un mentsh (tsvey forlezungen)," 2:103–186, "Di yidishe shprakh bavegung un di tshernivitser konferents," 4:111–121. "Di yidishe shprakh un di yidishe kultur," 4:165–183, and "Religiye un natsiye," 4:187–200, all in *Gezamelte shriftn* (New York: Dr. Hayim Zhitlovski Yubiley Komitet, 1912).

37. Fishman, *Rise of Modern Yiddish Culture,* 102. For Peretz's articulation of national-romantic Yiddishism, see his "Vos felt und zer literatur," and "Tsu di tsurikkumendike geyrim," in *Ale verk,* vol. 11, 53–64, 10–25.

38. The identification of national-romantic Yiddishism with Peretz and radical Yiddishism with Zhitlovsky is broadly schematic. In reality, this division was not always so neat. Thus, despite his calls for Yiddish literati to stop imitating European trends, Peretz himself stood at the forefront of importing European modernism and symbolism into Yiddish literature. Zhitlovsky, on the other hand, himself penned a national-romantic essay, calling on modern Jews to reappropriate the Jewish holidays from a secular-national perspective. He also called upon modern Jews to base their national identity upon Jewish history, even hinting that the Jews possessed a unique racial identity. See Zhitlovsky, "Di natsyonial-poetisher vidergeburt fun der yidisher religye," *Gezamelte shriftn* 4, 221–278. Also see Zhitlovsky, "Yid un mentsh."

39. Moss's excellent study, which focuses on the de-parochialization of Hebrew and Yiddish culture, deals primarily with Hebraist and Yiddishist aesthetes. See Moss, *Jewish Renaissance,* 101–141.

40. In building this book around these dates, I followed the lead of Jonathan Frankel, who in his *Prophecy and Politics* demonstrated the importance of the historical moment on individuals in their formation and revision of modern Jewish political ideologies.

1. Diaspora Nationalism and Yiddishism in Late Imperial Russia

1. For the significance of the 1905 Revolution in catapulting a young generation of Russian Jews to political prominence, see Jonathan Frankel, *Prophecy and Politics: Socialism, Nationalism and the Russian Jews, 1860–1917* (Cambridge: Cambridge University Press, 1981), 134–170, and Barry Trachtenberg, *The Revolutionary Roots of Modern Yiddish: 1903–1917* (Syracuse, NY: Syracuse University Press, 2008), 20–45. Also see the collection of essays, Stefani Hoffman and Ezra Mendelsohn, eds., *The Revolution of 1905 and Russia's Jews* (Philadelphia: University of Pennsylvania Press, 2008).

2. Frankel, *Prophecy and Politics,* 283–285.

3. For the emergence of public culture in the aftermath of the 1905 Revolution, see Jeffrey Veidlinger, *Jewish Public Culture in the Late Russian Empire* (Bloomington: Indiana University Press, 2009).

4. For a discussion of the Lithuanian Jewish synthesis of Orthodoxy and Zionism, see Ehud Luz, *Parallels Meet: Religion and Nationalism in the Early Zionist Movement, 1882–1904* (Philadelphia: Jewish Publication Society of America, 1988).

5. The *besmedresh* in Yiddish or *bet midrash* in Hebrew is the classical study house, in which Jewish men study the Talmud and other traditional texts. It held a primary place in traditional East European Jewish society. It was against the *besmedresh* that successive generations of East European Jewish men rebelled, embracing such movements as Haskalah, Zionism, and socialism.

6. Frankel, *Prophecy and Politics* , 134–143, 158–162.

7. For a discussion of Vozrozhdenie, see Frankel, *Prophecy and Politics,* 279–282; Trachtenberg, *Revolutionary Roots,* 35–36; Simon Rabinovitch, "Al-

ternative to Zion: The Jewish Autonomist Movement in Late Imperial and Revolutionary Russia" (PhD diss., Brandeis University, 2007), 40–43. For a memoir of the movement written by one of its founders, see Moyshe Zilberfarb, "Di grupe 'vozrozhdenye,'" *Royter pinkes* 1 (Warsaw, 1921), 113–130. Efroikin and Kalmanovitch both attended the group's second conference, held in September 1905. See Rabinovitch, "Alternative to Zion," 40n50. In his letters to his then girlfriend, Riva Teplitsky, the young Elias Tcherikower wrote about his attraction to Vozrozhdenie. Elias Tcherikower to Riva Teplitsky, February 16, 1906. Elias Tcherikower Archive RG 81, folder 1294, YIVO Archives New York.

8. For a general overview of the Revolution of 1905, see Abraham Ascher, *The Revolution of 1905: A Short History* (Stanford, CA: Stanford University Press, 2004). Also see Ascher's two longer works, *The Revolution of 1905: Russia in Disarray* (Stanford, CA: Stanford University Press, 1988), and *The Revolution of 1905: Authority Restored* (Stanford, CA: Stanford University Press, 1992).

9. Rabinovitch, "Alternative to Zion," 73–84. Also see Christolph Gassenschmidt, *Jewish Liberal Politics in Tsarist Russia, 1900–1914* (New York: NYU Press, 1995), 20–32, and Frankel, *Prophecy and Politics,* 158–169.

10. On the pogroms, see Shlomo Lambroza, "The Pogroms of 1903–1906," in *Pogroms: Anti-Jewish Violence in Modern Russian History,* ed. John Klier and Shlomo Lambroza (Cambridge: Cambridge University Press, 1992), 195–247; Frankel, *Prophecy and Politics,* 149–150. For Dubnov's reaction, see Simon Dubnov, *Pis'ma o starom i novom evreistvie (1897–1907)* (St. Petersburg: Obshchestvennaia Pol'za, 1907), 294–320; Frankel, *Prophecy and Politics,* 150–151.

11. Rabinovitch, "Alternative to Zion," 83, 110–111. The Jewish representatives to the first Duma, though members of the Kadet and Trudovik parties, sometimes were also members of other Jewish parties such as the Zionists or were affiliated with the Union for the Attainment of Full Rights.

12. Ibid., 84–89.

13. Frankel, *Prophecy and Politics,* 281–286; Rabinovitch, "Alternative to Zion," 116–117.

14. Rabinovitch, "Alternative to Zion," 125–128; Frankel, *Prophecy and Politics,* 283; Antony Polonsky, *The Jews in Poland and Russia,* vol. 2 *1881 to 1914* (Oxford: Littman Library of Jewish Civilization, 2010), 65.

15. Rabinovitch, "Alternative to Zion," 144–159.

16. Zilberfarb, "Neotlozhnyia zadachi evreiskoi obshchiny," *Evreiskii mir* (July, 1909): part 2, 4–6. For a discussion of this article, see Rabinovitch, "Alternative to Zion," 156–157; "Nashi zadachi," *Vestnik evreiskoi obshchiny* 1 (August 1913): 3; Y. Efren [Efroikin], "Kehile, folk, un inteligents," *Di idishe velt* 2 (April 1912): 47–54.

17. *Vekhi: sbornik statei o russkoi inteligentsii,* ed. Mikhail Gershenzon (Moscow, 1909), 2. For a discussion of *Vekhi,* see Christopher Read, *Revolution, Religion, and the Russian Intelligentsia, 1900–1912: The Vekhi Debate and Its Intellectual Background* (London: Macmillan, 1979), 106–120; Leonard

Schapiro, "The *Vekhi* Group and the Mystique of Revolution," in Leonard Shapiro, *Russian Studies,* ed. Ellen Dahrendorf, intro. Harry Willetts (New York: Viking Adult, 1987), 68–92. For a discussion of *Vekhi* in relationship to Russian Jewry in the years of reaction see Vladimir Levin, "Ha-politikah ha-yehudit ba-impiriyah ha-rusit be-idan ha-re'aktsiyah, 1907–1914" (PhD diss., Hebrew University, 2007), 2.

18. Veidlinger, *Jewish Public Culture;* Gassenschmidt, *Jewish Liberal Politics,* 97–105, 118–135; Rabinovitch, "Alternative to Zion," 179–189.

19. David E. Fishman, *The Rise of Modern Yiddish Culture* (Pittsburgh: University of Pittsburgh Press, 2005), 33–47; Gassenschmidt, *Jewish Liberal Politics,* 99–102. Levin, "Ha-politikah ha-yehudit," 83.

20. Gassenschmidt, *Jewish Liberal Politics,* 130–131.

21. Rabinovitch, "Alternative to Zion," 165–166.

22. Vladimir Levin, "The Jewish Socialist Parties in Russia in the Period of Reaction," in Hoffman and Mendelsohn, *Revolution of 1905,* 126–127. Among the other socialist nationalists who became folkists were Wolf Latski-Bartoldi, Shmuel Niger, and Nokhem Shtif.

23. Regarding the Czernowitz Conference, see Jess Olson, *Nathan Birnbaum and Jewish Modernity: Architect of Zionism, Yiddishism and Orthodoxy* (Stanford, CA: Stanford University Press, 2013), 176–208, and Emanuel Goldsmith, *Modern Yiddish Culture: The Story of the Yiddish Language Movement* (New York: Fordham University Press, 1997), 183–221. Regarding *Di literarishe monatsshriftn,* see "Tzu di lezer," *Di literarishe monatsshriftn* 1 (February 1908): 7–10; Kenneth Moss, "Jewish Culture between Renaissance and Decadence: *Di Literarishe Monatsshriftn* and Its Critical Reception," *Jewish Social Studies:* New Series 8, no. 1 (2001): 164–172. For the quotations from *Leben un visenshaft,* see "Tsu di lezer," *Leben un visenshaft* 1 (May 1909): 1, 3, 5.

24. "Tsu di lezer," *Di literarishe monatsshriftn* 1 (February 1908): 8; "Tsu di lezer," *Leben un visenshaft* 1 (May 1909): 3.

25. "Tsu di lezer," *Leben un visenshaft* 1 (May 1909): 3.

26. Moss, "Jewish Culture," 182.

27. Simon Dubnov, "Utverzhdenie golusa," *Evreiskii mir* 5 (May 1909): 58. Rabinovitch, "Alternative to Zion," 173–175.

28. Fishman, *Rise of Modern Yiddish Culture,* 14.

29. Rabinovitch, "Alternative to Zion," 177–178.

30. "Undzer veg," *Di idishe velt* 1 (March 1912): 3–5.

31. Ibid., 6.

32. Simon Dubnov, "Nokh draysik yeriken krig," *Di idishe velt* 1 (March 1912): 5–12.

33. Zalman Rejzen, "Tsherikover, Eliyohu," *Leksikon fun der yidisher literatur, prese un filologiye,* vol. 1 (Vilna: Vilner farlag fun b. Kletskin, 1928): 1208; Daniel Tsharni, "Di drayfakhe perzenlekhkeyt (tsum toyt fun eliyohu tsherikover)," *Idisher kempfer* (September 3, 1943): 11; Elias Tcherikower, "Ber borokhov vi ikh ken im," *Literarishe bleter* 52 (December 30, 1927):

1024; Tcherikower to Teplitsky, April 4, 1902 Tcherikower Archive RG 81, Folder 1291 YIVO Archives New York. Teplitsky to Tcherikower, August 19, 1902 Tcherikower Archive RG 81, Folder 1291 YIVO Archives; Tcherikower to Teplitsky, February 4, 1906 Tcherikower Archive RG 81, Folder 1294 YIVO Archives; Tcherikower to Teplitsky, June 27, 1908 Tcherikower Archive RG 81, Folder 1296 YIVO Archives; Teplitsky to Tcherikower, August 19, 1902 Tcherikower Archive RG 81, Folder 1291 YIVO Archives.

34. I. M. Cherikover [Elias Tcherikower], "Mendele-Moykher-Sforim: Opyt kriticheskoi otsenki," *Evreiskaia zhizn'* 6 (1905): 144.

35. Ibid., 156, 153.

36. Ibid., 159.

37. *Selikhes (seliḥot* in Hebrew*)* are the penitential prayers that traditional Jews recite during the High Holiday season and on fast days. *Kines (kinot* in Hebrew) are the dirges recited on Tisha B'av, the day of mourning for the destruction of the Temple. Both these prayers employ a poetic Hebrew that describes Jewish suffering in detail and calls upon God to forgive the Jewish people their sins and to redeem them from exile. Cherikover, "Mendele-Moykher-Sforim," 164.

38. Ibid., 167–168, 170.

39. Fishman, *Rise of Modern Yiddish Culture,* 52–53. Cherikover, "Mendele-Moykher-Sforim," 161.

40. I. Mikhailovitch [Tcherikower], "Bylom," *Svoboda i zhizn'* no. 11 (November 6 [19], 1906), 1; I. Mikhailovitch [Tcherikower], "Dvoriane iz 'narodnoi svobody,'" *Svoboda i zhizn'* no. 14 (November 27 [December10], 1906), 2.

41. Tcherikower to Teplitsky, February 4, 1906; March 3, 1906; February 17, 1906, and March 22, 1906; March 10, 1906; March 3, 1906 Tcherikower Archive RG 81, Folder 1294 YIVO Archives; Frankel, *Prophecy and Politics,* 140–141.

42. Tcherikower to Teplitsky, April 6, 1906; April 19, 1906; Tcherikower Archive RG 81, Folder 1294; undated Tcherikower Archive RG 81, Folder 1297 YIVO Archives; April 19, 1908 Tcherikower Archive RG 81, Folder 1296 YIVO Archives; Levin, "Ha-politikah ha-yehudit," 122.

43. Tcherikower, "Unparteyishkeyt," *Der tog,* November 5, 1916, 4; Tcherikower to Teplitsky, March 3, 1908 Tcherikower Archive RG 81, Folder 1296 YIVO Archives; Elias to Riva Tcherikower, March 26, 1910. Tcherikower Archive RG 81, Folder 1298 YIVO Archives; Tcherikower to Teplitsky, April 14, 1908. Tcherikower Archive RG 81 Folder 1296 YIVO Archives; Rejzen, 'Tsherikover, Eliyohu," 1208. Rabinovitch, "Alternative to Zion," 181.

44. S. M. Ginzburg, "Predislovie," in I. M. Cherikover, *Istoriia obshchestva dlia rasprostranea prosvieshcheniia mezhdu evreiami v Rossii (Kulturnoobschestvennyia techeniia v russkom evreistvie) 1863–1913* (St. Petersburg: I. Luria and Co., 1913), iii.

45. Tcherikower, *Istoriia* ix; 1–2, 123, 253.

46. Zalman Rejzen, "Efroykin, Yisroel," *Leksikon fun der yidisher literatur, prese un filologiye* vol. 2 (Vilna: Kletskin Press, 1927), 811–12; interview by author with Ron Efron (nephew of Yisroel Efroikin) July 2012; Rejzen, "Efroykin, Yisroel," 811–812; Leon Halpern, "Oyfn frishn keyver fun yisroel efroykin a"h," *Shriftn: Khoydeshlekhe oysgabe far integraler yidishkayt,* nos. 145-147(June-July-August 1954), 10.

47. Rejzen, "Efroykan, Yisroel," 811–812.

48. Levin, "Ha-politikah ha-yehudit," 25, 55–89. For Efroikin's description of his involvement in both these fields, see A. Litovski [Efroikin], "Vitebsker briv," *Di folksshtime,* no. 7 (June 12, 1907): 39–45.

49. Levin, "Ha-politikah ha-yehudit," 22, 90–91. Bazin [Moyshe Zilberfarb], "Der arbayter politik in der idisher gemeynde," *Di folksshtime,* no. 15 (August 10, 1907): 8–16.

50. A. Litovski, "Vitebsker briv," *Di folksshtime,* no. 14 (August 3, 1907): 41, 46.

51. A. Litovski, "Vitebsker briv," *Di folksshtime,* no. 7: 39.

52. A. Litovski, "Vitebsker briv," *Di folksshtime,* no. 14: 41, 46; A. Litovski, "Vitebsker briv," *Di folksshtime,* no. 7: 39–40.

53. A. Litovski, "Vitebsker briv," *Di folksshtime,* no. 7 (1907): 42; A. Litovski, "Vitebsker briv," *Di folksshtime,* no. 14: 44–45. For the background regarding this incident, see Levin, "Ha-politikah ha-yehudit," 90.

54. Levin, "Ha-politikah ha-yehudit," 14. Levin explained that at the end of the nineteenth century, such administrative bodies, representing the leadership of the local communities, developed in Kherson, Ekateranislav, Vitebsk, and other localities. Although not officially recognized by the government, the government related to them de facto.

55. A. Litovski, "Vitebsker briv," *Di folksshtime,* no. 7: 43–44. A *kahal shtibl* refers to the traditional meeting place of the premodern East European *kahal.* A *shtibl,* literally a "small house," refers in Yiddish most commonly to a small synagogue but in this case refers to the cramped, backroom quarters of the communal oligarchs. *Balebatim* literally means "house owners" but within a Jewish socialist context indicates the bourgeoisie and petite bourgeoisie.

56. Ibid., 44–45.

57. Levin, "Ha-politikah ha-yehudit," 316. For the original articles, see M. Borisov [Mark Ratner], "Dos funanderlozen fun der dume," *Di folksshtime,* no. 7: 1–7; M. Borisov, "Farvos nit boykot," *Di folksshtime,* no. 12 (July 18, 1907): 1–11; Y. Solomonov, "Dos naye vahl gezets," *Di folksshtime,* no. 8 (June 19, 1907): 1–11; Y. Solomonov, "Tsu der frage vegen di vahlen in der driter dume," *Di folksshtime,* no. 10 (July 4, 1907): 1–10; N. Sh. [Nokhem Shtif], "Tsu der boykot-frage," *Di folksshtime,* no. 11 (July 11, 1907): 1–12.

58. A. Litovski, "Vitebsker briv," *Di folksshtime,* no. 14: 41.

59. Levin, "Ha-politikah ha-yehudit," 309, 317.

60. A. Litovski, "Vitebsker briv," *Di folksshtime,* no. 14: 41–43; Levin, "Ha-politikah ha-yehudit," 317–318.

61. Yakobson, *Di folksshtime*, no. 5 (March 16, 1907): 71–74. I cannot identify with any certainty the true identity of the pseudonym Yakobson. Given the similarity of his views with those expressed by Efroikin in the article discussed below, it is possible that it is Efroikin. For a discussion of Yakobson's speech, see Levin, "Ha-politikah ha-yehudit," 25.

62. Levin, "Ha-politikah ha-yehudit," 26, 319–320. For a major Bundist's call for the creation of this bureau, see P. R. (Pavel Rosental), "Opmakhungen un a gemeynzame tekhnishe byuro," *Folkstsaytung* 388 (June 24, 1907): 1.

63. Yisroel Efroikin, "Unparteyishe arbeter komitetn (Diskutsiye artikel)," *Di folksshtime*, no. 14: 19–20.

64. Ibid., 23.

65. Ibid., 21.

66. Ibid., 23–24.

67. Ibid., 27.

68. Ibid., 25.

69. Ibid., 26–27.

70. Efroikin, "Unparteyishe," 19–27; Frankel, *Prophecy and Politics*, 167–169, 283–286.

71. Y. Solomonov, "Di vahlen—un di arbayter komitetn," *Di folksshtime*, no. 15 (August 10, 1907): 16–23.

72. For a discussion of the Jewish autonomists' view of co-territorial nationalists such as the Poles, see Rabinovitch, "Alternative to Zion," 121–124. For a discussion of the SERP's presence at this conference, see Levin, "Ha-politikah ha-yehudit," 23n18. Efroikin listed the participants from SERP under their party names. Zhitlovsky, for instance, went by the name Gaydrov. Ratner was Borisov, and Zilberfarb, Bazin. Shmuel Luzinsky similarly went by Lozov. Here, Efroikin used his party name, Manin. See Y. Manin [Efroikin], "Fun der konferents fun der natsionale sotsialistishe parteyn, ershter tog," *Di folksshtime*, no. 8: 3. For Levin's identification of the various party names, see Levin, "Ha-politikah ha-yehudit," 23n18.

73. Y. Manin, "Fun der konferents fun di natsionale sotsialistishe parteyn, Ershter tog," 3–19; Y. Manin, "Fun der konferents fun di natsionale sotsialistishe parteyn: Forzetsung," *Di folksshtime*, no. 9 (June 27, 1907): 3–10; Y. Manin, "Fun der konferents fun di natsionale sotsialistishe parteyn II: Di farteydigung fun di rekhtn fun di natsionale minderhaytn bay di vahlen," *Di folksshtime*, no. 15: 3–14; Y. Manin, "Fun der konferents fun di natsionale sotsialistishe parteyn III: Natsionale un teritoriale ovtonomiye," *Di folksshtime*, no. 16 (August 17, 1907): 3–26.

74. Levin, "Ha-politikah ha-yehudit," 112–113; A. Litovski, "Di zitsungen fun der ruslendisher sektsiye (A briv fun shtutgart)," *Di shtime zamelbukh* (August 1907): 23, 31–32, 34. The argument with Trotsky revolved around the number of trade union representatives in the Second International.

75. Levin, "Ha-politikah ha-yehudit," 50, 100, 119–122.

76. Efroikin to Zhitlovsky, January 2, 1908, and June 1908; August 3, 1909 Chaim Zhitlovsky Papers RG 208, folder 700 YIVO Archives New York.

77. Efroikin to Zhitlovsky, January 27, 1909; February 2, 1909; February 7, 1909; July 16, 1908; July 29, 1908; August 8, 1908; November 5, 1908; July 16, 1908; January 27, 1909; August 3, 1909. Chaim Zhitlovsky Papers RG 208, folder 700 YIVO Archives.

78. Frankel, *Prophecy and Politics,* 285–286. For Zhitlovsky's turn to Yiddishism during these years and the Czernowitz Conference, see Goldsmith, *Modern Yiddish Culture,* 161–221, and Olson, *Nathan Birnbaum,* 176–208; Zhitlovsky, "Di natsyonal-poetisher vidergeburt fun der yidisher religye," *Gezamelte shriftn* 4 (New York: Dr. Hayim Zhitlovski Yubiley Komitet, 1912), 221–278; Zhitlovsky, "Yid un mentsh (tsvey forlezungen)," in Zhitlovsky, *Gezamelte shriftn* 2 (New York: Dr. Hayim Zhitlovski Yubiley Komitet, 1912), 103–186; Yehuda Bernstein, "Jew and Mensch or Mensch and Jew? History and Race in Chaim Zhitlovsky's 'Yid un Mensch'," (unpublished paper); Tony Michels, *A Fire in Their Hearts: Yiddish Socialists in New York* (Cambridge, MA: Harvard University Press, 2005), 136–152.

79. Efroikin to Zhitlovsky, August 8, 1908; June 1908. Chaim Zhitlovsky Papers RG 208, folder 700 YIVO Archives; Y. Efren [Efroikin], "Tsayt fragen: Di idishe sotsialistishe parteyn un di idishe folks masn," *Dos naye leben,* vol. 1 no. 1 (December 1908): 28–35; Y. Efren, "Tsayt fragen 2: Di idishe folks-ideologiye un der idisher sotsializm," *Dos naye leben,* vol. 1 no. 3 (February 1909): 39–43.

80. Y. Efren, "Tsayt fragen: Di idishe sotsialistishe parteyn," 35.

81. Y. Efren, "Tsayt fragen 2: Di idishe folks-ideologiye," 39–40.

82. Ibid., 40–42; Efroikin to Zhitlovsky, January 12, 1909. Chaim Zhitlovsky Papers RG 208, folder 700 YIVO Archives.

83. Y. Efren, "Tsayt fragen 2: Di idishe folks-ideologiye," 43.

84. Y. L. Peretz, "Vegen der yidisher literatur," *Ale verk fun y. l. perets,* ed., intro. Nakhmen Mayzel (Vilna: Vilner farlag fun b. Kletskin, 1929), 253–258.

85. Y. Efren, "Tsayt fragen, driter kapitel: Di emigratsiyon un di organizirung fun di idishe folksmasen," *Dos naye leben,* vol. 1 no. 7 (June 1909): 1–7.

86. Ibid., 5–7; Levin, "Ha-politikah Ha-yehudit," 24–25.

87. Bazin [Moyshe Zilberfarb], "Zelbst kritik oder zelbst mord?" *Dos naye leben,* vol. 1 no. 7 (June 1909): 32–37

88. Z. K. [Zelig Kalmanovitch], "Vegen efrenes 'tsayt fragen,'" *Dos naye leben,* vol. 1 no. 5 (April 1909): 59–60; Shimoni, "Misht nit di parshiyes," *Dos naye leben,* vol. 1 no. 10 (August 1909): 49–50; Shimoni, "Misht nit di parshiyes (Ende)," *Dos naye leben,* vol. 1 no. 12 (November 1909): 46.

89. Levin, "Ha-politikah ha-yehudit," 112. Ab. Goldberg, "Di konferents fun di dray idish national-sotsialistishe parteyn," *Dos naye leben,* vol. 1 no. 5 (April 1909): 47–53.

90. Zhitlovsky, "Vegen fereynigung. Ershter artikel: Bundizm un tsionizm," *Dos naye leben,* vol. 1 no. 5 (April 1909): 2.

91. Zhitlovsky, "An ofener brief tsu di poale tsiyen in amerike (tsveyter artikel fun der seriye 'Vegen fereynigung,'" *Dos naye leben*, vol. 1 no. 6 (May 1909): 1–15.

92. Levin, "Ha-politikah ha-yehudit," 112; Efroikin to Zhitlovsky, February 21, 1909. Chaim Zhitlovsky Papers RG 208, folder 700 YIVO Archives; Efroikin listed Moyshe Shalit, Shtif, and Kalmanovitch as those on his side of the debate who supported the unification program. Efroikin to Zhitlovsky, August 3, 1909; October 14, 1909. Chaim Zhitlovsky Papers RG 208, folder 700 YIVO Archives.

93. Efroikin to Zhitlovsky, January 1, 1910. Chaim Zhitlovsky Papers RG 208, folder 700 YIVO Archives. *Bal habos* is the singular of *balebatim*.

94. Ibid. For his report on the congress, see I. Efren [Efroikin], "Pyati cyezd russkikh sionistov vi gamburg: Pervii den—Utrennie zasedeniie: Otchert tsentralnago komiteta," *Evreiskii mir*, no. 1 (January 8, 1910): 47–53; Efren, "Debati po otchetu tsentralnago komiteta, *Evreiskii mir*, no. 1 (January 8, 1910): 53–58; Efren, "Pyati cyezd russkikh sionistov: Evreiskii yazik pered sudom russkikh sionistov," *Evreiskii mir*, no. 3 (January 21, 1910): 41–43; Efren, "Debati o Gegenwartsarbeit," *Evreiskii mir*, no. 3 (January 21, 1910): 43–47; Efren, "Gomburgskii kongress: Pis'mo II— Generalnie debati," *Evreiskii mir*, no. 3 (Janaury 21, 1910): 47–50; Efren, "Pis'mo III: Palestinskaiia rabota," *Evreiskii mir*, no. 3 (January 21, 1910): 50–54; Efren, "Gamburgskii kongress: Pis'mo IV: Palestinskaiia rabota (Prodolzhenie), *Evreiskii mir*, no. 4 (January 28, 1910): 44–48; Efren, "Gamburgskii kongress: Pis'mo V: Posledsnee srazhenie," *Evreiskii mir* no. 4 (January 28, 1910), 48–51. *Gegenwartsarbeit* literally means "work in the present." It is the term that the members of the Helsingsfor Conference used to describe their call for national work in the Diaspora in addition to efforts for the establishment of a Jewish homeland in Palestine.

95. Efroikin to Zhitlovsky, February 6, 1910. Chaim Zhitlovsky Papers RG 208, folder 700 YIVO Archives; Zhitlovsky, "An ofener brief."

96. Efroikin to Zhitlovsky, October 14, 1909. Chaim Zhitlovsky Papers RG 208, folder 700 YIVO Archives.

97. Efroikin to Zhitlovsky, February 15, 1910; October 14, 1909. Chaim Zhitlovsky Papers RG 208, folder 700 YIVO Archives.

98. Levin, "Ha-politikah ha-yehudit," 109–115.

99. Dubnov, *Kniga zhizni: Vospominaniia i razmyshleniia, materiali dlia istorii moego vremeni* vol. 2 (Riga: "Jaun‡tnes Gr‡mata," 1935), 132. In Yiddish, see Dubnov, *Dos bukh fun mayn leben: Zikhroynes un meditatsiyes materialn tsu der geshikhte fun mayn tsayt*, vol. 2 (1903–1922) (New York: Alveltlekher yidisher kultur-kongres, 1961), 128. For the impact of former socialists on the platform of the reconstituted Folkspartey, see Levin "Ha-politikah ha-yehudit," 167. For Efroikin's call for a democratic movement, see N. Landau, "Di 'demokratishe grupe' un der tsuzamenfor: Entfer dem h. efren un andere," *Der fraynd* (February 13, 1913): 10.

100. Efroikin to Zhitlovsky, August 1910. Chaim Zhitlovsky Papers RG 208, folder 700 YIVO Archives. According to Rejzen, Efroikin left university in Switzerland because of financial difficulties. See Rejzen, "Efroykin, Yisroel," 811. Levin, "Ha-politikah ha-yehudit," 105, 107.

101. Yekhiel Hirshhoyt, "Efroykin, Yisroel," in *Leksikon fun der nayer yidisher literatur: Biographical Dictionary of Modern Yiddish Literature,* ed. Efrayim Oyerbakh, Yankev Birnboym, Eliyohu Shulman, Moyshe Shtarkman (New York: Congress for Jewish Culture, 1968), 30.

102. Efren, "Kehile, folk, un inteligents," *Di idishe velt* 2 (April 1912): 47–49, 51–52.

103. Y. Efren, "Dos yidishe leben in rusland," *Di yudishe velt* (January 1914): 119–122, 130–134.

104. Y. Efren, "Dos yudishe leben in rusland," *Di yudishe velt* (February 1914): 291.

105. Y. Efren, "In der idisher velt," *Di idishe velt* 2 (April 1912): 119–120. A "ma-yofis yid" served as the equivalent in East European Jewish culture to the epithet "Uncle Tom" in African American culture. The term referred to Jews who would sing and dance the Sabbath melody, beginning with the Hebrew words "Mah-yofis," to entertain the Polish *porits,* or noble. Among modern Jews, this act represented the epitome of debasement.

106. Levin, "Ha-politikah ha-yehudit," 376–379.

107. Y. Efren, "In der idisher velt," 120.

108. Ibid., 120, 124–126.

109. Y. Efren, "Politik un birgerlekhkeyt," *Di yudishe velt* 1 (January 1913): 105–106, 109. In this imagery, Efroikin invoked the language of Psalm 126, recited by traditional Jews on the Sabbath and holidays before the Grace after Meals. This psalm, which speaks of the return to Zion after the Babylonian exile, states, "Those who sow in tears will reap in song."

110. Polonsky, *Jews in Poland and Russia,* 72–74; Levin, "Ha-politikah ha-yehudit," 377–378. For an example of an article that interpreted the verdict of the Beilis trial in this light, see A. I. (A. Idelsohn), "Istekshii god," *Rassvet* (January 4, 1915): 1. For a discussion of this article, see Levin, "Ha-politikah ha-yehudit," 377.

111. Y. Efren, "Yudishe politik un di yuden-frage in der ferter duma," *Di yudishe velt* 7 (July 1913): 124–126, 131–132, 134.

112. Y. A. [Yisroel Efroikin], "In der yudisher velt," *Di Yudishe velt* 11 (November 1913): 133–134.

113. Ibid., 137.

114. Ibid., 137–139.

115. Ibid., 142.

116. I am indebted to Dr. Ruth Wisse for this insight, which she articulated in her paper "A Personal Statement: Simon Dubnow in My Life," at the international conference "Historicizing the Jewish People: Simon Dubnow at 150" (Leipzig, November 2010).

117. Brian Porter, *When Nationalism Began to Hate: Imagining Modern Politics in Nineteenth-Century Poland* (New York: Oxford University Press, 2000), see esp. 3–14, 129–134, 227–238.

118. Polonsky, *Jews in Poland and Russia,* 107–111. For a discussion about the conflict over Warsaw's representation in the fourth Duma, see Stephen David Corrsin, *Warsaw before the First World War: Poles and Jews in the Third City of the Russian Empire, 1880–1914* (Boulder, CO: East European Monographs, distributed by Columbia University Press, 1989). Also see Levin, "Ha-politikah ha-yehudit," 370–371.

119. Y. Efren, "In dem yudish-poylishn khoos," *Di yudishe velt* (April 1913): 101–116; Y. Efren, "Fun der zayt (tsum sakh hakol fun der boykot-bavegung in poyln)," *Di yudishe velt* (May 1914): 277–278.

120. Y. Efren,"Fun der zayt (tsum sakh hakol)," 283, 285–286.

121. Y. Efren, "Der ferter duma," 132–134. Y. Efren, "Dos yudishe leben in rusland," *Di yudishe velt* (April 1914): 122.

122. Shalom Luria, "Zelig Hirsh Kalmanovitsh: Ha-ish ve-'olamo," in Zelig Hirsh Kalmanovitch, *Yoman be-geto vilna u-khetavim min ha- 'izavon shenimtseu ba-harisot* ed. and intro. Shalom Luria (Tel Aviv: Moreshet Bet 'Edut 'al shem Mordekhai Anilevits," 1977), 13. For Kalmanovitch's reference to his learning in the Libave *besmedresh,* see his article "Farshilmelte taynes," *Letste nays,* March 19, 1925, 4. For a short biography of Kalmanovitch's early years, see Zalman Rejzen, "Kalmanovitch, Zelig," *Leksikon fun der yidisher literatur, prese un filologiye,* vol. 3 (Vilna: Vilner farlag fun b. Kletskin, 1929): 693–696; Joseph Kruk, *Tahat diglan shel shalosh mahpekhot:(Rusim, polanim, yehudim): ishim ve-tenu'ot be-dori: zikhronot* (Tel Aviv: Mahbarot le-sifrut, 1968), 115, 118.

123. In 1999, Shalom Luria told me in a conversation that his father was briefly arrested for revolutionary activity. I know no more details about Kalmanovitch's brush with tsarist law. For his interest in class struggle and his strident Marxist tone at the beginning of his reportage on the International Socialist Congress in Stuttgart see K. [Kalmanovitch], "Der internatsionaler kongres in shtutgart: Algemeyner berikht," *Di shtime zamelbukh* (August 1907): 5. Also see his disparaging remarks about the hypocrisy and violence of bourgeois regimes in his report on striking vineyard workers in France, in K. [Kalmanovitch], "Oyslendishe khronik," *Di folksshtime,* no. 11 (July 11, 1907): 41.

124. Rabinovitch, "Alternative to Zion," 124–125. Polonsky, *Jews in Poland and Russia,* 138–145. K-N [Kalmanovitch], "Di vahlen in estraykh," *Di folksshtime,* no. 7 (June 12, 1907): 35–39. K., "Oyslendishe khronik," 37–39. Kalmanovitch,"A bletl fun der geshikhte fun der estraykhisher sotsialdemokratiye," *Leben un visenshaft* 1 (May 1909): 62–64; Kalmanovitch, "Di tsentralizirung in der daytsher profesioneler bavegung," *Leben un visenshaft* 2 (June 1909): 129–134.

125. Kalmanovitch, "Fun der yidisher literatur: Dr. khayim zhitlovskis shriften," *Di yudishe velt* 8 (August 1913): 139.

126. Luria, "Zelig Hirsh Kalmanovitsh," 13–15; Rejzen, "Kalmanovitch, Zelig," 694–695. Kalmanovitch, "Fun der yidisher literatur," 141.

127. Y. L. Peretz, "Oyf der tshernivitser shprakh konferents," *Ale verk fun y. l. perets* 11 (New York, 1948): 293–296. Also see Peretz's articulation of the

role of Hebrew as the national language and of Yiddish as the folk language as quoted in Goldsmith, *Modern Yiddish Culture*, 192.

128. P. Kleyn [Kalmanovitch], "Di yudishe shprakh-lehre," *Di literarishe monatsshriftn* 3 (April 1908): 60–63. Goldsmith, *Modern Yiddish Culture*, 173.

129. P. Kleyn, "Di yudishe shprakh-lehre," 63.

130. Goldsmith, *Modern Yiddish Culture*, 173.

131. P. Kleyn, "Di yudishe shprakh-lehre," 64–76. The *Tsene-rene*, written by Yaakov ben Yitzhak Ashkenazi of Janów, presented the Pentateuch and liturgically read sections of the Prophets and the Writings in Yiddish translation. Not a straight translation, the *Tsene-rene* rather interpreted the biblical text according to rabbinic midrashim, the Talmud, and medieval commentaries. The *Tsene-rene* became synonymous with its female reading audience. For a discussion of *Tsene- rene*, see Jacob Elbaum and Chava Turniansky, "Tsene-Rene," *The YIVO Encyclopedia of Jews in Eastern Europe* vol. 2, editor in chief, Gershon David Hundert (New Haven: Yale University Press, 2008): 1912–1913. In a letter to Niger in which he discussed the fate of the neuter article "dos" in future Yiddish literary language, Kalmanovitch once again argued that it was the Hebrew component that influenced Yiddish syntax the most. Kalmanovitch to Niger, June 1913 Shmuel Niger Collection RG 360, Folder 34 YIVO Archives New York.

132. Kenneth Moss, review of Barry Trachtenberg, *The Revolutionary Roots of Modern Yiddish, 1903–1917*, in *East European Jewish Affairs* 40, no. 2 (2010): 196–197. Trachtenberg, *Revolutionary Roots*, 108–134. Ber Borochov, "Di oyfgaben fun der yidisher filologye," in *Der pinkes: Yorbukh far der geshikhte fun der yidisher literatur un shprakh, far folklor, kritik un bibliografye* (1913): 1–22; Borochov, "Di bibliotek funem yidishn filolog (400 yor yidishe shprakh-forshung)," ibid., 1–66.

133. Borokhov, "Di bibliotek funem yidishn filolog," 2.

134. Ibid., 43.

135. Kalmanovitch, "Bibliografishe notitsen," *Di literarishe monatsshriftn* 4 (May 1908): 153–156.

136. Kalmanovitch to Niger, December 9, 1912; January 25, 1913; August 11, 1913; July 14, 1914 Shmuel Niger Collection RG 360, Folder 34 YIVO Archives.

137. Shimon Dubnov, "Hakdome," *Algemeyne idishe geshikhte fun dem ur-elter biz der nayer tsayt, mit a nayer hakdome fun mekhaber. In 4 teylen. Ershter teyl* (Vilna: Vilner farlag fun b. Kletskin, 1909): i.

138. Dubnov, "Hakdome," ii.

139. Ibid., iv.

140. Kalmanovitch, "A nay verk iber der geshikhte fun yuden," *Di yudishe velt* (February 1915): 199–202.

141. Ibid., 199.

142. *Di idishe milkhomes fun yoysef ben matsiyahu hakoyhen (Yosifus flavius): Ale 7 bikher in 2 teyl Ibergesetst tsum ershtn mol oyf idish b'shleymes fun z. kamanovitsh* (Vilna: Vilner farlag fun b. Kletskin, 1914).

143. This introduction does not appear in the 1914 translation of Josephus's work. However, it appears in the later excerpts from the translation that Kalmanovitch published after World War I. See Kalmanovitch, "Yosifus flavius," in Kalmanovitch, *Di letse teg fun yerusholoyim aroysgenumen fun zekstn bukh fun yosifus flavius "Yudishe milkhomes"* (Berlin: Klal-farlag, 1922), 3–6. Given that Kruk speaks about reading this introduction during World War I, it is fair to assume that Kalmanovitch had written it at the time that he published the translation.

144. Kalmanovitch, "Yosifus flavius," 6.

145. Kruk, *Taḥat diglan,* 116–117. Kruk pointed out the socialist nationalist perspective of Kalmanovitch's portrayal of Josephus.

146. Kalmanovitch, "Hakdome (funem iberzetser)," in Emil Schürer, *Geshikhte fun yudishn folk in der tsayt fun bayis sheyni,* translation and intro. Zelig Kalmanovitch (Vilna: Vilner farlag fun b. Kletskin, 1914): viii.

147. Ibid., ix.

148. Ibid., i.

149. Ibid., iii.

150. Ibid., v.

151. Kalmanovitch to Niger, January 1913 Shmuel Niger Collection RG 360, Folder 34 YIVO Archives.

152. Kalmanovitch, "Hakdome (funem iberzetser)," viii.

153. For a discussion of Aḥad Ha-ʿAm's view on religion and its relationship to Jewish identity, see Gideon Shimoni, *The Zionist Ideology* (Hanover, NH: Brandeis University Press, 1995): 269–78. Dubnov's classical formulation of his view on the national nature of Jewish identity appears in his *Pis'ma;* Kalmanovitch, "Hakdome (funem iberzetser)," viii.

154. Kalmanovitch, "Hakdome (funem iberzetser)," viii.

155. Steven J. Zipperstein, *Imagining Russian Jewry: Memory, History, Identity* (Seattle: University of Washington Press, 1999), 41–62.

156. For the first year of publication, the periodical was printed in St. Petersburg under the title *Di idishe velt.* In 1913, however, the periodical began to be printed in Vilna under the title *Di yudishe velt.* I do not know what precisely compelled the editors to change the orthography of the journal's name. Kalmanovitch to Niger, August 11, 1913. Shmuel Niger Collection RG 360, Folder 34 YIVO Archives.

157. A. Vayter, "Dos teater: Fragmenten," *Di literarishe monatsshriftn* (February 1908): 123–132. In this piece, Vayter attributed what he perceived as the low level of the Yiddish theater to the fact that the Jewish religious culture of the Middle Ages forcibly had suppressed the theatrical traditions of the ancient Jewish past. Without an authentic national tradition to draw upon, modern Yiddish theater devolved into the realm of slapstick and farce. The Jewish middle class, moreover, poisoned the Yiddish theater with its crass

materialism and its disdain for Yiddish. The linguistic acculturation of the aesthetically refined audience of Russian Jews doomed Yiddish theater to this cultural poverty. Only by returning to the suppressed secular tradition of Jewish theater could Yiddish theater attract a highbrow audience, thereby escaping its cultural poverty.

158. Kalmanovitch to Niger, August 11, 1913 Shmuel Niger Collection RG 360, Folder 34 YIVO Archives.

159. Ibid.

160. Kalmanovitch to Niger, undated (probably from summer 1912), January 14, 1913 Shmuel Niger Collection RG 360, Folder 34 YIVO Archives.

161. Kalmanovitch to Niger, December 2, 1912; January, n.d., 1913; January 25, 1913; undated (1913); March 3, 1913; August 11, 1913; March 5, 1913; January 28, 1913; December 9, 1912 Shmuel Niger Collection RG 360, Folder 34 YIVO Archives.

162. Kalmanovitch to Niger, January, n.d., 1913; January 25, 1913; March 5, 1913 Shmuel Niger Collection RG 360, Folder 34 YIVO Archives.

163. Kalmanovitch to Niger, January 25, 1913 Shmuel Niger Collection RG 360, Folder 34 YIVO Archives.

164. Kalmanovitch to Niger, July 14, 1914 Shmuel Niger Collection RG 360, Folder 34 YIVO Archives.

165. Kalmanovitch to Niger, December 9, 1912 Shmuel Niger Collection RG 360, Folder 34 YIVO Archives. Hillel Tsaytlin (1871–1942) was a Yiddish journalist and thinker, who began to return to his Hasidic roots during the first decade of the twentieth century. At the time, he engaged in a sharp polemic with Peretz over the secular nature of Peretz's vision. Although intimately connected to Yiddish culture, he resisted its secularism.

166. Ibid.

167. Kalmanovitch to Niger, July 14, 1914. Shmuel Niger Collection RG 360, Folder 34 YIVO Archives.

2. Catastrophe and Renaissance during World War I

1. Shmuel Niger, "Di milkhome un mir yuden," *Di vokh*, no. 3 (January 22, 1915): 5–9; *Di vokh*, no. 4 (January 29, 1915): 5–10; *Di vokh*, no. 5 (February 5, 1915): 11–13; *Di vokh*, no. 6 (February 12, 1915): 5–9; *Di vokh*, no. 7 (February 19, 1915): 6–9; *Di vokh*, no. 8 (February 26, 1915): 6. The article slated to appear on February 26 was blocked by the censor. Kalmanovitch also expressed a similar sentiment to Niger in a letter immediately following the outbreak of the war (Zelig Kalmanovitch to Shmuel Niger, August 1, 1914; Shmuel Niger Collection RG 360, folder 34 YIVO Archives).

2. Steven J. Zipperstein, "The Politics of Relief: The Transformation of Russian Jewish Communal Life during the First World War," *Studies in Contemporary Jewry* 4 (1988): 24. Also see Semion Goldin, "Deportation of Jews by the Russian Military Command, 1914–1915," *Jews in Eastern Europe* 41, no. 1 (2000): 40–73. Simon Rabinovitch, "Alternative to Zion: The Jewish

Autonomist Movement in Late Imperial and Revolutionary Russia" (PhD diss., Brandeis University, 2007), 200–201. David G. Roskies, *Against the Apocalypse: Responses to Catastrophe in Modern Jewish Culture* (Cambridge, MA: Harvard University Press, 1984), 116.

3. Zipperstein, "Politics of Relief," 26; Rabinovitch, "Alternative to Zion," 203, 210–211.

4. This chapter contains a detailed discussion of Efroikin's disparaging attitude toward EKOPO for this reason. See Zipperstein, "Politics of Relief," 30–31, and Rabinovitch, "Alternative to Zion," 203–207.

5. Zipperstein, "Politics of Relief," 32.

6. Ibid., 27. Rabinovitch, "Alternative to Zion," 202–203, 212–213.

7. Vladimir Levin, "Ha-politikah ha-yehudit ba-impiriyah ha-rusit be-idan ha-re'aktsiyah, 1907–1914" (PhD diss., Hebrew University, 2007), 373–378; Rabinovitch, "Alternative to Zion," 221–222.

8. Jonathan Frankel, "An Introductory Essay: The Paradoxical Politics of Marginality; Thoughts on the Jewish Situation during the Years 1914–1921," *Studies in Contemporary Jewry* 4 (1988): 4.

9. Elias and Riva Tcherikower to family, August 7 [20], 1914; Riva Tcherikower to family, December 31, 1914; Elias and Riva Tcherikower to family, August 7 [20], 1914; Elias Tcherikower to family, July 20, 1915 Elias Tcherikower Archive RG 81, folder 1294, YIVO Archives.

10. Tcherikower to family, July 20, 1915 Elias Tcherikower Archive RG 81, file 1294, YIVO Archives. In this otherwise Russian letter, Tcherikower wrote this phrase "Yerusholayim deamerike" in Yiddish.

11. Tcherikower, "Ber borokhov vi ikh ken im," *Literarishe bleter* 52 (December 30, 1927): 1024.

12. As representative of the articles that Tcherikower wrote at this time, see the following articles in *Der idisher kongres:* "Di rusishe iden un der idisher kongres" (September 4, 1915): 3; "Der idisher rekht-kamf in 19tn yorhundert" (October 22, 1915): 5; "Idishe rekht un di frantsoyzishe revolutsiye" (October 29, 1915): 5; "Tsi vil dos rusishe identum natsionale rekht?" (December 10, 1915): 3. Regarding the struggle of American Jewish socialist nationalists on behalf of East European Jewry during World War I, see "Tsu ale idishe arbayter fun amerike: Deklaratsion fun natsional-sotsialistishen agitatsions komitet," *Der idisher kongres* (August 6, 1915): 1.

13. Jonathan Frankel, *Prophecy and Politics: Socialism, Nationalism and the Russian Jews, 1860–1917* (Cambridge: Cambridge University Press, 1981), 188–263, 453–551. Ber Borochov, "Forvort," in *In kampf far idishe rekht: A blik in der idisher rekhtlozinkeyt un in der geshikhte fun der idisher emantsipatsions bavegung,* ed. Ber Borochov (New York: Idish natsionaler arbeter farband fun amerike, 1916), 3–6. Borochov, "Birgerlikhe glaykhberekhtigung," ibid., 73–93.

14. Salo Baron, "Ghetto and Emancipation: Shall We Revise the Traditional View?" *Menorah Journal* 14, no. 6 (1928): 515–526.

15. See Joshua M. Karlip, "Between External Persecution and National Renaissance: Simon Dubnov's Lachrymose Vision of Russian-Jewish History," in *Jews in the East European Borderlands: Daily Life, Violence, Memory: Essays in Honor of John D. Klier,* ed. Eugene M. Avrutin and Harriet Murav (Brighton, MA: Academic Studies Press, 2012), 202–223.

16. Dubnov, "Di velt frage," *Dos yudishe vort (zamelbukh)* (January 1916): 8–9. The quotation is Lamentations 5:1.

17. Tcherikower, "Di geshikhte fun idisher emantsipatsiye in mayriv-eyrope," in Borochov, *In kampf,* 15.

18. Ibid., 17.

19. Tcherikower, "Der idisher rekht-kamf in 19tn yorhundert," *Der idisher kongres* (October 22, 1915): 5.

20. Simon Dubnov, *Pis'ma o starom i novom evreistvie (1897–1907)* (St. Petersburg: Obschestvennaia Pol'za, 1907), 74–112.

21. Tcherikower, "Di idishe rekhtlozikeyt in rusland," in Borochov, *In kampf,* 34.

22. Ibid., 42.

23. Ibid., 43–45.

24. Tcherikower, "Idishe proyekten vegen sibir," *Der idisher kongres* (November 12, 1915): 2–3.

25. Ibid.

26. Tcherikower, "Der shvartser yortsayt," *Der tog,* November 2, 1915, 4.

27. Tcherikower, "Tsvey yor milkhome un di idn," *Di tsukunft* 21, no. 8 (1916): 657.

28. Dubnov, *Pis'ma,* 281. For a discussion of this comparison, see Jonathan Frankel, "S. M. Dubnov: Historian and Ideologist," in Sophie Dubnov Ehrlich, *The Life and Work of S. M. Dubnov* (Bloomington: Indiana University Press, 1991), 19. For Dubnov's 1912 comparison of the year 1881 to years of Jewish cataclysms, see Dubnov, "Nokh draysik-yehrign krig," *Di idishe velt* 1 (1912): 8.

29. Tcherikower, "Tsvey yor milkhome un di idn," 657.

30. Tcherikower, "Der shvartser yortsayt," 7.

31. Tcherikower, "Khmelnitskis oyfshtand un der idisher khurbn," *Der tog,* April 23, 1916, 4; "Fun der finsterer fargangenheyt momentn fun di idishe khurbones in 17tn yorhundert," *Der tog,* May 13, 1916, 7; "Fun der fintserer fargangenheyt," *Der tog,* May 20, 1916, 8; Tcherikower, "Momenten fun der haydatshine," *Der tog,* June 4, 1916, 7.

32. Tcherikower, "Khmelnitskis oyfshtand"; Tcherikower, "Di zamel arbet," *Der idisher kongres* (September 27, 1915): 2. For the appeal by Peretz, Dinezon, and An-sky, see "Ruf tsu zamlen materialen vegen der velt krig," reprinted in *YIVO bleter* 36 (1952): 350–351. The original appeared in the Warsaw daily *Haynt* on January 1, 1915. For an English translation, see *The Literature of Destruction: Jewish Responses to Catastrophe,* ed. David G. Roskies (Philadelphia: Jewish Publication Society of America, 1989): 209–210.

33. Tcherikower, "Tsvey yor milkhome un di idn," 658.
34. Tcherikower, "Di kulturele bavegung tsvishen di idn in rusland," *Tsukunft*, no. 11 (November 1916): 952; Tcherikower, "Tsvey yor milkhome un di idn," 658. "In your blood shall you live" comes from Ezekiel 16:6. Tcherikower, "Ven der malakh hamoves hot keyn shlite nit" *Der idisher kempfer* (April 28, 1916): 8. Two Talmudic passages relate this story as occurring with two Amoraim, Talmudic sages, rather than Tannaim, Mishnaic sages, as Tcherikower stated. A better-known version of the story has it occurring between the Angel of Death and King David. The first two stories about Amoraim appear in the Babylonian Talmud Moded Katan 28a and Bava Metsia 86a. The story about King David occurs in BT Shabbat 30b. Also see Louis Ginzberg, *The Legends of the Jews*, vol. 4, *Bible Times and Characters from Joshua to Esther* (Philadelphia: Jewish Publication Society of America, 1954), 113–114, and vol. 6, *Notes to Volumes III and IV—From Moses in the Wilderness to Esther* (Philadelphia: Jewish Publication Society of America, 1959): footnotes 125 and 126. My thanks to Dr. Shneyer Z. Leiman for helping me to find these sources.
35. Tcherikower, "Ven der malakh hamoves."
36. Ibid. For a discussion of the affinities between Jewish cultural nationalism and traditional religious categories, see David E. Fishman, *The Rise of Modern Yiddish Culture* (Pittsburgh: University of Pittsburgh Press, 2005), 113.
37. Tcherikower, "Di kulturele bavegung," 952.
38. Ibid., 952–956.
39. Nahman Syrkin, "Undzer shprakhn frage," *Der tog*, May 27, 1916, 4.
40. Syrkin, "Yidish oder hebrayish," *Der tog*, June 3, 1916, 4.
41. Tcherikower, "Der kampf lustiker hebrayizm," *Der tog*, June 19, 1916, 4.
42. Ibid.
43. Tcherikower, "Ver hot vemen geroydeft? Tsu der frage vegen hebeyish un idish," *Der tog*, June 24, 1916, 6.
44. Ibid.; Tcherikower, "In der velt fun teater: Di neveyle," *Der idisher kempfer* (March 9, 1917): 5.
45. Tcherikower, "Oyfn shvel fun besmedresh," *Der tog*, October 13, 1916, 4.
46. Haim Nahman Bialik, "Al saf bet ha-midrash," *Kol kitve Ḥ.N. Bialik* (Tel Aviv: Dvir, 1956). This poem was written in 1895. For a discussion of the term *hurban bet ha-midrash* see David G. Roskies, *Against the Apocalypse: Responses to Catastrophe in Modern Jewish Culture* (Cambridge, MA: Harvard University Press, 1984).
47. Tcherikower, "Oyfn shvel."
48. Jonathan Frankel, "The Jewish Socialists and the American Jewish Congress Movement," *YIVO Annual of Jewish Social Science*, vol. 16, *Essays on the American Jewish Labor Movement*, ed. Ezra Mendelsohn (1976): 202–341; "Tsu ale idishe arbayter," 1.
49. "Tsu ale idishe arbayter," 1.
50. Nahman Syrkin, "Folks eynheyt," *Der idisher kongres* (August 6, 1915): 5; Chaim Zhitlovsky, "Di idishe arbayter un der idisher kongres," *Der idisher*

kongres (August 6, 1915): 5–6. In early 1917, *Der idisher kempfer* ran an editorial welcoming Zhitlovsky to the party. The editorial stated that it had taken Zhitlovsky a while to accept the party's Zionist platform but that the war had finally convinced him of its truth. Even though Zhitlovsky still differed with some of the party's official positions, the editorial still greeted his arrival with excitement. See "Undzer nayer khaver—Dr. kh. zhitlovski," *Der idisher kempfer* (March 30, 1917): 4.

51. Tcherikower, "Di grenitsen fun undzer sholem bayis," *Der idisher kongres* (October 15, 1915): 6.

52. Ibid., 6.

53. Frankel, "Jewish Socialists," 235.

54. Tcherikower, "Der alter un der nayer internatsional," *Der tog*, November 23, 1915, 2.

55. Tcherikower, "Der internatsional in 1916," *Der idisher kempfer* (December 29, 1916): 5–6; Der internatsional in 1916 II," ibid. (January 12, 1917): 5–6.

56. Tcherikower, "Der ruf tsu friden," *Der idisher kempfer* (February 2, 1917): 1.

57. Tcherikower, "Dos folk vos lebt eynzam," *Der tog,* September 30, 1916, 6. "'Om le-vodod yishkon" (A people that dwells alone) is a quotation from Numbers 23:9. It is part of Balaam's unwitting blessing of the Israelites.

58. Tcherikower, "Di fareynigung fun unterdrikte natsionen," *Der idisher kongres* (November 19, 1915): 8; "Der tsuzamenfor fun unterdrikte felker," *Der idisher kempfer* (September 1, 1916): 5; "Di tragediye fun di unterdrikte felker," *Der tog,* May 13, 1916, 6. Tcherikower, "Leon Bakst (A kharakteristik funem barimten idishen kinstler)," *Der tog,* April 15, 1916, 16.

59. Kalmanovitch to Niger, August 1, 1914. Shmuel Niger Collection RG 360, Folder 34 YIVO Archives New York. The rabbis of the Talmud preached the acceptance of suffering with love (*kabalat yisurin be-ahavah*). This quotation from the Talmud comes from the Babylonian Talmud, Yevamot 121a.

60. A. Y. Goldshmidt, "Di yidishe prese in vilne," in *Pinkes far der geshikhte fun vilne in di yorn fun milkhome un okupatsiye,* ed. Zalman Rejzen, Dr. Avrom Virshubski, Shmuel-Leyb Tsitron, Dr. Tsemakh Shabad (Vilna: B. Tsiyoynson un komp., 1922), 579; *Di vokh,* no. 1 (January 15, 1915): 32. His name also was listed as editor in every issue after this one. See *Di vokh,* front page; For the issue dedicated to the commemoration of Peretz, see *Di vokh,* no. 12 (April 2, 1915).

61. On relief organizations, see Baal Dimyen [Nokhem Shtif], "A trit faroys," *Di vokh,* no. 1 (January 15, 1915): 1–4; Baal Dimyen, "Yesoymim," *Di vokh,* no. 4 (January 29, 1915): 1–4; Nokhem Shtif, "Di goylim," *Di vokh,* no. 4 (January 29, 1915): 3–4; N. S. [Nokhem Shtif], "Krig un kultur," *Di vokh,* no. 4 (January 29, 1915): 11–16; N.S., "Kinderheymen un psukim," *Di vokh,* no. 13 (April 16, 1915). For Niger's series of articles in *Di vokh,* see Shmuel Niger, "Di milkhome un mir yuden," no. 3 (January 22, 1915): 5–9; no. 4 (January 29, 1915): 5–10; no. 5 (February 5, 1915): 11–13; no. 6 (February 12, 1915):

5–9; no. 7 (February 19, 1915): 6–9; no. 8 (February 26, 1915): 6. For a brief discussion of these articles, see Goldshmidt, "Di yidishe prese," 580–581.

62. K-n [Kalmanovitch]., "Mobilizatsiye fun der industriye," *Di vokh,* no. 23 (June 25, 1915): 12–15; Z. [Kalmanovitch], "Di neytralitet fun itlayen," *Di vokh,* nos. 9–10 (March 8, 1915): 15–20; K. [Kalmanovitch], "Tsum aroys-trit fun italalyen," *Di vokh,* nos. 17–18 (May 21, 1915): 21–24.; "K.M.," [Kalmanovitch] "Daytshland un amerike," *Di vokh,* no. 21 (June 11, 1915): 18–21; K., "Di virkung fun der milkhome oyf der folksvirtshaft in england un daytshland," *Di vokh,* no. 23 (June 25, 1915): 15–16; Z., "Di balkon lender," *Di vokh,* no. 11 (March 15, 1915): 16–19.

63. Kalmanovitch to Niger, July 14, 1915. Shmuel Niger Collection RG 360, folder 34, YIVO Archives.

64. Kalmanovitch to Yankev Dinezon, March 26, 1915, Shmuel Niger Collection RG 360, Folder 34, YIVO Archives.

65. Niger, "Y. l. perets," *Di vokh,* no. 12 (April 2, 1915): 5–6.

66. Khayim Gilden and P. Kats, "Peretses levaye," *Di vokh,* no. 12 (April 2, 1915): 17–24; "Der troyer nokh perets'n in vilne," ibid., 24–26; "A perets-ovent in peterburg (fun undzer korespondent)," *Di vokh,* no. 14 (April 16, 1915): 25–28; "Tsum perets-troyer," *Di vokh,* no. 16 (April 29, 1915): 28.

67. K-N. [Kalmanovitch], "Fun perets's leben," *Di vokh,* no. 12 (April 2, 1915): 11, 15–16.

68. Peretz, "Oyf der tshernovitser shprakh-konferents," in *Briv un redes fun y. l. perets,* ed. Nakhmen Mayzel (New York, Ikfun, 1944), 369–374. Also see Emanuel Goldsmith, *Modern Yiddish Culture: The Story of the Yiddish Language Movement* (New York: Fordham University Press, 1997), 196–199; K-N., "Fun peretses leben," 16–17.

69. Yudel Mark, "Di ershte yorn fun yivo (a kapitl zikhroynes)," *Di tsukunft* 81, no. 4 (April 1975): 131–132; Z"K [Kalmanovitch], "Di hilfs-arbayt far di korbones fun der milkhome," *Dos yudishe vort (zamelbukh)* (January 1916), 25–30.

70. Levin, Ha-politikah ha-yehudit," 125; Theodore Norman, *An Outstretched Arm: A History of the Jewish Colonization Association* (London: Routledge and Kegan Paul, 1985), 46–47. This book was written as an institutional history of the EKA. An academic study of this institution and its role in Russian Jewish society remains a desideratum. Also see Christolph Gassenschmidt, *Jewish Liberal Politics in Tsarist Russia, 1900–1914* (New York: NYU Press, 1995), 122.

71. L. Zak, "Ver iz a kooperator?" *Di yudishe kooperatsiye,* nos. 1–2 (January–February 1914): 9–12.

72. "Undzere tsiln," *Di yudishe kooperatsiye,* nos. 1–2 (January–February 1914): 4.

73. Efroikin, "Di milkhome un di yudishe kooperatsiye," *Di vokh,* no. 4 (January 29, 1915): 28–32.

74. Efroikin, "Shtendige kreditn oder rates-tsolungen?" *Di yudishe kooperatsiye* (December 1914): 7–10.

75. Efroikin, "Di milkhome un di yudishe kooperatsiye," 28–32.
76. Y. Efren, "Kooperatsiye un tsedoke," *Di vokh,* no. 8 (February 26, 1915): 1–6.
77. Y. E. [Yisroel Efroikin], "Kredit hilf," *Di vokh,* no. 20 (June 4, 1915): 5–8; Y. Efroikin, "Di halvoes operatsiye in der milkhome-tsayt," *Di yudishe kooperatsiye,* no. 7 (July 1915): 24–27.
78. Y. E., "Di milkhome hizkes un di yudishe bafelkerung," *Di vokh,* no. 7 (February 19, 1915): 1–6.
79. Y. Efren, "Der petrograder hilfs-komitet un di yudishe gezelshaft," *Tsum moment* (1916): 6.
80. Ibid., 12.
81. A. Litovski [Efroikin], "Vitebsker briv," *Di folksshtime,* no. 14 (1907): 43–44.
82. Efren, "Tsayt fragen: In dem gebentshtn land poyln," *Di yudishe velt* (January 1915): 355–357, 360–363; Y. Efren, "Arbayt un organizatsiye: Tsu di vahlen in di shtotishe zelbstfarvaltung in poylen," *Di vokh,* nos. 17–18 (May 15, 1915): 3–6. In the first article, he expressed his hope in the transformation of Poland into a state for all its nationalities. In the second of these articles, Efroikin urged Jewish democratic forces in Poland to organize for the elections to the city councils.
83. Efren, "A vikhtige oyfgabe," *Di vokh,* no. 1 (January 8, 1915): 1–7.
84. A. Litovski, "In tavrishn palats," *Di vokh,* no. 5 (February 5, 1915): 4–11.
85. Y. Efren, "Der progresiver blok un di yudishe politik," *Dos yudishe vort (zamelbukh)* (1916): 10–14.
86. "Executive Committee," Central State Archives of St. Petersburg, Fond 2049, M. I. Sheftel Papers, o. 1, d. 192. As quoted and translated in Rabinovitch, "Alternative to Zion," 223–224.
87. Rabinovitch, "Alternative to Zion," 224.
88. Jeffrey Veidlinger, *Jewish Public Culture in the Late Russian Empire* (Bloomington: Indiana University Press, 2009), 1–23. For an analysis of how young Russian Jewish revolutionaries transmuted their religious messianism into a secular revolutionary messianism, see Frankel, *Prophecy and Politics,* 2.
89. Veidlinger, *Jewish Public Culture,* 283–291.
90. Frankel, "Paradoxical Politics of Marginality," 4.

3. Losing Russia as a Base

1. Zvi Gitelman, *A Century of Ambivalence: The Jews of Russia and the Soviet Union, 1881 to the Present,* expanded 2nd ed. (Bloomington: Indiana University Press, 2001), 60–63.
2. Richard Pipes, *The Russian Revolution* (New York: Alfred A. Knopf, 1990): 537–555; Gitelman, *Century of Ambivalence,* 60; Henry Abramson, *A Prayer for the Government: Ukrainians and Jews in Revolutionary Times, 1917–1920* (Cambridge, MA: Harvard University Press, 1999), 33–66.
3. Gitelman, *Century of Ambivalence,* 64–70.

4. Ibid., 71; Ezra Mendelsohn, *The Jews of East Central Europe between Two World Wars* (Bloomington: Indiana University Press, 1983): 11–85, 171–213, 213–241, 241–255. These pages include the chapters on interwar Poland, Romania, Lithuania, Latvia, and Estonia.

5. Kenneth B. Moss, *Jewish Renaissance in the Russian Revolution* (Cambridge, MA: Harvard University Press, 2009), 253–279, and Gitelman, *Century of Ambivalence*, 73.

6. Tcherikower, "Baym 'soyne' oyf der khasene," *Der tog,* March 20, 1917, 4.

7. Simon Dubnov, *Chego khotiat evrei* (Petrograd: Akt. S. Ovo "Muravei," 1917), 5–10.

8. Tcherikower, "Di dinastiye romanov un di idn," *Di tsukunft* (March 1917): 201, 204.

9. Tcherikower, "Di natsionale oytonomiye far di rusishe idn (di inerlikhe problemen funem rusish-idishn leben," *Der tog,* June 5, 1917, 4; Simon Rabinovitch, "Alternative to Zion: The Jewish Autonomist Movement in Late Imperial and Revolutionary Russia" (PhD diss., Brandeis University, 2007), 252.

10. Tcherikower, "Di tsukunft fun di bafrayte idn," *Der tog,* April 10, 1917, 4.

11. Ibid.; "Di groyse revolutsion un der nayer idisher yishuv," *Di tsukunft* (May 1917): 329–332.

12. Elias Tcherikower, "Idishe proyekten vegen sibir," *Der idisher kongres* (November 12, 1915): 2–3.; Tcherikower, "Di tsukunft," 4; Tcherikower, "Di groyse revolutsion," 329–332. Tcherikower, Tcherikower, "Tsvey yor milkhome un di idn," *Di tsukunft* 21, no. 8 (1916): 657; Tcherikower, Tcherikower, "Der shvartser yortsayt," *Der tog,* November 2, 1915, 4.

13. Rabinovitch, "Alternative to Zion," 238; Zalman Rejzen, "Efroykin, Yisroel," *Leksikon fun der yidisher literatur, prese, un filologiye,* vol. 2 (Vilna, Kletskin Press, 1927): 811–812.

14. Rabinovitch, "Alternative to Zion," 243–244; flyer for the Russian Jewish Congress: "No. 4 Idishe folkspartey: Iden!" Revolutionary Russia RG 30, folder 221, YIVO Archives New York.

15. Flyer, "No. 7 Idishe folkspartey. Di idishe folksmasen un di valen tsu der grindungs-farzamlung," Revolutionary Russia RG 30, folder 221, YIVO Archives New York; and general flyer "Z.G.H.," Revolutionary Russia RG 30, folder 223 YIVO Archives New York; flyer "Tsu der grindungs-farzamlung," Revolutionary Russia RG 30, folder 221, YIVO Archives New York.

16. Flyer, "Idishe folkspartey: Tsu di valen in der petrograder kehile," Revolutionary Russia RG 30, folder 221, YIVO Archives New York.

17. Simon Dubnov, *Pis'ma o starom i novom evreistvie (1897–1907* (St. Petersburg: Obshchestvennaia Pol'za, 1907), 83–92, 313–315. In Yiddish, see Dubnov, *Briv vegn altn un nayem yidntum* (Mexico City: Shloyme Mendelson fond, bay der gezelshaft far kultur un hilf, 1959), 103–114, 340–341.

18. Dubnov, *Pis'ma,* 83–92, 313–315; flyer "In der petrograder kehile," and flyer for the Russian Jewish Congress; general flyer "Z.G.H." For a discussion of the evolution of the conception of the revitalized, secularized *kehile*

by Dubnov and prominent SERP and Bundist intellectuals, see David E. Fishman, The *Rise of Modern Yiddish Culture* (Pittsburgh: University of Pittsburgh Press, 2005), 62–79.

19. Jonathan Frankel, *Prophecy and Politics: Socialism, Nationalism and the Russian Jews, 1860–1917* (Cambridge: Cambridge University Press, 1981), 171–257; Rabinovitch, "Alternative to Zion," 254–266.

20. Tcherikower, "Borukh she-petorani," *Der tog,* May 23, 1917, 4.

21. Ibid.; Tcherikower, "Oyfn tsuzamenfor fun 'bund' (ayndruken)," *Undzer togblat,* December 21, 1917, 2. In this passage, Tcherikower used rabbinic language to satirize Bundist orthodoxy. In his words, A. Litvak's view that autonomy pertained to more than cultural matters broke "the *din* [Jewish law] of the Bundist *Shulḥan Arukh* [Code of Jewish Law]."

22. Pipes, *Russian Revolution,* 385–438; Tcherikower, "Kerenski," *Der tog,* June 1, 1917, 4.

23. Tcherikower, "Vegen a separaten friden," *Der tog,* April 16, 1917, 4; Tcherikower, "An entfer oyf an entfer," *Der tog,* May 24, 1917, 5.

24. Rex A. Wade, *The Russian Revolution, 1917* (Cambridge: Cambridge University Press, 2000), 213–215, and Orlando Figes, *A People's Tragedy: The Russian Revolution, 1891–1924* (London: Penguin Books, 1996), 464–469.

25. "Yidishe redes oyf der demokratisher baratung: Y. Efroykin (yidishe folks-spartey)," *Di yidishe folksblat* 1 (October 3, 1917), 29–30; Efroikin, "Der krisis (Tsu der demokratisher baratung)," *Di yidishe folksblat* 1 (October 3, 1917), 4–5.

26. "Rech' predstavitslia 'Evreiskoi Narodicheskoi Partii' I. R. Efroikina na Demokraticheskom Soveschanii," *Evreiskaia nedelia* , nos. 38–39 (September 29 1917): 5–6. Here I use Rabinovitch's translation of this passage. Rabinovitch, "Alternative to Zion," 246–247.

27. Efroikin, "Der krisis," 6; "Yidishe redes," 31.

28. Rabinovitch, "Alternative to Zion," 272–275, 296–297; "Der onheyb fun der val kompaniye in volin (A briv fun zhitomir)," *Di yidishe folksblat* 5 (November 3, 1917): 19–21.

29. Efroikin, "Yidishe redes," 30.

30. Ibid., 31.

31. Tcherikower, "Di natsionale oytonomiye far di rusishe idn (di inerlikhe problemen funem rusish-idishn leben)," *Der tog,* June 5, 1917, 4, 10; Rabinovitch, "Alternative to Zion," 236–237.

32. Tcherikower, "Di daytshe sotsial-demokratiye un der bolshevizm," *Undzer togblat,* March 5, 1918, 2; Tcherikower, "Di daytshe sotsial-demokratiye un der bolshevizm III," *Undzer togblat,* March 11, 1918, 2.

33. Pipes, *Russian Revolution,* 635–646.

34. Tcherikower, "Di levaye fun di linke sren," *Undzer togblat,* July 16, 1918, 3.

35. Tcherikower, "Tsi velen di bolshevikes aynhaltn di makht," *Undzer togblat,* March 17, 1918, 2.

36. Tcherikower, "Der dekadans fun der rusisher gezelshaft," *Undzer togblat,* April 9, 1918, 2–3.

37. Efroikin and Nokhem Shtif, "Di vokh: Di 'tsveyte revolutsiye,' " *Di yidishe folksblat* 5 (Petrograd, November 3, 1917): 3–7; Efroikin, "Di letste treyst," *Di yidishe folksblat* 6 (Petrograd, November 14, 1917): 6–8.

38. Efroikin, "Di internatsionale yidishe frage I: Der nayer goles un di yidishe ume," *Di yidishe folksblat* 8 (December 1, 1917): 8–9.

39. Ibid., 9–10. Whereas Efroikin's predictions concerning the political and economic fate of the Jews in the nationalizing successor states of Eastern Europe proved correct, he was wrong regarding the future of Jewish national culture in these countries. The lack of a high culture in independent Lithuania and the Polish *kresy* to which the Jews were attracted actually proved a stimulus to the thriving of Yiddish and Hebrew cultures.

40. Efroikin, "Di internatsionale yidishe frage: Der yidisher velt-farband," *Di yidishe folksblat* 10 (December 20, 1917), 7–8.

41. Ibid., 9.

42. Ibid.

43. Jonathan Frankel, "An Introductory Essay: The Paradoxical Politics of Marginality; Thoughts on the Jewish Situation during the Years 1914–1921," *Studies in Contemporary Jewry* 4 (1988): 4. Horace Kallen, *The Structure of Lasting Peace* (Boston: Marshall Jones Co., 1918), 34. See Noam Pianko's discussion of this quotation, as well as the phenomenon that he labeled the "counterstatist" school of Zionist thought that emerged in the aftermath of World War I, in Noam Pianko, *Zionism and the Roads Not Taken* (Bloomington: Indiana University Press, 2010), 26–59.

44. Pianko, *Zionism,* 59. Zimmern and Kallen credited Aḥad Ha-'Am for their autonomist vision, though in reality it shared more with Dubnov. See Pianko, *Zionism,* 45–48.

45. Gitelman, *Century of Ambivalence,* 60–63.

46. Dubnov, "Der nayer mabul II: Meshiakhs tsaytn," *Di yidishe folksblat* 1–2 (January 20, 1918): 10–13. David Shumsky, "Brith Shalom's Uniqueness Reconsidered: Hans Kohn and Autonomist Zionism," *Jewish History* 25 (2011): 339–353. The collapse of Jewish national autonomy and the rise of chauvinistic anti-Semitism in Eastern Europe joined with Arab rejection of the Jewish presence in Palestine to relegate this vision of autonomy for both Jews and Arabs to the periphery of Zionism. It is interesting that Dubnov, unlike Zimmern and Kallen, envisioned the granting of national autonomy to the Arabs in Palestine. Linking their vision of international Jewish solidarity with British imperialism, Zimmern and Kallen viewed the relationship of Jews to Arabs in Palestine from a condescending, imperial perspective that Dubnov did not share. See Pianko, *Zionism,* 52–55.

47. Efroikin, " 'Asḥalto de-geulo,' " *Di yidishe folksblat* 7 (November 21, 1917): 4–8; Sh. Rozenfeld, "Vos vilen yidn (azoy gut vi an ofener brif dem h. efroykin)," *Di yidishe folksblat* 1–2 (January 20, 1918): 13–15; Efroikin, "Goles, tsionizm un erets yisroel (A tshuve h. sh. rozenfeld un andere oponenten)," *Di yidishe folksblat* 1–2 (January 20, 1918): 15.

48. Efroikin, "Goles, tsionizm un erets yisroel," 16.

49. Pianko, *Zionism*, 26–59.

50. Z"K [Kalmanovitch], "Yidishe oyszikhten in erets-yisroel," *Di yidishe folks-blat* 7 (November 21, 1917), 12–15.

51. Moss, *Jewish Renaissance*, 32–33; Yudl Mark, "Di ershte yorn fun yivo (a kapitl zikhroynes)," *Di tsukunft* 81, no. 4 (April 1975): 131–132.

52. Mark, "Zelig Kalmanovitsh (Zikhroynes)," *Goldene keyt* (Tel Aviv, 1977): 128.

53. Kof [Kalmanovitch], "Vu zaynen di tuer," *Du yidishe folksblat* 7 (November 21, 1917): 8–11.

54. Moss, *Jewish Renaissance*, 32–38, 79–81.

55. For the definitive biography of An-sky that speaks about his expedition at length, see Gabriella Safran, *Wandering Soul: The Dybbuk's Creator, S. An-sky* (Cambridge, MA: Harvard University Press, 2011). An-sky's ethnographic questionnaire was recently translated into English for the first time. See Nathaniel Deutsch, *The Jewish Dark Continent: Life and Death in the Russian Pale of Settlement* (Cambridge, MA: Harvard University Press, 2011). Also see the collection of essays, *The Worlds of S. An-sky, A Russian Jewish Intellectual at the Turn of the Century*, ed. Gabriella Safran and Steven J. Zipperstein (Stanford, CA: Stanford University Press, 2006). Another very perceptive analysis of An-sky's ethnographic expedition is Mark Kiel, "A Twice Lost Legacy: Ideology, Culture, and the Pursuit of Jewish Folklore in Russia until Stalinization (1930–1931)" (PhD diss., Jewish Theological Seminary of America, 1991), 401–24. Moss, *Jewish Renaissance*, 73–74.

56. Y. L. Peretz, "Vos felt undzer literatur," in *Ale verk fun y. l. perets*, vol. 7 (New York: "CYCO" Bicher Farlag, 1947), 270–279; Peretz, "Far di tsurikgekumene a drite eytse," *Ale verk*, vol. 9 (New York: "CYCO" Bicher Farlag, 1947), 129. Also see Kiel, "Twice Lost Legacy," 421. Peretz, "Der lebens protses," *Ale verk*, vol. 6 (New York: "CYCO" Bicher Farlag, 1947), 389–399. In the last essay, Peretz argued that even as secular Yiddish culture would combat the conservatism of the traditionalists, it would thank them for their embodiment of Jewish values. Comparing Jewish civilization to a tree, Peretz explained that whereas modern Yiddish culture represented the leaves, Orthodoxy represented the trunk. If the trunk were to be cut down, the leaves would wither. See esp. pp. 395–396 of the essay.

57. Kiel, "Twice Lost Legacy," 183–213.

58. Ibid., 183–230; David N. Myers, *Re-inventing the Jewish Past: European Jewish Intellectuals and the Zionist Return to History* (New York: Oxford University Press, 1995): 133–134; Moss, *Jewish Renaissance*, 173–180.

59. Moss, *Jewish Renaissance*, 282–283.

60. Ibid., 74, 282–283.

61. K-N [Kalmanovitch], "A bukh vegen tanakh in yidish," *Di yidishe folksblat* 4 (October 25, 1917): 22–24. For the attempt by some during the revolutionary era to root modern Yiddish culture in a secular-nationalist under-

standing of the Bible, see Kenneth Moss, "'A Time to Tear Down, a Time to Build Up': Recasting Jewish Culture in Eastern Europe, 1917–1921" (PhD diss., Stanford University, 2003), 122–125. For a discussion of Kalmanovitch's interest during this time in all periods of Jewish history, see Mark, "Zelig Kalmanovitsh," 128–129. Yet Mark recalled that Kalmanovitch differed with Dubnov in the latter's view of Jewish history as a direct continuity from biblical Israelites to medieval martyrs to modern secular Jews. Kalmanovitch envisioned Jewish history more as an interrupted chain of reformulated values and lifestyles. His vision thus remained poised between that of Dubnov and Zhitlovsky.

62. "Te 'udat He-'avar," *He-'avar: Riv 'on le-divre yeme ha-yehudim ve-yahadut* 1 (November, December 1917) (ḥeshvan-Tevet, TRAKH). For a definition and discussion of the term "usable past," see David G. Roskies, *The Jewish Search for a Usable Past (The Helen and Martin Schwartz Lectures in Jewish Studies)* (Bloomington: Indiana University Press, 1999), esp. 1–16.

63. For a discussion of *Reshumot* see Kiel, "Twice Lost Legacy," 17–81, and Kiel, "Ideologies of Jewish Folklore: 'Reshumot'—the Russian Years," in *Text and Context: Studies in Modern Jewish History and Historiography in Honor of Ismar Schorsch* (New York: Jewish Theological Seminary, 2005), 256–282. For a discussion of the Russian Zionist turn to autonomist concerns during the revolution, see Rabinovich, "Alternative to Zion," 256–257.

64. Tcherikower, "Me-yerushat mishpaḥah patriarkhalit," *He-'avar* 3 (December 1918): 117.

65. Ibid., 128–129.

66. Peretz, "Fir doyres fir tsavoes," in *Di verk fun yitskok leybush perets,* ed. Dovid Pinski (New York: Farlag "Idish," 1920), 4:235–241; Tcherikower, "Me-yerushat," 118, 130.

67. Tcherikower, "Me-yerushat," 130.

68. Ibid., 117. For Peretz's assertion that modern national Jews had to rescue the values of traditional Judaism for their culture, see Peretz, "Vos felt."

69. Moss, *Jewish Renaissance,* 36–37; Moss, "'Time to Tear Down,'" 86–89.

70. Moss, *Jewish Renaissance,* 53–54, 93, 169–171.

71. Ibid. 53, and 316n88. The quote comes from Moyshe Katz, "Di kultur-lige in ukrayne," *Di tsukunft* 3 (March 1921): 183; "Takones fun der Kultur-Lige," TsDAVO (Central State Archives of the Higher Organs of State Government Administration of Ukraine), RG 3304, finding aid 1, folder 2, doc. 1 Kiev.

72. Moss, *Jewish Renaissance,* 90–95. Also see Ben-Zion Dinur, "Ba-merkaz ha-kiuvi (Reshimot ve-zikhronot me-shnot 1918–1920)," *He-'avar* 7 (1960): 15–17.

73. Moss, *Jewish Renaissance,* 54–56, 87.

74. Throughout his career, Dinaburg (later known as Dinur) returned to "chrestomathies" often. Interested both in serious historical scholarship and in the popularization of a Zionist historical consciousness, Dinaburg believed that "chrestomathies," historical *kinusim,* served as an appropriate medium to

accomplish these two tasks. Although presented as objective compilations of primary sources, these chrestomathies helped to build Dinaburg's larger meta-historical narrative based upon the themes of Jewish national activity in the Diaspora and the centrality of the land of Israel throughout all periods of Jewish history. For a discussion of the importance of this genre in Dinaburg's work, see Myers, *Re-inventing the Jewish Past,* 129–150. Tcherikower, "Retsenziye fun B. Dinaburg, *Yidishe geshikhte (historishe khrestomatye)—kveln un dokumentn . . . fun onheyb funem folk yisroel biz di hayntike tsaytn,"* *Bikhervelt* (August 1919): 83–87.

75. Tcherikower, "Retsenziye fun B. Dinaburg, Program far yidisher geshikhte, far shuln, lerer un zelbstbildung," *Shul un lebn* (March–April 1919): 87, 83. Dinaburg's authorship in Yiddish of a Jewish history program that concentrated on the land of Israel bespeaks a central tension that punctuated his whole career. A conscious proponent of "Palestinocentrism" who sought to prove the centrality of the land of Israel to all epochs of Jewish history, Dinaburg nonetheless spent much of his scholarly energy researching the Diaspora experience. Although he believed that the Jewish future would occur only in Palestine and then the State of Israel, he nonetheless reacted positively to Diaspora Jewish culture and to Yiddish. See Myers, *Re-inventing the Jewish Past,* 129–150. Also see Dinur, ed., *Yisra'el ba-golah,* 10 vols. (Tel Aviv: Devir, 1958–1972/73).

76. Pipes, *Russian Revolution,* 537–555; "Tsu undzere fraynd lezer," *Di yidishe folksblat* 8 (December 1, 1917), back page. On Yiddish culture in Russia in the months immediately following the October Revolution, see Moss, *Jewish Renaissance,* 223–224. On Efroikin's involvement with the Folks-Farlag, see Dinur, "Ba-merkaz ha-kiuvi," 26–27. In the end, the Folks-Farlag dropped this project, which was not realized until the interwar years.

77. A. Strashun to Niger (postscript, Shimen), December 29, 1917, RG 360, Shmuel Niger Collection, Folder 34, YIVO Archives.

78. Moss, *Jewish Renaissance,* 94, 317n101.

79. Dinur, "Ba-merkaz ha-kiuvi," 16–17.

80. Kalmanovitch to Niger, November 13, 1918, Shmuel Niger Collection RG 360, folder 34, YIVO Archives New York.

81. Kalmanovitch to Vayter, September 3, 1918, Shmuel Niger Collection RG 360, folder 34, YIVO Archives.

82. Ibid.

83. Kalmanovitch to Vayter, September 6, 1918, Shmuel Niger Collection RG 360, folder 34, YIVO Archives.

84. Moss, *Jewish Renaissance,* 90–92, 94, 317n101; Dinur, "Ba-merkaz ha-kiuvi," 16–17; Kalmanovitch to Niger, November 13, 1918; Kalmanovitch to Vayter, September 3, 1918; Kalmanovitch to Vayter, September 6, 1918. Shmuel Niger Collection RG 360, folder 34 YIVO Archives.

85. Kalmanovitch to Niger, November 13, 1918; September 3, 1918. Shmuel Niger Collection RG 360, folder 34 YIVO Archives.

86. Dinur, "Ba-merkaz ha-kiuvi," 26.

87. Kalmanovitch to Niger, November 13, 1918, and Kalmanovitch to Vayter, September 3, 1918. Shmuel Niger Collection RG 360, folder 34 YIVO Archieves. Dinur, "Ba-merkaz ha-kiuvi," 26. Here, Dinur discussed these translation projects. For Kalmanovitch's translation of Dubnov's history see Simon Dubnov, *Algameyne idishe geshikhte fun di elste tsaytn biz dem talmudishn un mitlalterikhn periyod* (Vilna: Kletskin Press, 1920). For Kalmanovitch's description of his dictionary project, see Kalmanovitch to Niger, May 25, 1920. Shmuel Niger Collection, RG 360, folder 34 YIVO Archives.

88. Jonathan Frankel, "The Dilemmas of Jewish Autonomism: The Case of Ukraine, 1917–1920," in *Ukrainian-Jewish Relations in Historical Perspective,* ed. Peter J. Potichnyj and Howard Astor (Edmonton: Canadian Institute of Ukrainian Studies, University of Alberta, 1988), 267–270.

89. Abramson, *Prayer for the Government,* 143; Frankel, "Dilemmas," 274.

90. Flyer "'Idishe folks-partey.' Zhitomir guberniye-komitet: Tsu der ukraynisher grindungs-farzamlung," Revolutionary Russia RG 30, folder 223, YIVO Archives New York. The other candidates running on this ticket were Pinkhes Dubinski and Nakhmen Rasaski. For information about the Ukrainian Jewish Constituent Assembly, see Abramson, *Prayer for the Government,* 98. For Efroikin's previous opposition to Ukrainian independence, see "Yidishe redes," 30.

91. Moss, "'Time to Tear Down,'" 372–373.

92. Quoted by Zosa Szajkowski, "Di geshikhte fun dem itstiken bukh," in Tcherikower, *Di ukrainer pogromen in yor 1919* (New York: YIVO, 1965), 339. Unfortunately, Szajkowski quoted from this letter without citing where it can be found in the Tcherkower archive.

93. Szajkowski, "Di geshikhte," 335–336, 338; Tcherikower, *Tog-bukh fun redaktsiye oyf oysforshen di pogrom materialn* (July 19, 1919), 10. Elias Tcherikower Collections RG 80, folder 664 YIVO Archives.

94. Szajkowski, "Di geshikhte," 333–339. In an article for the Warsaw Yiddish daily *Moment* about the archive and its perilous journey, the Yiddish writer H. D. Nomberg wrote: "All hands were stretched forth to take the material. Each 'regime' that entered Kiev wanted to obtain it. . . . Some—so that the larger world not know about their deeds—sought the material in order to destroy it; others, in contrast [wanted the material] in order to blacken the faces of their enemies." Quoted by Szajkowski, "Di geshikhte," 339n16.

95. Moss, *Jewish Renaissance,* 272–277; Kalmanovitch to Niger, September 9, 1921, Shmuel Niger Papers RG 360, folder 34 YIVO Archives.

96. Quoted by Szajkowski, "Di geshikhte," 339.

97. Tcherikower, *Antisemitizm un pogromen in ukraine in di yorn 1917–1918 (tsu der geshikhte fun ukrainish-yidishe batsihungen)* (Berlin: Yidisher literarisher farlag, 1923). Only in 1965 did the second volume in this series appear, written by Tcherikower and titled, *Di ukrainer pogromen in yor 1919* (New York: YIVO, 1965). (The pogroms in the year 1919). Apparently, Tcherikower had written this manuscript throughout the 1920s and 1930s. See Szajkowski, "Di geshikhte," 344–348.

98. M. Grosman, Y. Grinfeld, Elias Tcherikower, Wolf Latski, Joseph Schecht-
    man, "Araynfiv," *Di idishe avtonomiye un der natsionaler secretariat in
    ukraine: Materialn un dokumentn* (Kiev: Idisher folks-farlag, 1920): v–vii.

99. Tcherikower, ed. *In der tkufe fun revolutsiye (Memyarn, materialn, doku-
    mentn) Zamelbikher* (Berlin: Yidisher literarisher farlag, 1924). Tcherikower
    divided this book into two sections. The first consisted of memoirs and dia-
    ries of the years of the revolution and civil war by such prominent figures as
    Dubnov, Z. Revutski, A. Mukdoyni, and Alexander Khomski. The second
    section, titled "Materials and Documents," consisted of historical essays on
    such topics as Jewish Communists and Jewish society in 1919 Ukraine (writ-
    ten by Tcherikower), essays by Tcherikower and others on the persecution of
    Hebrew, Zionism, and Jewish religion, a historical essay by Tcherikower on
    the Red Army's complicity in pogroms, as well as specific historical documents.
    Tcherikower himself wrote three essays, one on the Jewish Communists in the
    Ukraine, one on Communist advocates of Hebrew in Turkistan, and one on
    the Soviet regime and pogroms. An advertisement at the book's end promised
    a second volume in this series. Among other historical essays promised was a
    work by Tcherikower to be titled "Di kiever grupe shrayber un kinstler un ir
    farzukh aroystsuraysn zikh fun ukraine 1920 (loyt dokumentn)" (The Kiev
    group of writers and artists and its attempt to escape from the Ukraine in
    1920, document based)." This second volume never appeared in print.

100. Tcherikower, "Araynfir," *In der tkufe fun revolutsiye*, v.

101. Ibid., v–viii.

102. Moss, " 'Time to Tear Down,' " 310–311. Moss, *Jewish Renaissance*, 231,
     235–238, 244–246. A. Litvak, "Literatur un lebn," *Baginen* (1919). It is in-
     teresting that both Rafes and Litvak were once considered nationalists
     within the Bundist party.

103. Dovid Bergelson, "Dikhtung un gezelshaftlekhkeyt," *Bikhervelt* 4–5 (Au-
     gust 1919): 5–16. For a discussion of this essay, see Moss, *Jewish Renais-
     sance*, 247–252. Here I used Moss's translation of the article's title.

104. Kalmanovitch to Niger, May 25, 1920. Shmuel Niger Collection RG 360,
     folder 34 YIVO Archives. Kalmanovitch invoked these passages of rebuke
     in the following words: "And in the evening you shall say, 'Would it were
     morning,' and in the morning you shall say, 'Would it were evening'—in gen-
     eral a whole *toykhekhe* (rebuke) with a surplus." These words come from the
     rebuke in Deuteronomy 28:67. Clearly Kalmanovitch, versed in the Bible,
     quoted this verse by heart without consulting the original text. If he had, he
     would have realized that he accidentally had reversed the verse. The original
     verse reads: "And in the morning you shall say, 'Would it were evening.' And
     in the evening you shall say, 'Would it were morning.' " The term *sameah be-
     helkam*, which Kalmanovitch used in reference to his mother's generation,
     comes from the tractate of the Mishna, Pirke Avot (Sayings of the Fathers).
     There (chap. 4, Mishna 1), Ben Zoma taught, "Who is wealthy? He who is
     satisfied with his lot [*ha-sameah be-helko*]." In this passage, Kalmanovitch
     expresses remorse for his generation's revolutionary spirit, which brought the
     current catastrophe of the civil war, Bolshevism, and the pogroms upon itself.

Although Kalmanovitch perhaps consciously meant this religious outburst, directed toward the "Master of the Universe," humorously, there is a certain level of seriousness in his comparison of the restless spirit of his generation with the religious satisfaction of the generation of his religious mother.

105. Kalmanovitch to Niger May 25, 1920 Shmuel Niger Collection RG 360, folder 34 YIVO Archives. I partially relied on Moss's translation of this passage. See Moss, "'Time to Tear Down,'" 410, and *Jewish Renaissance,* 253. However, I changed several aspects of the translation. I also translated several sentences from this passage that Moss did not.

106. Kalmanovitch to Niger, October 22, 1921, Shmuel Niger Collection RG 360, folder 34 YIVO Archives.

107. Moss, "'Time to Tear Down,'" 410.

108. Kalmanovitch to Niger, October 22, 1921. Shmuel Niger Collection RG 360, folder 34 YIVO Archives.

109. Kalmanovitch to Niger, May 25, 1920; September 9, 1921 Shmuel Niger Collection RG 360, folder 34 YIVO Archives; Kalmanovitch, *Yidishe gramatik: Konspekt fun lektsiyes, gelernt far minsker lerer Marts, 1921.* (Minsk: Gozisdat Belorussia, 1921).

110. Dubnov, "Der nayer mabul II," 10.

111. Ibid. Both Dubnov and Efroikin made the comparison to Sabbateanism. See Dubnov, "Der nayer mabul II," 12, and Efroikin, "Ashalto de-geulo," 7–8.

112. In his introduction, Frankel wrote: "But the Jewish people in Russia had been molded far less completely by the emancipation era and, with the reversal of 1881, it moved, as it were, directly from a preliberal to a postliberal stage of development, from medieval community to projects for national revival, from a religious to a social and secular messianism." See Frankel, *Prophecy and Politics,* 2.

113. See Tcherikower, "Di dinastiye romanov," 201.

114. Rabinovitch, "Alternative to Zion," 303–305.

4. At the Crossroads

1. Elias Tcherikower and Yisroel Efroikin, "A vort tsu di leyener," *Oyfn sheydveg* 1 (April 1939): 4.

2. Regarding Efroikin's financing of the journal, see Avrom Golomb, "Yisroel efroykin eynenu," *Shriftn: Khoydeshlekhe oysgabe far integraler yidishkayt,* nos. 145–147 (June–July–August 1954): 5–6; for the articles in *Oyfn sheydveg* regarding Jewish participation in general politics, see Stefan Zweig, "Yidn inem algameynem politishn lebn," *Oyfn sheydveg* 1 (April 1939): 103–105; Max Brod, "Tsi zoln yidn zikh farnemen nor mit yidishe politik?" *Oyfn sheydveg* 1 (April 1939): 106–111. For Tcherikower's letter to Zweig asking for an article on this topic, see Tcherikower to Zweig, Tcherikower Archive RG 80, folder 1281 YIVO Archives New York.

3. See, for example, Tcherikower, "Opklaybn oder tsugreytn?" *Di idishe emigratsiye* 7–8 (July–August 1925): 5–7.

4. Regarding how Efroikin became a travel agent, see Leon Halpern, "Oyfn frishn keyver fun yisroel efroykin a"h," *Shriftn: Khoydeshlekhe oysgabe far*

integraler yidishkayt nos. 145–147 (June-July-August 1954): 12. For Tcherikower's involvement in the Schwartzbard trial, see Kenneth B. Moss, "Tsherikover, Elye," *The YIVO Encyclopedia of Jews in Eastern Europe* on-line edition http://www.yivoencyclopedia.org/article.aspx/Tsherikover_Elye.

5. Tcherikower, "Mit vos kumen mir tsum kongres? (Program-forshlagn), *Der yidisher velt kongres* 1–2 (February 1934): 10. Efroikin, "Der meyn funen idishen kongres," *Der yidisher velt kongres* 1–2 (February 1934): 7.

6. M. Regalski, "Tsum ondenk fun yisroel efroykin," *Shriftn*, nos. 145–147 (June–July–August 1954): 24.

7. For Efroikin's vision of the afternoon schools, see "Dos identun in frankraykh darf hobn a fareynigte farshteyershaft: A geshprekh mitn prezident fun der federatsiye h. y. efroykin," *Parizer haynt,* April 10, 1935, 2. For his desire to unify the two communities, see Efroikin, "Undzer tsuzamenarbet mit di fran-soyzishe yidn," *Pariz,* April 12, 1935, 1. For Efroikin's retreat from general politics, see David H. Weinberg, *A Community on Trial: The Jews of Paris in the 1930s* (Chicago: University of Chicago Press, 1977), 113, 141n51. Regarding Efroikin's visit to Palestine, see Avrom Golomb, "Yisroel Efroykin—eynenu," *Shriftn*, nos. 145–147 (June-July-August, 1954): 5.

8. For a recent, comprehensive survey of Jewish national autonomy in Lithuania, see Šarūnas Liekis, *A State within a State? Jewish Autonomy in Lithuania, 1918–1925* (Vilnius: Versus Aureus, 2003). Kalmanovitch battled for the autonomist Yiddishist position in 1922 at the *Kehile tsuzamenfor* (convention). For a published version of his speech, see Kalmanovitch, *Undzer shul-frage: A fortrog gehaltn oyfn tsveytn kehiles tsuzamenfor in lite* (Kaunas: Farlag Likht, 1922). For Kalmanovitch's musings on the redemptive nature of Yiddish culture and on the relationship between Yiddishism and the Jewish religious tradition from this period, see Kalmanovitch, "Nokh a mol yidishizm," *Nays,* October 16, 1921, 3; Kalmanovitch, "Di yidishe natsionale bavegung un di ortodoksiye," *Nays,* March 23, 1923, 5–6; Kalmanovitch, "Religiye un politik," *Nays,* May 2, 1922, 2; Kalmanovitch, "Tsi iz faran a yidishe religiyeze bavegung?" *Nays,* May 9, 1922, 3; Kalmanovitch, "Der vog fun der yerushe," *Nays,* June 21, 1922, 2–3. When in Riga, Kalmanovitch tried to convince his readership that Yiddish was the national language of Latvian Jewry. See Kalmanovitch, "Idishe avtonomiye un ire bashitser," *Letste nays,* February 27, 1925, 4, and March 1, 1925, 3; Kalmanovitch, "Farshilmelte taynes," *Letste nays,* March 17, 1925, 4; Kalmanovitch, "Farshimilte taynes: Vi zaynen gevorn idishe dialektn," *Letste nays,* March 18, 1925, 4; "Farshimilte taynes: Voser shprakh reydn kurledner idn?" *Letste nays,* March 19, 1925, 4.

9. Cecile E. Kuznitz, *YIVO and the Making of Modern Jewish Scholarship* (New York: Cambridge University Press, forthcoming), especially the introduction. For Tcherikower's continued faith in YIVO in 1938, see Tcherikower, "Undzer kultur-oyfshtayg (rede fun e. tsherikover oyf der grindungs-farzamlung fun der opteylung fun yivo in frankraykh" (February 21, 1938), Tcherikower Archive RG 80, folder 1140 YIVO Archives New York.

10. Kalmanovitch, "Perspektivn far yidish in ratnfarband," *Literarishe bleter* 3 (January 16, 1931): 40–41; 4 (January 23, 1931): 61–62; 5 (January 30, 1931): 79–80; 6 (February 6, 1931): 100–102; 8 (February 20, 1931): 139–141. On a sojourn in Paris in 1934, Kalmanovitch wrote to his fourteen-year-old son, Sholem, about his turn to territorialism. Kalmanovitch to Sholem [Kalmanovitch] Luria, December 4, 1933. I would like to express my gratitude to the late Dr. Shalom Luria, who in 1999 provided me with a copy of this and other of his father's letters. Also see Kalmanovitch, "A literararisher tiken far der neshome fun s's (V. Latski-Bertoldi: 'Erdgayst.' Ershter band geklibene shriftn)," *Frayland* 1–2 (September–October 1934): 47–54.

11. David Vital, *A People Apart: The Jews of Europe, 1789–1939* (Oxford: Oxford University Press, 1999), 812–816, 820–823.

12. Ezra Mendelsohn, *The Jews of East Central Europe between the World Wars* (Bloomington: Indiana University Press, 1987), 32–36, 69–73. For a history of Agudas Yisroel in Poland, see Gershon C. Bacon, *The Politics of Tradition: Agudath Yisrael in Poland, 1916–1939* (Jerusalem: Magnes Press, Hebrew University, 1996).

13. Mendelsohn, *Jews,* 48–49, 53–56, 76–79, 213–239, 241–254.

14. Ibid., 65–68, 59, 76, 233–235, 250–252. TsISHO was an acronym for Tsentrale yidishe shul organizatsye (Central Yiddish School Organization).

15. Zvi Gitelman, *A Century of Ambivalence: The Jews of Russia and the Soviet Union, 1881 to the Present,* expanded 2nd ed. (Bloomington: Indiana University Press, 2001), 134–135, 142, 160–165, 173.

16. Walter Laqueur, *The History of Zionism* (New York: Schocken Books, 1972): 508–510, 525–530. Vital, *People Apart,* 881–892.

17. The poem first appeared under the title "A gute nakht, velt," *Inzikh* 3 (April 1938): 66–67. For an English translation, see David G. Roskies, *The Literature of Destruction* (Philadelphia: Jewish Publication Society of America, 1989), 374–375. For an overview of the crisis of Yiddishist intellectuals in the late 1930s written by one of its participants, see Tcherikower, "Der yidisher gaystiker krisis in shayn fun der prese (iberblik)," *Oyfn sheydveg* 1 (April 1939): 201–217. For a historical-literary analysis of Glatstein's poem, see Anita Norich, *Discovering Exile: Yiddish and Jewish American Culture during the Holocaust* (Stanford, CA: Stanford University Press, 2008). For Glatstein's article, see Glatstein, "Tsvishen eygene," *Inzikh* 46 (May 1938): 120–122.

18. Shmuel Feigin, "Nakhon le-yeme ha-benayim," *Ha-'Olam* 27, nos. 1–2 (October 6, 1938): 4–7; Chaim Lieberman, *In tol fun toyt: Gedanken vegen undzer tsayt un undzer shikzal in ir* (New York: H. Lieberman, 1938). H. Leivick, "Fun vanen kon kumen di hilf," *Der tog,* October 23, 1938, 7; "Fun vanen kon kumen di hilf: tsveyer artikel, "*Der tog,* October 30, 1938, 5; "Mir shteyen vider baym onheyb: Driter artikel fun der seriye: Fun vanen kon kumen di hilf, "*Der tog,* November 6, 1938, 5; "Vegen gehn tsurik in geto. Fun der seriyen: Fun vanen kon kumen hilf, "*Der tog,* November 13,

1938, 7, 3; "An entfer oyf briv: Letster artikel fun der seriye: Fun vanen kon kumen di hilf? "November 19, 1938, 5. Yoysef Opotashu, "Vos iz yidishkeyt?" *Yidishe kultur: Khoydesh-shrift fun dem alveltlekhn yidishn kulturfarband* 2 (December 1938): 1-6; Shmuel Niger, "Kenen mir zikh sheyden mit der velt?" *Der tog*, October 21, 1938, 4; "Mir zaynen nit aleyn," *Der tog*, November 19, 1938, 6. Chaim Zhitlovsky, "Di naye 'geto-iden' un di geto kegner," *Der tog*, November 13, 1938, 6. For an overview of most of these articles and others pertaining to this debate in the Yiddish press, see Tcherikower, "Der yidisher gaystiker krisis," 200–211.

19. A. M. Fuchs, "A brokhe le-vatole," *Parizer haynt*, July 3, 1938, 3. For a discussion of the question of "return to the ghetto" in the French Yiddish press, see Weinberg, *Community on Trial*, 189–195.

20. A. Kremer, "Tsurik in geto?" *Parizer haynt*, July 12, 1938, 3.

21. The additional participants were Charles Rappaport, Dovid Einhorn, and Dr. A. Sengalowski. "Tsurik in geto?" *Parizer haynt*, December 21, 1938, 2, and December 22, 1938, 3.

22. "Tsurik in geto?" December 21, 1938.

23. Ibid. Golomb, "Yisroel Efroykin enenu," *Shriftn*, nos. 145–147 (June–July–August 1954), 5. Efren, "Dos yudishe leben in rusland," *Di yudishe velt* (February 1914): 291.

24. Paula Hyman, *From Dreyfus to Vichy: The Remaking of French Jewry, 1906–1939* (New York: Columbia University Press, 1979), 230.

25. Weinberg, *Community on Trial*, 183.

26. Hyman, *From Dreyfus to Vichy*, 230. Weinberg, *Community on Trial*, 183, 148–170.

27. Guy Miron, *The Waning of Emancipation: Jewish History, Memory, and the Rise of Fascism in Germany, France, and Hungary* (Detroit: Wayne State University Press, 2011), 83–118.

28. Weinberg, *Community on Trial*, 186–188, 191–193.

29. Jacques Jefroykin, "Affirmation," *Oyfn sheydveg* 1 (April 1939): 225.

30. Tcherikower, "Di tragediye fun a shvakhn dor," *Oyfn sheydveg* 1 (April 1939): 20–22.

31. Efroikin, "Vu haltn mir in der hayntiker velt," *Oyfn sheydveg* 2 (August 1939): 15.

32. Ibid., 17–22; Kalmanovitch, "Untern hamer fun der geshikhte," *Oyfn sheydveg* 1 (April 1939): 73–74.

33. Tcherikower, "Di tragediye," 6.

34. Ibid., 6, 8–9, 11–13. Referring to the Nuremberg Laws and other Nazi restrictions, Tcherikower stated that German Jews should have viewed the off-limits German cafés and restaurants as "muktsah meḥmat mius," a Talmudic term that means "set aside (not permissible to move on the Sabbath) because of repulsiveness" and metaphorically means "loathsome." Just like Dubnov, Tcherikower imagined German Jewry as the symbol of Jewish assimilation and national self-abnegation. Recently, Michael Brenner challenged this portrait by writing of a "renaissance" of Jewish culture, including a turn to Jewish nationalism, in Weimar Germany. Brenner's unbiased

account belies the depiction of interwar German Jewry as thoroughly as-similated and demoralized, which pervades not just Tcherikower's essay but also much of the historiography written after World War II about interwar German Jewry. See Michael Brenner, *The Renaissance of Jewish Culture in Weimar Germany* (New Haven, CT: Yale University Press, 1998). Kalmano-vitch, "Untern hamer," 32. Efroikin, "Vu haltn mir," 25.

35. Kalmanovitch, "Untern hamer," 43–44. Tcherikower, "Di tragediye," 13.

36. Tcherikower, "Di tragediye," 9.

37. Tcherikower, "Idishe buntn gegen di gezeyres fun nikolay dem ershten (di idishe masen, di maskilim, un zeyere politishe shtimungen," *Tsukunft* (March 1939): 174–179; Tcherikower, "Di maskilim, nikolay der ershter un di idishe masn," *Tsukunft* (July 1939): 408–413.

38. Tcherikower, "Di tragediye," 14–17. Tcherikower wrote, "and one truly becomes an ignoramus [*am hoorets*] when he warms himself in the Jewish shtetls around the foreign fire of Christmas trees." Ibid., 17.

39. The first quote, about "a death by a kiss" *(mise beneshike)* serving as the "ugliest death of a nation" comes from Tcherikower, "Di tragediye," 17. The second quote, about the meaningless of Yiddish culture in the absence of national or religious content, from ibid., 15.

40. Kalmanovitch, "Untern hamer," 30.

41. Lucy S. Dawidowicz, *From That Time and Place: A Memoir, 1938–1947*, introduction by Nancy Sinkoff (New Brunswick, NJ: Rutgers University Press, 2008), 100.

42. Ibid., 114.

43. Transcribed from a letter that Dawidowicz wrote Leibush Lehrer, October 25, 1938. Dawidowiciz Papers, box 51, folder 4 American Jewish Histori-cal Society, New York. Quoted in Nancy Sinkoff, "Introduction: *Yidishkayt* and the Making of Lucy S. Dawidowicz," in Dawidowicz, *From That Time and Place,* xxvi.

44. Through the words "And you shall live by them" Kalmanovitch is referring here to Leviticus 18:5: "You shall keep My laws and My rules, by the pursuit of which man shall live; I am the Lord." The rabbis in the Talmud interpreted the words "ve-ḥai ba-hem," and you shall live by them," as permission to vi-olate most of the Torah's commandments in order to save one's life. My translation here is from the *JPS Hebrew–English Tanakh* 249. Kalmanovitch to Tcherikower, April 9, 1939, Tcherikower Archive RG 82, folder 2183, YIVO Archives New York.

45. Transcribed from letter from Dawidowicz to Lehrer, October 25, 1938. Dawidowicz dated this statement to January 15, 1939. Quoted in Sinkoff, "Introduction: *Yidishkayt* and the Making of Lucy S. Dawidowicz," xxvi. Joseph Kruk, *Taḥat diglan shel shalosh mahpekhot:(Rusim, polanim, ye-hudim): ishim ve-tenu'ot be-dori: zikhronot* (Tel Aviv: Maḥbarot le-sifrut, 1968), 118.

46. Sinkoff, "Introduction," xxvii. Transcribed from a letter from Dawidowicz to Lehrer, February 13, 1939, Dawidowiciz Papers, box 51, folder 4 Ameri-can Jewish Historical Society. Dawidowicz dated this statement to January

15, 1939. The conclusion that Yiddish and its culture only could survive in a political and economic ghetto, she confided to Lehrer, "is pretty dangerous stuff."

47. Kalmanovitch to Yudl Mark, December 8, 1938, YIVO-Vilna Administration Records RG1.1, box 9, folder 161 YIVO Archives New York.

48. For an explanation of Sabbatean theology, see Gershom Scholem, *Sabbetai Ṣevi: The Mystical Messiah* (Princeton, NJ: Princeton University Press, 1973).

49. Kalmanovitch to Mark, December 8, 1938. YIVO-Vilna Administration Records RG 1.1, box 9, folder 161 YIVO Archives.

50. Kalmanovitch, "Untern hamer," 29–46, quote p. 44.

51. Ibid., 36.

52. Ibid., 29, 46.

53. Tcherikower, "Di tragediye," 10. Many Talmudic passages begin with the words, "The Holy One Blessed be He made a blessing for Israel." Here, Tcherikower invoked this traditional construction in order to emphasize the providential role of racial anti-Semitism in bringing assimilated Jews back to the fold.

54. Efroikin, "Vu haltn mir," 26. Kalmanovitch, "Untern hamer," 29. For this Talmudic quotation, see page 1 of this book.

55. Kalmanovitch, "Untern hamer," 46.

56. Simon Dubnov to Tcherikower, March 2, 1939, RG 81 Tcherikower Archive, Folder 1759 YIVO Archives New York.

57. Dubnov to Tcherikower May 4, 1939; June 11, 1939 Tcherikower Archive RG 81, Folder 1759 YIVO Archives.

58. Dubnov, "Vos darf men ton in homen's tsaytn? A briv tsu der redaktsiye fun Oyfn sheydveg," *Oyfn sheydveg* 2 (August 1939): 3–7. For an English translation, see Simon Dubnow, *Nationalism and History: Essays on Old and New Judaism,* ed. Koppel S. Pinson (Philadelphia: Jewish Publication Society of America, 1958), 354–359. Here, I used Pinson's translation.

59. This English translation comes from Dubnow, *Nationalism and History,* 358; for the original Yiddish see Dubnov, "Vos darf men ton," 6.

60. Tcherikower, "Vegn sheydveg un vegn 'shlakhtfeld' (A frayndlikher entfer oyf a frayndlikher kritik)," *Oyfn sheydveg* 2 (August 1939): 8–12.

61. Dubnov, "Vos darf men ton in homen's tsaytn," 6; Tcherikower, "Vegn sheydveg un vegn 'shlakhtfeld,'" 12.

62. Tcherikower, "Vegn sheydveg un vegn 'shlakhtfeld,'" 13.

63. I thank Samuel Kassow for bringing Dubnov's "Vuhin gehen mir?" to my attention when speaking about it in his conference paper, "What should we do in Haman's Times: The Public Intellectual on the Eve of War," International Conference. *Historicizing the Jewish People: Simon Dubnow at 150* (November 5, 2010, Leipzig Germany). Kassow disagreed with Jonathan Frankel's assessment that by the late 1930s, Dubnov proved an intellectual refugee of the nineteenth century doomed to have lived too far into the twentieth. See Jonathan Frankel, "S. M. Dubnov: Historian and Ideologist,"

in Sophie Dubnov Ehrlich, *The Life and Work of S. M. Dubnov* (Bloomington: Indiana University Press, 1991), 26–27. Dubnov, "Vuhin gehen mir? Troyerige batrakhtungen vegen undzer troyeriger tsayt," *Tsukunft* (July 1935): 392–398.

64. Dubnov, "Vuhin gehen mir?" 398.
65. Efroikin, "Vu haltn mir," 26.
66. Tcherikower, "Di tragediye," 28.
67. Ibid., 26.
68. Tcherikower, "Undzer kultur-oyfshtayg."
69. Ibid., 25. *Tfilin* are the phylacteries worn by traditional Jewish men on the arm and head during morning prayers. "Yontev" (yom tov in Hebrew) is the Yiddish word for religious holiday. Compare this passage to Tcherikower's "Oyfn shvel fun besmedresh," written in the midst of World War I. See Tcherikower, "Oyfn shvel fun besmedresh," *Der tog*, October 13, 1916, 4.
70. Tcherikower, "Di tragediye," 7. In this passage, Tcherikower conjured up several powerful images of medieval Jewry dying proudly for the sanctification of God's name. When Jews died at the stake in Blois, France, as a result of a blood libel in 1171, it is reported that they sang the words of "Alenu le-shabe'aḥ," the central prayer that affirms Jewish superiority over pagans and idol worshippers. Similarly, "Elokim 'al dami ledami" (O God, do not be silent to my blood) was a liturgical penitential poem written in the aftermath of the First Crusade, when many Jews of the Rhineland chose to kill themselves and their children rather than fall into the hands of the Crusaders. The author of this poem, R. David ben R. Mushulam, expressed the hope that the blood of these victims would spur God to vengeance. See Shimon Bernfeld, *Sefer ha-dem'aot Me'oraot ha-gezerot ve-ha-redifot ve-hashmadot*, vol. 1 (Berlin: Eschkol, 1923), 199–202. Similarly, the story of R. Simḥah Ha-Kohen appeared in the Mainz Anonymous Crusade Chronicle, which told the story of the martyrdom of Rhineland Jewry in 1096. According to the chronicle, when the Crusaders broke into the bishop's castle where many of the Jews of Worms had sought refuge, R. Simḥah Ha-Kohen feigned interest in conversion and asked to be brought to the room of the bishop. As the conversion began, R. Simḥa gnashed his teeth at the bishop's nephew, as a lion toward his prey, and then stabbed him to death. R. Simḥah succeeded in killing two others before his knife broke and the Christians overpowered and killed him. The chronicle concludes, "There was killed the young man who sanctified the Name, and did what the rest of the community did not—he killed three uncircumcised ones with his knife." Quoted in Bernfeld, *Sefer ha-dem'aot*, 155–156. Also see A. M. Haberman, "M 'a'aseh ha-gezerot ha-yeshanot-anonimi," in *Sefer gezerot ashkenaz ve-tsarfat* (Jerusalem: Tarshish Books, 1945), 97. Through these powerful images of martyrdom, Tcherikower sought to portray the spiritual heroics of premodern Jewry, which he described earlier in the essay with the Talmudic expression that it "loved afflictions." See Tcherikower, "Di tragediye," 5. Not having attended synagogue services regularly since his youth, Tcherikower

probably discovered the liturgical poem to which he referred in the Bernfeld collection. I thank Dr. Shneyer Z. Leiman for helping me to find these references.

71. Sophie Dubnov-Erlich, *The Life and Work of S. M. Dubnov,* trans. Judith Vowles (Bloomington: Indiana University Press, 1991): 237–240.

72. Dubnov, "*Inter-arma* (1940): Gedanken fun a yidishn historiker vegen di tsiln fun krig un friden," in: *Oyfn sheydveg* 3 [never appeared in print, written in spring 1940], Tcherikower Archive RG 81, folder 1283: 1–4, YIVO Archives.

73. Ibid., 5.

74. Ibid.

75. Ibid., 6.

76. Ibid., 7. Dubnov then ended with a postscript stating that the World Jewish Congress together with the American Jewish Congress should serve as the representatives of the Jewish people at a future peace conference.

77. Dubnov, "Vos darf men ton in homen's tsaytn," 4. Frankel, "S. M. Dubnov," 18–26.

78. Tcherikower diary, July 10, 1940, and July 18, 1940, Tcherikower Archive RG 81, folder 1283 YIVO Archives.

79. Tcherikower diary, July 13, 1940 Tcherikower Archive RG 81 folder 1148 YIVO Archives.

80. Ibid., and Tcherikower diary, July 11, 1940, Tcherikower Archive RG 81, folder 1148 YIVO Archives.

81. Ibid., July 13, 1940. The statement "There is no wise man like the tested man" probably appeared for the first time in the sixteenth century in the writings of the Maharal (R. Yehudah Loew ben Betsalel) of Prague.

82. Ibid., July 10, 1940 Tcherikower Archive RG 81, folder 1148 YIVO Archives. Here, Tcherikower paraphrased 2 Kings 4:13.

83. Richard I. Cohen, *The Burden of Conscience: French Jewry's Response to the Holocaust* (Bloomington: Indiana University Press, 1987), 13–17; Tcherikower diary, July 11, 1940 Tcherikower Archive RG 81, folder 1148 YIVO Archives; Tcherikower, "Undzer kultur-oyfshtayg," Tcherikower Archive RG 80, folder 1140 YIVO Archives; Tcherikower diary July 13, 1940 Tcherikower Archive RG 81, folder 1148 YIVO Archives.

84. Tcherikower diary, July 13, 1940, and July 23, 1940 Tcherikower Archive RG 81, folder 1148 YIVO Archives.

85. Ibid., July 17, 1940, and July 18, 1940 Tcherikower Archive RG 81, folder 1148 YIVO Archives.

86. Ibid., July 17, 1940 Tcherikower Archive RG 81, folder 1148 YIVO Archives.

87. Ibid., August 6, 1940. Tcherikower Archive RG 81, folder 1148 YIVO Archives.

88. Ibid., July 23, 1940.

89. Ibid., July 16, 1940. Cohen, *Burden of Conscience,* 13–17.

90. Tcherikower diary, July 23, 1940.

91. Ibid., August 6, 1942.

92. Ibid., July 26, 1942.
93. Ibid., July 20, 1940, and July 16, 1940. HICEM, founded in 1927, was a merger of HIAS (the Hebrew Immigrant Aid Society), the EKA (Jewish Colonization Association) and Emigdirekt.
94. Ibid., July 16, 1940, and August 6, 1940.
95. Ibid., September 7, 1940.
96. Ibid., July 20, 1940.
97. Ibid., September 7, 1940.
98. See Thedor Herzl, "The Jewish State," in *The Zionist Idea: A Historical Analysis and Reader,* ed. Arthur Herzberg (Philadelphia: Jewish Publication Society of America, 1997), 220–222.
99. B. Y. Bialostotski, "Bay a bagegenish mit undzere gest," *Kultur un dertsiung: A monatlekher shul-un kultur zshurnal,* no. 6 (October 1940): 7. Regarding the *Algemeyne entsiklopedye,* see Barry Trachtenberg, "From Edification to Commemoration: "Di Algemeyne Entsiklopedye," the Holocaust and Changing Mission of Yiddish Scholarship," *Journal of Modern Jewish Studies* 5, 3 (2006): 285–300.
100. Tcherikower, "Yidishe martirologiye un yidishe historiografiye," *YIVO bleter* 17, no. 2 (March–April 1941): 97–112. The English translation of this article appeared as "Jewish Martyrology and Jewish Historiography," *YIVO Annual of Jewish Social Science* 1 (1946): 9–23. For Tcherikower's discussion of the divide between collective memory and historiography, see Tcherikower, "Yidishe martirologiye," 97–99.
101. Tcherikower, "Yidishe martirologiye," 102–112.
102. This translation comes from Tcherikower, "Jewish Martyrology," 23. For the original Yiddish, see Tcherikower, "Yidishe martirologiye," 112. It is unclear to which statement of the Vilna Gaon Tcherikower is referring. However, if the Vilna Gaon made this statement, he based it on the following passage in the Babylonian Talmud, Berakhot 5a: "We learned: Rabbi Shimon ben Yoḥai said, 'The Holy Blessed Be He bestowed three gifts upon Israel and He did not give any of them except through afflictions. They are as follows: the Torah, the land of Israel, and the World to Come. From where do we learn [this in reference to] the Torah? For it says (Psalms 94:12): "Happy is the man whom You afflict, Lord, and for whom You teach from Your Torah . . ."'" (translation my own).
103. Yosef Yerushalmi, *Zakhor: Jewish History and Jewish Memory* (Seattle: University of Washington Press, 1982). See esp. chap. 4, "Modern Dilemmas: Historiography and Its Discontents," 81–103. Other historians have questioned the extent to which modern Jewish historiography indeed has liberated itself from meta-historical narratives rooted in collective memory. See Amos Funkenstein, *Perceptions of Jewish History* (Berkeley: University of California Press, 1993), esp. introduction, 1–21.
104. Tcherikower, "Yidishe martirologiye," 106. According to Ismar Schorsch, it was Bernfeld's extreme portrayal of Jewish history as a series of persecutions and acts of Jewish martyrdom that led Baron to react against what he termed "the lachrymose conception" just several years after the publication

of *Sefer Ha-dem'aot*. See Ismar Schorsch, "The Lachrymose Conception of Jewish History," in Schorsch, *From Text to Context: The Turn to History in Modern Judaism* (Boston: Brandeis University Press, 1994), 376–388.

105. Tcherikower, "Jewish Martyrology," 19. For the Yiddish original, see Tcherikower, "Yidishe martirologiye," 108.

106. Tcherikower, "Jewish Martyrology," 23. For the Yiddish original, see Tcherikower "Yidisha martirologiye," 112. *Shevet Yehudah* is a work of sixteenth-century Jewish historiography written by Solomon Ibn Vergah. Through imaginary dialogues, the author sought to explore the social and natural causes behind Jewish suffering. He applied these methods especially to his analysis of the Spanish Expulsion. Azriel Shochat, ed., *Sefer Shevet Yehudah le-Rabi Shelomoh ibn. Vergah* (Jerusalem: Mosad Bialik, 1946 or 1947). Tcherikower implied here that Ibn Verga made the statement quoted from the book about the Jewish people. In reality, however, Tcherikower took this quotation completely out of context. In *Shevet Yehudah,* this statement appears as part of an imaginary conversation between King Alfonso of Spain and his adviser Thomas regarding the interpretation of a dream. See Shochat, *Sefer Shevet Yehudah,* 149–151. According to Shochat, this comparison of the Jews to a torch served as a regular polemical tool of medieval Christians. Also see Shochat, *Sefer Shevet Yehudah,* 225n18. The fact that Tcherikower took this quotation so out of context speaks to his limited knowledge of medieval Hebrew sources, which he probably studied not in their original context but in anthologies and secondary sources.

107. Tcherikower, "Jewish Martyrology," 23. For the statement in the original Yiddish, see Tcherikower, "Yidishe martirologiye," 112.

108. Tcherikower, "Di amolike anarkhistn in gerangl kegn idishn got (a kapitl kultur-geshikhte mit 50 yor tsurik)," *Der idisher kempfer* (March 7, 1941): 9–11; March 14, 1941: 10–12.

109. Dov Levin, *The Lesser of Two Evils: Eastern European Jewry under Soviet Rule, 1939–1941* (Philadelphia/Jerusalem: Jewish Publication Society, 1995), 198–217. Kalmanovitch to Naftoli Feinerman, October 23, 1939, YIVO Archive of American Department RG100a, Folder 26, YIVO Archives New York. Kalman Weiser, "The Jewel in the Yiddish Crown: Who Will Occupy the Chair in Yiddish at the University of Vilnius?" *Polin* 24 (2012): 224. I would like to thank Dr. Kalman Weiser for sharing this article with me before publication.

110. Max Weinreich to Naftoli Feinerman, October 14, 1939, Max Weinreich 1930s–1968 RG 584, folder 293b, YIVO Archives. For a discussion of this perspective, see Weiser, "Jewel in the Yiddish Crown," 237.

111. Kalmanovitch to Niger, November 19, 1939. Shmuel Niger Collection RG 360, file 34 YIVO Archives.

112. Weiser, "Jewel in the Yiddish Crown, 232–233. Also see Liekis, "Jewish-Polish Relations and the Lithuanian Authorities in Vilna, 1939–1940," *Polin* 19 (2007): 521–536; Marek Wierzbicki, "Polish-Jewish Relations in Vilna and the Region of Western Vilna under Soviet Occupation, 1939–1941," *Polin* 19 (2007): 487–516.

113. Kalmanovitch to Feinerman, January 1940. Max Weinreich 1930s–1968 RG 584, folder 293b, YIVO Archives New York.

114. "Protokol fun der zitsung fun der tsaytvayliker farvaltung fun yivo, 9tn detsember 1939: Fun der tsveyter zitsung, shabes dem 9tn detsember, 5 a zeyger nokh mitog," YIVO-Vilna Administration Records RG 1.1 box 3.1, folder 631, 13, YIVO Archives.

115. Ibid.

116. Ibid., 15.

117. "Protokol fun der zitsung," 31.

118. Ibid., 32–33.

119. Ibid., 33–34, 40.

120. "Protokol fun der zitsung fun der tsaytrayliker farvaltung fun yivo, vilne, dem 27th yanuar 1940," p20 YIVO-Vilna Administration Records RG 1.1, box 31, folder 631 YIVO Archives.

121. Ibid., 16–21. Weiser, "Jewel in the Yiddish Crown," 242. "Zitsung fun der tsaytvayliker farvaltung fun yivo, 10tn marts 1940," RG 1.1, box 3.1, folder 631, 3–5, YIVO Archives.

122. "Zitsung fun der tsaytvayliker farvaltung fun yivo, 10tn marts 1940," 19.

123. Ibid., 32–33.

124. Ibid., 15. See Weiser, "Jewel in the Yiddish Crown," 242n71.

125. Kalmanovitch, "Bay vos haltn yidn haynt?" *Ringen* (Kaunas, 1940): 30–31. I would like to thank Dr. David G. Roskies for bringing this article to my attention.

126. Ibid., 32–33.

127. Ibid., 33.

128. Ibid.

129. Ibid., 35. Kalmanovitch, "Untern hamer," 39. For a discussion of the early embrace by the Bund of a demand for cultural autonomy and of the ideology of *doikeyt,* see Jonathan Frankel, *Prophecy and Politics: Socialism, Nationalism and the Russian Jews, 1860–1917* (Cambridge: Cambridge University Press, 1981), 171–257, and Henry Tobias, *The Jewish Bund in Russia from Its Origins to 1905* (Stanford, CA: Stanford University Press, 1972). For Kalmanovitch's discussion of Polish Jewry's lack of options and his dismissal of the search for Polish political allies as futile, see Kalmanovitch, "Bay vos haltn yidn haynt?" 35–36. For an articulation of the position that Polish Jewry turned to the Bund in the late 1930s because of this party's connection to Polish politics, see Mendelsohn, *Jews.* Also see Emanuel Melzer, *No Way Out: The Politics of Polish Jewry, 1935–1939* (Cincinnati: Hebrew Union College Press, 1997). Recently, Jack Jacobs proposed a reason for the growing popularity of the Bund closer to that proposed by Kalmanovitch. He argued that the Bund in interwar Poland had succeeded in producing a counterculture that attracted ever-increasing numbers of young Polish Jews to its cultural, social, and political program. See Jack Jacobs, *Bundist Counter-Culture in Inter-war Poland* (Syracuse, NY: Syracuse University Press, 2009).

130. Kalmanovitch, "Bay vos haltn yidn haynt?" 38.

131. Ibid. The verse is found in Isaiah 6:11. In Kalmanovitch's article, he wrongly cited it as Isaiah 11. Also, he indicated that the translation of the verse that he used came from Yehoyash's Yiddish Bible translation.

132. Kalmanovitch to Niger, June 16, 1940. Shmuel Niger Collection RG 360, folder 34, YIVO Archives New York.

133. "Oykh der 'yivo' vert endlekh aroysgetsoygn fun zumf," *Togblat*, August 16, 1940; Leyzer Ran, *Ash fun yerushalayim de-lite* (New York: Vilner farlag, 1959), 176–179; Weiser, "Jewel in the Yiddish Crown," 246 and 246n88.

134. Kalmanovitch to Niger, April 4, 1941. Shmuel Niger Collection RG 360, folder 34 YIVO Archives New York. Also see Shmerke Kaczerginski, *Tsvishn hamer un serp. Tsu der geshikhte fun der likvidatsye fun der yidisher·kultur in sovetn-rusland* (Buenos Aires: Der emes, 1950), 28.

135. Weiser, "Jewel in the Yiddish Crown," 17.

136. Kalmanovitch to Niger, April 12, 1941. Shmuel Niger Collection RG 360, folder 34 YIVO Archives New York.

137. David G. Roskies, *Against the Apocalypse: Responses to Catastrophe in Modern Jewish Culture* (Cambridge, MA: Harvard University Press, 1984), 196–197.

138. Efroikin, "Vu haltn mir," 26.

5. The Holocaust

1. Regarding Efroikin's withdrawal from public life at the beginning of his stay in Montevideo, see Dr. Avraham Mivshan, "Yisra'el 'Efroykin enenu," *Shriftn: Khoydeshlekhe oysgabe far integraler yidishkayt*, 145–147 (June–July–August 1954): 8.

2. Ibid., 7; Elias Tcherikower, "Fun der historisher sektsiye," in *Yidn in frankraykh: Shtudies un materialn*, vol. 1, ed. Elias Tcherikower Ershter Band (New York: YIVO, 1942), 7–8.

3. Tcherikower, "Di frantseyzishe revolutsye un yidn (150 yor nokh der yidisher emantsipatsye)," in *Yidn in frankraykh: Shtudies un materialn*, ed. Tcherikower (New York: YIVO, 1942), 109.

4. Ibid., 111–112.

5. See Arthur Hertzberg, *The French Enlightenment and the Jews* (New York: Columbia University Press, 1968).

6. Tcherikower, "Di frantseyzishe revolutsye un yidn," 119.

7. Tcherikower, "Di yidishe aktsiyes far rekht beys der frantseyzisher revolutsye (1789–1791)," in *Yidn in frankraykh*, vol. 2, ed. Tcherikower (New York: YIVO, 1942), 35–38, 41–49, 141.

8. Ibid., 21–22.

9. Ibid., 27. Tcherikower translated the statement from "Adresse présentée à l'Assemblée nationale, le 31 août 1789, par les députés réunis des Juifs . . ."

10. Ibid., 28.

11. Ibid., 41–49.

12. Tcherikower, ""Di frantseyzishe revolutsye un yidn," 115.

13. Ibid., 36.

14. Tcherikower, "Dos folk vos lebt eynzam," *Der tog*, September 30, 1916, 6.

Tcherikower, "Der idisher rekht-kamf in 19tn yorhundert," *Der idisher kongres* 12 (October 22, 1915): 5.

15. Tcherikower, "Di yidishe aktsiyes," 49.

16. Ibid., 50–51.

17. Ibid., 55.

18. Over a decade after Tcherikower's death, Tcherikower's onetime colleague from Kiev, the historian Ben-Zion (Dinaburg) Dinur, translated this work into Hebrew and published it in Israel. See Tcherikower, *Yehudim be'itot ha-mahpekhah,* trans. and intro. Ben-Zion Dinur (Tel Aviv: Am Oved, 1957). For an analysis about how the rise of the modern press and its relative freedom from government censorship contributed to the rise of modern anti-Semitism, see Jonathan Frankel, *The Damascus Affair: "Ritual Murder," Politics, and the Jews in 1840* (Cambridge: Cambridge University Press, 1997).

19. For Tcherikower's feeling of distance from the Jewish tragedy, see Daniel Tsharni, "Di drayfakhe perzenlekhkeyt (tsum toyt fun eliyohu tsherikover)," *Idisher kempfer* (September 3, 1943): 11. For his volumes on the Jewish labor movement in America, see *Geshikhte fun der yidisher arbeter-bavegung in di fareynikte shtatn:* vol. 1: *Der historisher hintergrunt un di sotsial-ekonomishe faktorn,* ed. E. Tcherikower (New York: YIVO, 1943); *Geshikhte fun der yidisher arbeter-bavegung in di fareynikte shtatn:* vol. 2: *Fun di onheybn biz 1890,* ed. E. Tcherikower (New York: YIVO, 1945).

20. Tcherikower, "Ven der malakh hamoves hot keyn shlite nit" *Der idisher kempfer* (April 28, 1916): 8; Tsharni, "Di drayfakhe perzenlekhkeyt."

21. Mivshan, "Yisra'el efroykin-enenu!," 8; Avrom Golomb, "Yisroel efroykin-enenu!" *Shriftn* nos. 145–147 (June–July–August 1954): 6; M. Yolis, "Yisroel efroykin un di 'shriftn,'" *Shriftn* nos. 145–147 (June–July–August 1954): 26–27.

22. Yosef Friedlander, "Halvayato shel R. Ḥayim Ozer Grodzenski," in *Vilner zamlbukh, Me'asef Vilnah,* ed. Yisrael Rudnitzki (Tel Aviv: Igud yotse vilnah ve-ha-sevivah be-Tel-Aviv, 1974), 44. For an English translation, see Shnayer Z. Leiman, "The Day Vilna Died," *Tradition* 37, no. 2 (2003): 91. I am grateful to Dr. Shnayer Z. Leiman for making me aware of this source.

23. Editorial, "Dray yor—lamed vov shriftn," *Shriftn* 36 (May 1945): 2.

24. Ibid.

25. Efroikin, *In kholem un oyf der vor: Esayen vegn alte problemen in a nayer tsayt* (New York: Farlag Oyfn sheydveg, 1944), 11–24. In this chapter's opening statement regarding the ten measures of illusion, Efroikin consciously paraphrased a statement in the Babylonian Talmud Kiddushin 49b that stated that women took nine of the ten measures of speech and Jerusalem nine of the ten measures of beauty in the world.

26. Samuel Kassow, *Who Will Write Our History? Emanuel Ringelblum, the Warsaw Ghetto, and the Oyneg Shabes Archives* (Bloomington: University of Indiana Press, 2007), 230–239.

27. Efroikin, *In kholem,* 77–83, 113–121, 84–100, 117–118, 101–107.

28. Ibid., 131.

29. Ibid., 162–72. This quote comes from p. 167.

30. Ibid., 177–178.
31. For a recent study that argues that Dubnov remained true to his Diaspora nationalist principles throughout the interwar period, see Simon Rabinovitch, "The Dawn of a New Diaspora: Simon Dubnov's Autonomism, from St. Petersburg to Berlin," *Leo Baeck Institute Year Book* 50 (2005): 267–288.
32. Efroikin, *In kholem,* 181–190.
33. Ibid., 34–56.
34. Efroikin, "Di internatsionale yidishe frage: Der yidisher velt-farband," *Di yidishe folksblat* 10 (December 20, 1917): 7–8.
35. Efroikin, *In kholem,* 41. Emphasis in the original.
36. Ibid., 368.
37. Ibid., 179–180.
38. Ibid., 236, 244–246.
39. Ibid., 207–208.
40. Ibid., 211–214.
41. Ibid., 218–219.
42. Ibid., 239–240.
43. For a definition of the "new Jewish politics," see Ezra Mendelsohn, *The Jews of East Central Europe between the World Wars* (Bloomington: Indiana University Press, 1983), 48–49. For the failure of these politics in interwar Poland, see p. 56.
44. Efroikin, *In kholem,* 368. *Kabtsansk* means "Paupersville." It is the name of the hometown of Hershele, the protagonist of Mendele Moykher Sforim's novel *Dos vinshfingerl (The Wishing Ring).*
45. Ibid., 191–199.
46. Ibid., 198–200, 205. Klatzkin made this argument in his book *Krisis und Entscheidung im Judentum: Der Probleme des modernen Judentums* (Berlin: Jüdischer Verlag, 1921).
47. Efroikin, *In kholem,* 200.
48. Ibid., 302–304.
49. Ibid., 291–300. The quotation regarding equal rights meaning responsibility for "pillage and wars, murder and terror" comes from p. 293. In particular, Efroikin concentrated on the pillage of "yellow-brown and black-skinned human beings who are oppressed by the white nations."
50. Ibid., 332–366, 308–321, 322–331.
51. Ibid., 248–269.
52. Ibid.
53. Ibid., 270–290, 344–349.
54. Yitzhak Arad, *Ghetto in Flames: The Struggle and Destruction of the Jews in Vilna in the Holocaust* (Jerusalem and New York: Yad Vashem Martyrs' and Heroes' Remembrance Authority, Anti-Defamation League of B'nai B'rith, 1980), 29–79, 101–119.
55. Ibid., 120; Mark Dworzecki, *Yerusholayim de-lite in kamf un umkum: Zikhroynes fun vilner geto* (Paris: Yidishn folksfarband in frankraykh un yidishn natsionaln arbeter-farband in amerike, 1948), 64.

56. Arad, *Ghetto in Flames,* 125.
57. Ibid., 133–163, 172–199. For a table listing the estimated number of victims per each *Aktion,* see pp. 216–217.
58. Ibid., 138, 164–171.
59. Ibid., 273–338. For a discussion of Gens as the internal ruler of the ghetto and of the role of the Jewish police in *Aktionen,* see Dworzecki, *Yerusholayim de-lite,* 303–312.
60. Arad, *Ghetto in Flames,* 339–351. For a depiction of the *Aktion* in Oszmiana, see Dworzecki, *Yerusholayim de-lite,* 414–416. For Kalmanovitch's perspective on these events, see Zelig Kalmanovitch, *Yoman be-geto vilnah u-khetavim min ha- 'izavon she-nimtseu ba-harisot* ed. and intro. Shalom Luria (Tel Aviv: Moreshet Bet 'Edut 'al shem Mordekhai Anilevits, 1977), 85–86. Dworzecki cited ghetto reports that placed the number of Jews that the Nazis demanded to be handed over at fifteen hundred.
61. Arad, *Ghetto in Flames,* 221–262.
62. Ibid., 377–400.
63. Ibid., 355–372, 401–440.
64. David G. Roskies, "Jewish Cultural Life in the Vilna Ghetto," in *Lithuania and the Jews—the Holocaust Chapter* (Center for Advanced Holocaust Studies: United States Holocaust Memorial Museum, 2005), 3.
65. Kassow, *Who Will Write Our History?,* 127–128, 230–239.
66. Roskies, "Jewish Cultural Life in the Vilna Ghetto," 38–40. For a discussion of the essence of Jewish identity in the pages of *Shriftn,* see Rambam [Maimonides], "Yigdal," *Shriftn* nos. 5-6-7 (20-21-22) (January–February–March1944): 199; Rambam, "Di draytsn ikorim (ani ma'amin)," *Shriftn* nos. 5-6-7 (20-21-22) (January–February-March 1944): 200–201. "Yigdal" is a poem that poetically lists Maimonides's thirteen principles of faith. The actual author of the poem, however, is not Maimonides [Rambam], as stated wrongly in *Shriftn,* but rather probably R. Daniel ben Yehudah Hadayyan; Aḥad Ha-'Am, "Loy sa'aseh lekho pesel ve-khoyl temuno," *Shriftn* nos. 5-6-7 (20-21-22) (January–February-March 1944): 202–203; Kh. Grinberg, "Kol hatoro kulo al regel aḥas," (di gantse toyre oyf eyn fus)," *Shriftn* nos. 5-6-7 (January–February-March 1944): 196–198; Dr. Sh. Ravidovitsh, "Ikh un nisht der sholiakh," *Shriftn* nos. 5-6-7 (January–February-March 1944): 204–207; Avrom Golomb, "Kol hatoyre kule fun hayntiker tsayt," *Shriftn* nos. 5-6-7 (20-21-22) (January-February-March 1944) 209–210; A. Gordon, "Di filosofiye fun der toyre," *Shrifn* nos. 5-6-7 (20-21-22) (January–February-March 1944): 207–208. For a discussion of the debate over the nature of Jewish identity among intellectuals in the Vilna ghetto, see Dworzecki, *Yerusholayim de-lite,* 263–264.
67. David E. Fishman, *The Rise of Modern Yiddish Culture* (Pittsburgh: University of Pittsburgh Press, 2005), 141–148. For a general description of the unit's work, see Shmerke Kaczerginski, *Partizaner geyen* (Bamberg: "Oyf der vakh," 69); Kaczerginski, *Ikh bin geven a partizan (di grine legende)* (Buenos Aires: "Kultur" fun mushkat un zaslavski, 1952), 41–42. For Kalmanovitch's

statement defending the smuggling of books into the ghetto, see Reizl Korchak, *Lehavot ba-efer,* 3rd expanded ed. (Merḥavyah: "Moreshet" and "Sifriyat Poʻalim," 1965), 95.

68. Herman Kruk, *The Last Days of the Jerusalem of Lithuania: Chronicles from the Vilna Ghetto and the Camps, 1939–1944,* ed. and intro Benjamin Harshav, trans. Barbara Harshav (New Haven, CT: Yale University Press, 2002), 270; Kruk, *Togbukh fun vilner geto,* ed. Mordekhai V. Bernshteyn (New York: YIVO, 1961), 242–243.

69. Kruk, *Last Days,* 269; Kruk, *Togbukh,* 242.

70. Dworzecki, *Yerusholayim de-lite,* 261.

71. Kalmanovitch, "Problemen fun literarisher geshikhte tsivshn yidn," 3–7. Only fragments of this essay were found in the ruins of the ghetto at the end of the war. I am grateful to the late Shalom Luria for sharing with me his transcription of this essay.

72. Ibid., 4–7; Kalmanovitch, *Yoman,* 103. For an English translation, see Kalmanovitch, "A Diary of the Nazi Ghetto in Vilna," *YIVO Annual of Jewish Social Science,* vol. 7 (New York, 1953), 50. Here, it translates *agadat Mosheh Rabenu* simply as "the Moses legend." For a Yiddish translation see Kalmanovitch, "A togbukh in vilner geto," *YIVO bleter* 35 (1951): 59.

73. Kalmanovitch, "Aḥad Ha-ʻam u-tehume ha-sifrut ha-ʻivrit," in Kalmanovitch, *Yoman,* 145–160. As examples of Aḥad Ha'Am's disparaging attitude toward belles lettres, Kalmanovitch referred to Aḥad Ha'Am's following articles: "Ha-lashon ve-sifrutah," *Luaḥ Aḥi'asaf* (1893): 17–30, and "Te'udat ha-shiloaḥ," *Ha-Shiloaḥ* 1 (October 1896): 1–6. For a discussion of the debate between Aḥad Ha-ʻAm and his students on the pages of *Ha-Shiloaḥ,* see Steven J. Zipperstein, *Elusive Prophet: Ahad Ha'am and the Origins of Zionism* (Berkeley: University of California Press, 1993), 115–124. Also see Arnold Band, "The Ahad Ha-am and Berdyczewski Polarity," in *At the Crossroads: Essays on Ahad Ha-am,* ed. Jaques Kornberg (Albany: SUNY Press, 1983), 49–59. As an example of Klausner's rejection of Aḥad Ha-ʻAm's disparaging attitude toward belletristics, see Joseph Klausner, "Megamatenu," *Ha-Shiloaḥ* 11 (1903), and Klausner, *Ha-zeramim ha-ḥadashim shel hasifrut ha-ʻivrit hatse'irah* (New York: Hotsa'at "Ivriyah," 1906 or 1907).

74. Kalmanovitch, "Aḥad Ha'am," 151–152, 164.

75. Ibid., 157.

76. Kenneth B. Moss, *Jewish Renaissance in the Russian Revolution* (Cambridge, MA: Harvard University Press, 2009), 283. Kalmanovitch, *Undzer shul-frage: A fortrog gehaltn oyfn tsveytn kehiles tsuzamenfor in lite* (Kaunas: Farlag Likht, 1922), 20–21.

77. Kalmanovitch, "Ahad Ha-ʻAm," 163.

78. Ibid., 164.

79. Peretz expressed these thoughts in the following essays: Y. L. Peretz, "Der lebens protses," *Ale verk fun y. l. perets,* vol. 11, *Gedanken un ideen* (Vilna: Vilner farlag fun b. kletskin), 239–251; "Vegen der yidisher literatur," *Ale verk,* vol. 19, *Briv un redes,* ed., intro., and annotation Nakhmen Mayzel

(Vilna: Vilner farlag b. kletskin, 1929), 299–304; "Vos felt undzer literatur," *Ale verk,* vol. 11 (Vilna: Vilner farlag b. kletskin, 1925), 53–64; "Vegn, vos firn op fun yidishkayt," *Ale verk,* vol. 11 (Vilna: Vilner farlag b. kletskin, 1925), 65–98. For a discussion of these articles, see Ruth R. Wisse, *I. L. Peretz and the Making of Modern Jewish Culture* (Seattle: University of Washington Press, 1991).

80. Kalmanovitch, "Y. l. peretses kuk oyf der yidisher literatur," *Di goldene keyt* 2 (1949): 122.

81. Kalmanovitch, "Y. l. peretses kuk oyf der yidisher literatur," *YIVO bleter* 33 (1950): 61. For Peretz's original quotation, see Peretz, "Der lebens protses," 247–248.

82. Kalmanovitch, "Y. l. peretses kuk oyf der yidisher literatur," *YIVO bleter* 33, p. 50, *Di goldene keyt,* p. 119.

83. Ibid., *Di goldene keyt,* 126, 121–122.

84. Kruk, *Last Days,* 496. For Yiddish original, see Kruk, *Togbukh,* 494.

85. Kruk, *Last Days,* 474. For Yiddish original, see Kruk, *Togbukh,* 470. Barbara Harshav, the translator of Kruk's diary, spelled Kalmanovitch's name Kalmanowicz. Since this passage comes from her translation, I spell his name here in this manner.

86. The translation comes from Kalmanovitch, "Diary," 64–65; for the Hebrew original, see Kalmanovitch, *Yoman,* 116; for the Yiddish, see Kalmanovitch, "A togbukh in vilner geto," 74–75.

87. The translation comes from Kalmanovitch, "Diary," 12; for Hebrew original, see *Yoman,* 66; for the Yiddish, see "A togbukh," 19.

88. Kalmanovitch, "Diary," 46; for Hebrew original, *Yoman,* 99; for Yiddish translation, "A togbukh," 55.

89. Yehuda Bauer, *Jewish Reactions to the Holocaust* (Tel Aviv: MOD Books, 1989), 86–95.

90. Kalmanovitch, "Der gayst fun geto," *YIVO bleter* 30 (1947), 169–172. Kalmanovitch wrote the words "happy end" in English. The long quotation comes from p. 172.

91. Kalmanovitch, "[Hebreyisher originel] Togbukh fun vilner geto (fragment)," *YIVO bleter naye seriye* 3 (1997): 91; for the Yiddish translation, see "[Yidishe iberzetsung] Togbukh fun vilner geto (fragment)," 61.

92. See Babylonian Talmud 'Eruvin 54a: "Rabbi Eliezer said, "What is the meaning of the verse, 'His pallet like a bundle of spices' (Song of Songs 10)? If a person makes himself like this bundle that everyone treads and like these spices from which everyone takes fragrance, his learning will endure and if not, his learning will not endure." For a classical formulation of this praise of those who accept their afflictions happily, see Baylonian Talmud Yoma 23a.

93. Kalmanovitch, "[Hebreyisher originel] Togbukh," 101; for a Yiddish translation, see "[Yidishe iberzetsung] Togbukh," 75.

94. Kalmanovitch, "[Hebreyisher originel] Togbukh," 100; for the Yiddish, see "[Yidishe iberzetsung] Togbukh," 74.

95. Translation from Kalmanovitch, "Diary," 47; for the Hebrew original, see *Yoman*, 99; for Yiddish, "A togbukh," 56.

96. Kalmanovitch, *Yoman*, 100; for the English translation, see "Diary," 47; for the Yiddish translation, "A togbukh," 56.

97. Dworzecki, *Yerusholayim de-lite*, 261. Regarding Kalmanovitch's joining in services as Rabbi Shaulke's *kloyz*, see Shmerke Kaczerginski, *Khurbn vilne: Umkum fun di yidn in vilner gegnt, der harige-tol ponar. Perzenlekhe iber-lebungen, zamlung fun eydes bavayzn oder dokumentn* (New York: Tsiko bikher-farlag, 1947), 209. A facsimile of the yeshiva's invitation to Kalmanovitch for the *siyum* appeared in Asher Katzman, "Khurbn vilne," *Dos idishe vort*, no. 220 (Heshvan 5741) (November 1981): 32. Regarding Kalmanovitch's involvement in and intercession on behalf of the *daf yomi* group, see Yehoshua Eibshitz, *Bi-kedushah u-vi-gevurah: Pirke Kidush Hashem u-Mesirut Nefesh: Asufah ti'udit 'al ha-emunah ke-gorem mashpi'a be-tekufat ha-shoah* (Tel Aviv: n.p., 1976), 295–296. I thank Dr. Shneyer Z. Leiman for pointing me toward these last two sources.

98. For an example of Kalmanovitch's referring to the Soviets as the *gedoylim*, see Kalmanovitch, *Yoman*, 69; for an English translation, see "Diary," 16; for a Yiddish translation, "A togbukh," 23. A letter from Kalmanovitch to Niger attests to the fact that he was using this epithet as early as 1920. See Kalmanovitch to Niger, May 25, 1920, RG 360 Shmuel Niger Collection, Folder 34, YIVO Archives New York. For Kalmanovitch's reference to the Poles and Lithuanians as "the children of the handmaiden" see Kalmanovitch, *Yoman*, 81; for English, "Diary," 28; for Yiddish, "A togbukh," 36. Throughout the diary, Kalmanovitch refers to the Germans as the "masters." For Kalmanovitch's identification of the Nazis with demonic forces, see Kalmanovitch, *Yoman*, 89; for English, "Diary," 36; for Yiddish, "A togbukh," 44. For his reference to the Nazis as Armilius, see Kalmanovitch, *Yoman*, 113; for English, "Diary," 62; for Yiddish, "A togbukh," 71. Armilius is the name of the wicked king who, according to the aggadah, will kill Messiah son of Joseph only to be killed himself by Messiah son of David. Shalom Luria pointed out that Isaiah 11:4 reads, "and with the spirit of his lips will he smite the wicked." Targum Yonatan translates this verse based on the aggadic interpretation as follows: "And through the articulation of his lips will he kill Armilius the wicked." See Luria's explanation in Kalmanovitch, *Yoman*, 113n223.

99. Kalmanovitch, *Yoman*, 82–83; for English, "Diary," 30; for Yiddish, "A togbukh," 38. The first quote has its origins in Psalms 25:6. It further was incorporated into *Taḥanun*, a prayer recited daily but elongated on Mondays and Thursdays in which Jews pray for deliverance from the persecutions of the exile. The second quote comes from the Sabbath song traditionally recited at the Friday night table, "Tsur mi-shelo," which thanks God for sustenance and ends with a prayer for deliverance.

100. Kalmanovitch, *Yoman*, 88–89; for English, "Diary," 36; for Yiddish, "A togbukh," 44.

101. Kalmanovitch, *Yoman*, 113; for English, "Diary," 61; for Yiddish, "A togbukh," 70.

102. Kalmanovitch, *Yoman*, 110; for English, "Diary," 58; for Yiddish, "A togbukh," 68. This string of verses is a close paraphrase of Psalm 37:12–15. However, because he was quoting from heart, Kalmanovitch misquoted several phrases in these verses. I have translated the passage including Kalmanovitch's errors. I have indicated the original, correct phrases in brackets. Here, I adapted the translation not from the English translation of the diary but rather from the *JPS Tanakh*. See *JPS Tanakh* (Philadelphia: Jewish Publication Society, 1999), 1455. Regarding the misquotation at the end of the passage, see Kalmanovitch, "Diary," 58n161.

103. Kaczerginski, *Khurbn vilne*, 209. Kalmanovitch, *Yoman*, 123; for English, "Diary," 72; for Yiddish, "A togbukh," 82. Kalmanovitch, *Yoman*, 125; for English, "Diary," 74; for Yiddish, "A togbukh," 84. For the biblical reference, see Lamentations 4:9. Kalmanovitch, *Yoman*, 123–24; for English, "Diary," 72; for Yiddish, "A togbukh," 82–83.

104. Kalmanovitch, *Yoman*, 125; for English, "Diary, 74–75; for Yiddish, "A togbukh," 85. This statement of Hillel appears in *Pirke Avot* (The Sayings of the Fathers) Chap. 2, Mishna 6.

105. Kalmanovitch, *Yoman*, 121–22; for English, "Diary," 70; for Yiddish, "A togbukh," 80–81.

106. Kalmanovitch, *Yoman*, 123; for English, "Diary," 72; for Yiddish, "A togbukh," 82. Kalmanovitch, *Yoman*, 124; for English, "Diary," 73; for Yiddish, "A togbukh," 84.

107. Kaczerginski also attended the service. In his memoir, he wrote about Kalmanovitch, "I saw him in the *besmedresh* on Simḥat Torah, how he danced in ecstasy [*dveykes*] with a Torah scroll around the *bimah*." Kaczerginski, *Khurbn vilne*, 209.

108. Although *YIVO bleter* translated the word *'avon* as "aims," I would translate the word more accurately and literally as "sins." The translation here comes from Kalmanovitch, "Diary," 30–31. For the Hebrew original, see Kalmanovitch, *Yoman*, 83; for the Yiddish, "A togbukh," 38–39.

109. Dworzecki, *Yerusholayim de-lite*, 260. Dworzecki wrote, "An enthusiastic wonderment for all the holy sparks, which revealed themselves in the ghetto-person—and a sharp, cutting, merciless lesson [*lere*] of the events, gave him impulses toward fiery speeches of love and rebuke, and transformed him into the *Prophet of the Ghetto*—such was his name in the ghetto of the Jerusalem of Lithuania." Dworzecki, *Yerusholayim de-lite*, 263. Also see Avrom Sutzkever's poem "Der novi," begun in the Vilna ghetto and completed in Moscow, which he dedicated to the memory of Kalmanovitch. Sutzkever, "Der novi: Geheylikt dem ondenk fun z. kalmanovitsh," in *Lider fun yam hamoves: Fun vilner geto, vald, un vander [geshribn in di yorn 1936–1967]* (Tel Aviv: Farlag bergen-belzen, 1968), 127–130.

110. For the midrash that states that the future of all future Jews stood at Sinai, see Genesis Rabba 84:4.

111. Kalmanovitch, *Yoman*, 103–104; for the original Yiddish, see Kalmanovitch, *Yoman*, 137–138, and Kalmanovitch, "A togbukh," 59–60; for the English, see "Diary," 50–51. For the *Oyfn sheydveg* article, see Kalmanovitch, "Untern hamer fun der geshikhte," *Oyfn sheydveg* 1 (April 1939): 46.

112. This translation comes from Kalmanovitch, "Diary," 52; for the Yiddish original, see *Yoman*, 139–140, and "A togbukh," 61; for the Hebrew, see *Yoman*, 104–105.

113. I. Tishby, "Kudsha-berikh-hu orayta ve-yisra'el kola had: Mekor ha-imra be-ferush 'Idra raba le-Ramkhal," *Kiryat Sefer*, June 1975, 480–492. For this reference I rely on David G. Roskies, *Against the Apocalypse: Responses to Catastrophe in Modern Jewish Culture* (Cambridge, MA: Harvard University Press, 1984), 218 and 340n70.

114. Kalmanovitch, "Dapim keru'im me-tokh masah," *Huliyot: Dapim le-mehkar besifrut yidish ve-zikoteha le-sifrut ha-'ivrit* 3 (Spring 1996): 297–299. The quotation comes from p. 299. This passage from the diary was found in the Lithuanian Archive in Vilnius and sent to Luria in Israel. The date of this entry, therefore, is unknown. Regarding the image of the Jews in Nazi-occupied Europe as a vanquished camp of an eternal people, see Babylonian Talmud Pesahim 87b: Rabbi Oshaiah said, ". . . The Holy One Blessed Be He performed righteousness for Israel that He scattered them among the nations." The Talmudic commentator Rashi explained this line as meaning that given the scattered nature of the exile, the nations cannot destroy the entire Jewish people together at once.

115. The translation of these phrases comes from Kalmanovitch, "The Spirit of the Ghetto," *YIVO bleter* 30 (1947): 328. For the Yiddish original, see Kalmanovitch, "Der gayst fun geto," *YIVO bleter* 30 (1947), 172.

116. Kalmanovitch, *Yoman*, 93; for English, see "Diary," 40; for Yiddish, "A togbukh," 49.

117. Kalmanovitch, "Bay vos haltn yidn haynt?" *Ringen* (Kaunas, 1940). For the original Hebrew, see Kalmanovitch, *Yoman*, 72; for English, see "Diary," 19; for Yiddish, "A togbukh," 26–27.

118. Translation comes from Roskies, "Jewish Cultural Life in the Vilna Ghetto," 37. For the Hebrew original, see Kalmanovitch, "[Hebreyisher originel] Togbukh," 102–103; for Yiddish translation, see "[Yidishe iberzetsung] Togbukh," 76–78. I only disagree with the translation in one point. In the Hebrew original, when referring to Rabbi Grodzenski 's archive, he referred to it not as "Chaim Oyzer's archive" but rather as "the archive of Rabbi Chaim Ozer of blessed memory." See Kalmanovitch, "[Hebreyisher originel] Togbukh," 102.

119. For Kalmanovitch's disillusionment with the Yiddishist intelligentsia for its alleged pro-Soviet sympathies, see Kalmanovitch to Naftoli Feinerman, January 1940, RG 584 Max Weinreich 1930s–1968, folder 293b, YIVO Archives New York. For his preferences during the Russian Civil War for the Whites and Ukrainian nationalists over the Soviets, see Kalmanovitch to Niger, May 25, 1920, RG 360 Shmuel Niger Collection, folder 34, YIVO

Archives New York. Much of the analysis in this passage comes from Roskies, "Jewish Cultural Life in the Vilna Ghetto," 36–38.

120. For a discussion of the appropriation of the Vilna Gaon's memory by Jewish nationalists of all stripes, see Fishman, *Rise of Modern Yiddish Culture*, 114–125. For a Talmudic statement that even one righteous person can sustain the world, see BT Yoma 38b.

121. Roskies, "Jewish Cultural Life in the Vilna Ghetto," 38.

122. Kalmanovitch, "[Hebreyisher original] Togbukh," 93; for Yiddish, see Kalmanovitch, "[Yidishe iberzetsung] Togbukh," 65.

123. The translation here comes from Kalmanovitch, "Diary," 44; for the Yiddish original, see *Yoman*, 135–136, and "A togbukh," 52–53; for the Hebrew, see *Yoman*, 96–97.

124. For Kalmanovitch's embrace of the "work for life," see *Yoman*, 106; for English, "Diary," 54; for Yiddish, "A togbukh," 63. For his belief that Jewish productivity led the Nazis to bless the Jews against their will, see, for instance, *Yoman*, 117; for English, "Diary," 65; for Yiddish, "A togbukh," 75. For an instance where a Nazi official expressed wonder at the creation of the sports field, see Kalmanovitch, "[Hebreyishe original] Togbukh," 100; for Yiddish "[Yidishe iberzetsung] Togbukh," 74.

125. Kalmanovitch, "[Heybreyisher originel] Togbukh," 86–87; for Yiddish, "[Yidishe iberzetsung] Togbukh," 54–56. The biblical quotation comes from Deuteronomy 17:13.

126. Ibid., 87. For Yiddish, see Kalmanovitch, "[Yidishe iberzetsung] Togbukh," 56.

127. Kalmanovitch, *Yoman*, 84; for English, "Diary," 31; for Yiddish, "A togbukh," 39.

128. Kalmanovitch, *Yoman*, 85–86; for English, "Diary," 33–34; for Yiddish, "A togbukh," 41–42.

129. The translation here comes from Kalmanovitch, "Diary," 34; for Hebrew original, *Yoman*, 86–87; for Yiddish, "A togbukh," 42.

130. Yitzkhok Kharlash, "A shite vos ken aropfirn fun zinen," *Undzer tsayt* (April–May 1952): 57–59. Luria, in Kalmanovitch, *Yoman*, 87n94. For Dina Porat's suggestion that Kalmanovitch wrote in such an extreme manner in order to convince himself, see Dina Porat, "The Vilna Ghetto Diaries," in *Holocaust Chronicles: Individualizing the Holocaust through Diaries and Other Contemporaneous Personal Accounts*, ed. Robert Moses Shapiro (New York: Ktav, 1999), 167.

131. *Jerusalem Talmud Terumut*, chap. 8. Maimonides's codification of the law appears in his *Mishneh Torah* Yesodei HaTorah 5:5.

132. Kalmanovitch, *Yoman*, 116; for English, "Diary," 64; for Yiddish, "A togbukh," 74.

133. Roskies, *Against the Apocalypse*, 4–5.

134. Kalmanovitch, *Yoman*, 116–117; for English, "Diary," 64–66; for Yiddish, "A togbukh," 74–76.

135. Kalmanovitch, "Diary," 64–65.

136. Kassow, *Who Will Write Our History?* 232–233.

137. Kaczerginski, *Khurbn vilne*, 210.
138. Ibid.
139. Dworzecki, *Yerusholayim de-lite*, 264. For accounts of Kalmanovitch's experience in the camps of Estonia, also see Kaczerginski, *Khurbn vilne*, 210, and Shalom Luria, "Zelig Hirsh Kalmanovitsh: Ha-ish ve-'olamo," in Kalmanovitch, *Yoman*, 56–59.

Conclusion

1. Samuel Kassow, *Who Will Write Our History? Emanuel Ringelblum, the Warsaw Ghetto, and the Oyneg Shabes Archives* (Bloomington: University of Indiana Press, 2007), 386.
2. Dan Diner made this comment in his introduction to my paper at the conference that he convened at the Simon Dubnow Institute in Leipzig, Germany, on the 150th anniversary of Dubnov's birth. Dan Diner, Opening Comments to the Session, "On the Eve of Turmoil" (featuring my paper "At the Crossroads: Simon Dubnow and His Disciples on the Eve of World War Two," and Samuel Kassow, "What Should We Do in Haman's Times: The Public Intellectual on the Eve of War"), November 5, 2010, Leipzig.
3. For a discussion of Dubnov's belief in the emergence of two new hegemonic centers of Jewish life in America and Palestine, see Simon Rabinovitch, "The Dawn of a New Diaspora: Simon Dubnov's Autonomism, from St. Petersburg to Berlin," *Leo Baeck Institute Year Book* 50 (2005), 267–288.
4. David Roskies used this term to describe Tcherikower, Efroikin, and Kalmanovitch's negotiated return to religious tradition in his comments to my doctoral dissertation defense in 2006.
5. Leslie Poles Hartley began his novel *The Go-Between* with these words. Historian David Lowenthal adopted the words as an apt characterization of modern society's estrangement from the collective memories of traditional societies. See Leslie Poles Hartley, *The Go-Between* (New York: New York Review of Book Classics, 2002), and David Lowenthal, *The Past Is a Foreign Country* (Cambridge: Cambridge University Press, 1985).
6. Efroikin, *A kheshbn hanefesh* (Paris: A. B. Cerata Publishers, 1948); Efroikin, *Kdushe un gvure bay yidn amol un haynt: gzeyres tov"shin- tov shin"hey* (New York: Farlag *Oyfn Sheydveg*, 1949); Efroikin, "Vu haltn mir in der hayntiker velt," *Oyfn sheydveg* 2 (August 1939): 15.
7. For a discussion of the contradictions between Efroikin's embrace of religious thought and traditional rabbinic authority and his continued secular political action, see A. L. Shusheym, "Yisroel Efroykin," *Shriftn: Khoydeshlekhe oysgabe far integrater yidishkayt* nos. 145–147 (June–July–August 1954): 14–19, esp. 18–19. In June 2012, Michel Jefroykin, Efroikin's grandson, informed me of his grandfather's financing of *Aliyah Bet*. For Efroikin's activity in Poale Zion–Hitaḥdut, see Avrom Golomb, "Yisroel Efroykin Eynenu," *Shriftn*: nos. 145–147 (June–July–August 1954): 5; M. Regalski, "Tsum ondenk fun yisroel efroykin," *Shriftn* nos. 145–147 (June-July-August 1954): 23–24.

8. Lucy S. Dawidowicz to Irving Howe, December 6, 1974. Dawidowicz Papers, box 77, folder 14. American Jewish Historical Society, New York. Quoted in Nancy Sinkoff, "Introduction: Yidishkayt and the Making of Lucy S. Dawidowicz," in Lucy S. Dawidowicz, *From That Place and Time: A Memoir, 1938–1947* (New Brunswick, NJ: Rutgers University Press, 2008), xxxi–xxxii.

9. Jess Olson made a similar point in the introduction to his book. I thank him for sharing his introduction with me before the publication of his book. See Jess Olson, *Nathan Birnbaum and Jewish Modernity: Architect of Zionism, Yiddishism, and Orthodoxy* (Stanford, CA: Stanford University Press, 2013), 1–17.

Acknowledgments

Many people made this work possible. I owe thanks to JoAnne Brown, Robert Forster, and Dorothy Ross, all formerly of the Johns Hopkins University, for igniting my passion for the discipline of history. The Jewish history faculty of the Jewish Theological Seminary of America honed my skills as a historian. Above all I want to thank David E. Fishman for sharing his vast knowledge of Jewish history and Yiddish culture, for his methodological rigor, and for his continued friendship. Also instrumental to my studies were Benjamin Gampel, David G. Roskies, Ismar Schorsch, and Seth Schwartz. At the Uriel Weinreich Program in Yiddish Language, Literature, and Culture, I gained the Yiddish fluency necessary for this study. I wanted to thank my colleagues at Yeshiva University for commenting on my manuscript at various stages, particularly David Berger, Steven Fine, Jeffrey Gurock, Debra Kaplan, Jess Olson, and William Stenhouse.

I also have benefited greatly from the wisdom and generosity of Elisheva Carlebach, Dan Diner, Sam Kassow, Shneyer Z. Leiman, David N. Myers, Avrom Novershtern, Nancy Sinkoff, Jeffrey Veidlinger, Ruth Wisse, and Steven Zipperstein. Discussions with the following colleagues enriched my book's arguments: Cecile Kuznitz, Lisa Leff, Natan Meyer, Kenneth Moss, Simon Rabinovitch, Joshua Shanes, David Shneer, and Kalman Weiser. I also thank Oksana Fedorko, Diana Nakeeb, and Lyudmila Sholokhova for assisting me in my research. I am particularly grateful to Kathleen McDermott, my editor at Harvard University Press, for her confidence in this project. I also thank the readers for Harvard University Press, whose comments sharpened my analysis.

I owe gratitude to the following institutions for their financial support: the Graduate School of JTS; the Charles H. Revson Foundation; the Golomb Fund of the Committee Pro-Yiddish; the YIVO Institute for Jewish Research, which awarded me a Natalie and Mendel Racolin Memorial Fellowship; and the Center for Jewish History, which awarded me a doctoral fellowship. I am particularly grateful to the Center for Jewish Studies of Harvard University for a yearlong Harry Starr Fellowship in Judaica during which I wrote most of this book. Special thanks go to Ruth Wisse, Eric Nelson, and to Rachel Rockenmacher. I also thank my deans, Barry Eichler (Yeshiva College) and David Berger (Bernard Revel Graduate School), for allowing me to take this leave and for their ongoing support. I write these lines as a summer fellow at the Simon Dubnow Institute of Jewish History and Culture in Leipzig, Germany. I am grateful to the Institute and to its director, Dan Diner, for this fellowship.

I am grateful to the staffs of the YIVO library and archives, the reading room of the Center for Jewish History, the Dorot Jewish Division of the New York Public Library, Yeshiva University and JTS libraries, and the Widener Library of Harvard University. I especially want to recognize the late Shalom Luria, son of Zelig Kalmanovitch, for sharing some of his father's letters with me. Yuval Luria generously provided me with images of his grandfather. Sections of chapter 4 were excerpted from my articles "At the Crossroads between War and Genocide: A Reassessment of Jewish Ideology in 1940," in *Jewish Social Studies* 11, no. 2 (Winter 2005): 170–201. I thank Indiana University Press for permission to reuse the material here. Parts of chapter 4 were also first published in my article "In the Days of Haman: Simon Dubnow and His Disciples at the Eve of World War II," in Simon Dubnow Institute Yearbook 4 (2005), Göttingen: Vanderhoeck & Ruprecht 2005, 531–564. Sections of chapters 2 and 4 were excerpted from my article "Between Martyrology and Historiography: Elias Tcherikower and the Making of a Pogrom Historian," in *East European Jewish Affairs* 38:3 (December 2008): 257–280 (http://dx.doi.org/10.1080/13501670802450863).

I never could have completed this book without the loving support of my family. My parents, Fred and Dina Karlip, raised me to love knowledge, encouraged my interest in East European Jewry, and always offered their support. In addition to her devotion, my grandmother, Rosalie Michelson Wolfson, constantly encouraged my pursuit of an academic career. The completion of this book would have been impossible without the support of my in-laws, Ira and Rochelle Langer. Finally, I cannot express in words my gratitude to my wife, Shoshana, both for her steady companionship and love and for the numerous sacrifices that she made to ensure the completion of this work. I dedicate this book to her. She and our daughters have enriched my life beyond measure.

Index